Communications
in Computer and Information Science   1861

Rationale

The CCIS series is devoted to the publication of proceedings of computer science conferences. Its aim is to efficiently disseminate original research results in informatics in printed and electronic form. While the focus is on publication of peer-reviewed full papers presenting mature work, inclusion of reviewed short papers reporting on work in progress is welcome, too. Besides globally relevant meetings with internationally representative program committees guaranteeing a strict peer-reviewing and paper selection process, conferences run by societies or of high regional or national relevance are also considered for publication.

Topics

The topical scope of CCIS spans the entire spectrum of informatics ranging from foundational topics in the theory of computing to information and communications science and technology and a broad variety of interdisciplinary application fields.

Information for Volume Editors and Authors

Publication in CCIS is free of charge. No royalties are paid, however, we offer registered conference participants temporary free access to the online version of the conference proceedings on SpringerLink (http://link.springer.com) by means of an http referrer from the conference website and/or a number of complimentary printed copies, as specified in the official acceptance email of the event.

CCIS proceedings can be published in time for distribution at conferences or as postproceedings, and delivered in the form of printed books and/or electronically as USBs and/or e-content licenses for accessing proceedings at SpringerLink. Furthermore, CCIS proceedings are included in the CCIS electronic book series hosted in the SpringerLink digital library at http://link.springer.com/bookseries/7899. Conferences publishing in CCIS are allowed to use Online Conference Service (OCS) for managing the whole proceedings lifecycle (from submission and reviewing to preparing for publication) free of charge.

Publication process

The language of publication is exclusively English. Authors publishing in CCIS have to sign the Springer CCIS copyright transfer form, however, they are free to use their material published in CCIS for substantially changed, more elaborate subsequent publications elsewhere. For the preparation of the camera-ready papers/files, authors have to strictly adhere to the Springer CCIS Authors' Instructions and are strongly encouraged to use the CCIS LaTeX style files or templates.

Abstracting/Indexing

CCIS is abstracted/indexed in DBLP, Google Scholar, EI-Compendex, Mathematical Reviews, SCImago, Scopus. CCIS volumes are also submitted for the inclusion in ISI Proceedings.

How to start

To start the evaluation of your proposal for inclusion in the CCIS series, please send an e-mail to ccis@springer.com.

Nirbhay Chaubey · Sabu M. Thampi ·
Noor Zaman Jhanjhi · Satyen Parikh ·
Kiran Amin

Editors

Computing Science, Communication and Security

4th International Conference, COMS2 2023
Mehsana, Gujarat, India, February 6–7, 2023
Revised Selected Papers

Editors
Nirbhay Chaubey 🆔
Ganpat University
Mehsana, India

Noor Zaman Jhanjhi 🆔
Taylor's University
Subang Jaya, Malaysia

Kiran Amin 🆔
Ganpat University
Mehsana, India

Sabu M. Thampi 🆔
Kerala University of Digital Sciences,
Innovation and Technology
Trivandrum, India

Satyen Parikh 🆔
Ganpat University
Mehsana, India

ISSN 1865-0929   ISSN 1865-0937 (electronic)
Communications in Computer and Information Science
ISBN 978-3-031-40563-1   ISBN 978-3-031-40564-8 (eBook)
https://doi.org/10.1007/978-3-031-40564-8

© The Editor(s) (if applicable) and The Author(s), under exclusive license
to Springer Nature Switzerland AG 2023

This work is subject to copyright. All rights are reserved by the Publisher, whether the whole or part of the material is concerned, specifically the rights of translation, reprinting, reuse of illustrations, recitation, broadcasting, reproduction on microfilms or in any other physical way, and transmission or information storage and retrieval, electronic adaptation, computer software, or by similar or dissimilar methodology now known or hereafter developed.
The use of general descriptive names, registered names, trademarks, service marks, etc. in this publication does not imply, even in the absence of a specific statement, that such names are exempt from the relevant protective laws and regulations and therefore free for general use.
The publisher, the authors, and the editors are safe to assume that the advice and information in this book are believed to be true and accurate at the date of publication. Neither the publisher nor the authors or the editors give a warranty, expressed or implied, with respect to the material contained herein or for any errors or omissions that may have been made. The publisher remains neutral with regard to jurisdictional claims in published maps and institutional affiliations.

This Springer imprint is published by the registered company Springer Nature Switzerland AG
The registered company address is: Gewerbestrasse 11, 6330 Cham, Switzerland

Preface

This volume contains the papers presented at the 4th International Conference on Computing Science, Communication and Security (COMS2), held at the beautiful campus of Ganpat University, India during February 6–7, 2023. COMS2 2023 was held in hybrid mode, wherein the invited guests, keynote speakers, dignitaries, session chairs, paper presenters, and attendees joined a two-day international conference online using Zoom video conferencing. The online conference forum brought together more than 255 delegates including leading academics, scientists, researchers, and research scholars from all over the world to exchange and share their experiences, ideas, and research results on aspects of Computing Science, Network Communication, and Security.

The conference was inaugurated on the first day by the National Anthem "Jana Gana Mana" with the presence of academic leaders and luminaries: Shri Ganpatbhai I. Patel (Padma Shri), President and Patron in Chief of Ganpat University; the invited guest of the program Ashok Jhunjhunwala, Padmashri and institute professor, IIT Madras, India; Jyotika Athavale President-Elect of the IEEE Computer Society, Technical Leader at NVIDIA, USA; Hironori Washizaki Dean of Research, Waseda University, Japan; Priyanka Sinha, IoT Analytics, Zenatix Solutions, India; Mahendra Sharma, Pro Chancellor and Director General of Ganpat University; Noor Zaman from Taylor's University, Malaysia; Sabu M. Thampi, IIIT, Trivandrum, India; Kiran Amin, Executive Dean of the Faculty of Engineering and Technology, Ganpat University, India; Satyen Parikh, Executive Dean of Computer Science, Ganpat University, India; and Nirbhay Chaubey, Dean of Computer Science, Ganpat University, India, who declared the conference open.

There were four plenary session talks held covering the different areas of the conference: Ashok Jhunjhunwala delivered a keynote talk on "Strategy Towards Low-Carbon Transition Driving India Towards Net-Zero", Hironori Washizaki addressed the conference on "Machine Learning Software Engineering and ML Design Pattern", Jyotika Athavale spoke about "Standard for Functional Safety Data Format for Interoperability Within The Dependability Lifecycle", and Priyanka Sinha talked on "IPv6 Neighbour Discovery Protocol Enhancements for Wireless Network".

The conference accepted 20 papers as oral presentations (out of 190 full papers received and critically peer reviewed using the Springer EquinOCS system), which were presented during the two days. The conference committee formed six expert session chairs, all expert professors in their fields and from reputed universities in India and abroad.

The session track had panel members and session chairs: Savita Gandhi, Dean of Computer Science, GLS University, Ahmedabad, India; Nikhil J. Kothari, professor from Dharmsinh Desai University, Nadiad, India; Jagdish M. Rathod, Professor from Birla Vishvakarma Mahavidyalaya, Vallabh Vidyangar, India; Maulika Patel, professor from CVM University, Vallabh Vidyangar, India; Nilesh Modi, Dr. Bhimrao Ambedkar Open University, Ahmedabad, India; and Rutvij Jhaveri, from Pandit Deendayal Energy University, India.

All the accepted papers were peer reviewed by three qualified reviewers chosen from our conference Scientific Committee based on their qualifications and experience. The proceedings editors wish to thank the dedicated Scientific Committee members and all the other reviewers for their contributions. We also thank Springer for their trust and for publishing the proceedings of COMS2 2023.

The conference was organized by Ganpat University, a well reputed state private university, with a campus that spreads out over more than 300 acres of land with world class infrastructure and more than 12,000 students on campus. In consideration of its contribution to education in only a short period of time, the university has been given membership of the Association of Indian Universities (AIU).

The conference was full of fruitful discussions, igniting the spirit of research. It was indeed a remarkable, memorable, and knowledgeable virtual conference. The success of COMS2 2023 means that planning can now proceed with confidence for the 5th International Conference on Computing Science, Communication and Security (COMS2) scheduled for February 2024 at Ganpat University, India.

February 2023   Nirbhay Chaubey
                                                   Sabu M. Thampi
                                                Noor Zaman Jhanjhi
                                                     Satyen Parikh
                                                       Kiran Amin

Organization

Scientific Committee

Ganpatbhai Patel (Patron-in-Chief & President)	Ganpat University, India
Mahendra Sharma (Pro Chancellor)	Ganpat University, India
Rakesh Patel	Ganpat University, India
Amit Patel	Ganpat University, India
Saurabh Dave	Ganpat University, India
Girish Patel	Ganpat University, India
Rajkumar Buyya	University of Melbourne, Australia
K. S. Dasgupta	DAIICT, India
Mohammed Atiquzzaman	University of Oklahoma, USA
Arup R. Dasgupta	Space Application Centre, ISRO, India
Akshai Aggarwal	University of Windsor, Canada
Om Prakash Vyas	IIIT, Allahabad, India
Savita R. Gandhi	GLS University, India
Sabu M. Thampi	IIITM-K, India
Deepak Mathur	IEEE Asia Pacific Region 10, Singapore
Sartaj Sahni	University of Florida, USA
Maniklal Das	DA-IICT, India
S. Venkatesan	IIIT, Allahabad, India
Deepak Garg	Bennett University, India
Mohit Tahiliani	NIT, Karnatka, India
Nilesh Modi	Dr. Babasaheb Ambedkar Open University, India
Kevin Dami	University of Detroit, USA
Bala Natarajan	Kansas State University, USA
Virendra C. Bhavsar	University of New Brunswick, Canada
G. Sahoo	Birla Institute of Technology, India
Kiran Amin	Ganpat University, India
Satyen Parikh	Ganpat University, India
Hemal Shah	Ganpat University, India
Nirbhay Chaubey	Ganpat University, India
Rakesh D. Vanzara	Ganpat University, India
Hamid R. Arabnia	University of Georgia, USA
Sanjay Madria Missouri	University of Science and Technology, USA
Arvind Shah	Georgia Southwestern State University, USA

P. Balasubramanian	Nanyang Technological University, Singapore
Xing Liu	Kwantlen Polytechnic University, Canada
Kalpdrum Passi	Laurentian University, Canada
Ratvinder Grewal	Laurentian University, Canada
Ali Mostafaeipour	Yazd University, Iran
Ramesh Bansal	University of Sharjah, UAE
Neville Watson	University of Canterbury, New Zealand
Yuan Miao	Victoria University, Australia
Shah Miah	Victoria University, Australia
Mohan Kolhe	University of Agder, Norway
Akhtar Kalam	Victoria University, Australia
Pao-Ann Hsiung	National Chung Cheng University, Taiwan
Prateek Agrawal	University of Klagenfurt, Austria
Anatoliy Zabrovskiy	University of Klagenfurt, Austria
Valentina Emilia Balas	University of Arad, Romania
Ashok Karania	EMEA, UK
D. P. Kothari	VIT University, India
H. S. Mazumdar	Dharmsinh Desai University, India
Debajyoti Mukhopadhyay	Bennett University, India
Ashok R. Patel	Florida Polytechnic University, USA
Ruoyu Wang	Arizona State University, USA
Kevin Gary	Arizona State University, USA
Tatyana Ryutov	University of Southern California, USA
George Sklivanitis	Florida Atlantic University, USA
Koushik A. Manjunatha	Idaho National Laboratory, USA
Sathyan Munirathinam	ASML Corporation, USA
Yogesh Patel	Salesforce, USA
Priyanshukumar Jha	Amazon, USA
El Sayed Mahmoud	Sheridan College, Canada
Jigisha Patel	Sheridan College, Canada
Pawan Lingra	St. Mary's University, Canada
Muhammad Dangana	University of Glasgow, UK
Gisa Fuatai Purcel	Victoria University of Wellington, UK
Gyu Myoung Lee	Liverpool John Moores University, UK
Stefano Cirillo	University of Salerno, Italy
Flavio Vella	Free University of Bozen, Italy
Alessandro Barbiero	Università di Milano, Italy
Lelio Campanile	Università Vanvitelli, Italy
Asmerilda Hitaj	University of Milano Bicocca, Italy
Abdallah Handoura	Ecole Nationale Supérieure des Télécommunications, France
Gua Xiangfa	National University of Singapore, Singapore

Raman Singh	Trinity College Dublin, Ireland
Ahmed M. Elmisery	Waterford Institute of Technology, Ireland
Shahzad Ashraf	Hohai University, China
Moharram Challenger	University of Antwerp, Belgium
Dragi Kimovski	Klagenfurt University, Austria
Iwan Adhicandra	University of Sydney, Australia
Payal Mahida	Victorian Institute of Technology, Australia
Tarandeep Kaur Bhatia	Deakin University, Australia
Siddharth Patel	Eaton Corporation, Australia
Marcin Paprzycki	Polish Academy of Sciences, Poland
Sabyasachi Chakraborty	Inje University, South Korea
Sayan K. Ray	Manukau Institute of Technology, New Zealand
Ahmed Al-Sa'di	Auckland University of Technology, New Zealand
Clementine Gritti	University of Canterbury, New Zealand
Samaneh Madanian	Auckland University of Technology, New Zealand
Aravind Nair	KTH Royal Institute of Technology, Sweden
Yehia Abd Alrahman	Chalmers University of Technology, Sweden
Karl Andersson	Luleå University of Technology, Sweden
Jose M. Molina	Universidad Carlos III de Madrid, Spain
Manuel Chica	University of Granada, Spain
Jose Angel Diaz-Garcia	University of Granada, Spain
Carlos Fernandez-Basso	University of Granada, Spain
George Papakostas	Eastern Macedonia and Thrace Institute of Technology, Greece
Dimitris Karampatzakis	International Hellenic University, Greece
Ioannis Tollis	University of Crete, Greece
Christos J. Bouras	University of Patras, Greece
Loannis Tollis	University of Crete, Greece
Zitong Yu	University of Oulu, Finland
Akien Paul	University of the West Indies, West Indies
Rakhee	University of the West Indies, West Indies
Ammar Muthanna	Saint Petersburg State University of Telecommunications, Russia
Noor Zaman Jhanjhi	Taylor's University, Malaysia
Irdayanti Mat Nashir	Universiti Pendidikan Sultan Idris, Malaysia
Jing Rui Tang	Universiti Pendidikan Sultan Idris, Malaysia
Zaliza Hanapi	Universiti Pendidikan Sultan Idris, Malaysia
Encik Ong Jia Hui	Tunku Abdul Rahman University College, Malaysia
Qusay Medhat Salih	Universiti Malaysia Pahang, Malaysia
Dalal A. Hammood	Universiti Malaysia Perlis, Malaysia
Muhammad Asif Khan	Qatar University, Qatar

Ashraf A. M. Khalaf	Minia University, Egypt
Dimiter G. Velev	University of National and World Economy, Bulgaria
Pahlaj Moolio	Pannasastra University of Cambodia, Cambodia
Mudassir Khan	King Khalid University, Saudi Arabia
Lamia Berriche	Prince Sultan University, Saudi Arabia
Lal Bihari Barik	King Abdulaziz University, Saudi Arabia
Shermin Shamsudheen	Jazan University, Saudi Arabia
Tran Cong Hung	Posts and Telecomunication Institute of Technology, Vietnam
Anand Nayyar	Duy Tan University, Vietnam
Pao-Ann Hsiung	National Chung Cheng University, Taiwan
Seyyed Ahmad Edalatpanah	Ayandegan Institute of Higher Education, Iran
Aws Zuheer Yonis	Ninevah University, Iraq
Razan Abdulhammed	Northern Technical University, Iraq
Moharram Challenger	Ege University, Turkey
Sandeep Kautish	LBEF, Kathmandu, Nepal
A. A Gde Satia Utama	Universitas Airlangga, Indonesia
Eva Shayo	University of Dar es Salaam, Tanzania
Anil Audumbar Pise	University of the Witwatersrand, South Africa
Sarang C. Dhongdi	BITS Pilani, India
Satyabrata Jit	IIT(BHU), India
Pratik Chattopadhyay	IIT(BHU), India
Amrita Chaturvedi	IIT(BHU), India
Amit Kumar Singh	IIT(BHU), India
Amrita Mishra	IIIT Naya Raipur, India
Panchami V.	IIIT, Kottayam, India
Bhuvaneswari Amma N. G.	IIIT, Una, India
Jitendra Tembhurne	IIIT, Nagpur, India
Renjith P.	IIIT, Kurnool, India
Sachin Jain	IIIT, Jabalpur, India
Priyanka Mishra	IIIT, Kota, India
Chetna Sharma	IIIT, Kota, India
Eswaramoorthy K.	IIIT, Kurnool, India
Pandiyarasan Veluswamy	IIITDM, Kancheepuram, India
Sahil	IIIT, Una, India
Sanya Anees	IIIT, Guwahati, India
Suvrojit Das	NIT, Durgapur, India
Aruna Jain	Birla Institute of Technology, India
Amit Kumar Gupta	DRDO, Hyderbad, India
R. Kumar	SRM University, India
B. Ramachandran	SRM University, India

Iyyanki V. Muralikrishna	J.N. Technological University, India
Apurv Shah	M.S. University, India
Manoj Kumar	Infliblnet University Grants Commission, India
U. Dinesh Kumar	IIM, Bangalore, India
Saurabh Bilgaiyan	KIIT, India
Raja Sarath Kumar Boddu	Jawaharlal Nehru Technological University, India
Kiran Sree Pokkuluri	SVECM, India
Devesh Kumar Srivastava	Manipal University, India
P. Muthulakshmi	SRM University, India
R. Anandan	VELS University, India
Amol Dhondse	IBM India Software Labs, India
R. Amirtharajan	SASTRA Deemed University, India
Padma Priya V.	SASTRA Deemed University, India
Deepak H Sharma	K.J. Somaiya College of Engineering, India
Ravi Subban	Pondicherry University, India
Parameshachari B. D	Visvesvaraya Technological University, India
Nilakshi Jain	University of Mumbai, India
Archana Mire	University of Mumbai, India
Sonali Bhutad	University of Mumbai, India
Anand Kumar	Visvesvaraya Technological University, India
Jyoti Pareek	Gujarat University, India
Sanjay Garg	Indrashil University, India
Madhuri Bhavsar	Nirma University, India
Vijay Ukani	Nirma University, India
Mayur Vegad	BVM Engineering College, India
N. M. Patel	BVM Engineering College, India
J. M. Rathod	BVM Engineering College, India
Maulika Patel	CVM University, India
Nikhil Gondalia	CVM University, India
Priyanka Sharma	Raksha Shakti University, India
Digvijaysinh Rathod	Gujarat Forensic Science University, India
Kalpesh Parikh	Intellisense IT, India
Balaji Rajendran	CDAC, Bangaluru, India
Mehul C. Parikh	Gujarat Technological University, India
G. R. Kulkarni	Gujarat Technological University, India
Amol C. Adamuthe	Shivaji University, India
Shrihari Khatawkar	Shivaji University, India
Snehal Joshi	Veer Narmad South Gujarat University, India
Ambika Nagaraj	Bengaluru Central University, India
Ashok Solanki	Veer Narmad South Gujarat University, India
Aditya Sinha	CDAC, India
Harshal Arolkar	GLS University, India

Binod Kumar	University of Pune, India
Maulin Joshi	Savajanik University, India
Vrushank Shah	Indus University, India
Manish Patel	Sankalchand Patel University, India
Ankit Bhavsar	GLS University, India
Seema Mahajan	Indus University, India
S. K. Vij	ITM University, India
Vishal Jain	Sharda University, India
D. B. Choksi	Sardar Patel University, India
Paresh Virpariya	Sardar Patel University, India
Priti Srinivas Sajja	Sardar Patel University, India
C. K. Bhensdadia	Dharmsinh Desai University, India
Vipul K. Dabhi	Dharmsinh Desai University, India
N. J. Kothari	Dharmsinh Desai University, India
Narayan Joshi	Dharmsinh Desai University, India
S. D. Panchal	Gujarat Technological University, India
M. T. Savaliya	Gujarat Technological University, India
Vinod Desai	Gujarat Vidyapith, India
Jignesh Doshi	Gujarat Technological University, India
Bhaveshkumar Prajapati	Gujarat Technological University, India
Nisha Somani	Gujarat Technological University, India
Desai Archana Natvarbhai	Gujarat Technological University, India
Akhilesh Ladha	Gujarat Technological University, India
Jaymin Bhalani	Gujarat Technological University, India
Dhananjay Yadav	Gujarat Technological University, India
Keyur Jani	Gujarat Technological University, India
Jeegar Trivedi	Sardar Patel University, India

Organizing Committee

Ajay Patel	Ganpat University, India
Ketan Patel	Ganpat University, India
Anand Mankodia	Ganpat University, India
Paresh M. Solanki	Ganpat University, India
Savan Patel	Ganpat University, India
Jigna Prajapati	Ganpat University, India
Pravesh Patel	Ganpat University, India
Ketan Sarvakar	Ganpat University, India

Contents

An Efficient Signal Detection Technique for STBC-OFDM in Fast Fading Channel

Jyoti P. Patra[1]([✉]) [iD], Bibhuti Bhusan Pradhan[2] [iD], S. Thulasi Prasad[1] [iD], and Poonam Singh[3] [iD]

[1] Vidya Jyothi Institute of Technology, Hyderabad 500075, Telegana, India
jyotiprasannapatra@gmail.com, sthulasiprasad@vjit.ac.in
[2] Malla Reddy Engineering College, Hyderabad 500100, Telegana, India
bibhu.iisc@gmail.com
[3] National Institute of Technology, Rourkela 769008, Odisha, India
psingh@nitrkl.ac.in

Abstract. In frequency selective fading channel, the STBC-OFDM system achieves optimal performance. Unfortunately, the STBC-OFDM system performance is degraded due to co-channel interference (CCI) in time selective fading channel. To suppress CCI effects various signal detection techniques are investigated including diagonalized zero forcing detection (DZFD), successive interference cancellation (SIC), decision feedback detection (DFD), List-SIC, and maximum likelihood (ML) methods. Although ML detection technique achieves optimal performance, it results into very high computational complexity. In this paper, the STBC-OFDM systems performance is analyzed under the influence of time selective channels. In particular, we proposed a suboptimal ordered iterative decision feedback (OIDF) detection technique based on dual combining scheme of DZFD and SIC with iterations. Finally, the performance evaluation is carried out for proposed OIDF method and various standard conventional signal detection methods based on complexity and bit error rate (BER). The results show that BER performance of OIDF method nearly approaches to ML method with substantial reduction in complexity.

Keywords: Signal Detection · STBC-OFDM · Co-channel Interference · Low Complexity · Fast Fading Channel

1 Introductions

Next generation wireless communication offers a wide range of applications starting from telephonic service to high quality video signal streaming. These causes major challenges due to high data rate and link reliability. Recently, the transmit diversity schemes have gained tremendous interest due to the improvement of link reliability without requiring extra transmitting power or bandwidth [1,2]. Alamouti in [3] first proposed transmit diversity technique known as space time

© The Author(s), under exclusive license to Springer Nature Switzerland AG 2023
N. Chaubey et al. (Eds.): COMS2 2023, CCIS 1861, pp. 1–14, 2023.
https://doi.org/10.1007/978-3-031-40564-8_1

block code (STBC). After that, the STBC becomes one of the popular signal processing technique for many applications such as Wi-Fi [6,7], WiMAX, LTE [4,5], and radio receiver applications [8]. The STBC scheme is appropriate for flat fading channel. However, frequency selective channel is converted by OFDM technique into numerous narrow parallel flat channels. Thus STBC and OFDM techniques can be combined together to resolve the frequency selctive problem [9]. But, in fast fading channel, the system performance of STBC-OFDM degrades because of the occurrence of co-channel interference (CCI) effects and inter-carrier interference (ICI) effects. The ICI effects arise due to orthogonality loss between OFDM subcarriers. The CCI arise due to the channel variation among adjacent OFDM symbol blocks. It is shown that the power loss is 7–8 dB larger in CCI effcts as compared to ICI effects [10]. Therefore, many researches have been taken place to cancel the CCI effects rather than ICI [10–16]. In [11], based on the transform matrix, diagonalized maximum likelihood detection technique (DMLD) was proposed. However, the complexity of DMLD method significantly increases with the higher order modulation. A successive interference cancellation (SIC) detection technique was proposed based on difference in diversity gain [10]. However, it suffers from the issue of error propagation. In [12], the decision feedback detection (DFD) technique was proposed. This DFD method achieves better performance as compared to DMLD method as it avoids noise enhancement problem. Based on Cholesky decompostion [13,14], three signal detection methods e.g. DF, ZF and ML methods were proposed. To suppress error floor in SIC, a List-SIC method is proposed in [15] and thus significantly improves the system performance. In [16], A diagonalized zero forcing detection (DZFD) technique was proposed. This method performs exactly same as DMLD with lower complexity. The maximum likelihood (ML) detection technique was investigated in [13,14]. Typically, the performance of ML technique has the optimal value, however the complexity of ML method grows exponentially with modulation order. A QR decomposition based signal detection method was proposed for space time scheme in [17]. A low-complexity ML decoder for STBC based spatial permutation modulation system was proposed in [18] by exploiting the STBC orthogonality code. A multiple-input multiple-output signal detection algorithm using VBLAST based on lowest mean square error was proposed in [19]. Neuman series approximation-based signal detection method was proposed in [20] to avoid matrix inversion for massive MIMO systems. A modified ZF based method was proposed for underwater STBC-OFDM acoustic communication system in [21]. However, all these signal detection techniques provide trade-off between complexity and performance in comparison with ML technique. In this work, we proposed a suboptimal ordered iterative DF (OIDF) detection technique based on DZFD and SIC with iterations. This OIDF achieves performance similar to ML method with significantly reduction in complexity.

The rest of paper is organized as follows. In Sect. 2, the STBC-OFDM system model is described. In Sect. 3 several signal detection techniques are described to cancel the CCI effects. In Sect. 4, suboptimal OIDF method is discussed. In Sect. 5, the proposed and conventional methods have been analyzed based on complexity. The performances of several signal detection methods are evaluated based on BER for various mobile velocity in Sect. 6. At the end, the conclusion about paper is discussed in Sect. 7.

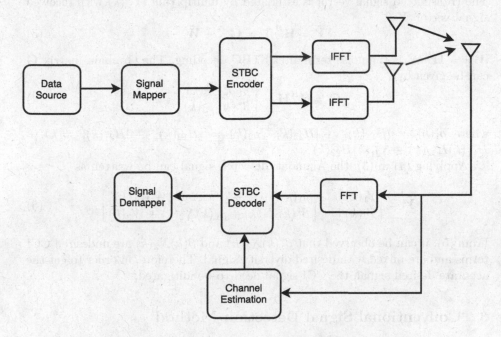

Fig. 1. Block diagram of STBC-OFDM system model.

2   System Model

We consider an STBC-OFDM system model as shown in Fig. 1. At the transmitter side, random binary data sequence is generated, mapped into data symbols using any finite constellation and then forwarded to STBC block where it encodes the data symbol vector, $X = \begin{bmatrix} X_1(k) & X_2(k) \end{bmatrix}^T$ into the STBC encoded matrix $\mathbf{S}$ as per the Alamouti scheme as given by

$$\mathbf{S} = \begin{bmatrix} X_{11}(k) & X_{12}(k) \\ X_{21}(k) & X_{22}(k) \end{bmatrix} = \begin{bmatrix} X_1(k) & X_2(k) \\ -X_2^*(k) & X_1^*(k) \end{bmatrix} \tag{1}$$

The symbol $X_{ji}(k)$ is the transmitting data signal from the ith transmitting antenna for the jth symbol period at the kth subcarrier. Then, the STBC encoder signals are processed using IFFT operation. Finally, after addition of cyclic prefix (CP), the signals are transmitted through the antennas. At the receiver side, after performing of signal manipulation such as deletion of cyclic prefix and FFT operations, the received signal is written as

$$\mathbf{Y} = \begin{bmatrix} Y_1(k) \\ Y_2^*(k) \end{bmatrix} = \begin{bmatrix} H_{11}(k,k) & H_{12}(k,k) \\ H_{22}^*(k,k) & -H_{21}^*(k,k) \end{bmatrix} \begin{bmatrix} X_1(k) \\ X_2(k) \end{bmatrix} + \begin{bmatrix} W_1(k) \\ W_2^*(k) \end{bmatrix} = \mathbf{H}X + W \tag{2}$$

where $\boldsymbol{Y} = [Y_1(k)\ Y_2^*(k)]^T$ and $\boldsymbol{X} = [X_1(k)\ X_2(k)]^T$, are received and transmitted signal vectors respectively. Symbol $\boldsymbol{W} = [W_1(k)\ W_2^*(k)]$ is noise vector. The transmitted signal vector is estimated by multiplying $\mathbf{H}^H(k)$ with received signal vector $\boldsymbol{Y}$

$$\tilde{\boldsymbol{Y}} = \mathbf{H}^H \boldsymbol{Y} = \mathbf{G}X + \tilde{\boldsymbol{W}} \tag{3}$$

$[\tilde{\boldsymbol{W}}] = \mathbf{H}^H \mathbf{W}$ is the noise term after STBC decoding. The Gramain matrix $\mathbf{G}$ can be given by

$$\mathbf{G} = \mathbf{H}^H \mathbf{H} = \begin{bmatrix} \rho_1(k) & \beta(k) \\ \beta^*(k) & \rho_2(k) \end{bmatrix} \tag{4}$$

where $\rho_1(k) = |H_{11}(k)|^2 + |H_{22}(k)|^2, \rho_2(k) = |H_{12}(k)|^2 + |H_{21}(k)|^2, \beta(k) = H_{11}^*(k)H_{12}(k) - H_{21}^*(k)H_{22}(k)$

Applying (4) in (3), the Alamouti detected signal can be written as

$$\tilde{\boldsymbol{Y}} = \begin{bmatrix} \tilde{Y}_1(k) \\ \tilde{Y}_2(k) \end{bmatrix} = \begin{bmatrix} \rho_1(k)X_1(k) + \beta(k)X_2(k) + \tilde{W}_1(k) \\ \beta^*(k)X_1(k) + \rho_2(k)X_2(k) + \tilde{W}_2(k) \end{bmatrix} \tag{5}$$

From (5), it can be observed that $\beta^*(k)X_1(k)$ and $\beta(k)X_2(k)$ are undesired CCI terms and are mixed with desired diversity signal. Therefore, in order to get the accurate desired signal, the CCI signal need to be mitigated.

3   Conventional Signal Detection Method

The conventional signal detection techniques are discussed in this section which includes SIC method, DZFD method, List-SIC method, DF method and ML method to suppress the CCI effects.

3.1   DZFD Method

In fast fading channel, the Gram matrix $\mathbf{G} = \mathbf{H}^H \mathbf{H}$ is not orthogonal matrix. Hence, to obtain a diagonal matrix, transform $\boldsymbol{\Omega}$ matrix is multiplied with $\mathbf{H}$ matrix as proposed in [16]. Multiplying $\boldsymbol{\Omega}$ with the received signal $\boldsymbol{Y}$, we have

$$\breve{\boldsymbol{Y}} = \boldsymbol{\Omega}\boldsymbol{Y} = diag(\phi_1(k), \phi_2(k))\boldsymbol{X} + \boldsymbol{\Omega}\boldsymbol{W} \tag{6}$$

where $\phi_i(k)$ is a complex number. After solving (6), the $\boldsymbol{\Omega}$ matrix can be written as

$$\boldsymbol{\Omega} = \begin{bmatrix} H_{21}^*(k) & H_{12}(k) \\ H_{22}^*(k) & -H_{11}(k) \end{bmatrix} \tag{7}$$

The value of $\phi_i(k)$ can be obtained by multiplying $\boldsymbol{\Omega}$ with $\mathbf{H}$ matrix as follows

$$\begin{aligned} \phi(k) &= \phi_1(k) = \phi_2(k) \\ &= H_{11}(k)H_{21}^*(k) + H_{12}(k)H_{22}^*(k) \end{aligned} \tag{8}$$

The required transmitted signal is obtained by dividing $\phi(k)$ on either side of (6) followed by hard decision as given by

$$\hat{X}_1(k) = \Pi \ (\breve{Y}_1(k)/\phi(k) \ ) \tag{9}$$

$$\hat{X}_2(k) = \Pi \ (\breve{Y}_2(k)/\phi(k) \ ) \tag{10}$$

This method cancels the CCI term to zero and thus, theoretically there is no CCI effects present in the system. However it suffers from noise enhancement.

3.2 SIC Method

The SIC method is performed based on the higher diversity gain term for detection of transmitted data signal and is given as follows.

[*Step* 1]: *Initialization*: Perform Alamouti signal detection

$$\tilde{Y}_1(k) = \rho_1(k)X_1(k) + \beta(k)X_2(k) + \tilde{W}_1(k) \tag{11}$$

$$\tilde{Y}_2(k) = \beta^*(k)X_1(k) + \rho_2(k)X_2(k) + \tilde{W}_2(k) \tag{12}$$

[*Step* 2]: Compare the diversity gain

$$if \rho_1(k) \geq \rho_2(k) \ , \ \text{set subscripts } a = 1, \ b = 2$$
$$else \ \ \rho_1(k) < \rho_2(k) \ , \ \text{set subscripts } a = 2, \ b = 1$$

[*Step* 3]: Detect data signal according to larger diversity gain

$$\hat{X}_a(k) = \Pi(\tilde{Y}_a(k)/\rho_a(k)) \tag{13}$$

[*Step* 4]: Detect other data signal by cancelling the CCI term

$$\hat{X}_b(k) = \Pi([\tilde{Y}_b(k) - \beta^*(k)\hat{X}_a(k)]/\rho_b(k)) \tag{14}$$

here Π denotes the hard decision function.

3.3 DFD Method

The decision feedback (DF) method obtain first signal and assume that the this is estimated correctly. Then cancels the contributions of first signal to obtain second signal. The algorithm of DF method is illustrated below.

[*Step* 1]: Obtain first data signal using zero forcing method

$$\hat{X}_1(k) = \Pi \ (\breve{Y}_1(k)/\phi(k) \ ) \tag{15}$$

[*Step* 2]: Cancel the contribution of first signal $(\hat{X}_1(k))$ from Alamouti detected signal $(\tilde{Y}_2(k))$ to obtain second $\hat{X}_2(k)$

$$\hat{X}_2(k) = \Pi([\tilde{Y}_2(k) - \beta^*(k)\hat{X}_1(k)]/\rho_2(k)) \tag{16}$$

The DFD method gives better performance as compared to DZFD method as it avoids noise enhancement problem.

3.4 List-SIC Method

The List-SIC method was proposed in [15] to suppress the CCI effects. Unlike hard decision in SIC, this method preserves all possible constellation points and passes it to the next step for effective CCI cancellation. The description of list SIC is given as follows

[*Step* 1]: Compare the diversity gain:

$$if \rho_1(k) \geq \rho_2(k), \qquad \text{set subscripts } a = 1, \text{ and } b = 2$$
$$else \rho_1(k) < \rho_2(k), \quad \text{set subscripts } a = 1, \text{ and } b = 2$$

[*Step* 2]: Preserve the symbol vector constellation with higher diversity gain

$$\tilde{\boldsymbol{X}}_a = \boldsymbol{C}_M, \tag{17}$$

where $\boldsymbol{C}_M$ is the constellation mapping and for QPSK $\boldsymbol{C}_M = [C_0, C_1, C_2, C_3]$.

[*Step* 3]: Cancel the CCI term according to diversity gain

$$\tilde{\boldsymbol{R}}_b = [\hat{Y}_b(k) \otimes \boldsymbol{1}_M - \beta^*(k)\tilde{\boldsymbol{X}}_a(k)]/\rho_b(k) \tag{18}$$

where $\boldsymbol{1}_M$ is of size $1 \times M$ with all element equals to 1.

[*Step* 4]: Construct matrix candidates by taking hard decision on $\tilde{\boldsymbol{R}}_b$

$$\tilde{\boldsymbol{X}}_b = \Pi[\tilde{\boldsymbol{R}}_b] \tag{19}$$

[*Step* 5]: Construct the candidates symbol matrix according to ordering

$$if \ \ a = 1, \ b = 2 \ \ \tilde{\boldsymbol{X}}_{candidate} = \begin{bmatrix} \tilde{\boldsymbol{X}}_a^T & \tilde{\boldsymbol{X}}_b^T \end{bmatrix}$$

$$if \ \ a = 2, \ b = 1 \ \ \tilde{\boldsymbol{X}}_{candidate} = \begin{bmatrix} \tilde{\boldsymbol{X}}_b^T & \tilde{\boldsymbol{X}}_a^T \end{bmatrix}$$

[*Step* 6] Detect the data symbol from the candidate list

$$\hat{\boldsymbol{X}}(k) = \arg\min_{\tilde{X}(k)} \left\| \boldsymbol{Y}(k) - \mathbf{H}(k)\tilde{\boldsymbol{X}} \right\|^2 \tag{20}$$

where $\tilde{\boldsymbol{X}}$ is the column vector of $\tilde{\boldsymbol{X}}_{candidate}$. As the list-SIC method depends on constellation mapping to estimate the data signal, the complexity of the List-SIC method grows linearly with higher order modulation.

3.5 ML Method

The ML detection chooses the best appropriate signal after estimates all possible combination. Mathematically, it can be expressed as

$$\hat{X}(k) = \arg\min_{X_1, X_2 \in C_M} \left\| \boldsymbol{Y}(k) - \mathbf{H}(k) \begin{bmatrix} X_1 \\ X_2 \end{bmatrix} \right\|^2 \tag{21}$$

where $\boldsymbol{C}_M$ denotes constellation mapping. The ML method perform $|C_M|^2$ times matrices operations to obtain transmitted data signal.

4   Proposed OIDF Method

The proposed OIDF method is an iterative dual combining scheme of DZFD and SIC. Although the DZFD cancel the CCI effects by forcing them to zero, it provides less diversity gain. At first we calculate the absolute value of the diversity gain of the DZFD method for kth subcarrier given by

$$
\begin{aligned}
E[|\phi(k)|] &= E[|H_{11}(k)H_{21}^*(k) + H_{12}(k)H_{22}^*(k)|] \\
&= E[|H_{11}(k)H_{21}^*(k)|] + E[|H_{12}(k)H_{22}^*(k)|] = 2J_0(2\pi f_d T_s)
\end{aligned}
\tag{22}
$$

It is to note that, the performance of DZFD method is based on correlation parameter and is always less than one i.e. $J_0(2\pi f_d T_s) \leq 1$. Therefore, the diversity gain of DZFD method is less than the gain of Almouti method i.e. $|\phi| \leq \rho$. The performance of DZFD method drastically decreases as normalized Doppler frequency $(f_d N T_s)$ increases. The DFD method obtains the initial signal from the DZFD and then cancels the contribution to get the other transmitted signal without any ordering, thus it may lead to error propagation problem. This motivates to propose the suboptimal OIDF method which eliminates the problem of error propagation. The OIDF method iteratively cancels the CCI effects to estimate the data signal. At first,this method obtain a rough estimate of the transmitted signal using DZFD method based on diversity gain and subsequently cancels the contributions in iterative process. The description of proposed OIDF technique is illustrated below.

[*Step* 1]: *Ordering*

  if $\rho_1(k) \geq \rho_2(k)$,   set subscripts $a = 1$, and $b = 2$
  else $\rho_1(k) < \rho_2(k)$,   set subscripts $a = 1$, and $b = 2$

[*Step* 2]: Obtain the rough estimates of data signal using DZFD method based on higher diversity gain

$$
\hat{X}_a(k) = \Pi\{(\tilde{Y}_a(k)/\phi(k)\}
\tag{23}
$$

[*Step* 3]: Obtain the refined data signal by cancelling the CCI effects in an iterative process

  for $t = 1: I$

$$
\hat{X}_b(k) = \Pi\{ [\tilde{Y}_b(k) - \beta^*(k)\hat{X}_a(k)]/\rho_b(k)\}
\tag{24}
$$

$$
\hat{X}_a(k) = \Pi\{ [\tilde{Y}_a(k) - \beta(k)(k)\hat{X}_b(k)]/\rho_a(k)\}
\tag{25}
$$

  end

---

where I stands for the number of iterations. The proposed OIDF method refines the estimated data signal by iteratively cancelling the CCI effects in each iteration. Therefore the interferences have been completely removed after few iterations and the desired diversity gain is improved.

Table 1. Number of complex multiplications for several signal detection methods.

	Alamouti	SIC	DZFD	DFD	List-SIC	OIDF	ML
Complexity	8	11	10	21	10+6 C_M	24	$4|C_M|^2$
QPSK	8	11	10	21	34	24	64
16QAM	8	11	10	21	106	24	1024

5   Computational Complexity

The complexity of various signal detection techniques are calculated in this section based on number of complex multiplications. The Almouti detection performs signal operation as $\tilde{Y} = \mathbf{H}^H \mathbf{Y}$ which needs 4 complex multiplications. In addition to that, calculation of $\rho_1(k)$ and $\rho_2(k)$ requires each two complexity. As $\rho_1(k)$ and $\rho_2(k)$ are integer value, the decision of Alamouti method i.e. $\hat{X}_i(k) = \Pi(\tilde{Y}_i(k)/\rho_i)$ does not have extra computational complexity. Thus, Alamouti method has total 8 complex multiplications. In SIC, 4 complex multiplication are required for $\tilde{Y}$ and $\rho_1(k)$, $\rho_2(k)$ and $\beta(k)$ requires each two complex multiplications. Comparing the diversity gain does not need complex computations as it is performed using shift operation. The SIC method perform either $\beta(k)X_2(k)$ or $\beta^*(k)X_1(k)$ to cancel the CCI signal. Thus total 11 complex multiplications are required for SIC signal detection method. In DZFD, the operation of $\breve{Y}(k) = \Omega(k)Y(k)$ needs a total 4 multiplications. Beside that, the calculation of ϕ requires 2 complex multiplications. Typically, a single complex division requires twice times complex multiplications. Dividing ϕ_i with $\breve{Y}_i(k)$, $\hat{X}_i(k) = \breve{Y}_i(k)/\phi_i(k)$ needs 2 complex multiplications. Thus, in DZFD, a total numbers of 10 complex multiplications are required. The DF detection technique estimate the first signal $\hat{X}_1(k)$ using DZFD method, thus needs 10 complex multiplication. In addition to that, $\tilde{Y}$ involves in 4 complex multiplication and each 2 multiplications are required for $\rho_1(k)$, $\rho_2(k)$, $\beta(k)$. The DFD also requires one complex multiplication for calculating $\beta^*(k)\hat{X}_1$. Thus, total 21 complex multiplications are involved in DFD method. The List-SIC method requires 4 complex multiplication for calculating $\tilde{Y}(k)$ and $\rho_1(k)$, $\rho_2(k)$ and $\beta(k)$ requires 6 complex multiplications. In List-SIC method, computations in [Step 3] and [Step 5] require $2C_M$ and $4C_M$ complex multiplications. Thus total $10 + 6C_M$ CM are required for List-SIC method. The ML detection method involves $4C_M^2$ complex multiplications to solve (21). The proposed OIDF method adopts DZFD method which requires 10 complex multiplications to obtain the initial data signal. To compute $\tilde{Y}(k)$ needs 4 complex multiplications, and $\rho_1(k)$, $\rho_2(k)$, $\beta(k)$ requires 6 complex multiplications. In addition to that, [Step 3] involves two complex multiplications i.e. $\beta^*(k)\hat{X}_1$ and $\beta^*(k)\hat{X}_1$ and if there are I number of iterations, the complexity in [Step 3] has $2.I$ computational complexity. Thus the proposed OIDF method involves $20 + 2.I$ complex multiplications. From simulation, it can be seen that the OIDF method saturated after $I = 2$ number of iteration. Therefore, the OIDF method requires 24 complex multiplication. Table 1 summarizes the number of complex multiplications for various signal detection techniques.

Table 2. Simulation Parameters.

Parameters	Value	
Configuration of Antenna	2 Tx, 1 Rx	
FFT Block size	128	
Number of OFDM Subcarrier	128	
Length of CP	16	
Type of Modulation	QPSK	
Frequency of Carrier (f_c)	2.5 GHz	
Bandwidth of OFDM Signal (B)	1 MHz	
Channel Model	Rayleigh Channel	
Number of Multipath Channel	8	
Delay Spread of Channel (d)	1.5	
Velocity of mobile (v)	200Km/h	400Km/h
Normalized Doppler Spread ($f_d N T_s$)	0.0593	0.1185

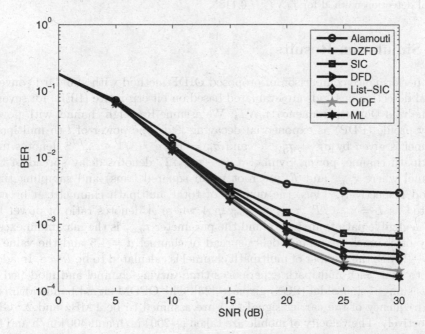

Fig. 2. BER performance comparison of proposed OIDF with various conventional signal detection method for $f_d N T_s = 0.0593$.

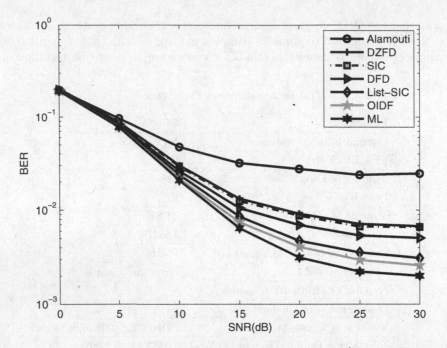

Fig. 3. BER performance comparison of proposed OIDF with various conventional signal detection method for $f_d NT_s = 0.1185$.

6   Simulation Results

The performance comparison of proposed OIDF method with standard conventional detection methods are evaluated based on bit error rate (BER) for several normalized Doppler frequency $f_d NT_s$. We assume Rayleigh channel with power delay profile (PDP) as exponential decaying [22]. The power of l-th multipath channel is given by $\sigma_l^2 = \sigma_0^2 e^{-l/d}$ and $\sigma_0^2 = 1 - e^{-1/d}/1 - e^{-L/d}$ denotes first multipath channel power. Symbol $d = -\tau_{rms}/T_s$ denotes delay spread of the channel where τ_{rms} and T_s are root mean squared (rms) and sampling time period respectively. Thus, the number of total multipath channel can be calculated as $L = \tau_{\max}/T_s$, $\tau_{\max} = \tau_{rms} \ln A$ where A denotes ratio of power for non-negligible path to first path and the parameter τ_{max} is the maximum excess delay of channel. Assuming, delay spread of channel $d = 1.5$ and the value of $A = -20$ dB, the number of multipath channel is calculated to be $L = 8$. In addition to that, each multipath experiences time varying channel and modelled as Jakes sum- of-sinusoidal (SOS) given in [23]. The OFDM signal bandwidth (B) and frequency of the carrier signal (f_c) are assumed to be 1 MHz and 2.5 GHz respectively. The velocity of mobile are taken as 200 km/h and 400 km/h and for which the normalized Doppler frequency are calculated as $f_d NT_s = 0.0593$ and $f_d NT_s = 0.1185$ respectively. Table 2 shows the total simulation parameters for Monte-Carlo simulation.

Figure 2 and 3 show the performances comparison of various signal detection techniques for $f_d N T_s = 0.0593$ and 0.1185 respectively. It is observed that the signal detection of Alamouti method is severely degraded due to the presence of CCI effects. The SIC method provides better performance compared to Alamouti method but it has the problem of error propagation effects. The DZFD method provides better results than Alamouti. However, its diversity gain decreases with increases in Doppler frequency. The DFD gives better result than DZFD as it estimates the first signal using DZFD and cancels the contribution of first signal to obtain the second signal. The List-SIC method outperforms the DFD method, however its computational complexity is very high with higher order modulation. The OIDF method iteratively cancels the CCI effects by adopting DZFD and SIC method and thus achieves better performance as compared to all the conventional methods except ML method. The performance of OIDF is close to ML. The BER performances of signal detection techniques in ascending order are as follows: Alamouti, SIC, DZFD, DFD, List-SIC, OIDF and ML.

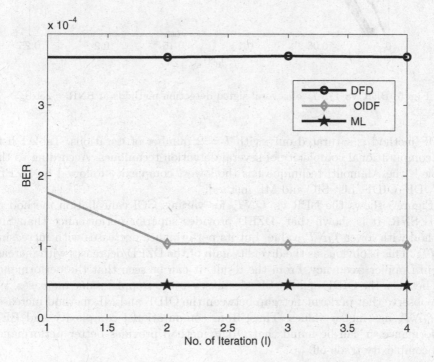

Fig. 4. BER Vs No. of Iterations (I) of DF, ML and OIDF method for $f_d N T_s = 0.0593$ at SNR $= 25$ dB.

Figure 4 shows the performance of DFD, ML and proposed OIDF techniques with several number of iterations (I) for $f_d N T_s = 0.0593$ at SNR $= 25$ dB. From the result, it can be observed that OIDF method outperforms DFD method and achieves performance near to ML method. From the Fig. 4, it is seen that the

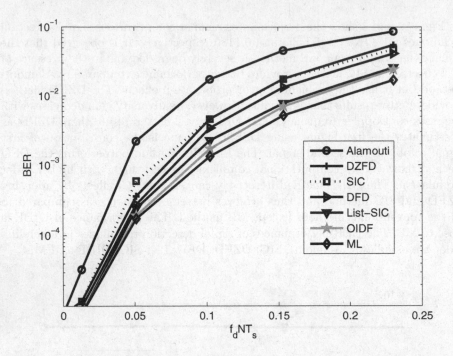

Fig. 5. BER Vs $f_d N T_s$ of several signal detection methods at SNR = 25 dB.

OIDF method is saturated only with $I = 2$ number of iterations. Table 1 lists the computational complexity of several detection techniques. According to the Table 1, the Alamouti technique has the lowest complexity followed by DZFD, SIC, DF, OIDF, List-SIC and ML method.

Figure 5 shows the BER vs $f_d N T_s$ for various CCI cancellation method at 25dB SNR. It is shown that, DZFD provides superior performance than SIC method with lower $f_d N T_s$ value, but its performance decreases with increasing $f_d N T_s$. This is obvious as the diversity gain of the DZFD decreases with increasing in Doppler frequency. From the result, it can be seen that the performance gap between the OIDF and list-SIC decreases as the Doppler value increases. We also observe that performance gap between the OIDF and ML method increases as $f_d N T_s$ has higher values. Thus, from computational complexity and BER performance, it can be found that OIDF method provides better performance and complexity trade-off.

7   Conclusions

In this paper, a sub-optimal signal detection technique is proposed for STBC-OFDM systems over fast fading channel. In frequency selective channels, the performance of STBC-OFDM is optimal but suffers from CCI effects in time selective channels. To cancel the CCI effects, various conventional methods are analyzed namely Alamouti, SIC, DZFD, List-SIC, DFD, and ML methods. We proposed suboptimal OIDF signal detection method based on iterative combining scheme of DZFD and SIC techniques. Finally, the comparison of proposed OIDF and various conventional methods are carried out based on BER and complexity. From the Monte-Carlo simulation, it can be demonstrated that the OIDF technique performs close to optimal ML with substantially lower complexity.

References

1. Paulraj, A., Gore, D., Nabar, R., Bolcskei, H.: An overview of MIMO communications- a key to gigabit wireless. Proc. IEEE **92**(2), 198–218 (2004)
2. Zhang, W., Xia, X.G., Letaief, K.B.: Space-time/frequency coding for MIMOOFDM in next generation broadband wireless systems. IEEE Wirel. Commun. **14**(3), 32–43 (2007)
3. Alamouti, S.M.: A simple transmit diversity technique for wireless communications (1998)
4. Li, Q., et al.: MIMO techniques in WiMAX and LTE: a feature overview. IEEE Commun. Mag. **48**(5), 86–92 (2010)
5. Pham, V.B.: Space-time block code design for LTE-advanced systems. Trans. Emerg. Telecommun. Technol. **26**(5), 918–928 (2015)
6. Bejarano, O., Knightly, E.W., Park, M.: IEEE 802.11 AC: from channelization to multi-user MIMO. IEEE Commun. Mag. **51**(10), 84–90 (2013)
7. Cisco: 802.11ac: The fifth generation of Wi-Fi technical white paper. Technical report, Cisco (2012)
8. Pham, Q.V., Nguyen, N.T., Huynh-The, T., Le, L.B., Lee, K., Hwang, W.J.: Intelligent radio signal processing: a survey. IEEE Access **9**, 83818–83850 (2021)
9. Lee, K.F., Williams, D.B.: A space-time coded transmitter diversity technique for frequency selective fading channels. In: Proceeding of IEEE Sensor Array and Multichannel Signal Processing Workshop, SAM, pp. 149–152 (2000)
10. Wee, J.W., Seo, J.W., Lee, K.T., Lee, Y.S., Jeon, W.G.: Successive interference cancellation for STBC-OFDM systems in a fast fading channel. In: Proceeding of IEEE 61st Vehicular Technology Conference, VTC-Spring, pp. 841–844 (2005)
11. Kanemaru, H., Ohtsuki, T.: Interference cancellation with diagonalized maximum likelihood decoder for space-time/space-frequency block coded OFDM. In: Proceedings of IEEE 59th Vehicular Technology Conference. VTC-Spring, pp. 525–529. IEEE (2004)
12. Suraweera, H.A., Armstrong, J.: Alamouti coded OFDM in Rayleigh fast fading channels-receiver performance analysis. In: TENCON 2005 IEEE Region 10, pp. 1–5. IEEE (2005)
13. Chiang, P.H., Lin, D.B., Li, H.J.: Performance of 2IMO differentially transmitdiversity block coded OFDM systems in doubly selective channels. In: Proceedings of IEEE Global Telecommunications Conference, GLOBECOM, pp. 3768–3773. IEEE (2005)
14. Lin, D.B., Chiang, P.H., Li, H.J.: Performance analysis of two-branch transmit diversity block-coded OFDM systems in time-varying multipath Rayleigh-fading channels. IEEE Trans. Veh. Technol. **54**(1), 136–148 (2005)
15. Tso, C.Y., Wu, J.M., Ting, P.A.: Iterative interference cancellation for STB-COFDM systems in fast fading channels. In: Proceeding of IEEE Global Telecommunications Conference, GLOBECOM, pp. 1–5 (2009)

16. Li, C.M., Li, G.W., Liu, H.Y.: Performance comparison of the STBC-OFDM decoders in a fast fading channel. J. Mar. Sci. Technol. **20**(5), 534–540 (2012)
17. Cortez, J., Palacio, R., Ramírez-Pacheco, J.C., Ruiz-Ibarra, E.: A very low complexity near ml detector based on QRD-M algorithm for STBC-VBLAST architecture. In: 2015 7th IEEE Latin-American Conference on Communications (LATIN-COM), pp. 1–5. IEEE (2015)
18. Tu, H.H., Lee, C.W., Lai, I.W.: Low-complexity maximum likelihood (ML) decoder for space-time block coded spatial permutation modulation (STBC-SPM). In: 2019 International Symposium on Intelligent Signal Processing and Communication Systems (ISPACS), pp. 1–2. IEEE (2019)
19. Zhao, G., Wang, J., Chen, W., Song, J.: A novel signal detection algorithm for underwater mimo-OFDM systems based on generalized MMSE. J. Sens. **2019**, 1–10 (2019)
20. Mousavi, S.H., Pourrostam, J.: Low computational complexity methods for decoding of STBC in the uplink of a massive MIMO system. EURASIP J. Wirel. Commun. Netw. **2020**(1), 1–17 (2020)
21. Akhondi, M., Alirezapouri, M.A.: A modified ZF algorithm for signal detection in an underwater MIMO STBC-OFDM acoustic communication system. Ann. Telecommun. 1–17 (2023)
22. Cho, Y.S., Kim, J., Yang, W.Y., Kang, C.G.: MIMO-OFDM Wireless Communications with MATLAB. Wiley, Hoboken (2010)
23. Zheng, Y.R., Xiao, C.: Simulation models with correct statistical properties for Rayleigh fading channels. IEEE Trans. Commun. **51**(6), 920–928 (2003)

Achieving Accurate Trajectory Control While Training Legged Robots Using Machine Learning

Amit Biswas[1]([✉]) [iD], Neha N. Chaubey[2] [iD], and Nirbhay Kumar Chaubey[3] [iD]

[1] Triassic Robotics Pvt Ltd., Delhi, India
amit@triassicrobotics.com
[2] Dharmsinh Desai University, Gujarat, India
nchaubey123@gmail.com
[3] Ganpat University, Gujarat, India
nirbhay@ieee.org

Abstract. Legged robots are a class of robotic systems designed to move and navigate using leg mechanisms, similar to how animals with legs move. Legged robots differ from other mobile robots primarily in their mode of locomotion. They can traverse various types of terrain, uneven surfaces and human made structures like stairs, steps etc. They have significant advantages over other forms of robotic locomotion, such as wheels or tracks, but they are complex to build and control. Designing and controlling legged robots can be complex due to the need for stability, balance, and coordination among multiple legs. Building these control mechanisms have always been a challenging task. In this paper we discuss about a four-legged robot that we built and how we trained and controlled its motion. We discuss how we can use latest techniques in Machine Learning (ML) to train locomotion skills to legged robots. We evaluate training directly in the cartesian space as compared to the more popular approach of using joint space. We also look at the challenges we faced in trajectory control and how we solved them. We discuss how we achieved accurate tracking of trajectories and explain the importance of accurate trajectory tracking in legged locomotion. We describe our experimental setup including the simulation environment we used, the tools and techniques used in setting up the experiments and how we built a real robot and used it for our experiments.

Keywords: Legged Robots · Legged locomotion · Motion Control · Trajectory Control · Cartesian Space · Joint Space · Machine Learning · Reinforcement Learning · Augmented Random Search

1 Introduction

Robotic locomotion is a challenging task especially on uneven or unstructured terrains. For legged robots, its even more of a challenge. Compared to other forms of robotic locomotion such as wheel or tracks, Legged locomotion is much more complicated

N. Chaubey et al. (Eds.): COMS2 2023, CCIS 1861, pp. 15–29, 2023.
https://doi.org/10.1007/978-3-031-40564-8_2

because of the need for stability, balance, and coordination between multiple legs. Legged locomotion is difficult to achieve because of the complexities involved in building and controlling the mechanisms that enable legged motion.

These complexities can be broadly classified into two categories: (i) Determining and synchronizing the leg movements that are required to achieve a desired motion and (ii) Accurately effecting the desired motion through a series of mechanisms including motor controllers, sensors etc. Achieving a fine balance between these components is also as critical as solving these complexities.

The challenge of legged locomotion also involves processing the large set of possible actions. The control of legged robots is inherently complex due to the coordination of multiple legs and joints. Achieving smooth and efficient locomotion while adapting to varying terrains and obstacles is a significant challenge. Legged robots often require substantial power to move and maintain stability. The mechanical design of legged robots needs to account for both structural integrity and flexibility. The robot's limbs and joints must be robust enough to withstand dynamic movements and external forces while being lightweight to conserve energy. Achieving the right balance between strength, weight, and flexibility can be a challenge. Compared to wheeled or tracked robots, legged locomotion consumes more energy. Efficient energy management and power supply systems are necessary to extend the operational time and range of legged robots, especially in field applications where recharging or refueling may be limited.

In legged robots, the body of the robot is supported by mechanical structures representing legs or limbs. These legs are used for movement of the robot as well. Sequence of leg movements are carefully synchronized to set the body in motion. Leg movements and their placements must be orchestrated to keep the body in motion while maintaining balance and stability. Computing the movement of the legs and then executing the motion in hardware, is the core of the challenge of legged locomotion [1].

The irregular nature of the terrain introduces more complexities in the process. If the surface is not even, support from legs becomes unpredictable. Not all possible positions may be suitable for footfall, and some of the possible positions may not even be achievable due to the uneven nature of the terrain. Sometimes the position determined by the controller may not be reachable due to surface irregularities. These unpredictable elements make planning the leg movements even more difficult. Uneven surface also creates unpredictable reactionary forces on contact. These reactionary forces vary in magnitude and direction and is difficult to factor in while planning leg movements. These challenges, arising from the interaction of the robot to the environment, introduces new set of complications in the walking process [2].

For the first part of the problem, ie. Determining and synchronizing leg movements, various different control mechanisms have been developed in the past. Most of these traditional methods relied heavily on purely physics-based controllers. These controllers are difficult to build and maintain and requires substantial amount of modifications to adapt for any change in the environment. These controllers are not versatile to subtle changes in the environment. A much more feasible solution is required to make legged motion effective. Recent advancements in the field of Artificial Intelligence (AI) and Machine Learning (ML) techniques have opened up new possibilities for controlling motion of legged robots and for training them as well. These new control systems that are based on Machine Learning, are found to be much more resilient to environmental factors.

Traditional controllers that were purely physics based took a different approach by attempting to control the robot by observing its state and then calculating the necessary changes required. These controllers would measure physical aspects of the robot such as joint positions, body state etc. and use these values to calculate a possible state for the legs. This approach can be further advanced to achieve complex movements such as walking. Similarly balance and stability can also be achieved while walking. These methods of controlling the robot worked well under ideal conditions but even minor changes in the environment would create problems. Small deviations in environment often give rise to conditions that are the controller cannot handle. Under challenging environments, these controllers fail to perform. In addition to the fragile nature of these controllers, they are also difficult to make. They require deep knowledge across multiple domains to understand and develop the control policies. After development they need a lot of fine-tuning as well.

Artificial intelligence and Machine Learning techniques have started playing a crucial role in controlling legged robots, enabling them to adapt, learn, and make autonomous decisions in complex environments. Algorithms based on machine learning techniques are used to plan and control the motions of legged robots. These algorithms learn from experience or simulate the robot's movements to find suitable control strategies that maximize stability, energy efficiency, and locomotion performance. By observing and imitating human movements or predefined motion sequences, legged robots can learn how to navigate and perform specific tasks. These algorithms allow legged robots to adapt their locomotion strategies in real-time based on sensor feedback. Reinforcement learning or adaptive control algorithms can adjust leg trajectories, foot placement, or gait patterns to optimize stability, maintain balance, and improve performance in response to changing terrain or external disturbances. This approach of controlling the robot makes it much more resilient as compared to traditional controllers.

The second part of the challenge is to accurately execute the desired leg movements. Accurate trajectory control becomes very necessary here. In-order to have accurate tracing of trajectories, several things have to be synchronized such as the motor controllers, the feedback sensors, the control algorithms etc. We found that minor discrepancies sensor feedback or motor control often leads to major deviations in the tracked trajectory. Under certain conditions such as at high velocities, the deviations are even more magnified. Higher inertia of the moving part also contributes to increased deviations and jittery movements. Maintaining the desired velocity and acceleration throughout the trajectory is often a challenge because of the discrepancies in the feedback or control loop as well. We found a solution by leading the positional value of the trajectory by a few steps ahead so that the acceleration and velocity can remain smooth and need not change abruptly at each step of control.

2 Related Work

Much research has been done in the field of robotic locomotion. Many different methods have been proposed and evaluated. The Cheetah robot, developed by MIT researchers, works by generating simple reference trajectories. In order to get desired contact forces, it performs model predictive control and then uses Jacobian transpose control to realize them [3]. The ANYmal robot [4] uses the inverted pendulum model to plan for footholds [3]. These control algorithms work well but require deep knowledge across multiple domains including the dynamics of the robot, physical aspects of the robot and its capabilities. Often these requirements become a limiting factor. In contrast, AI based control mechanisms can be used for training even without any prior know-how of the dynamics of the robot or its physical aspects. This can be achieved thorough Reinforcement Learning techniques.

Literature survey shows several instances where machine learning techniques have been used for robotic locomotion [5–8]. Multiple approaches have been proposed based on reinforcement learning techniques. They results vary on performance and success levels. Reinforcement Learning can be used to explore different leg trajectories and coordination patterns, these algorithms can discover gaits that minimize energy consumption, maximize stability, or adapt to varying terrains and are found to be much better than traditional methods of control [8]. Robots can be trained in simulation using techniques like Deep Reinforcement Learning. Simulations provide a valuable platform for training and optimizing legged robot controllers. AI-based algorithms can be applied to train legged robots in simulated environments, leveraging reinforcement learning. Simulations allow for faster and safer exploration of control policies, enabling legged robots to learn and improve their locomotion capabilities before deployment in the real world. However, simulation differs from the real world in several factors, and all of these factors cannot be accurately modelled in simulation. This creates discrepancies between the real world and the simulated environment.

The discrepancies between simulation and the real world create a gap that is sometimes referred to as the sim-to-real gap. Numerous solutions have been proposed to overcome this sim-to-real gap [9]. An easy solution would be to use a physical setting that represents the real-world setup very closely and train the robot in this environment. This approach effectively removes any sim-to-real gap because simulation has been removed from the process altogether. In most scenarios this approach is not feasible because of multiple factors such as it is not possible to collect training data from the physical environment, changing the robot's dynamics is now possible, and its time consuming to iterate. Using simulations for training can be a much more efficient solution. We can conduct the training process completely in a simulated environment and on successful training, we can transfer the trained policies to a hardware robot.

In our setup, we will evaluate a relatively newly proposed algorithm called Augmented Random Search (ARS) [10] that is claimed to be much more efficient than many existing algorithms. According to the algorithm's authors, ARS beats the fastest competing methods by about 15 times [10].

While using Machine Learning to train legged robots, selection of action space has large effect on both training time and quality of trained policies [11]. Most of the previous work has focused on learning in joint space. However, cartesian space can be an equally good action space and, in some studies, cartesian space control has been found to be better than joint space [11].

Most of the previous work does not focus on the challenges of executing the learned motion on real hardware. The trained policies were only validated on simulated environments. However, it is tricky process to transfer trained policies from a simulated environment to real-world hardware [9].

3 Using Machine Learning to Train Locomotion Policies

Machine Learning has emerged as the most successful method of training complex motion control behavior in robots [12]. Using Machine Learning we can virtually eliminate the need of any manual tuning or precise fine tuning of the control parameters. This is a great benefit especially for complex motion control systems like in legged robots because the system can be made to learn the intricacies by itself instead of being programmed by a human. Reinforcement learning (RL) is often used for training legged robots due to its ability to learn complex behaviors and adapt to dynamic environments. Einforcement learning enables legged robots to learn through trial and error. The robot explores its environment, takes actions, and receives feedback or rewards based on the outcomes. RL algorithms learn from these experiences and adjust the robot's behavior to maximize the cumulative reward over time. This iterative learning process allows legged robots to discover effective locomotion strategies and adapt to different terrains or tasks. Legged robots often undergo initial training in simulated environments before being deployed in the real world. RL is well-suited for simulated training as it enables legged robots to explore and learn in virtual environments without the risks or costs associated with real-world trials. Once a legged robot has learned locomotion skills in one setting, RL algorithms can help generalize and adapt those skills to new situations.

In recent research work, a lot of progress has been made in the field of Deep Reinforcement Learning [13–15]. RL algorithms, such as deep reinforcement learning, can learn hierarchical representations, allowing legged robots to generate complex and coordinated movements. Controlling legged robots is a challenging task due to the high-dimensional action spaces and the need for coordination among multiple limbs. Reinforcement learning can handle the complexity of learning control policies by searching and optimizing in large action spaces. In order to eliminate any discrepancies, we try to create a representation of the model as accurately as possible.

We evaluated two approaches while training our robot: first we used joint space by getting joint positions from position sensors and mapping them to the trajectory controller, and second approach is to map the position of the end points of the legs directly in the cartesian space. We observed that using cartesian space can be as effective as using joint space [16]. Whether joint space is used or cartesian space, accurate trajectory control was a crucial factor that determines performance (Fig. 1).

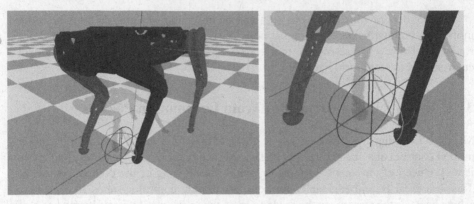

Fig. 1. Tracking trajectories in cartesian space

3.1 Learning in Cartesian Space

In our experimental setup, we trained our robot directly in the cartesian space. Joint space control is popularly used for such training, but cartesian space is also being studied in several studies [17]. We decided to use cartesian space because it was more closely related to real world mapping. A policy trained in cartesian space attempts to control the movements by reading and controlling the cartesian position of the end effector of each leg. This method of controlling, as compared to joint space, has some benefits such as higher sample efficiency and easier transfer between multiple simulation environments. We also found that changing the physical dimensions of the robots leg had less effect while using cartesian space than while using joint space.

Another advantage of cartesian space control is improved tracking of trajectories. We found that without using special techniques that maintain the end effector position at each step, joint space control did not tract the trajectories as accurately as cartesian space control did. This is because joint space control does not guarantee uniform amount of movement for all joints in motion although the end result was reached. With cartesian space control, the same end result was reached, but it guaranteed that every step in the trajectory is executed while the end effector remains placed in the trajectory [18]. This results into very accurate tracking performance.

4   Using Augmented Random Search for Training

Legged robots often operate in dynamic and uncertain environments. They need to make real-time decisions regarding gait selection, obstacle avoidance, and navigation. Highly dynamic maneuvers such as walking, running, jumping etc. require careful balancing and stability and are extremely difficult for robots to execute [9]. Developing efficient planning algorithms that can handle the complexity of legged locomotion while considering real-time sensory information is a significant challenge. Numerous applications of machine learning (ML) based techniques have been suggested to address these issues[19]. In our experiments we evaluate a relatively new algorithm named "Augmented Random Search" [10] to train basic locomotion skills such as walking to our custom built quadruped robot.

Augmented Random Search (ARS) is a reinforcement learning algorithm that combines elements of random search and policy gradient methods. It is a simple yet effective algorithm for training static, linear policies for continuous control problems [20]. ARS is an improvement over Basic Random Search (BRS) (Fig. 2).

Algorithm 1 Augmented Random Search (ARS): four versions **V1**, **V1-t**, **V2** and **V2-t**

1: **Hyperparameters:** step-size α, number of directions sampled per iteration N, standard deviation of the exploration noise ν, number of top-performing directions to use b ($b < N$ is allowed only for **V1-t** and **V2-t**)

2: **Initialize:** $M_0 = 0 \in \mathbb{R}^{p \times n}$, $\mu_0 = 0 \in \mathbb{R}^n$, and $\Sigma_0 = I_n \in \mathbb{R}^{n \times n}$, $j = 0$.

3: **while** ending condition not satisfied **do**

4:    Sample $\delta_1, \delta_2, \ldots, \delta_N$ in $\mathbb{R}^{p \times n}$ with i.i.d. standard normal entries.

5:    Collect $2N$ rollouts of horizon H and their corresponding rewards using the $2N$ policies

$$\mathbf{V1:} \begin{cases} \pi_{j,k,+}(x) = (M_j + \nu\delta_k)x \\ \pi_{j,k,-}(x) = (M_j - \nu\delta_k)x \end{cases}$$

$$\mathbf{V2:} \begin{cases} \pi_{j,k,+}(x) = (M_j + \nu\delta_k)\operatorname{diag}(\Sigma_j)^{-1/2}(x - \mu_j) \\ \pi_{j,k,-}(x) = (M_j - \nu\delta_k)\operatorname{diag}(\Sigma_j)^{-1/2}(x - \mu_j) \end{cases}$$

for $k \in \{1, 2, \ldots, N\}$.

6:    Sort the directions δ_k by $\max\{r(\pi_{j,k,+}), r(\pi_{j,k,-})\}$, denote by $\delta_{(k)}$ the k-th largest direction, and by $\pi_{j,(k),+}$ and $\pi_{j,(k),-}$ the corresponding policies.

7:    Make the update step:

$$M_{j+1} = M_j + \frac{\alpha}{b\sigma_R} \sum_{k=1}^{b} \left[r(\pi_{j,(k),+}) - r(\pi_{j,(k),-}) \right] \delta_{(k)},$$

where σ_R is the standard deviation of the $2b$ rewards used in the update step.

8:    **V2** : Set μ_{j+1}, Σ_{j+1} to be the mean and covariance of the $2NH(j+1)$ states encountered from the start of training.[2]

9:    $j \leftarrow j + 1$

10: **end while**

Fig. 2. Algorithm of Augmented Random Search [11]

5   Accurate Trajectory Control

Accurate trajectory control plays a fundamental role in achieving desired leg movements. Planning for joint trajectories may be achieved during the training process but it is responsibility of the controller to make sure that the planned trajectories are tracked accurately [21]. The accuracy achieved during training can be easily offset by inaccurate tracking.

In absence of appropriate trajectory control mechanisms in place, significant amount of tracking error was observed. Several factors contributed to the error including physical aspects such as the momentum of the leg or limitations of control accuracy, responsiveness of the motor and limitations in reading positional feedback. Accurate trajectory control allows robots to achieve precise movements and positions.

Inaccuracies in tracking the trajectory arises out of several factors including minor discrepancies in the control-feedback loop [22]. Delays in reading positions, or delays in motor controller contribute to tracking errors. However, one factor that contributed substantially was flaws in the trajectory control method. We noticed that at higher velocities and if mass of moving part is high, the momentum of the moving body becomes large enough to introduce substantial amount of tracking errors. The controller attempts to correct this by compensating the values of acceleration and velocity. This ends up being over compensated in the opposite direction and the process repeats again (Fig. 3).

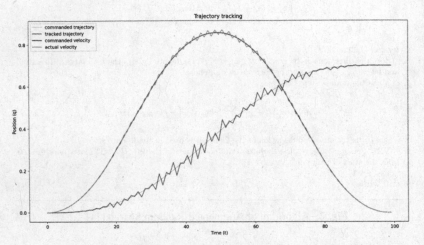

Fig. 3. Poor tracking of trajectories, jittery and abrupt movements

5.1 Using Positional Lead in Trajectory Control

We tested a new approach to solve the tracking errors. Out of the three parameters that are maintained during trajectory control, Acceleration, Velocity, and Position, we found that if the position value is led by n steps ahead, it resulted in better tracking performance [1]. The leading factor, n, starts with 0 at the beginning of the trajectory, reaches its maximum value at the middle of the trajectory and drops back to zero at the end of the trajectory. The maximum value is determined experimentally and requires some tuning (Figs. 4 and 5).

Algorithm 2: Trajectory Control with positional lead in every step

```
//Parameters:
pos_lead        //Factor of positional lead
s_list          //List of all steps in the trajectory
step            //One step in the list of steps s_list
acc             //Acceleration value at the current step
vel             //Velocity value at the current step
pos             //Position value at the current step

While s_list has steps, loop through each step
        step = current step
        acc = step.acc
        vel = step.vel
        if current step is less than total steps - pos_lead
                pos = (current step + pos_lead).pos
        else
                pos = step.pos
        Update motor controller(acc, vel, pos)
        state = Read state from motor controller
        update local state
End while
```

Fig. 4. Positional lead used while tracking trajectories

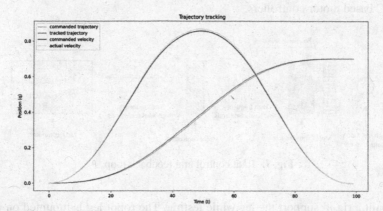

Fig. 5. Improved trajectory tracking and smooth movements due to positional lead

6 Experimental Setup

For our experimental setup, we built a real quadruped robot and also setup a simulation environment. We used the real robot to run experiments related to trajectory planning, testing tracking accuracy, and testing motion control. We also took measurements from the robot to get actual real-world values and compared them to our simulation results. Hidden discrepancies that are sometimes not encountered in simulation are often uncovered while testing on real hardware.

We built a fully articulated 4-legged robot. Each leg has 3 degrees of freedom. The joints are referred to as 'Abad' joint, the 'Femur' joint and the 'Tibia' joint. Each joint is powered by an electric motor that drives an actuator. The actuator consists of a set of gear reducers. A high resolution position sensor is attached to each joint, this provides accurate positional feedback to the motor controller (Figs. 6 and 7).

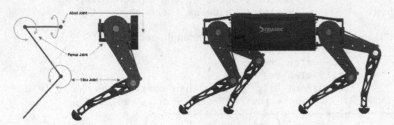

Fig. 6. Leg configuration of "Stego" the real quadrupedal robot built for our experiments

There is an onboard motor controller that receives positional feedback from the high-resolution position sensors connected to each joint. The motor controller uses this data to compute and control the velocities and joint angles. For this experimental setup, we used FOC based motor controllers.

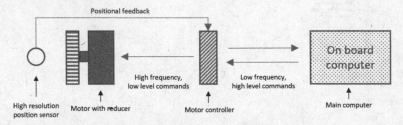

Fig. 7. Joint control and feedback loop

We built a rig to support the leg while testing. The robot leg is mounted on the rig in such a way that it is supported fully but allows vertical movement along the z axis and rotational movement for Femur and Tibia. This setup is connected to a simulated environment on a computer and can be controlled from there (Fig. 8).

6.1 Simulation Environment Setup

We built a simulation environment that represents real-world scenarios as closely as possible. We used this setup to test locomotion policies and to try out training sessions as well. On Windows machine, we used PyBullet for the simulation. We built an identical environment on a Ubuntu system using Gazebo for simulation. For modeling the robot, original CAD files were used that was created for making the real robot. URDF models were created out of these robot models and then it was used in simulation (Figs. 9 and 10).

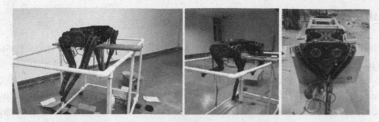

Fig. 8. Stego - The quadruped robot we built to experiment on real hardware

Fig. 9. The real robot leg mounted on the test rig and the simulation environment using PyBulllet

Fig. 10. A single robot leg controlled through the simulation environment

7 Results

We successfully used reinforcement learning methods to train a legged robot basic loco-motion skills such as walking. The trained robot successfully executed simple gait pat-terns such as in walking. We achieved this without requiring deep understanding of the robots. We were able to train the robot without prior domain knowledge. The simulation environment we used to train mimics real-world scenarios very closely. On completion of the training process, the robot was able to execute the trained policies such as walking gaits.

We also demonstrate the benefits of accurate trajectory control. In our experiments, we achieved very accurate trajectory tracking both in the real robot leg as well as in simulation. We demonstrated the benefits of using positional lead in trajectory control. With positional lead the controller continuously tries to reach the leading position while acceleration and velocity remain at the current step. By doing so, the controller does try to overcompensate in opposite direction. This results in much better tracking of trajectories and smoother movements.

We validated that training can be done directly in cartesian space as compared to the more common approach of using joint space. Using cartesian space has some ben-efits such as improved tracking of trajectories, better transferability between simulation environments and more resilient against any changes in the robots hardware.

We successfully built a fully articulated quadrupedal legged robot. We used this robot for running experiments on real hardware. We establish that controlling legged motion can be achieved by training in simulation and transferring the trained policies to real hardware. Several challenges remain while transferring policies from simulation to real hardware (Figs. 11 and 12).

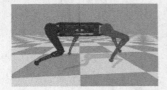

Fig. 11. Execution of walking gait in simulation

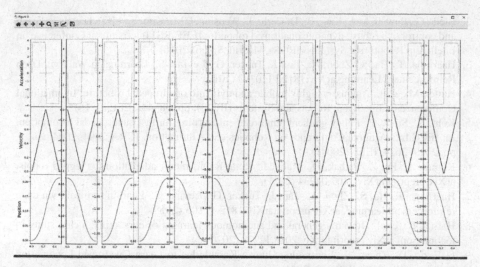

Fig. 12. Simultaneous planning of acceleration, velocity and position for all legs of the robot

8 Conclusion

Reinforcement learning offers a flexible and adaptive approach to training legged robots, enabling them to learn complex locomotion behaviors, adapt to dynamic environments, and generalize across tasks. Machine Learning allows legged robots to acquire robust and efficient locomotion skills that enhance their autonomy and versatility in real-world applications. Using Machine Learning we were successful in achieving complex dynamic gaits in simulation that would otherwise be difficult to achieve with any other approach. We evaluated controlling the joints by addressing them in joint space as well directly in cartesian space and we found that cartesian space motion control and learning is a viable alternative to joint space control. Under some circumstances, cartesian space control may be better suited than Joint space control. We found that accurate trajectory control is absolutely crucial in executing legged locomotion. Using positional lead while tracking trajectories improves tracking performance significantly. For future research we want to evaluate fixed-time trajectories in joint space and compare the performance with cartesian space. For trajectory control we want to verify if acceleration and velocity can be led along with position. This may improve tracking accuracy even more than what we achieved with positional lead. Transferring trained policies from the simulation environment to the real robot remains a challenge to be further explored in future.

References

1. Biswas, A., et al.: Training a legged robot to walk using machine learning and trajectory control for high positional accuracy. In: Kautish, S., et al., AI-Enabled Social Robotics in Human Care Services, IGI Global, pp. 172–187 (2023).https://doi.org/10.4018/978-1-6684-8171-4.ch006

2. Bledt, G., Powell, M.J., Katz, B., Di Carlo, J., Wensing, P.M., Kim, S.: MIT cheetah 3: design and control of a robust, dynamic quadruped robot. In: IEEE/RSJ International Conference on Intelligent Robots and Systems (IROS), Madrid, Spain (2018)

3. Haarnoja, T., Ha, S., Zhou, A., Tan, J., Tucker, G., Levine, S.: Learning to Walk via Deep Reinforcement Learning.arXiv:1812.11103v3 (2019)

4. Hutter, M., et al.: Anymal-a highly mobile and dynamic quadrupedal robot. In: International Conference on Intelligent Robots and Systems (IROS), pp. 38–44. IEEE (2016)

5. Kohl, N., Stone, P.: Policy gradient reinforcement learning for fast quadrupedal locomotion. In: IEEE International Conference on Robotics and Automation. ICRA 2004. 2004, vol. 3, pp. 2619–2624. IEEE (2004)

6. Kumar, A., Fu, Z., Pathak, D., Malik, J.: Rma: Rapid motor adaptation for legged robots. arXiv preprint arXiv:2107.04034 (2021)

7. Haarnoja, T., Ha, S., Zhou, A., Tan, J., Tucker, G., Levine, S.: Learning to walk via deep reinforcement learning. arXiv preprintarXiv:1812.11103 (2018)

8. Hafner, R., et al.: Towards general and autonomous learning of core skills: a case study in locomotion. arXiv preprintarXiv:2008.12228 (2020)

9. DeFazio, D., Zhang, S.: Leveraging Human Knowledge to Learn Quadruped Locomotion Policies.arXiv:2107.10969v2 (2021)

10. Tan, J., et al.: Sim-to-Real: Learning Agile Locomotion For Quadruped Robots.arXiv:1804.10332v2 (2018)

11. Mania, H., Guy, A., Recht, B.: Simple random search provides a competitive approach to reinforcement learning. arXiv:1803.07055 (2018)

12. Bellegarda, G., Chen, Y., Liu, Z., Nguyen, Q.: Robust High-speed Running for Quadruped Robots via Deep Reinforcement Learning. arXiv:2103.06484 (2021)

13. Bellicoso, C.D., Bjelonic, M., Wellhausen, L., et al.: Advances in real-world applications for legged robots. J. Field Rob. **35**, 1311–1326 (2018). https://doi.org/10.1002/rob.21839

14. Lillicrap, T.P., et al.: Continuous control with deep reinforcement learning. arXiv preprintarXiv:1509.02971 (2015)

15. Schulman, J., Wolski, F., Dhariwal, P., Radford, A., Klimov, O.: Proximal policy optimization algorithms. CoRR, abs/1707.06347 (2017)

16. Duan, Y., Chen, X., Houthooft, R., Schulman, J., Abbeel, P.: Benchmarking deep reinforcement learning for continuous control. In: Proceedings of the 33rd International Conference on International Conference on Machine Learning - Volume 48, ICML 2016, pp. 1329–1338. JMLR.org (2016)

17. Bellegarda, G., Nguyen, Q.: Robust Quadruped Jumping via Deep Reinforcement Learning.arXiv:2011.07089 (2020)

18. Xu, X., Chen, Y.: A method for trajectory planning of robot manipulators in Cartesian space. In: Proceedings of the 3rd World Congress on Intelligent Control and Automation (Cat. No.00EX393), Hefei, vol. 2, pp. 1220–1225 (2000).https://doi.org/10.1109/WCICA.2000.863437

19. Kaspar, M., Muñoz Osorio, J.D., Bock, J.: Sim2Real transfer for reinforcement learning without dynamics randomization. In: IEEE/RSJ International Conference on Intelligent Robots and Systems (IROS), pp. 4383–4388 (2020).https://doi.org/10.1109/IROS45743.2020.9341260

20. Smith, L., Kew, J.C., Peng, X.B., Ha, S., Tan, J., Levine, S.: Legged robots that keep on learning: Fine-tuning locomotion policies in the real world. arXiv preprintarXiv:2110.05457 (2021)

21. Tirumala, S., et al.: Gait Library Synthesis for Quadruped Robots via Augmented Random Search. arXiv:1912.12907v1 (2019)
22. Carpentier, J., Wieber, P.B.: Recent progress in legged robots locomotion control. Curr. Rob. Rep. **2**, 231–238 (2021). https://doi.org/10.1007/s43154-021-00059-0(2021)
23. Arm, P., et al.: SpaceBok: a dynamic legged robot for space exploration. In: 2019 International Conference on Robotics and Automation (ICRA), Montreal, QC, Canada, pp. 6288–6294 (2019). https://doi.org/10.1109/ICRA.2019.8794136

Relational Model and Improvised DSR Assisted Framework for Secure Wireless Communication

K. C. Rajani[1]([⊠]) ([iD]), S. Manjunatha[2], V. S. Rakesh[2], and P. Bhavana[2]

[1] Department of Artificial Intelligence and Machine Learning, Cambridge Institute of Technology, Bengaluru, India
rajanikcc009@gmail.com
[2] Department of Computer Science and Engineering, Cambridge Institute of Technology, Bengaluru, India

Abstract. Wireless communications offer a wide range of application with cost-effective communication establishment used in both commercial and domestic purpose. Owing to the presence of decentralized environment in Wireless Communications, it is quite a potential issue for monitoring the regular behavior of any wireless node while performing data propagation. The proposed study states that a wireless node in wireless communication environment plays a role of either normal node or malicious node with completely two different polarities of intention. However, the essential concern is mainly towards the selfish node, which is basically a normal node and owing to certain reason their behavior comes under suspicious zone. Irrespective of various forms of security attacks, identifying malicious node behavior is the most challenging security concern in wireless communication, which has yet not received a proper security solution. The proposed work presents a novel idea of security towards resisting adversarial impact of selfish node and routing mis-behavior present in wireless communications environment. The 1st-framework introduces a retaliation model where a novel role of node called as an auxiliary node is introduced to cater up the routing demands along with security demands. This module performs identification of a malicious routing mis-behavior based on evaluation carried out for the control message being propagated to the auxiliary node. The 2nd-framework further introduces a group friendly architecture where a probability-based modelling is carried out considering various possible set of actions to be executed by normal and selfish node. The model also presents a solution towards security threat prevention by encouraging the selfish node to perform cooperation. The study outcome is benchmarked with existing technique to see that proposed system offers a good balance between security performance and data transmission performance in wireless communication.

Keywords: Wireless Communications · Security · Dynamic Secure Routing · Re lational Model · Auxiliary Node · Selfish Node

1 Introduction

Establishing a secure communication protocol in decentralized environment of wireless communications (WIREL. COMMUN.) demands a clear understanding of the types as well as strategies of attacker [1, 2]. While majority of existing implementation uses predefined information of attacker, it is not practical to conclude its applicability in real world especially in presence of dynamic and unknown attacker. There is various recent implementation carried out in specific case studies of wireless Communication, which states that there is a need of performing attack modelling considering various latent and non-exclusive behavioral traits of attacker. According to these studies, the attackers' nodes do exhibit certain common traits of behavior just like regular nodes as well as it also has certain unique behavior which differentiate it from regular node. Unfortunately, such theory has not been subjected to exclusive series of experiments and analysis and hence no conclusive remarks do exist for such theory. There are also studies towards selfish node mis-behavior using trust-based approach, which offers more background as well as baseline towards developing a next series of research work [3, 4]. Hence, all this studies combinedly give a constructive guideline towards modelling the proposed system by addressing the identified research problem [5–8]. Majority of the security threats associated with the WIREL. COMMUN. is directly linked with the data transmission events, where routing protocols are the prime targets of vulnerability. The first essential demands to ensure this security effectiveness is to retain maximum *Confidentiality*, which is meant for restricting the access to the illegitimate members or nodes. Therefore, if the confidentiality is compromised than it will mean that the data associated with the routing is also in higher threat. Apart from this, the next essential demands to ensure proper security feature in WIREL. COMMUN. is associated with data *integrity* which will mean that routed data is not maliciously tampered to alter its content. The third prime demand of security is *availability* which is about letting an access to the data or service when demanded irrespective of any traffic or network condition. The fourth demand of security in WIREL. COMMUN. is *authorization* which will permit only the nodes that has been authorized to participate in data forwarding process keeping aside the unauthorized nodes. The fifth essential requirement of security is *non-repudiation* which ensure non-deniability of the service which balances the communication demands as well as secure validation demands at same time. Apart from this, *reliability* as well as *dependability* are another security requirements for WIREL. COMMUN. to ensure that better fault tolerance of the protocol in presence of adverse operational environment. All the above security requirements are necessary in order to ensure that a safer data communication and better resistance from attacker in WIREL. COMMUN.; However, it should be noted that all the mentioned security demands are very much difficult to be met in realistic implementation, whereas majority of the existing studies primarily focuses on meeting either one or two of such security requirements in WIREL. COMMUN. For a given condition of routing and attack environment [9–13]. Existing review of literatures witnesses that majority of the security solutions has narrowed scope of practical implementation due to multiple identified research problems. Apart from this, it is also noticed that studies towards Dynamic Source Routing (DSR) is quite less explored in this perspective WIREL.COMMUN security [14, 15]. The proposed research work is carried out Dynamic Source Routing (DSR) which is basically an on-demand routing scheme in WIREL COMMUN. The prime reason to emphasize on DSR is because of its scope for routing without any form of dependency to retain information of routing table within the node. Apart from this, it also assists in heavier communication by permitting multiple routes towards any receiver wireless devices while the transmitting nodes are flexible enough to be permitted to opt for any routes as well as control them. However, in spite of this beneficial features towards data transmission and routing, DSR protocol is said not to offer higher scalability especially to large scale form of network [16, 17]. There is a heavy consumption of processing time with less availability to address broken link maintenance. This inherited properties of DSR also calls for security threat that are found to be less address in existing system of routing protocol implementation. In such scenario, if there is a presence of any mis-behaving wireless devices, it is quite complex process to localize them and isolate them from the entire networks. Thereby, the prime, aim of the proposed study is to develop a novel framework which can incorporate secure communication system by resisting routing mis-behavior in WIREL.COMMUN. The secondary aim of the proposed study is to consider leveraging the security of Dynamic Source Routing (DSR) by introducing a novel security framework. Hence, this paper presents a novel combined security technique towards leveraging the relational model and improvised DSR protocol towards securing the data propagation in the context of WIREL. COMMUN. Section 2 discusses about the existing research work followed by problem identification in Sect. 3. Section 4 discusses about proposed methodology and its elaborated discussion. Finally, the comparative analysis of accomplished result is discussed under Sect. 5 followed by conclusion in Sect. 6.

2   Related Work

This section discusses about the existing research work being carried out toward techniques adopted for enhancing security performance in WIREL. COMMUN. At present, there are various studies being carried out towards securing the data transmission in WIREL. COMMUN. Different schemes have been evolved for accounting towards the security of the message as well as data packet; however, primary emphasis is given for the developing a scheme for unique data transmission in decentralized environment of WIREL. COMMUN. The work carried out by Liu et al. [18] have discussed about a unique authentication scheme that is responsible for maintaining anonymity while per forming communication. According to this scheme, a group signature is used in order to validate the legitimacy of the route request control message. The work carried out by El-Semary et al. [19] have presented a unique scheme towards securing blackhole attack in WIREL. COMMUN using conventional AODV routing scheme. According to this study, the implementation emphasizes towards harnessing AODV protocol integrated with the chaotic map function in order to protect cooperative blackhole attack. The work carried out by Veeraiah et al. [20] have used trust-based approach towards authenticating the legitimacy of the mobile nodes in WIREL. COMMUN.

The unique ness of the work is that it uses hybrid routing scheme where fuzzy logic has been used for ascertaining of legitimacy of the cluster head. Similar form of secure routing scheme in WIREL. COMMUN is the discussion by Tu et al. [21] where the issues associated with authentication is implemented. The implementation of this protocol is carried out in such a way that it is resistive against certain ranges of specific attacks in WIREL. COMMUN. Studies towards resisting blackhole attack has been also carried out by Hassan et al. [22] considering the case study of vehicular nodes. The ideas of this work is based on identification followed by identification of malicious nodes in vehicular network by assessing the control message. A unique study has been carried out by Khan et al. [23] where a security modelling is carried out towards resisting multi-collusion attack. The idea of this scheme is to identify the degree of mismatched routing where game theory plays a bigger role in modelling considering the wireless communication aspect of Internet-of-Things. Existing studies towards DSR protocol has been also carried out by Agarwal et al. [24–26], Chaubey [27], and Chaubey [28–32]. These studies have introduced simplified and unique approaches towards safeguarding communication in ad hoc environment with vehicular network mainly.

3 Problem Description

Majority of the existing approaches targeting towards securing WIREL. COMMUN is based on sophisticated encryption (encryption with highly iterative steps with inclusion of complex mathematical operation) process mainly. Also, there are significantly a smaller number of research work carried out towards securing DSR protocol in vulnerable and dynamic environment of WIREL. COMMUN. There are very a smaller number of studies being promoted towards usage of non-encryption-based security protocol for securing routing operation in WIREL. COMMUN. It is also noticed that it is computationally challenging task to confirm the identification of a selfish node just on the basis of preliminary trust value. Therefore, from the above stated points of research problem, the concluded statement of research problem is *"Developing a strategic solution towards identifying and preventing routing mis-behavior in wireless communications is quite a computationally challenging task."*

4 Proposed Methodology

The proposed system is emphasizing on developing a secure routing scheme for address the concern of routing mis-behavior in wireless communications. The complete implementation of the proposed scheme is carried out considering the analytical research methodology combining both empirical form and mathematical form for achieving the stated research objectives. The study in this paper introduces two distinct security frameworks for wireless communications which are- i) Novel Retaliation Model for identifying Routing Mis-Behavior and ii) Novel Group Architecture for promoting Selfish Node Cooperation respectively.

4.1 Novel Retaliation Model for Identifying Routing Mis-Behavior

The prime goal of the proposed system is to develop a novel computational framework that can identify the misbehavior of routing in WIREL.COMMUN environment by improving upon the conventional DSR protocol. The proposed research work is carried out towards securing Dynamic Source Routing (DSR) in WIREL. COMMUN where the conventional DSR scheme is considered as one of the efficient data forwarding protocol. This routing scheme is mainly meant for multi-hop data transmission in WIREL. COMMUN explicitly considering mobile nodes targeting towards rendering higher degree of self-configuring and self-organizing without any dependencies towards any form of infrastructure. DSR is basically a reactive protocol that operates on the theory of source routing where the sender node chooses all the sequence of the wireless nodes to be deployed for forwarding message. The complete operation of DSR protocol is carried out considering i) discovery of route and ii) maintenance of route.

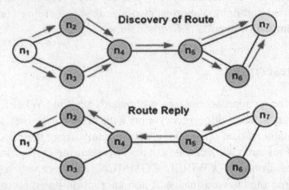

Fig. 1. DSR Protocol Operations Overview in Wireless Communications

The above Fig. 1 highlights discovery process of route as well as mechanism to transmit the route response in DSR. In order to carry out DSR based routing, it is essential to retain cache information of the routes considering a pair of that the source node and destination node. The cached information is used by the wireless node to make data transmission to the sender.

4.2   Reason for Adopting DSR in Proposed Scheme

The average routing and security demands in the proposed scheme arises during the mechanism of data transmission in vulnerable environment with presence of attacker. The idea is to balance the data transmission with energy efficiency as well as security demands in ad hoc ecosystem. The *primary reason* is associated with its beneficial characteristic of its reactive nature that truncates the dependencies towards flooding the network periodically considering all the updated message in the table that is needed in any non-reactive protocols in WIREL. COMMUN. The information of the route cache is utilized by an intermediate node in order to reduce an overhead. Hence all these properties of DSR makes it suitable to design and develop an application in WIREL. COMMUN. The secondary *reason* is that none of the broken communication links are being subjected for maintenance task in routing operation in DSR. This property can easily invite various entries of security threat as well as it also affects the communication performance. Apart from this, DSR is highly prone for any form of flooding attack as it encounters higher delay for just setting up a connection. This property can be easily misused by DoS attacker. The first step is associated with the initialization of the mobile nodes in WIREL. COMMUN environment, whereas the second step is associated with the monitoring of the malicious behavior and the third step is to carry out prevention technique. The first step of block operation is associated with providing a specific role to the wireless nodes in proposed WIREL. COMMUN system. The prime contribution of the proposed system is to formulate a new form of a node called as a retaliation node for assisting in preventing the attacker node after positively identifying them.

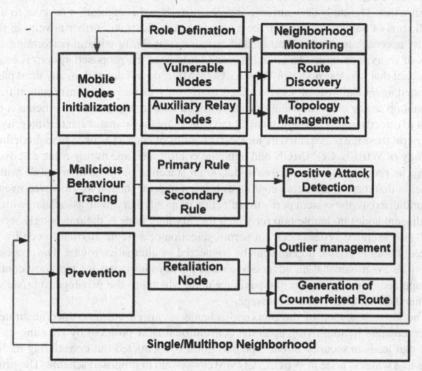

Fig. 2. Proposed Architecture of 1st –Framework

The complete implementation of the above highlighted research methodology is carried out in multiple steps as exhibited in Fig. 2.

4.3 Strategy Implementation

Different from any existing techniques of security using DSR protocol, the proposed scheme introduces two novel roles of wireless nodes i.e. vulnerable node and auxiliary node. The second step of block operation is responsible for constructing a set of rules in order to ascertain the presence of vulnerability condition of nodes influenced by an attacker. The responsibility of this ruleset is to evaluate the contents of the control message associated with the wireless nodes in WIREL. COMMUN with an aid of proposed algorithm of detection. Upon correctly identifying the attacker, the responsibility of last operational block is to resist them further to participate in routing operation using a retaliation node. However, the significant novelty of the proposed research methodology is its new technique to perform prevention against intruder node. This task is carried out by the retaliation node which doesn't existing physically in the communication environment and it is only evolved when the positive identification of malicious node is confirmed. The proposed scheme investigates the legitimacy of the information associated with the wireless nodes located in single and multi-hop communication channel. The adversaries are provided with an information about counterfeited nodes and hops that do not exists in the network and hence a sophisticated computation is carried out to ensure this. The study also carries out probability-based computation in order to find out all sorts of outliers involved in the process of identification. Further novelty of this security approach is its identification and resistivity capability without performing any forms of encryption in it. The complete methodology of the proposed system is based on the fact that wireless nodes in WIREL. COMMUN do not depend on any third party or trusted agent and instead it is permitted to use only its individual information from its own hop or any other information that is shared with it. The proposed scheme is not meant to directly assess the legitimacy of the control message; instead, it the integrity of the control message is evaluated by looking for forms of conflict between the predefined topology of WIREL. COMMUN and obtained control message during route discovery stage. The proposed system performs individual selection of an auxiliary node with a condition that there could be no conflict as briefed in prior statement. However, even if the conflict exists, the system performs selection of an auxiliary node associated with all the adjacent nodes in double hop for which the auxiliary node is the only single access point. However, the system does not permit selection of a single auxiliary node for all adjacent nodes in double hop that can be connected by alternative routes. The proposed system also consider that an adversary cannot perform intrusion for topology control message and can only capture the auxiliary node which has the privilege to broadcast command for topology control message.

The implementation of the proposed scheme is carried out on a specific strategy implementation by improving upon the conventional DSR protocol by covering up its flaws that leads to security threat. The execution is conducted out considering mobile nodes as a wireless node in WIREL. COMMUN system in proposed scheme. The prime novelty factor associated with the proposed scheme resides within the technique to prevent the attacker by falsified control message which direct them towards a path whose nodes doesn't have any physical presence. Following are the strategies adopted to shape the undertaken research methodology in proposed system:

- **Primary Strategy:** The primary strategy of the proposed scheme is to enhance the conventional DSR protocol by incorporating certain sets of novel features mainly focusing on decentralized aspect of routing.
- **Secondary Strategy:** The secondary strategy of the proposed scheme is to amend the DSR routing formulation in different way unlike the unlike the legacy version of it.
- **Ternary Strategy:** The ternary strategy of proposed scheme to improve DSR is to completely change the identification and prevention scheme.

With an adoption of the above three strategy, the proposed system is modelled to ensure that all its newly formulated schemes to improve upon conventional DSR doesn't fall vulnerable to any form of attack. Apart from this, the presented methodology can identify any form of malicious behavior of dynamic attacker without any a priori definition of it. With reference to Fig. 3, the proposed system considers a use case of with multiple node position with respect to single and multiple hops connected with vulnerable node.

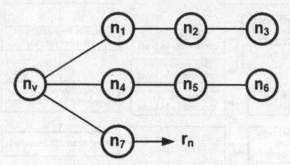

Fig. 3. Secure DSR Flow in 1st-Framework

The next part of the implementation is about deploying a retaliation node. However, in order to understand its full functionality, it is required to understand a changed topology to visualize the process being taking place in practical environment of WIREL. COMMUN. It is to be noted that proposed system performs identification of the conflicts between the route discovery control message as well as network topological changes as recorded by the vulnerable node during the propagation of route discovery control message.

4.4 Novel Group Architecture for Promoting Selfish Node Cooperation

The prime target of the proposed system is to design and develop a novel computational framework called as a friendly group architecture which is meant for further improvising the security capabilities of DSR protocol illustrated in prior segment. Apart from security perspective, the proposed system also emphasizes on developing a novel security methodology that can has lesser dependencies towards involved resources to carry out routing task in WIREL. COMMUN environment. The inclusion of the term *friendly* states that proposed system let the normal node to identify the selfish node without any computational complexity and communication overhead; while the system let it permit to carry out data propagation unlike any existing security protocols in WIREL. COM-MUN. However, this is only carried out upon comprehensive probability computation to confirm of the identified selfish node will carry out data forwarding task in its next set of action. Fig. 4 highlights the friendly architecture and the methodological flow adopted to implement it. The complete work implementation is classified into two stages of development i.e. confirming the identification of a selfish node and unique prevention strategy toward such identified selfish node.

The probability-based evaluation is carried out for this purpose towards detecting the presence of selfish node followed by cooperation of it, unlike any existing studies in literatures.

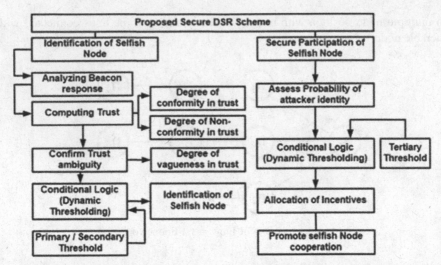

Fig. 4. Proposed Methodology for Identification and Prevention of Selfish Node in 2nd -Framework

4.5 Threat Detection Technique

This is the first part of the implementation which is meant for confirming the positive identity of the selfish node present in WIREL. COMMUN environment. This module is operation only after the communication is being carried out by the nodes while the system never has any form of predefined information about the identity of the selfish node. The complete operation of the threat detection in this part of proposed system is carried out by following operational blocks:

Identification of a Selfish Node: The proposed system of friendly architecture is designed considering three types of wireless nodes in WIREL. COMMUN viz. Regular node, selfish node and attacker node. However, for simplification, selfish node and attacker node is considered to play a similar role in this part. It is because a selfish node as well as attacker node characteristic are nearly similar whereas selfish node is completely governed by the attacker node.

The actions performed by regular node are viz.

i) NAct1: it can assist in forwarding the data to neighboring nodes, ii) NAct2: it can choose to drop the data packet in case it drains its energy more or for security reason, and iii) NAct3: it can perform disseminating the report of positively identified selfish node. Similarly, the selfish node will also have operational features viz. i) SAct1: it can assist in forwarding the data as a relay node in order to gain trust from other nodes, ii) SAct2: it can drop the data packets in order to mimic similar characteristic of normal node, and iii) SAct3: it can launch malicious codes in the network. A closer look into this set of characteristics will exhibit following expression:

$$NAct1 = SAct1 \& NAct2 = SAct2 \tag{1}$$

$$NAct2 \neq SAct3 \tag{2}$$

According to the above-mentioned expression, it will mean that Eq. (1) will mean common characteristic of both normal and selfish node, while Eq. (2) will mean a distinct characteristic that differentiate normal node from selfish node. This Eq. (1) represent the complexity associated in identification process when regular and selfish node start adopting similar set of actions while Eq. (2) represent a different set of action adopted by regular node and that is completely different from selfish node which acts as an indicator of two different nodes. Hence, the identification of the selfish node is primarily carried out based on occurrences of Eq. Mainly. However, the problem arises when the frequency of Eq. (1) is comparatively more than that of Eq. (2) as in such case, it is quite difficult to differentiate normal node from selfish node. Therefore, further computation is carried out in order to confirm the identity of the selfish node in WIREL. COMMUN environment.

- **Analyzing Beacon Response:** This is the next succeeding operation carried out by proposed system, where the beacons or the control messages are subjected to analysis. However, it is to be noted that existing system has reported a significant problem of overhead in conventional DSR protocol. This problem is addressed in proposed work by not accessing the contents of the beacons and rather it finds the frequency of operation associated with the implication of beacons.
- **Computing Trust:** Basically, the trust computation is carried out by the proposed system in order to ascertain any report of vulnerability from the neighboring nodes of the target nodes (whose trust is being evaluated). All the nodes after accomplishment of operation (obtaining the data, forwarding the data, dropping the data, or inducing malicious codes) are allocated with trust values in the form of 0 and 1 by the neighboring nodes. All the trust values are stored in local memory system of the wireless nodes. The trust value is considered as 1 if the node has priorly forwarded the data to the assigned destination node while it allocates a trust value of 0 if the node has not forwarded the data to assigned destination node because of any reason.
- **Confirm Trust Ambiguity:** This operation block is another layer of computation towards trust when the behavior of normal n ode as well as selfish node are found to be same. In such case, there is a rise of ambiguity and this trust factor associated with presence of ambiguity is computed based on new empirical expression.
- **Conditional Logic:** The proposed system formulates certain conditional logic that assists in confirming the presence of vulnerability situation. It should be noted that majority of the conformation of the selfish node is carried out by the prior block of operation; however, the final conformation also depends upon multiple statistics e.g., environment, state of nodes, topology, network, resources, etc. For this purpose, the proposed system formulates three different types of thresholds viz. Primary, secondary, and tertiary threshold.

The core cut-off value is basically configured by the normal node and on that basis, it starts evaluating the target nodes on the basis of degree of conformity. Upon receiving the response from the beacon evaluation block operation, the normal start initiates its probability computation for the trust as well as it attempts its best to differentiate the node on the basis of conformity and non-conformity-based trust factor which is them compared with primary and secondary cut-off value. Better optimal results are further obtained in the next stage where the regular node carry out NAct3 operation using the third cut-off value.

4.6 Threat Prevention Technique

This module is responsible for performing prevention of all possible threat caused due to presence of selfish node. However, this prevention technique is completely different in contrast to any existing security solution in WIREL. COMMUN which performs singular operation of isolating them from rest of the part of network. The novelty of proposed scheme is that it encourages the selfish node to participate in data forwarding operation which was never seek as an alternative option in any existing literature.

5 Results Discussion

This section discusses about the results being obtained after conducting a simulation-based analysis. Discussion of this section is carried out with respect to simulation environment being considered, adopted strategy to perform analysis, and discussion of simulation results.

5.1 Experimental: Novel Retaliation Model

The complete scripting of the proposed system is carried out using MATLAB as it offers less emphasis on coding scheme and more flexibility to implement any form of user formulated logic with enriched analysis tools. The simulation is carried out considering 500–1000 wireless mobile nodes with a speed of each node in WIREL. COMMUN fixed to 2 m/s. This node mobility speed is generalized for mobile wireless network which can be amended on the basis of any specific application. Within the simulation area of $1000 \times 1000 \ m^2$, the deployment of the wireless nodes is carried out with an algorithm implementation while they are executed for around 1000 times. The proposed system carries out the simulation using MATLAB where data is programmatically generated by initializing to 2500 bytes of data. Similar data is also used for comparing proposed scheme with existing scheme.

Retaliation node plays a significant role in diverting the malicious node toward a counterfeited routes as a proposed prevention mechanism. With every event of attacks on multiple location of a simulation area, there are also fair possibilities towards evolution of multiple number of retaliation node. Fig. 5 (a) highlights the trends of usage of retaliation nodes evaluated in increasing number of node densities in order to assess the increase/decrease in number of retaliations with increasing load of traffic. The trend exhibited in Fig. 5(a) highlights that number of retaliation nodes minimizes with increasing number of node density (or network traffic) in a progressive fashion. The prime reason behind this trend is that there is no physical existence of retaliation node and it is only advertised when the system performs true identification of an attacker node. The graphical outcome exhibited in Fig. 5 (b) shows that proposed secured DSR scheme offers better throughput compared to conventional DSR protocol. It should be noted that x-axis for node density is scaled up where one unit represents 100 for node density.

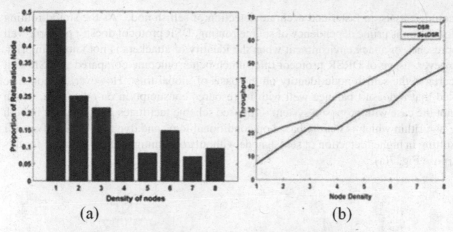

Fig. 5. Graphical Outcome of Comparative Performance Analysis

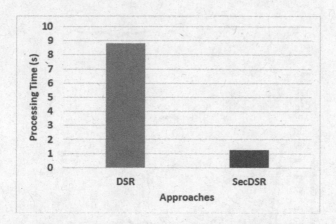

Fig. 6. Analysis of Algorithm Processing Time (sec)

Figure 6 highlights that proposed secured DSR offers potentially reduced algorithm processing time as compared to existing DSR protocol. The justification behind this outcome is that there is no involvement of an iterative steps for confirming the presence of attacker by proposed scheme, instead, all the routing behavior is progressively observed and three different rules are executed sequential to ensure that identification of malicious nodes doesn't encounter a greater number of steps or resources.

5.2 Experimental: Group Architecture for Selfish Node Cooperation

This performance parameter is basically an execution of first module which is about identification of a selfish node. After the detection of selfish node is monitored, they are analyzed with respect to all the three system to assess the detection performance. It should be noted that conventional DSR was meant for routing and not for security and hence when they are deployed in exchanged of proposed secured DSR protocol, it couldn't assist in faster and accurate detection of selfish node. As the stored routing information is prime dependency of source routing, DSR protocol doesn't perform well in presence of attack environment when the identity of attackers is not known in prior. However, usage of DRSR protocol offer much better outcome compared to DSR as it ascertains the selfish node identity on the basis of global trust. However, it should be noted that it doesn't balance well with its resource consumption on other side, which is not the case with proposed system. Proposed scheme facilitates identification in both the algorithm which is mainly based on conditional logic and dynamic usage of cut-off resulting in higher detection of selfish node without consuming higher resources for this purpose Fig. 7(a).

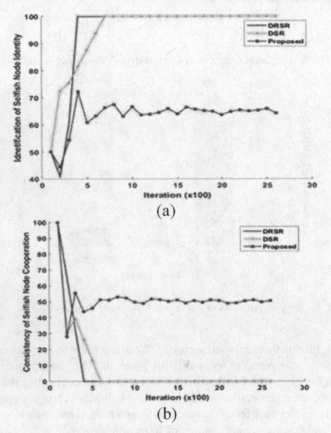

(a)

(b)

Fig. 7. Graphical Outcome of Comparative Performance Analysis

The outcome exhibited in Fig. 7(b) shows that proposed scheme offers potential better consistency as compared to existing schemes with respect to consistency. The prime reason behind this are as follows: conventional DSR protocol exhibited a scalability problem where much of the processing effort as well as time is spent towards finding a secure route. This is not much a big problem in case of small network or network with similar form of an attacker. However, when a dynamic and multiple attackers are deployed in simulation environment, DSR protocol offers higher scalability problem and hence consistency potentially degrades right from the preliminary stages of iteration. On the other hand, DRSR protocol will be required to consistently perform computation of a trust which is applicable only for static attacker and needs the system to know its identity. However, when an unidentified selfish node is present, DRSR protocol fails to update the old trust value with new one and hence its consistency too drops down just like DSR protocol. On the other hand, proposed scheme offers allocation of incentives and doesn't need much internal computation within the wireless nodes in WIREL. COMMUN causing to react faster in presence of selfish node. Further, a highly flexible form of incentive allocations scheme is presented which are not static but is computed and hence they offer equal performance irrespective of change of attack strategy. Hence, proposed scheme offers better consistency performance as compared to existing scheme.

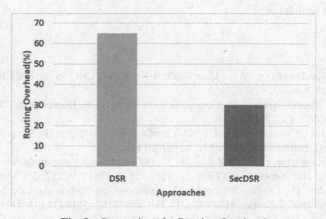

Fig. 8. Comparison for Routing Overhead

Figure 8 highlights the comparative analysis of routing overhead where it can be seen that proposed scheme offers 35% reduced overhead in contrast to conventional DSR.

6 Conclusion

The complete study has been focused towards implementing a novel security technique focusing on monitoring the routing mis-behavior in WIREL. COMMUN. The prime contribution of the proposed study resides in architectural design where two modules of implementation is carried out towards this architecture development associated with retaliation model and friendly architecture model. Both the model acts as an overlay architectural design with each other, where granular information extraction associated with data transmission and control message transmission, where the authentication towards ascertaining the legitimacy of the node is carried out based on probability computation, unlike existing security approaches in WIREL. COMMUN. The 1st-Framework addresses the research problem of unbiased emphasis towards detecting behavior in WIREL. COMMUN. The behavior tracing operation is carried out using primary and secondary set of rules on the basis of understanding the intention of an attacker. The prevention features are developed to safeguard such auxiliary node from the malicious access of an attacker The 2nd-Framework is an extension of prior module of implementation with an extended focus on addressing problems associated with emphasis towards static attacker identity, development of adversarial model, conventional prevention system, and less emphasis of resource involvement. The identification of selfish node is carried out by neighborhood monitoring where the response of control messages is analyzed followed by dual form of trust computation. The quantized simulation outcome shows that proposed system offers approximately 35% of better throughput, 29% of reduced dependencies of auxiliary nodes, and 96.41% of reduced processing time in 1st-Framework.On the other for 2nd-Framework, it exhibits approximately 47.15% of reduction in traffic overhead, 38.06% of reduced energy consumption, 69.82% of better identification rate for selfish node, and 78.92% of higher consistency in confirming cooperation of selfish node.

References

1. Ilyas, M.: The Handbook of Ad Hoc Wireless Networks, CRC Press, Boca Raton (2017). ISBN: 781351836159, 1351836153
2. Mitra, P.: Recent Trends in Communication Networks, IntechOpen (2020). ISBN: 9781838805067, 1838805060
3. Westcott, D.A., Coleman, D.D.: CWNA Certified Wireless Network Administrator Study Guide (2021). ISBN: 9781119736332, 1119736331
4. Singh, N., Kaiwartya, O., Rao, R.S., Jain, V.: IoT and Cloud Computing Advancements in Vehicular Ad-Hoc Networks IGI Global (2020). ISBN: 9781799825722, 1799825728
5. Kanellopoulos, D., Cuomo, F.: Recent Developments on Mobile Ad-Hoc Networks and Vehicular Ad-Hoc Networks, MDPI (2021). ISBN: 9783036511627, 3036511628
6. Yu, B., Hu, S.: Big Data Analytics for Cyber-Physical Systems, Springer, Cham (2020). https://doi.org/10.1007/978-3-030-43494-6, ISBN: 9783030434946, 303043494X
7. Foschini, L., El Kamili, M. (eds.): ADHOCNETS 2020. LNICSSITE, vol. 345. Springer, Cham (2021). https://doi.org/10.1007/978-3-030-67369-7
8. Molinaro, A., Campolo, C., Scopigno, R.: Vehicular Ad Hoc Networks Standards, Solutions, and Research, Springer, Cham (2015). https://doi.org/10.1007/978-3-319-15497-8, ISBN: 9783319154985, 3319154982, 2015
9. Khatib, M., Alsadi, S.: Wireless Mesh Networks-Security, Architectures and Protocols, Intech Open (2020). ISBN: 9781789852035, 178985203X
10. Chen, X.: Randomly Deployed Wireless Sensor Networks, Elsevier, Amsterdam (2020). ISBN: 9780128227718, 0128227710
11. Banerjee, I., Warnier, M., Brazier, F.M.T.: Self-organizing topology for energy-efficient ad-hoc communication networks of mobile devices. Complex Adapt. Syst. Model. 8(7), 1–21 (2020)
12. Islam, N., Shaikh, Z.A.: A Study of Research Trends and Issues in Wireless Ad Hoc Networks. IGI Globals-Handbook of Research on Progressive Trends in WIREL. COMMUN and Networking (2014)
13. Al Mojamed, M.: Integrating mobile ad hoc networks with the internet based on OLSR. Wirel. Commun. Mob. Comput. **2020**, 1–16 (2020)
14. Kumar, K., Verma, S.: A survey of the design and security mechanisms of the wireless networks and mobile adhoc networks. In: IOP Science-Open Access (2020).https://doi.org/10.13140/RG.2.2.31396.09609

15. Rajeswari, A.R.: A Mobile Ad Hoc Network Routing Protocols: A Comparative Study", IntechOpen-Open access peer-reviewed chapter (2020). https://doi.org/10.5772/intechopen.92550

16. Boulaiche, M.: Survey of secure routing protocols for wireless ad hoc networks. Wireless Pers. Commun. **114**(1), 483–517 (2020). https://doi.org/10.1007/s11277-020-07376-1

17. Liu, W., Yu, M.: AASR: authenticated anonymous secure routing for MANETs in adversarial environments. IEEE Trans. Veh. Technol. **63**(9), 4585–4593 (2014). https://doi.org/10.1109/TVT.2014.2313180

18. El-Semary, A.M., Diab, H.: BP-AODV: blackhole protected AODV routing protocol for MANETs based on chaotic map. IEEE Access **7**, 95197–95211 (2019). https://doi.org/10.1109/ACCESS.2019.2928804

19. Veeraiah, N., et al.: Trust aware secure energy efficient hybrid protocol for MANET. IEEE Access **9**, 120996–121005 (2021). https://doi.org/10.1109/ACCESS.2021.3108807

20. Tu, J., Tian, D., Wang, Y.: An active-routing authentication scheme in MANET. IEEE Access **9**, 34276–34286 (2021). https://doi.org/10.1109/ACCESS.2021.3054891

21. Hassan, Z., Mehmood, A., Maple, C., Khan, M.A., Aldegheishem, A.: Intelligent detection of black hole attacks for secure communication in autonomous and connected vehicles. IEEE Access **8**, 199618–199628 (2020). https://doi.org/10.1109/ACCESS.2020.3034327

22. Khan, B.U.I., Anwar, F., Olanrewaju, R.F., Kiah, M.L.B.M., Mir, R.N.: Game theory analysis and modeling of sophisticated multi-collusion attack in MANETs. IEEE Access **9**, 61778–61792 (2021). https://doi.org/10.1109/ACCESS.2021.3073343

23. Aggarwal, A., Gandhi, S., Chaubey, N.: Performance Analysis of AODV, DSDV and DSR in MANETs. ArXiv [Cs.NI] (2014). https://doi.org/10.48550/ARXIV.1402.2217

24. Aggarwal, A., Gandhi, S., Chaubey, N., Jani, K.A.: Trust based secure on demand routing protocol (TSDRP) for MANETs. In: 2014 Fourth International Conference on Advanced Computing & Communication Technologies, pp. 432–438. IEEE (2014)

25. Aggarwal, A., Gandhi, S., Chaubey, N., Tada, N., Trivedi, S.: NDTAODV: Neighbor Defense Technique for Ad Hoc On-Demand Distance Vector (AODV) to mitigate flood attack in MANETS.ArXiv [Cs.NI] (2014). https://doi.org/10.48550/ARXIV.1405.6216

26. Gandhi, S., Chaubey, N., Shah, P., Sadhwani, M.: Performance evaluation of DSR, OLSR and ZRP protocols in MANETs. In: 2012 International Conference on Computer Communication and Informatics, pp. 1–5. IEEE (2012)

27. Chaubey, N.K.: Security analysis of vehicular ad hoc networks (VANETs): a comprehensive study. Int. J. Secur. Appl. **10**(5), 261–274 (2016). https://doi.org/10.14257/ijsia.2016.10.5.25

28. Chaubey, N.K., Yadav, D.: A taxonomy of Sybil attacks in vehicular ad-hoc network (VANET). In IoT and Cloud Computing Advancements in Vehicular Ad-Hoc Networks, pp. 174–190. Hershey, PA: IGI Global. (2020)

29. Chaubey, N.K., Yadav, D.: Detection of Sybil attack in vehicular ad hoc networks by analyzing network performance. Int. J. Electr. Comput. Eng. (IJECE) **12**(2), 1703 (2022). https://doi.org/10.11591/ijece.v12i2.pp1703-1710

30. Rajani, K.C., Aishwarya, P., Meenakshi, S.R.: A review on multicasting routing protocols for mobile ad-hoc wireless networks. In: 2016 International Conference on Communication and Signal Processing (ICCSP), Melmaruvathur, India, pp. 1045–1052 (2016). https://doi.org/10.1109/ICCSP.2016.7754309

31. Rajani, K.C., Aishwarya, P.: Securing dynamic source routing by neighborhood monitoring in wireless adhoc network. Int. J. Adv. Comput. Sci. Appl. (IJACSA), **13**(2) (2022). https://doi.org/10.14569/IJACSA.2022.0130243

32. Rajani, K.C., Aishwarya, P., Manjunath, S.: Friendly group architecture for securely promoting selfish node cooperation in wireless ad-hoc network. Int. J. Adv. Comput. Sci. Appl. (IJACSA), **13**(12) (2022). https://doi.org/10.14569/IJACSA.2022.0131263

DEEC Protocol with ACO Based Cluster Head Selection in Wireless Sensor Network

Renu Jangra[1]([⊠])(iD) and Ramesh Kait[2](iD)

[1] University of Engineering and Management, Jaipur, Rajasthan, India
renu.jangra@uem.edu.in
[2] Kurukshetra University, Kurukshetra, Haryana, India
ramesh.kait@kuk.ac.in

Abstract. When it comes to wireless sensor networks, the routing protocols have a major bearing on the network's power consumption, lifespan, and other metrics. Cost-based, chaining, and clustering models are just a few of the many that inform the creation of routing protocols. It can be challenging to keep track of all of the nodes in Wireless Sensor Networks because there are so many of them. The optimal strategy is to form a cluster out of several nodes. By grouping together, sensor nodes are able to conserve energy and reduce their overall impact on the network. Management and coordination of the cluster's nodes are performed by the cluster head. In its current configuration, the DEEC functions well during transmissions and has been around for some time in the network. However, a probability strategy based on ACO is used in this research to determine which node within a cluster will serve as the cluster's leader. It is the responsibility of the cluster head to collect data from each of the individual nodes and then transmit that data to the home station. The ACO-DEEC protocol chooses a leader for the cluster by putting a probability rule that is based on the parameters of the distance between the nodes and the quantity of power they have. As a consequence of this, this algorithm performs better than the conventional DEEC protocol in terms of energy efficiency, the number of packets reached at the base station, and the count of the nodes that fail entirely.

Keywords: Wireless sensor Network (WSN) · Ant Colony optimization (ACO) · Ant Colony Optimization-Distributed Energy Efficient Clustering protocol (ACO-DEEC) · Cluster Head · DEEC Protocol

1 Introduction

Without the sensor nodes, the wireless sensor network would be nothing more than a theory. Because the sensor nodes only have a limited amount of battery life, the network won't be able to function for as long as it could. A BS exists within or outside the sphere of influence of the node [1]. There are a wide variety of routing strategies that can be used to reduce network downtime, packet/data overflow, and node mortality. To achieve this, we used routing protocols based on clustering. When several nodes join together to form a cluster, one of them is designated as the CH, and the others become cluster nodes.

N. Chaubey et al. (Eds.): COMS2 2023, CCIS 1861, pp. 46–57, 2023.
https://doi.org/10.1007/978-3-031-40564-8_4

Exchange of information between the higher-ups in the cluster. One such clustering-based protocol is the "Distributed energy efficient clustering" (DEEC) protocol. As one possible representation of the relationship between residual and node average energy [2, 3], DEEC employs the cluster leader. The cluster's leader will almost certainly be the node with the highest residual and average energies. Clustering-based routing protocols define a mechanism for selecting the cluster head as well as cutting down on the distance travelled by the communication path between the cluster node (CH) and the base station. This enables the transmission of data to be carried out in a manner that is both more effective and less dependent on the consumption of power. There is now a bio-inspired clustering methodology available for use in selecting appropriate CHs. Some people have doubts about the dependability of wireless connections and prefer hardwired networks instead. Recently, WSNs have become increasingly interested in biomimetic design principles [4]. Swarm-theory based routing algorithms are highly resilient to unexpected topological changes. Seeing a group of ants foraging for food sparked the idea. In this paper, we introduced the ACO-DEEC algorithm, which determines a cluster head's probability of being chosen by analyzing the cluster's strength and its proximity to other nodes. In comparison to the DEEC protocol that is currently in use, the method that has been suggested improves energy efficiency, reduces the number of packets that are transmitted to the base station, and brings the number of dead nodes down.

1.1 ACO

Communal behaviors in insects and other animals serve as inspiration for swarm intelligence. It's a different way of thinking about fixing the issue at hand. In particular, many approaches and procedures make use of the idea of ant behavior. Ant colony optimization stands out as the most effective and methodical of these approaches (ACO). ACO was motivated by the foraging strategies of various ant species. Pheromone, a chemical substance, is laid down by the ants. The other ants in the colony should follow this substance because it indicates the right course of action. Optimization issues can be tackled with the help of a similar method used in ant colony optimization [5]. An example of a swarm intelligence technique is the ACO algorithm. This method uses probabilistic reasoning to locate a solution that is close to optimal. Dorigo.M, Maniezzo.V, and Colomi are the Italian researchers who carried out this study. A use the foraging behavior of ant colonies as the basis for their simulated evolutionary algorithm ACO Ant Colony Optimization. This method examines the evolution of an ant colony, which represents a pool of potential solutions, in order to identify the optimal one. This algorithm has shown excellent performance over the past decade in a wide range of settings, including Combinatorial optimization, routing in network, mining of data, functional optimization, and robot path development are just a few examples of the many optimization techniques available today. This algorithm possesses excellent robustness, as well as a reliable mechanism for distribution and an efficient mechanism for calculation. When combined with other approaches, ACO performs admirably in solving difficult optimization problems. More so than other approaches, it excels at optimizing composite environments. As a result, the development of theoretical analysis and valid study of ACO has enormous pedagogical significance and engineering value. The application of ACO has been beneficial to a variety of different industries, including the electrical power, mining operations, chemical, water conservancy, architectural, and traffic industries, amongst others. When dealing with the optimization of the travelling salesman route, the self-organization of ants can be put into play in four distinct ways. By searching the route in TSP iteratively, multiple ants are able to communicate with one another at once. Each ant is assumed to deal with its own issues on its own. Good comments: More pheromone on a path or along a graph edge results in more ants taking that route in the travelling salesman problem. It draws the conclusion that, in subsequent iterations, a larger number of ants will take that route. The following fictitious rule serves as the basis for the positive feedback system. The pheromone's value determines whether or not there will be a graph edge along the ant's path; in other words, the pheromone's value is directly proportional to the ant's path. Inversely proportional to the length of a path is the concentration of pheromones at its edge. More ants will use pheromones in the construction of new paths because the shorter path contains more pheromone than the longer path on the corresponding edges of the graph. Only considering positive responses leads to a situation known as stagnation, in which all of the ants take the same, inefficient route. Pheromone evaporation is thought of as a way to prevent the unfavorable reaction. Pheromone evaporation should not take place at an excessively high rate. if the bar is set too high, there will be no need to reduce in size and scope. If it happens too quickly, the ant colony will lose sight of the progress it has made in the past too soon (memory loss), undermining the efficacy of the ants' social support [4].

1.2 DEEC

The DEEC protocol is an efficient energy-saving method that operates in clusters. Network nodes are organized hierarchically, with CH collecting data from cluster nodes and relaying it to the base station. We take into account both "advanced" and "normal" nodes in the DEEC. Both the advanced node and the standard node have an initial energy of. As an example of the network's total initial energy, consider:

$$E_{total} = N(1-x)E_0 + NxE_0(1+a) = NE_0(1+ax)$$

Each DEEC cluster has its own CH because the network is divided into multiple smaller clusters. The network's residual energy and the nodes' initial energies are used to determine which CH to use. The probability function is defined as the product of these two quantities [5]. The probability function with a high value is more likely to produce a CH. The optimum count $C(T_i)$ of CHs in DEEC for each round is computed from the following equations.

$C(T_i) = p_{opt}E_i(r)/(1+axE'(r))$, if $T(i)$ is a normal node. $C(T_i) = p_{opt}(1+a)E_i(r)/(1+ax)E'(r)$, if $T(i)$ is an advanced node.

Where, the average energy $E_{energy}(r)$ of the network at round r and is stated by.

$$E_i(r) = \sum_{i=1}^{N} r/N \quad E_i(r) \text{ is the residual energy of the node at round r.}$$

1.3 ACO-DEEC

Ant colony optimization is functional to the DEEC protocol in the proposed ACO-DEEC method. The DEEC uses a probability rule to determine who will serve as CH. This rule has its foundation in the comparison of the energy left with the nodes to the average energy across the network. When determining which node should serve as the cluster head, the ACO-DEEC takes into account the probability function as well as the energy level of the node and its distance from the base station. Large paths are assumed to have more energy than short ones between nodes, and vice versa. The following are the procedures followed by the ACO-DEEC ants: Ants use the start rule to choose the next cluster head and the revise rule to pick the best candidate.

Start Rule: When there is an ant on the cluster head node named i, use Eqs. 1 and 2 to determine which cluster head node j should be selected as the next cluster head node.

$$P = \frac{Dis \tan ce_i * \alpha + Phero_i * \beta}{\sum_{i=0}^{N_i} (Dis \tan ce_i * \alpha + Phero_i * \beta)} \tag{1}$$

where the probability function P assists the node in selecting the cluster head, and $Phero_i$ refers to the value of the pheromone.

$$Phero_i = \frac{\tau_{i,j}^{\alpha} * \eta_i^{\beta}}{\sum_{i=0}^{N_i} \tau_{i,j}^{\alpha} * \eta_i^{\beta}} \tag{2}$$

where, pheromone intensity denotes by $\tau_{i,j}^{\alpha}$, η_i denotes the heuristic information and α & β denotes controlling parameters,

$$\eta_i = \frac{1}{I_e - e} \tag{3}$$

where, I_e is the energy initially provided to the node and e is present energy that a node has. The node that has a power level that is lower than its actual energy level has a lower probability of being selected as a Cluster Head.

Revision Rule: There is an update in the current value of pheromone when an ant selects the next CH. This update is done by the rule given in Eq. 4.

$$\tau_{i,j}(t + 1) = (1 - \rho)\tau_{i,j}(t) + \rho \Delta \tau_{i,j}(t) \tag{4}$$

The change in the pheromone value is represented by $\Delta \tau_{i,j}(t)$ and ρ denotes the parameter that helps to stop the extra accumulation of the pheromone.

2 Literature Review

An E-DEEC algorithm with normal, advanced, and super nodes was proposed by P. Saini and A.K. Sharma [6]. The introduction of a super node, which is more powerful than both regular and advanced nodes, introduces heterogeneity into the network. E-DEEC performed better in simulations than SEP did. The proposed algorithm improves the network's longevity and reliability.

S. B. ALLA and colleagues [7] developed the BCDEEC protocol for use in WSN that have varying degrees of homogeneity. In the algorithm, it was suggested that the Base Station should ensure that the nodes with the most energy could act as a path and a becomes a CH in order to save the average amount of energy that the nodes consume. This was done in a direction to lessen the entire volume of energy that was consumed by the nodes. Data is delivered to the base station using cluster head to gateway routing, which results in lower overall power consumption and a smaller number of faulty nodes. The findings of the simulation made it abundantly clear that Balanced and Centralized DEEC performed well than SEP and DEEC, thereby extending the lifetime of the network.

Distributed Energy-Efficient Clustering, Developed DEEC, Enhanced DEEC, and Threshold DEEC were the four protocols that were compared by T. N. Qureshi et al. [8] using scenarios that ranged from top to bottom levels of heterogeneity. Although both EDEEC and TDEEC performed admirably under the test conditions, the outcomes exhibited that TDEEC was superior in way of stability and longevity.

The new MDEEC, which was proposed by C.Divya et al. [9], makes it possible to transmit more data from the BS to CH within a specified time gap than the conventional DEEC does. In comparison to DEEC, the results of the simulation demonstrated that MDEEC possessed 15% higher message throughput and 15% lower delay in data transmission. As a direct consequence of this, the energy efficiency of the network increased.

ITDEEC is a novel method that was introduced by Mostafa Bogouri et al. [10]. It enhances the threshold DEEC for heterogeneous WSN by removing the nearer nodes to the BS during the clustering process. These closer nodes consumed extra energy than the other nodes. According to the results of the MATLAB simulation, the network lifetime in ITDEEC had increased by 46% when compared to TDEEC, and the amount of data that could be transmitted had increased by 184%.

In WSN, many sensor nodes equipped with modest computing and sensing capabilities perform the necessary tasks. The benefits and drawbacks of routing protocols were discussed by K. Yaeghoobi et al. [11]. They compared the protocols SEP, HEED, LEACH, and DEEC in simulations and found similar outcomes. The outcome proved that HEED outperformed LEACH and SEP in both heterogeneous and unified settings.

Sarin Vencin and Ebubekir Erdem proposed TBSDEEC (Threshold balanced sampled DEEC) for three-level heterogeneous clustering [12]. Our model competed against the DEEC, EDEEC, and EDDEEC in two MATLAB scenarios on quality metrics like number of packets reached at the BS, the average latency, the number of nodes that were online, and the amount of energy that was consumed. In order to evaluate how effective our new method is, we evaluate it in relation to two other methods: the artificial bee colony optimization algorithm and the energy harvesting WSN clustering method. In simulations, the proposed model demonstrates superior performance to alternative protocols and significantly increases the lifetime of sensor networks.

To be more specific, "AM-DisCNT" and "iAM-DisCNT" were both developed by Akbar et al. [13]. In the first iteration of the algorithm, nodes were dispersed across the space in a circular pattern to ensure that each one consumed an equal amount of power. The second algorithm increased throughput by combining mobile and fixed base stations in the most efficient way possible. It was discovered that both proposed algorithms are superior to DEEC and LEACH in extending the stability period by 32% and 48%, respectively, then those two other compounds.

The authors of this work proposed [14] a modified heterogeneous algorithm that takes distance of the super nodes to the Base station as well as its the average distance of the nodes. The goal of this algorithm is to determine which nodes should serve as cluster heads. They have considered various levels of amplification energy for use in communication both within and between clusters, as well as between the cluster head and the BS, in an effort to diminish the quantity of power that is consumed. The simulation results that were tested in MATLAB 2017a show that the one that was proposed performs better than E-DEEC across all three parameters that were evaluated.

S. Kurumbanshi and S. Rathkanthiwar [15] discussed about the problems, routing, probabilistic approaches and issues exist in wireless sensor network with their solution. They also describe various operations by setting them one can get the better network with better energy level. When working with large networks, delay is taken as a metric. There are many applications of the wireless sensor network, but still there are many challenges in it. The issue with channel state information is explained which is used for operation in the network and processing of the signal. The neural network is used by the authors to set the threshold and particle swarm optimization is used to adjust the weight. They use the Pareto distribution of energy saving.

Silki Baghla and Savina Bansal [16] explained that the energy saving concept is very critical issue in a heterogeneous network. The new technology arises in which mobile are equipped with multiple networks at the same time. All these consume more energy. So, vertical handover technique is used by authors t handle this issue. A new algorithm is proposed VIKOR to manage the handover. This will consume less energy when work with WLAN, cellular network and WiMax simultaneously.

Sowjanya Ramisetty, Mahesh Murthy, and Anand S. Reddy [17] Using the moth flame optimisation al-gorithm, we found the optimal placements for the sensor nodes in the partitioned network to improve throughput, range, and power consumption (OPS-MFO). The proposed model has been shown to perform better than state-of-the-art algorithms in experimental evaluations.

3 Proposed Algorithm (ACO-DEEC)

Start

1. Make the network that have some parameters like initial probability (p), node count (n), round count $r_{\max}$, initial energy E_0, $rho(\rho)$, $E_{f,s}$, E_{amp}, E_{TX}, E_{RX}.
2. Determine the network's typical energy consumption.
3. Compute the probability function for each node by basing it on the node's strength as well as its distance from the base station.
4. A formula is used to calculate the probability function

$$P = \frac{Distance_i * \alpha + Phero_i * \beta}{\sum\limits_{i=0}^{N_i} (Distance_i * \alpha + Phero_i * \beta)}$$

$$Phero_i = \frac{\tau_{i,j}^{\alpha} * \eta_i^{\beta}}{\sum\limits_{i=0}^{N_i} \tau_{i,j}^{\alpha} * \eta_i^{\beta}}$$

$$\eta_i = \frac{1}{I_e - e}$$

5. The set G contains all of the nodes that could potentially become CHs. If a node in the previous round was a cluster head, it is added to G. A node is a member of that cluster and has an obligation to contribute data to the proper CH if it is not a member of group G.
6. If the condition holds (choose random number > threshold function), then the node can be selected as a CH. If it is not meeting the condition, it will continue to function as a member of the cluster and report its data to the correct CH.
7. Figure out how much power is left in the node, how many nodes have died, and how many packets have been sent back to the hub.
8. One round/cycle has ended.
9. Stop

4   Flowchart of Proposed Algorithm

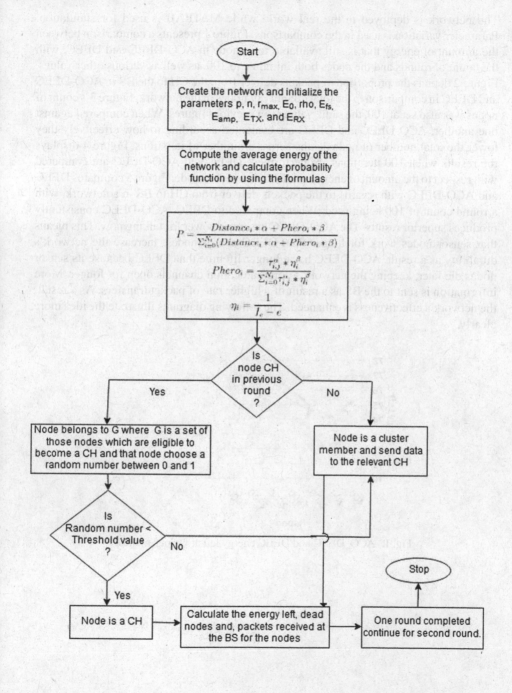

Start

Create the network and initialize the parameters p, n, r_{max}, E_0, rho, E_{fs}, E_{amp}, E_{TX}, and E_{RX}

Compute the average energy of the network and calculate probability function by using the formulas

$$P = \frac{Distance_i * \alpha + Phero_i * \beta}{\sum_{i=0}^{N_i}(Distance_i * \alpha + Phero_i * \beta)}$$

$$Phero_i = \frac{\tau_{i,j}^\alpha * \eta_i^\beta}{\sum_{i=0}^{N_i} \tau_{i,j}^\alpha * \eta_i^\beta}$$

$$\eta_i = \frac{1}{J_e - \epsilon}$$

Is node CH in previous round ?

Yes

No

Node belongs to G where G is a set of those nodes which are eligible to become a CH and that node choose a random number between 0 and 1

Node is a cluster member and send data to the relevant CH

Is Random number < Threshold value ?

No

Yes

Node is a CH

Calculate the energy left, dead nodes and, packets received at the BS for the nodes

One round completed continue for second round.

Stop

5 Experimental Result

The network is deployed in the real world while MATLAB is used for simulation. Parameter variation is used in the comparisons. Figure 1 presents a comparison between the amount of energy that is still available for a node in ACO-DEEC and DEEC, with the count of rounds and the nodes both initialize to 100, as well as various other values. Figure 2 depicts the proportion of packets deliver from the CH to the BS in ACO-DEEC and DEEC in comparison to the total quantity of nodes in the network. Figure 3's count of nodes was also set at 100, the same value as in previous figures. When compared against one another, ACO-DEEC and DEEC are evaluated according to how effectively they lower the total number of node deaths across a number of iterations. Figure 4 displays the results when 100 iterations are performed. DEEC and ACO-DEEC are compared with respect to the amount of energy available to a sensor node. Figure 5 compares DEEC and ACO-DEEC with regards to the packets deliver from CH to BS in a network, with a round count of 100 being used. When compared to DEEC, ACO-DEEC consistently produces superior results. The ACO-DEEC has more power for talking now. This means that sensor nodes work for longer than DEEC sensor nodes. Increase the network's durability as a result. ACO-DEEC has a longer lifetime than DEEC because its sensor nodes die later, keeping the network's communication channels open for longer. More information is sent to the BS as a result of a higher rate of packet transfers. As a result, the network's effectiveness is enhanced. The following diagrams illustrate the idea more clearly.

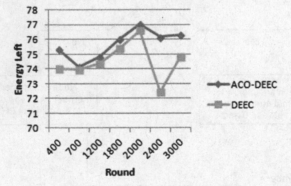

Fig. 1. ACO_DEEC and DEEC energy left at various rounds.

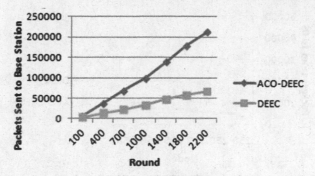

Fig. 2. Packets deliver to the BS at various rounds, comparing ACO-DEEC and DEEC.

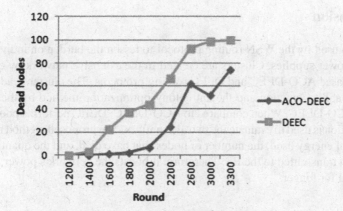

Fig. 3. ACO-DEEC and DEEC comparison of dead nodes at various iterations.

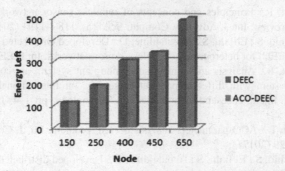

Fig. 4. Energy dissipated compared between ACO-DEEC and DEEC at various nodes.

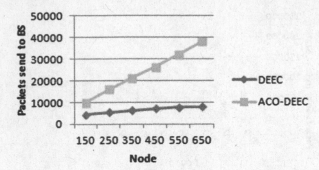

Fig. 5. Different nodes in ACO-DEEC and DEEC packets are compared.

6 Conclusion

Clustering is used by the WSN routing protocol to lessen the burden on individual sensor nodes' power supplies. Clusters are created in the extensive network by employing the energy-based ACO-DEEC and DEEC routing protocols. The cluster head is chosen using a probability function and the ant colony optimization method by the proposed algorithm ACO-DEEC. When compared to ACO-DEEC, DEEC performs poorly. MATLAB simulation is used to evaluate the two alternatives. The proposed method minimizes the amount of energy used, the number of nodes that have died, and the quantity of data that has been transmitted to the BS. Therefore, it boosts the network's power and keeps it operational for longer.

References

1. Jangra, R., Kait, R.: Principles and concepts of wireless sensor network and ant colony optimization: a review. Int. J. Adv. Res. Comput. Sci. **8**(5), 1180–1191 (2017)
2. Elbhiri, B., Rachid, S., Elfkihi, S., Aboutajdine, D.: Developed Distributed Energy-Efficient Clustering (DDEEC) for heterogeneous wireless sensor networks. In: IEEE (2010)
3. Jangra, R., Kait, R.: Analysis and comparison among ant system; ant colony system and max-min ant system with different parameters setting. In: International Conference on "Computational Intelligence and Communication Technology, pp 1–4. IEEE, Ghaziabad (2017)
4. Jangra, R., Kait, R.: ACO parameters analysis of TSP problem. Int. J. Comput. Sci. Mob. Appl. **5**(8), 24–29 (2017)
5. Elbhiri, B., Rachid, S., El fkihi, S., Aboutajdine, D.: Developed distributed energy-efficient clustering (DDEEC) for heterogeneous wireless sensor networks. In: IEEE, pp.1–4 (2010)
6. Saini, P., Sharma, A.K.: E-DEEC- enhanced distributed energy efficient clustering scheme for heterogeneous WSN. In: 1st International Conference on Parallel, Distributed and Grid Computing, pp 2015–210. IEEE, Solan (2010)
7. Alla, S.B., Ezzati, A., Mouhsen, A., Hssane, A.B., Hasnaoui, M.L.: Balanced and centralized distributed energy efficient clustering for heterogeneous wireless sensor networks. In: 3rd International Conference on Next Generation Networks and Services, pp 39–44. IEEE, Hammamet (2011)

8. Qureshi, T.N., Javaid, N., Malik, M., Qasimm, U., Khan, Z. A.: On performance evaluation of variants of DEEC in WSNs. In: Seventh International Conference on Broadband, Wireless Computing, Communication and Applications, 162–169. IEEE, Victoria (2012)

9. Divya, C., Krishnan, N., Krishnapriya, P.: Modified distributed energy-efficient cluster for heterogeneous wireless sensor networks. In: International Conference on Emerging Trends in Computing, Communication and Nanotechnology, pp. 611–615 IEEE, Tirunelveli (2013)

10. Bogouri, M., Chakkor, S., Hajraoui, A.: Improving threshold distributed energy efficient clustering algorithm for heterogeneous wireless sensor networks. In: Third IEEE International Colloquium in Information Science and Technology, pp 430-435. IEEE, Tetouan (2014)

11. Kaebeh Yaeghoobi, S.B., Soni, M.K., Tyagi, S.S.: performance analysis of energy efficient clustering protocols to maximize wireless sensor networks lifetime. In: International Conference on Soft Computing Techniques and Implementations, pp 170–176. IEEE, Faridabad (2015)

12. Vançin, S., Erdem, E.: Threshold balanced sampled DEEC model for heterogeneous wireless sensor networks. Wirel. Commun. Mob. Comput. **2018**, 1–12 (2018)

13. Akbar, M., Javaid, N., Imran, M., Rao, A.: Muhammad Shahzad Younis and Iftikhar Azim Niaz", A multi-hop angular routing protocol for wireless sensor networks". Int. J. Distrib. Sens. Netw. **12**(9), 1–13 (2016)

14. Jibreel, F.: Improved enhanced distributed energy efficient clustering (iE-DEEC) scheme for heterogeneous wireless sensor network. Int. J. Eng. Res. Adv. Technol, **5**(1), 6–11 (2019). E-ISSN: 2454–6135, 2019

15. Kurumbanshi, S., Rathkanthiwar, S.: Increasing the lifespan of wireless adhoc network using probabilistic approaches: a survey. Int. J. Inf. Technol. **10**, 537–542 (2018)

16. Baghla, S., Bansal, S.: An approach to energy efficient vertical handover technique for heterogeneous networks. Int. J. Inf. Technol. **10**(3), 359–366 (2018). https://doi.org/10.1007/s41 870-018-0115-2

17. Ramisetty, S., Anand, D., Kavita, Verma, S., Jhanjhi, N.Z., Humayun, M.: Energy-efficient model for recovery from multiple cluster nodes failure using moth flame optimization in wireless sensor networks. In: Peng, SL., Hsieh, SY., Gopalakrishnan, S., Duraisamy, B. (eds.) Intelligent Computing and Innovation on Data Science. Lecture Notes in Networks and Systems, vol. 248, pp 491–499. Springer, Singapore(2021). https://doi.org/10.1007/978-981-16-3153-5_52

Performance Analysis of Recovery Methods for Loss of Target in Wireless Sensor Network Following TDNN Prediction Algorithm

Alpesh Sankaliya[1](✉) and Maulin Joshi[2]

[1] Gujarat Technological University, Gujarat, India
alpeshrs@gmail.com
[2] Sarvajanik College of Engineering and Technology, Surat, India

Abstract. The efficient target tracking framework can save the network lifetime by reducing a sensor node burden. Energy is very important aspect in tracking of target in WSN. Compared to other prediction methods, the efficiency of the TDNN is better. By considering target velocity and geometrical shapes, lost target recovery can be improved further in terms of energy efficiency. Performance of different methods based on circular and contour geometrical shapes and taking target velocity into consideration is evaluated and compared based on energy efficiency.

Keywords: Wireless Sensor Network (WSN) · Time Domain Neural Network (TDNN) · Target Tracking · Target Recovery · Energy Efficient Target Recovery

1 Introduction

WSN are being used mostly for target tracking in applications such as military and crime activities. Smart cities without sensors are impossible to forecast in the upcoming years. An automatically reconfigurable sensor network composed of tiny but strong sensors that can function without human assistance can be used to save human time and labor. In vital sectors of several fields, such as vehicle position monitoring, logistics management, and anti-terrorism, WSN have been mostly used in military and civic industries, particularly for tracking targets in important locations. In WSN, a variety of tracking techniques can be applied [1, 2]. Based on research it can be said that Time domain neural networks method provides better solution in terms of target tracking as compared to other methods. Target is monitored while taking into account the fixed region and fixed number of nodes where it is expected to be present. Targets can occasionally lose because of network flaws or any other circumstances, such as the absence of nearby nodes in few area [3]. In that case target recovery algorithm is being used. Different target recovery algorithms has been analyzed in this work based on circular and contour geometrical shapes with target velocity also being used to specify the predicted region of lost target.

N. Chaubey et al. (Eds.): COMS2 2023, CCIS 1861, pp. 58–69, 2023.
https://doi.org/10.1007/978-3-031-40564-8_5

2   Literature Survey

The most popular use of wireless sensor networks is target tracking. Sensing, localisation, prediction, and communication are crucial components of a comprehensive racking mechanism. [3].

Sensing: The nodes have a limited sensing range. They can sense the target presence only when it enters into the sensor's vicinity. The sensed information is sent to a central entity using a transceiver.

Localization and prediction: The central entity is responsible for a localization task. Once the target presence is detected in an area being monitored, an exact location must be estimated to take further actions. The trilateration method is applied to estimate the target location on data received from sensor nodes. It needs information from at least three sensor nodes. Using a prediction method, the target's future location is anticipated based on its current direction and velocity.

Communication: The central entity reports a target location to the action center.

The network architecture that governs how sensors communicate with one another affects how well a tracking algorithm performs. In distant applications, tiny, powerful sensor nodes are typically dropped through the air, resulting in the deployment of sensors at random. The location of the nodes has a direct impact on network coverage and a secondary impact on sensing operations. Nodes located near a network's edge can identify intrusions as target enters the tracking region [6]. The surrounding nodes cannot identify the existence of the target if there is a coverage hole in that area, which affects tracking performance. The trilateration or triangulation method can be used to estimate the target location if a at least three nodes detect the existence of the target [9]. Figuere1 shows flowchart of target tracking and recovery system.

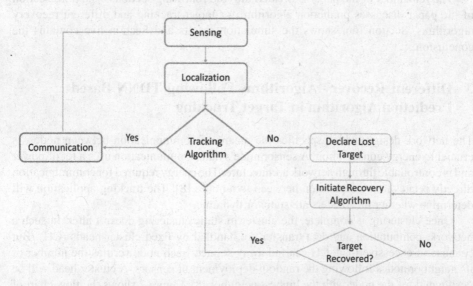

Fig. 1. Flowchart of target tracking and recovery system

Many dynamic and static duty cycle-based approaches have been presented in the literature to alter sensor motes' sleep time when target is unlikely to be surrounding area [1]. To conserve energy, Nodes can be put to sleep, however this increases the odds of missing the target. The sensor node's energy usage while in sleep mode keeps rising as the product of time and energy usage while in sleep mode per second rises. An energy-saving prediction method can reduce transmission that isn't essential. Prediction is a problem of sensor combination. The objective is to select nodes which are closer to projected target location in order to save energy. The kalman-based method fails when the target travels more quickly [4]. The kalman-based method is suitable for predicting on the future situation of moving vehicles with almost no acceleration [9, 10]. When tracking a maneuvering target, A kalman method causes divergence due to acceleration of target. The state transition matrix selected affects how well the prediction algorithm performs. Time is only injected into TDNN through its inputs. Time delays are set at the start of training and do not change, but Time delays in tracking applications must be adaptable to change acceleration properties. TDNN found more accurate in prediction algorithm in WSN.

Even so there have been attempts to improve tracking performance by altering these filters, tracking in the presence of holes has not received much attention. The existence of a hole severely impedes network tracking. When it goes through the hole, the target is momentarily lost. Failure of communication as a result of network holes, Node Failures, Location Estimation Errors, Prediction Errors, Random Maneuvering and Faulty Node are Various causes of losing the target [5, 3]. As a result, these factors must be taken into account when building the tracking with recovery process. We show how filter-based tracking algorithms and recovery algorithms function in the presence of holes in this article.

The remainder of the paper is divided into the following sections. The third section of the paper discusses prediction algorithm for target tracking and different recovery algorithms. Section four shows the simulation results and Section five contains the conclusion.

3 Different Recovery Algorithms Following TDNN Based Prediction Algorithm in Target Tracking

The network design, which specifies the means of communication between nodes, is crucial to energy conservation. A sensor node's data communication uses a lot of power and is controllable through network architecture. The energy required for communication directly relates to the separation between two nodes [8]. The tracking application will determine whether the clusters are static or dynamic.

Once clustering is complete, the cluster in static clustering doesn't alter. In such a network, computation and data transfer are handled by fixed cluster heads (CH). But because of excessive load, CH can fad away sooner. Each node verifies the number of its neighbor nodes following the random deployment of sensors. A cluster head will be designated for the node with the highest neighbor [8]. Figure 2 shows the flow chart of static clustering in wireless sensor network [14, 15].

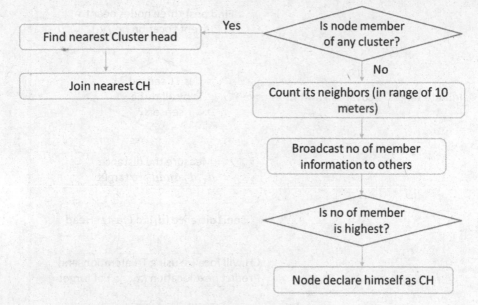

Fig. 2. Static Clustering in sensor Network

The target is first tracked by the three closest nodes. Using the trilateration method, the cluster head will localise the target and forecast its subsequent position [11, 12]. The target location is predicted using a variety of prediction techniques. For instance, TDNN, Kalman, and interacting multiple models [13]. In this work, here we have used TDNN as a prediction algorithm. Figure 3 shows the flowchart of tracking target in WSN.

In event of a lost target, the cluster head first verified the target's previous location. If the target is still not located, start the recovery algorithm. Once the target has been recovered, the prediction system will monitor and predict the target. The Recovery Algorithm flowchart is shown in Fig. 4.

Here we have implemented Time delayed neural network (TDNN) as a prediction algorithm in simulation. Neural networks outperform Kalman or other mathematically-based methods as model-free estimators. During tracking, a variety of sensor nodes are employed to find travelling target. The core of information processing is a cluster head node that has been chosen. Sensor nodes give data to the CH, which applies a neural networks based algorithm to anticipate. Nonparametric nature of neural network method eliminates the need for information source knowledge [1].

In spite of past values, FFNNs react to an input. Traditional back propagation algorithms include inefficient response times, delayed convergence, and the potential to get caught in local minima. Back propagation requires memory in a dynamic network and is independent of time series. Dynamic models may contain memory by utilising time delays. Movement of target is a random process that evolves over time. Time delay neural networks, often known as TDNNs, are FFNNs with a delayed input. The TDNN method attempts to determine the correlation between the current samples and the delayed input samples [8]. Following are various recovery techniques in the event of target loss.

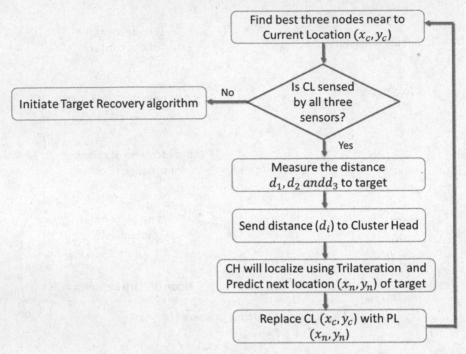

Fig. 3. Flowchart of Target tracking

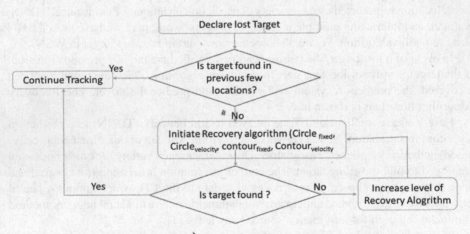

Fig. 4. Flowchart of Recovery Algorithm

3.1 Circle_fixed

In a circular method, all nodes that are within the first radius (R1) are first activated. If the target is not located, all nodes are activated into a larger radius (R2), and so on, as shown in Fig. 1. As more nodes are activated, more energy is required to recover the target [5].

The drawback of this method is that a big area has been covered by the circle, activating a large number of nodes and making it an energy-intensive method. Even if the target is close by, this strategy will cover a wide area [6, 7] (Fig. 5).

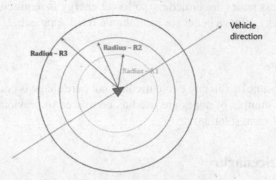

Fig. 5. Conceptual diagram of Circle$_{fixed}$ Method

3.2 Contour$_{fixed}$

The contour, taking into account the kinematics of the vehicle, is the region that the target can visit to obtain its current position, speed, and direction during refresh time. It eliminates the least likely portion of the tracking circle. Figure 2 shows the contour approach (Fig. 6).

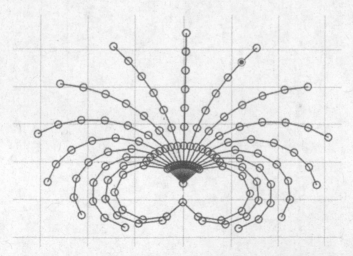

Fig. 6. Specific instance of fixed contour technique for recovery

3.3 Circle_{velocity}

The only difference between this method and Circle Fixed is that target velocity is calculated before creating active area with a twice the radius of target velocity. As less space is covered, less nodes are turned on so lower energy is required during recovery of target, this strategy offers a better solution than a fixed approach.

3.4 Contour_{velocity}

This method work same as velocity circle method but here shape is contour. Because of contour shape less number of nodes are used as compared to previous methods and it provides energy efficient solution.

4 Simulation Scenario

100 x 100 m2 area is used in which there are 14 clusters and 600 nodes as shown in Fig. 7. Different recovery methods following TDNN algorithm are analyzed using track shown in Fig. 8. Energy parameters are defined below. To determine whether the nodes can follow the target location, cluster heads communicate with nodes [3, 8]. A message is sent to neighboring cluster heads by the current cluster head. Then cluster heads use nodes to determine location of target. Nodes first process the message than sense if target is available in their range and can be located or not [9]. Then message is sent back to

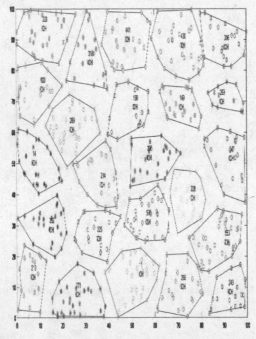

Fig. 7. Typical scenario for node and cluster formation experimental Network

cluster heads. Neighbor cluster head then sends the message back to the current cluster head. Energy parameters are defined in Table 1 [8].

Table 1. Simulation parameters [2]

Parameter	Value
Initial Energy of node	2 J
Sensing Energy	9.6×10^{-3} J/Second
Transmission Energy	5.76×10^{-3} J/Byte
Receiving Energy	0.88×10^{-3} J/Byte
processing Energy	4.0×10^{-9} J/Instruction
sleep Energy	0.33×10^{-3} J/Second
Message size	64 Byte

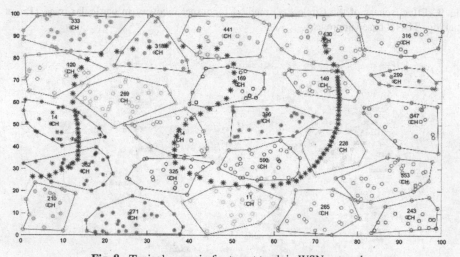

Fig. 8. Typical scenario for target track in WSN network

Typical scenario for track in WSN is as shown in above Fig. 8 where target is shifting at constant speed.

Figure 9 illustrates the results for the fixed circle (Circle $_{fixed}$) method. As observed, a recovery mechanism has been initiated because the target has become lost in some places. In level 1 recovery, the target is not tracked by the Circle $_{fixed}$ approach. Target is tracked in level 2 as shown in Fig. 9. However, more nodes are engaged for target recovery due to the circle's large area.

Figure 10 illustrates the results for the velocity-based circle (Circle $_{velocity}$) method. With this method, level 1 recovery includes the region surrounding a circle whose radius is equal to the target velocity. After that, the radius of a circle is determined for each level increment by multiplying the level by the velocity.

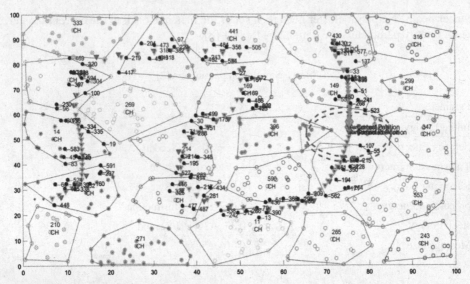

Fig. 9. Effectiveness of the Circle fixed method for target recovery in particular track (Target tracking- TDNN based approach)

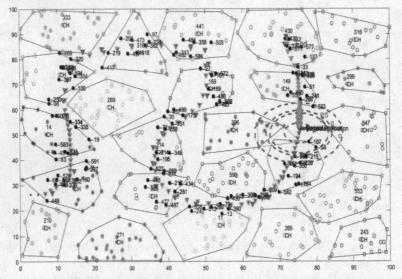

Fig. 10. Effectiveness of the Circle velocity method for target recovery in particular track (Target tracking- TDNN based approach)

Figure 11 illustrates the results for the Fixed contour (Contour_fixed) method. In this large area is being used as compared to previous cases so more energy being used to recover the target. Figure 12 illustrates the results for the velocity based contour(Contour velocity) method. Contour are made based on velocity so it covers less area as compared to previous approaches and provides better solution in terms on energy efficiency. Table 2 shows the energy analysis of different recovery algorithms. As is apparent from Table 2, the velocity based contour (Contour $_{velocity}$) method can save more energy while recovering the loss target. Figure 13 shows the graphical representation of energy analysis of recovery methods for loss target in WSN.

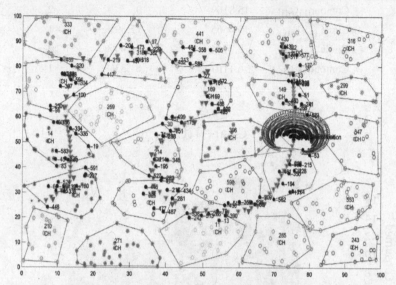

Fig. 11. Effectiveness of the Contour $_{fixed}$ method for target recovery in particular track (Target tracking- TDNN based approach)

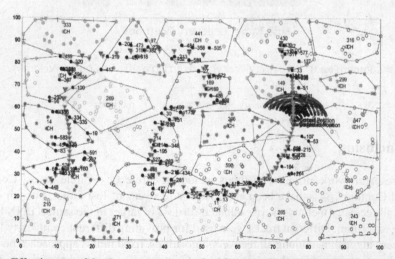

Fig. 12. Effectiveness of the Contour $_{velocity}$ method for target recovery in particular track (Target tracking- TDNN based approach)

Table 2. Saving of energy analysis for particular track

METHOD USED FOR TRACKING	METHODS USED FOR RECOVERY	ENERGY USED IN RECOVERY (Joules)	Percentage of energy saved compared to Contour$_{fixed}$	No of Times Target Lost
TDNN	Contour$_{(Fixed)}$	15.8169	0	2
	Circle $_{(velocity)}$	13.0665	17.39%	1
	Circle $_{(fixed)}$	8.7944	44.40%	2
	Contour$_{(velocity)}$	6.1167	61.33%	1

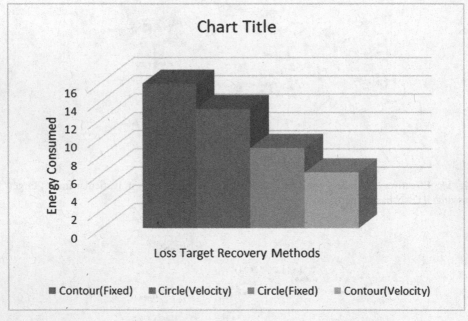

Fig. 13. Energy analysis of recovery methods

5   Conclusion

In this research work, different methods including Circle $_{fixed}$, Circle $_{velocity}$, Contour $_{fixed}$ and Contour $_{velocity}$ have been analysed for recovery of lost target. For fair comparison all recovery methods were evaluated for loss of target in the same TDNN based tracking algorithm. Different tracks were used for providing different complexity levels to recovery algorithm. Among all recovery algorithms, fixed radius approaches perform better when there is sudden change in velocity. Contour $_{velocity}$ algorithm performs better under constant velocity conditions as compared to other methods.

References

1. Munjani, J.H., Joshi, M.: Target tracking in WSN using time delay neural network. J. Mach. Intell. **2**(2), 16–22 (2017)
2. Bhagat, D.P., Soni, H.: Target tracking in a wireless sensor network using a multi-step KF-PSO model. Int. J. Comput. Appl., 1–12 (2019)
3. Wang, Y., Feng, X.: Maneuvering target tracking in wireless sensor network with range only measurement. J. Phys.: Conf. Ser. **1325**(1) (2019)
4. Patil, S., Gupta, A., Zaveri, M.: Recovery of lost target using target tracking in event driven clustered wireless sensor network. J. Comput. Netw. Commun. (2014)
5. Asmaa, E.Z., Said, R., Lahoucine, K.: Review of recovery techniques to recapture lost targets in wireless sensor networks. In: Proceedings of 2016 International Conference on Electrical and Information Technologies, ICEIT (2016)
6. Demigha, O., Hidouci, W.K., Ahmed, T.: On Energy efficiency in collaborative target tracking in wireless sensor network: a review. IEEE Commun. Surv. Tutorials **15**(3), 1210–1222 (2013)
7. Ahmad, T., Abbas, A.M.: EEAC: an energy efficient adaptive cluster based target tracking in wireless sensor networks. J. Interdisc. Math. **23**(2), 379–392 (2020)
8. Bhavsar, M.A., Munjani, J.H., Joshi, M.: Target tracking in WSN using dynamic neural network techniques. In: Bhattacharyya, P., Sastry, H., Marriboyina, V., Sharma, R. (eds.) Smart and Innovative Trends in Next Generation Computing Technologies, NGCT 2017, vol. 828, pp. 771–789. Springer, Singapore (2018). https://doi.org/10.1007/978-981-10-8660-1_58
9. Jondhale, S.R., Deshpande, R.S.: Kalman filtering framework-based real time target tracking in wireless sensor networks using generalized regression neural networks. IEEE Sens. J. **19**(1), 224–233 (2019)
10. Xu, Y., Xu, K., Wan, J., Xiong, Z., Li, Y.: Research on particle filter tracking method based on Kalman filter. In: Proceedings of 2018 2nd IEEE Advanced Information Management, Communicates, Electronic and Automation Control Conference, IMCEC 2018, (Imcec), pp. 1564–1568 (2018)
11. Jondhale, S.R., Shubair, R., Labade, R.P., Lloret, J., Gunjal, P.R.: Application of supervised learning approach for target localization in wireless sensor network. In: Singh, P.K., Bhargava, B.K., Paprzycki, M., Kaushal, N.C., Hong, W.-C. (eds.) Handbook of Wireless Sensor Networks: Issues and Challenges in Current Scenario's. AISC, vol. 1132, pp. 493–519. Springer, Cham (2020). https://doi.org/10.1007/978-3-030-40305-8_24
12. Wang, X., Liu, X., Wang, Z., Li, R., Wu, Y.: SVM+ KF target tracking strategy using the signal strength in wireless sensor networks. Sensors **20**(14), 3832 (2020)
13. Yang, H., Sikdar, B.: A protocol for tracking mobile targets using sensor networks. In: Proceedings of the 1st IEEE International Workshop on Sensor Network Protocols and Applications, SNPA 2003, pp. 71–81 (2003)
14. Chaubey, N.K., Patel, D.H.: Energy efficient clustering algorithm for decreasing energy consumption and delay in wireless sensor networks (WSN). Int. J. Innov. Res. Comput. Commun. Eng. **4**(5), 8652–8656 (2016)
15. Chaubey, N., Patel, D.H.: Routing protocols in wireless sensor network: a critical survey and comparison. Int. J. IT Eng. **04**(02), 8–18 (2016). ISSN: 2321–1776

A Comparative Study of DWT and DCT Along with AES Techniques for Safety Transmission of Digital Bank Cheque Image

Sudhanshu Gonge[1,2](✉) (iD), Rahul Joshi[1,2] (iD), Ketan Kotecha[1,2] (iD), Milind Gayakwad[3] (iD), Rupali Gangarde[1,2] (iD), Gagandeep Kaur[1,2] (iD), and Kalyani Kadam[1,2] (iD)

[1] Symbiosis Institute of Technology, Lavale, India
{sudhanshu.gonge,rupali.gangarde,gagandeep.kaur,
kalyanik}@sitpune.edu.in, rahulj@sitpune.edu
[2] Symbiosis International (Deemed University), Lavale, Pune, Maharashtra, India
head@scaai.siu.edu.in
[3] College of Engineering, Bharati Vidyapeeth Deemed to Be University, Pune, India

Abstract. Security, copyright protection, and authenticity are important parameters used for data security. Data access can be either legally or illegal. However, many users are in the network & connected to it in different ways. Such as social media, mobile internet, mobile apps, mobile E-commerce, etc. There are varieties of data. Such as audio, image, video, message, text, special case characters, etc. These data can be sent in an encoded format and received at the destination after decoding like a digital bank image through the Cheque Truncation System for faster cheque clearance. An attack type can occur intentionally or unintentionally during the transmission of cheque images. A solution to this problem is to offer security, authenticity, and copyright protection to the cheque image. In this study, the discrete wavelet (DWT) and discrete cosine (DCT) transforms are integrated and implemented for watermarking using the AES technique with a maximum key length of '256 bits. In addition, the analysis is done for watermarking, for which AES is used for security against various attack types.

Keywords: DWT · DCT · Watermarking · AES · Security

1 Introduction

Data Communication is an important part of a digital communication system. This system utilizes network technology for data transmission and reception. However, the network criteria applied based on reliability, security & performance. Different data types are there based on their size and formats, to transfer it from source to receiver. An information Technology, banking, academics, and private and public sectors use data communication systems for data transmission and reception through the internet [1, 2]. The data bits can get corrupted due to different transmission impairment factors like noise, attenuation, delay distortion, etc. During data transmission, many unauthorized users in the network channel try to access the data intentionally or unintentionally through various applications based on the internet. Such as, the bank system transfers money through demand draft, mobile banking, net banking, debit card, credit card, & various secured payment gateway. However, payments done through cheques use a cheque truncation system. In this system, the cheque is cleared from the customer's home bank to the drawee bank via a clearinghouse of bank cheques. It helps in the fast clearance of cheques through CTS, while preventing physical efforts on the part of the employee. To maintain the confidentiality, integrity & availability of bank cheques, security, and copyright protection techniques are required. The C.I.A. uses different algorithms to provide security and copyright techniques for its services viz., (i) Encipher & decipher, (ii) Digital WMKING, (iii) Hashing Techniques, (iv) Blockchain Technology, etc. [3–5]. For confidentiality, integrity, authenticity, copyright protection services to BKCHIMGs, this research uses a combination of digital image WMKING with frequency domain along with AES using a 256-bit key. The research was conducted to determine the robustness of the WM and the quality check against several ATTYs used in this research [3–7].

2 Frequency Domain Watermarking Techniques

A digital WM is implanted in the image and then transmitted over the channel in this process. It helps us for indexing, identifying the authorized user, and avoiding the duplication of the data [6–10]. There are different transforms that are being used for frequency-domain WMKING techniques (viz). (i) Discrete cosine transforms, (ii) Discrete wavelet transform, (iii) Singular valued decomposition, and their combinations, etc. In this research work, the DCT and DWT WMKING as well as with the AES method using the 256-bit key are implemented and discussed in this work [1–8].

2.1 Discrete Cosine Transform

The frequency domain transforms that converts spatial domain signals into the frequency domain. Every signal data in the frequency domain is easy to compute. There are two types of DCT used in various applications. The 1-D Discrete cosine transforms are utilized to analyze the biomedical signal, speech/and audio compression [7, 8]. The 2-D DCT used in the JPEG encoder, MPEG-1, MPEG-2, image transformation, in its pattern recognition. In this research work, a 2-D discrete cosine transform is applied to BKCHIMGs [8–13]. It separates the image into different frequencies. Middle-frequency DC components are considered for implanting WM bits into BKCHIMGs. The 2-D DCT is referred to as WMKING because even part of the 2-D BKCHIMG converts it into its equivalent frequency co-efficient. The mathematical expression is as shown below in Fig. 1: -

2D DCT:

$$\text{DCT}(a, b) = \alpha(a, b)\alpha(b) \sum_{x=0}^{N-1} f(c, d)\cos[\frac{(2c + 1)a\pi}{2N}]\cos[\frac{(2d + 1)b\pi}{2N}] \qquad (1)$$

for $a,b = 0, 1, ..., N-1$
    for $c,d = 0, 1, 2....... N-1$.
      where $\alpha(a) = 1/\sqrt{2}$ $a = 0$
            Or
            $\alpha(a) = 1$ $a = 1, 2........., N-1$
            $\alpha(b) = 1/\sqrt{2}$ $b = 0$
            Or
            $\alpha(b) = 1$ $b = 1, 2........., N-1$

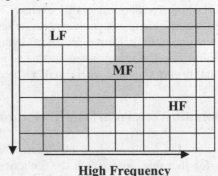

Fig. 1. A definition of DCT Regions used for digital WMKING.

2D IDCT:

It is an inverse DCT function, which reconstructs a sequence of DC coefficients from the 2D DCT BKCHIMG.

$$f(c, d) = \sum_{u=0}^{N-1} \alpha(a)\alpha(b)DCT(a, b)\cos[\frac{(2c + 1)a\pi}{2N}]\cos[\frac{(2d + 1)b\pi}{2N}] \quad (2)$$

2.2 Discrete Wavelet Transform

DCT and FFT cannot locate trends, drift, and abrupt changes at the beginning as well as during the termination of the data signal. DCT and FFT both use a complex number for computation and finding the solution. DWT consists of an average value in the form of the wave for a limited duration of time [11–15]. It works effectively as compared to DCT and FFT. It provides flexibility & has a possibility of time-shifting property using localized waves with zero integral value [16–22]. There are a variety of wavelets, viz.(i) Daubechies wavelet, (ii) Mallat wavelet, (iii) Fast Haar wavelet, (iv) Continuous wavelet, (v) Haar wavelet, etc. Every wavelet function developed with the help of its mother wavelet function. Mathematically, discrete wavelet transforms defined as:

$$\Theta_{u,v}(x) = \frac{1}{\sqrt{u}}\Theta\left(\frac{x - u}{v}\right) \quad (3)$$

Scaling is determined by 'u' while shifting by 'v'. In this work, the Discrete Haar wavelet function used. Computation of a 2-D Haar Wavelet, two steps need to be followed during image processing. The steps are:- (1) Compute the 1-D transform for each column; place the resulting vectors into a column-transformed image f'(x, y). (2) Each row of f'(x, y) is computed in the 1-D transform in row wise form, whereas x and y represent the image pixels. (3) Image f(x, y) divided into four sub-bands shown in Fig. 2. For implanting WM into the pixel, approximate sub-band is selected during the DWT WM implanting process.

$f(x, y) =$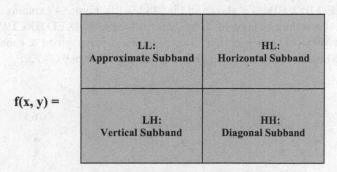

Fig. 2. Discrete Wavelet Transformed Image Sub-Bands

2.3 Digital Watermarking Process

The Fig. 3 shows the complete digital image WMKING process using frequency domain.

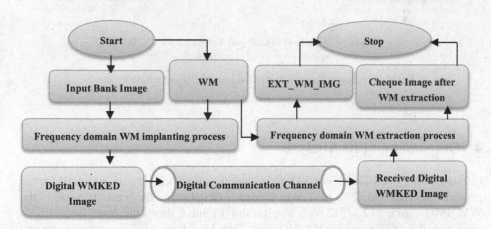

Fig. 3. Frequency Domain Watermarking Process.

3 Advanced Encryption Standard

AES is an important technique used for data encipher & decipher. The AES works using key size, viz. (i) "128 bits" key, (ii) "192 bits" key, & (iii) "256 bits" key. Each cycle includes four transformations: (i) Sub bytes; (ii) Shift Rows; (iii) Mix Columns; and (iv) Add Key. Enciphering and deciphering operations for keys of sizes "128 bits", "192 bits", and "256 bits" require 10, 12, and 14 rounds, respectively. The key size play vital role in AES Technique. If the key size is large, it will be difficult for attacker to decrypt and access data, but encryption & decryption time increases. The working of AES applied on digital WMKED BKCHIMG is shown in Fig. 4 [13–17]. Figure 4 explains working of 256-bit keys AES technique applied on frequency domain WMKED BKCHIMG. Many researcher for WMKED benchmarking used parameters like payload & capacity of key as well as WM used in different frequency domain applications [17–22].

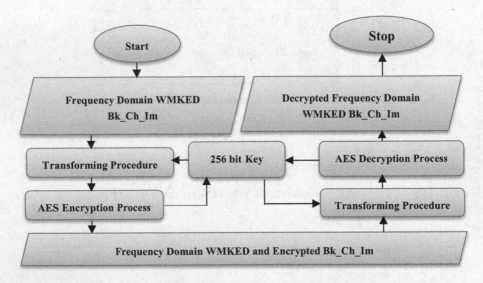

Fig. 4. Frequency Domain WMKING and AES Technique Process.

4 Outcomes and Its Analysis

In this work, the BKCHIMG of 512×512-pixel size with 24-bit dpi was used for the experiment. The WM_IMG bank logo is used for implanting the pixel. The size of the WM_IMG logo is 512×512 with 24-pixel dpi. Figure 5 shows the cover BKCHIMG, on which the DCT image WMKING with '256 bits' keys AES operation is carried out. Figure 6 shows the digital WM used for implanting WM pixels during the image WMKING process.

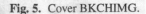

Fig. 5. Cover BKCHIMG.

Fig. 6. Digital WM_IMG.

The DCT BKCHIMG WMKING task is executed by implanting digital image WM bits in middle frequency i.e., dc component. The inverse of DCT is applied after the successful implanting process of bits. This results in Digital WMK_IMG. The resultant of DCT WMKED BKCHIMG is as shown in Fig. 7.

Fig. 7. DCT WMKED BKCHIMG.

Fig. 8. DCT WMKED & AES Encrypted BKCHIMG.

The AES algorithm with '256 bits' keys for the encryption process is implemented in Fig. 7, which results in combined discrete cosine transform WMKED encrypted BKCHIMG. It is as shown in Fig. 8.

Fig. 9. DCT WMKED & AES Encrypted BKCHIMG after applying Rotation ATTY with 45°.

There are various ATTYs are considered for this experiment, viz. (i) cropping ATTY, (ii) Gaussian blur ATTY with noise power of 0.04dB, (iii) JPEG compression ATTY with 50%, (iv) Median filtering ATTY, (v) Rotation ATTY with 45°, (vi) Salt and Pepper noise ATTY with the power of 0.04dB & (vii) Under normal mode ATTY. It observed that the image that appears after ATTY is similar to the image shown in Fig. 8, excluding against rotation ATTY. The rotation ATTY with 45° on the encrypted image will appear as shown in Fig. 9. After this step, the AES decryption operation is carryout and decrypted WMKED bank cheque obtained.

76   S. Gonge et al.

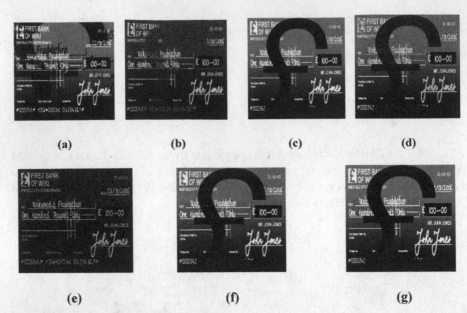

(a)   (b)   (c)   (d)

(e)   (f)   (g)

Fig. 10. DCT EXT_WM_IMG against various ATTY (a) Cropping ATTY (b) Gaussian ATTY (c) JPEG Compression ATTY (d) Median Filtering ATTY (e) Rotation ATTY (f) Salt & Pepper noise ATTY (g) Under normal mode.

Later on, the digital WM extraction task executed using the same pseudo-random number of WM pixels used during the implanting process. The discrete cosine transform WM extraction task executed by reconstructing the image pixel. The results of DCT-extracted WM_IMGs shown in Fig. 10(a)-to-Fig. 10(g). The evaluation parameter considered for this research are PSNR, MSE, Elapsed time & NCC i.e., normalized cross-correlation coefficient. The NCC used for checking the robustness of digital WM as shown in Eq. (6). Mathematically, these terms PSNR, MSE, and NCC explained in Eq. (4), Eq. (5) & Eq. (6)

$$PSNR_{dB} = 10Log_{10}\left\{(Maximum)_1^2 / (Mean\ Square\ Error)\right\}$$

$$= 20Log10\left\{(Maximum)_1 / \sqrt{(Mean\ Square\ Error)^{(1/2)}}\right\} \quad (4)$$

$$Mean\ Square\ Error = (1/A \times B).\sum x = 1\ to\ B.\sum y = 1\ to\ A\left[f(x,y) - f'(x,y)\right]^2 \quad (5)$$

The normalized cross-correlation coefficient is calculated as shown in Eq. (6). It is used to calculate the difference between EXT_WM_IMG and original WM.

$$NCC = \rho(Wm, \hat{W}m) = \frac{\sum_{i=1}^{N} Wm_i * \hat{W}m_i}{\sqrt{\sum_{i=1}^{N}(Wm_i)^2}\sqrt{\sum_{i=1}^{N}\left(\hat{W}m_i\right)^2}} \quad (6)$$

Equation (4) represents the imperceptibility of the image, whereas Eq. (5) explains about mean square error. It explains the difference between the original WM_IMG and exacted WM_IMG. These parameters are also considered for the discrete wavelet transform WMKING of BKCHIMG as well as with the AES technique. The observation tables explain the comparative study of DCT and DWT used for bank cheque WMKING as well as with the AES technique.

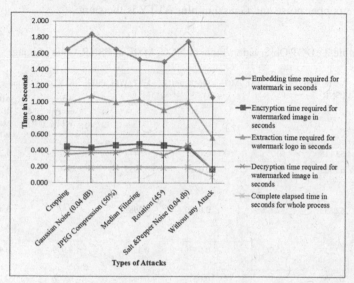

Fig. 11. DCT elapsed time for gain factor ($\alpha = 0.5$) taken against various ATTYs applied on the processed image.

Table 1. Observation table of computed time of DCT for Gain Factor (0.5)

ATTY	WEMT	WIET	WEXT	WDT	CTIS
Cropping	1.653	0.452	0.982	0.358	0.186
Gaussian Noise	1.840	0.436	1.076	0.374	0.186
JPEG Compression	1.653	0.468	0.998	0.374	0.189
Median Filtering	1.528	0.483	1.029	0.436	0.191
Rotation (45°)	1.497	0.468	0.904	0.343	0.188
Salt &Pepper Noise	1.749	0.436	0.998	0.468	0.198
Without any ATTY	1.060	0.171	0.561	0.171	0.077

The Table 1 explains the DCT elapsed time for gain factor ($\alpha = 0.5$) taken against various ATTY applied on the processed image. The graphical representation shown in Fig. 11. The implanting time of WM is higher than that of the decryption time. However, the time complexity i.e., the elapsed time found to be less under normal mode ATTY. The time taken for encrypting the WMKED BKCHIMG is less than its decrypting time. It is observed that the decryption time against JPEG compression and Salt & Pepper noise ATTY is the same, whereas the encryption time taken by the WMKED BKCHIMG against salt &pepper noise and Gaussian blur ATTY is the same.

Table 2. DCT Observation Table of NCC, MSE, & PSNR value of image

ATTY	WMK_IMG PSNR	EXT_WM_IMG PSNR	WMK_IMG MSE	EXT_WM_IMG MSE	NCC of WM image	
					After encryption & WMK_IMG	After decryption & extraction of WM
Cropping	58.115	50.771	0.1003	0.5444	1	0.2917
Gaussian Noise (0.04 dB)	62.333	50.396	0.0379	0.5935	0.964	0.2397
JPEG Compression (50%)	62.333	52.128	0.0379	0.3982	1	0.4782
Median Filtering	62.333	51.76	0.0379	0.4334	0.999	0.4124
Rotation (45 °)	62.333	49.9	0.0379	0.6653	0.008	0.1857
Salt & Pepper Noise (0.04 dB)	62.333	51.961	0.0379	0.4139	0.935	0.455
Without any ATTY	62.333	52.128	0.0379	0.3982	1	0.4782

The PSNR, MSE, and NCC values for gain factor (=0.5) applied against various ATTY on processed discrete cosine images are described in Table 2. The graph shows in Fig. 12, tells about the PSNR of WMKED BKCHIMG after extraction of WM against ATTY.

From Fig. 12, it observed that the DCT WMKED bank cheque PSNR is better than the PSNR value obtained after WM extraction. The PSNR value of JPEG compression and under normal ATTY i.e., without any ATTY found to be the same. Figure 13 explains the graphical representation of NCC & MSE value of DCT WMK_IMG as well as with AES encryption technique. It also explains NCC and MSE values of the WM after the extraction process. From this graph, the MSE value of DCT WMKED BKCHIMG with AES encryption techniques found to be less compared to that of MSE value obtained after decryption and WM extraction. Similarly, the Robustness i.e., the NCC value WM after DCT WMKING of BKCHIMG & AES encryption found to be better than that of the value obtained after AES decipher, extraction of WM.

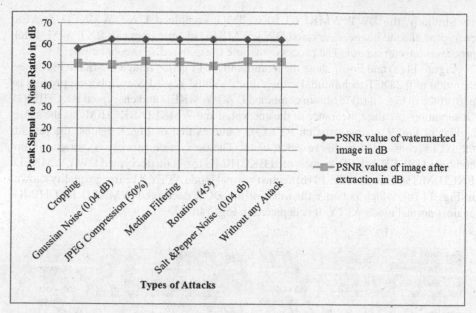

Fig. 12. PSNR value of image for gain factor ($\alpha = 0.5$) taken against various ATTYs applied on the processed image.

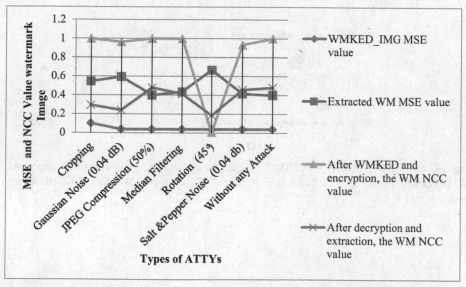

Fig. 13. NCC & MSE value of image for DCT gain factor ($\alpha = 0.5$) taken against various ATTY applied on processed image.

Similarly, the DWT WMKING BKCHIMG, combined DWT WMKED & AES encrypted cheque image, decrypted DWT WMKED cheque image & EXT_WM_IMG processes are carried out. The process outcome is discussed & shown below.

Figure 14 (a) and Fig. 7 show the feature of DWT cheque image WMKING is better than that of the DCT technique. Further, the '256 bits' key AES enciphering process is performed in Fig. 14 (a) to obtain combined DWT WMKED and encrypted BKCHIMG. Observations are the appearance of the encrypted and WMKED BKCHIMG is the same as that of Fig. 9 against rotation ATTY & same as that of Fig. 8 against the rest of the ATTY considered in this research work. The decryption process is carried out on combined DWT WMKED & encrypted BKCHIMG to obtain decrypted DWT WMKED BKCHIMG as shown in Fig. 14 (b) against normal mode ATTY. The image quality shown in Fig. 14 (b), which is better than that of the DCT, decrypted WMKED BKCHIMG against normal mode ATTY. It is depicted in Fig. 14(c).

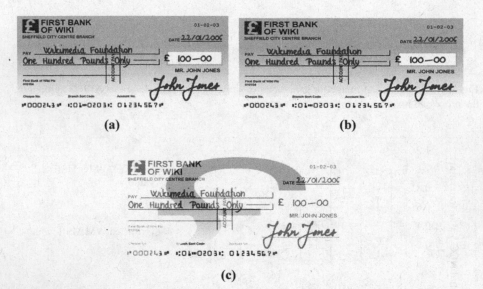

(a)   (b)

(c)

Fig. 14. (a). DWT WMKED BKCHIMG for gain factor ($\alpha = 0.5$) and (b). DWT decrypted WMKED BKCHIMG for gain factor ($\alpha = 0.5$). (c). DCT decrypted WMKED BKCHIMG for gain factor ($\alpha = 0.5$)

The extraction process of the WM is carried out on Fig. 14(b) by using the DWT WM extraction technique using the same seed of WM pixel used during at the time of implanting process. Figure 15 (a)-to-Fig. 15 (g), shows EXT_WM_IMG against various ATTY. Figure 15 (a)-to-Fig. 15 (g), shows that the quality of DWT EXT_WM_IMG is much better than that of DCT EXT_WM_IMG shown in Fig. 10. From Table.3, it is to observed that enciphering & decipher time is less than that of implanting and extraction time. However, the complete-elapsed time is also less than both AES encipher and decipher than that of the implanting & extraction time. This comparison of time is showed in the Fig. 16.

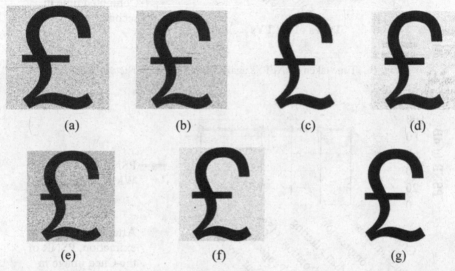

(a)   (b)   (c)   (d)

(e)   (f)   (g)

Fig. 15. DWT EXT_WM_IMG against various ATTY (a) Cropping ATTY (b) Gaussian ATTY (c) JPEG Compression ATTY (d) Median Filtering ATTY (e) Rotation ATTY (f) Salt & Pepper noise ATTY (g) Under normal mode.

Table 3. Computation Time for Gain Factor (0.5) against ATTYs using DWT

ATTY	WEMT	WIET	WEXT	WDT	CTIS
Cropping	1.683	0.421	0.998	0.405	0.182
Gaussian Noise	1.341	0.483	0.998	0.421	0.183
JPEG Compression	1.591	0.358	1.060	0.327	0.189
Median Filtering	1.497	0.452	1.076	0.483	0.184
Rotation (45 °)	1.482	0.468	0.967	0.358	0.184
Salt & Pepper Noise	1.357	0.608	1.014	0.421	0.186
Without any ATTY	1.965	0.483	1.060	0.452	0.193

82   S. Gonge et al.

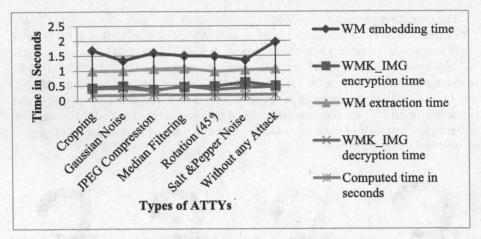

Fig. 16. Time taken by ATTYs against DWT for Gain Factor (0.5).

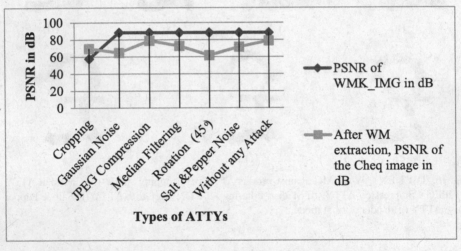

Fig. 17. PSNR value of DWT WMK_IMG and image after extraction.

Figure 17 shows that, the DWT WMKED bank cheque PSNR value is constant i.e., 88.410 dB for all ATTYs excluding cropping ATTYs. The DWT-processed image PSNR, MSE & NCC value against various ATTYs shown in Table 4.The Graph of NCC value and MSE value against various ATTYs using discrete wavelet transform shown in Fig. 18. From Table 4 shows that, the robustness after encryption & WMKING is 100% against cropping ATTY, JPEG compression ATTY and Without any ATTY. The MSE of WMKED BKCHIMG has same value against all ATTYs except cropping ATTY considered in this research paper. The quality of robustness of WM after decryption and extraction is 99.77% under normal mode it is 88.29% against rotation ATTY, which is minimal as compared to that of other ATTY.

Table 4. PSNR, MSE, & NCC value against various ATTY using DWT for Gain Factor (0.5).

ATTY	WMK_IMG PSNR value	EXT_WM_IMG PSNR value of image	WMK_IMG MSE value	EXT_WM_IMG MSE value	NCC value of WM image	
					After Encryption & WMK_IMG	After decryption & extraction of WM logo
Cropping	57.729	69.591	0.1096	0.0071	1	0.9809
Gaussian Noise	88.410	64.809	0.000093	0.0214	0.964	0.9472
JPEG Compression	88.410	78.909	0.000093	0.0008	1	0.9977
Median Filtering	88.410	72.613	0.000093	0.0035	0.999	0.9908
Rotation (45 °)	88.410	61.658	0.000093	0.0443	0.007	0.8829
Salt & Pepper Noise	88.410	71.457	0.000093	0.0046	0.934	0.9883
Without any ATTY	88.410	78.909	0.000093	0.0008	1	0.9977

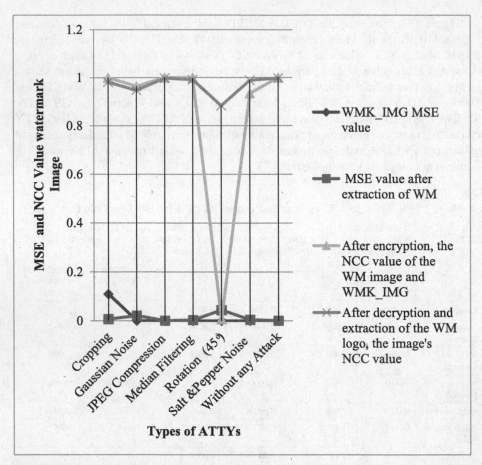

Fig. 18. NCC & MSE value of DWT image for gain factor ($\alpha = 0.5$) against various ATTYs applied on the processed image.

From the above result, it is clear that the PSNR, MSE, and NCC values obtained from DWT transform are better than that of the MSE, NCC & PSNR values obtained using the DCT Technique.

5 Conclusion

In this research work, a combination of frequency-domain digital BKCHIMG WMKING and '256 bits' keys AES technique explained. The DCT cheque image WMKING with '256 bits' keys AES technique reduces image quality and WM robustness. The DWT image WMKING techniques with '256 bits' key AES provide more confidentiality, integrity, and authentication. The DWT provides a good compression ratio as that of the DCT. It has been proved against JPEG compression ATTY. The DWT provides more flexibility to embed WM pixel as compared to that of the DCT. From Fig. 10, it proves that the DCT BKCHIMG WMKING provides less robustness up to 18% against rotation

ATTY as compared to that DWT image WMKING as well as with AES techniques. The Fig. 15 gives the best EXT_WM_IMG than DCT EXT_WM_IMG. This obtained results and its comparative study show that DWT and its combination with AES is better than that of the combo of DCT and AES technique.

Glossary

In this research paper, some symbols have been used as abbreviation. It is as.

Follows: -

Attacks Types: - ATTY.

Watermark implanting time: - WEMT.

Watermarked image encryption time: - WIET.

Watermark extraction time: - WEXT.

Watermarked decryption time: - WDT.

Computed time in seconds: - CTIS.

Cheque Truncation System: - CTS.

Watermark image: - WM_IMG.

Watermarked image: - WMK_IMG.

Extracted watermark: - EXT_WM_IMG.

Watermarking: - WMKING.

Bank Cheque Image: - Bk_Ch_Im.

WMKED: - WMKED.

Watermark: - WM.

AES encryption & decryption process: - AES Technique.

Normalized cross-correlation coefficient: - NCC.

References

1. Cox, I.J., Kilian, J., Leighton, T., Shamoon, T.: Secure spread spectrum wming for multimedia. IEEE Trans. Image Process. **6**(12), 1673–1687 (1997)
2. Voloshynovskiy, S., Pereira, S., Pun, T.: ATTYs on digital watermarks: classification, estimation-based ATTYs and benchmarks. Comm. Mag. **39**(8), 118–126 (2001)
3. Woo, C.-S.: Digital image watermarking methods for copyright protection and authentication. Faculty of Information Technology, Queensland University Of Technology (2007)
4. Nikolaidis, N., Pitas, I.: Robust image watermarking in the spatial domain. Signal Process. **66**, 385–403 (1998)
5. Langelaar, G.C., Setyawan, I., Lagendijk, R.L.: Watermarking digital image and video data. IEEE Signal Process. Mag. **17**(5), 20–46 (2005)
6. Barni, M., Bartolini, F., Cappellini, V., Piva, A.: A DCT-domain system for robust image watermarking. Signal Process. **66**(3), 357–372 (1998)
7. Na, L., Zheng, X., Zhao, Y., Wu, H., Li, S.: Robust algorithm of digital image watermarking based on discrete wavelet transform. In: Electronic Commerce and Security, International Symposium, 3–5, pp. 942–945 (2008)
8. Cox, I.J., Linnartz, J.P.: Some general methods for tampering with watermark. IEEE J. Sel. Areas Commun. **16**, 587–593 (2010)
9. Kumar, A., Santhi, V.: A review on geometric invariant digital image watermarking techniques. Int. J. Comput. Appl. **12**(14), 31–36 (2010)

10. Ali, A.H., Ahmad, M.: Digital audio watermarking based on the discrete wavelets transform and singular value decomposition. Eur. J. Sci. Res. **39**(1), 6–21 (2010)
11. Dhar, P.K., Khan, M.I.: A new DCT-based watermarking method for copyright protection of digital audio. Int. J. Comput. Sci. Inf. Technol. (IJCSIT) **2**(5), 91–97 (2010)
12. Lu, W., Lu, H., Chung, F.L.: feature based watermarking using watermark template match. Appl. Math. Comput. **177**(1), 886–893 (2011)
13. Gunjal, B.L., Mali, S.: Secured color image watermarking technique in DWT-DCT domain. Int. J. Comput. Sci. Eng. Inf. Technol. (IJCSEIT) 36–44 (2011)
14. Chaitanya, K., Sreenivasa Reddy, E., Gangadhara Rao, K. : Digital color image watermarking using DWTDCT coefficients in RGB planes. Glob. J. Comput. Sci. Technol. Graph. Vision **13**(5), 17–21 (2013)
15. Shaikh, S., Deshmukh, M.: Digital Image Watermarking In DCT Domain. Int. J. Emerg. Technol. Adv. Eng. **3**(4), 289–293 (2013)
16. Kelkar, Y., Shaikh, H., Khan, M.I.: Analysis of robustness of hybrid digital image watermarking technique under various ATTYs. Int. J. Comput. Sci. Mob. Comput. **2**(3), 137–143 (2013)
17. Lee, K.-H., Chiu, P.-L.: Digital image sharing by diverse image media. IEEE Trans. Inf. Forensics Secur. **9**(1) (2014)
18. Gonge, S.S., Ghatol, A.A., Thakare, V.: A secure digital watermarking technique using multiple transforms and advanced encryption standard technique used for security of bank cheque image. Int. J. Appl. Innov. Eng. Manage. (IJAIEM) **5**(9) (2016)
19. Gonge, S.S.: Digital image transmission using combination of DWT-DCT watermarking and AES technique. In: Thampi, S.M., Gelenbe, E., Atiquzzaman, M., Chaudhary, V., Li, K.-C. (eds.) Advances in Computing and Network Communications. LNEE, vol. 735, pp. 667–684. Springer, Singapore (2021). https://doi.org/10.1007/978-981-33-6977-1_49
20. Begum, M., Uddin, M.S.: Digital image watermarking techniques: a review. Information **11**, 110 (2020). https://doi.org/10.3390/info11020110
21. Wan, W., Wang, J., Zhang, Y., Li, J., Yu, H., Sun, J.: A comprehensive survey on robust image watermarking. Neurocomputing **488**, 226–247 (2022). ISSN 0925-2312. https://doi.org/10.1016/j.neucom.2022.02.083
22. Moad, M.S., Kafi, M.R., Khaldi, A.: A wavelet based medical image watermarking scheme for secure transmission in telemedicine applications. Microprocess. Microsyst. 90, 104490 (2022). ISSN 0141-9331. https://doi.org/10.1016/j.micpro.2022.104490, https://www.sciencedirect.com/science/article/pii/S0141933122000539

Advancement of Non-coherent Spectrum Sensing Technique in Cognitive Radio Networks - A Simulation-Based Analysis

Narendrakumar Chauhan$^{(\boxtimes)}$ ⓘ and Purvang Dalal ⓘ

Faculty of Technology, Dharmsinh Desai University, Nadiad, Gujarat, India
{nvc.ec,pur_dalal.ec}@ddu.ac.in

Abstract. This article provides a concise overview of commonly employed Spectrum Sensing methods in Cognitive Radio (CR). In practical situations where the receiver lacks access to information about the Primary User (PU) signal, the Energy-based detection approach proves to be more appropriate for Spectrum Sensing in CR. The article also explores the advancements made in the Non-coherent (Energy detection) spectrum sensing approach. Additionally, the effectiveness of spectrum sensing heavily relies on selecting the appropriate threshold. Consequently, the article presents a simulation-based analysis of the Static threshold and Adaptive double threshold algorithm, including their limitations. To enhance detection performance, the article proposes the Modified threshold as an alternative to the Static threshold and Adaptive double threshold algorithm. The performance of the Modified threshold is validated using a MATLAB simulator with a QPSK modulated Orthogonal Frequency Division Multiplexing (OFDM) signal. The results demonstrate that the Modified Threshold outperforms the Static and Adaptive double threshold algorithms, particularly at low Signal to Noise Ratio (SNR) levels.

Keywords: Cognitive Radio · Non-cooperative Spectrum Sensing · Detection Probability · Threshold

1 Introduction

The transition from using only voice communication to incorporating multimedia applications has created a need for higher data rates, resulting in a significant demand for radio spectrum resources. However, the allocation of these resources often lacks efficiency, leading to some parts of the spectrum being heavily used while others remain unused or rarely utilized, as shown in Fig. 1. Research studies indicate that approximately 70% of the total spectrum is not fully utilized [1]. This inefficient distribution of spectrum can result in service disruptions. The scarcity of available spectrum is a critical concern in network research that requires attention. To address this issue, CR technology has emerged as a promising solution by allowing opportunistic access to underutilized spectrum. In CR,

© The Author(s), under exclusive license to Springer Nature Switzerland AG 2023
N. Chaubey et al. (Eds.): COMS2 2023, CCIS 1861, pp. 87–102, 2023.
https://doi.org/10.1007/978-3-031-40564-8_7

secondary users (SUs) can utilize the spectrum band opportunistically without causing interference to the PUs. CR techniques enable efficient utilization and opportunistic sharing of the spectrum.

CR empowers users to (1) Assess the accessibility of various spectrum segments and identify the existence of authorized users while operating within a licensed frequency range, (2) Select the optimal available channel, (3) Facilitate collaborative access to this channel among multiple users, and (4) Exit the channel when a registered user is identified.

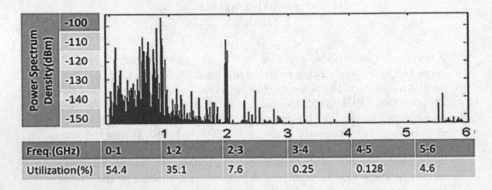

Freq.(GHz)	0-1	1-2	2-3	3-4	4-5	5-6
Utilization(%)	54.4	35.1	7.6	0.25	0.128	4.6

Fig. 1. Spectrum Utilization.

In order to function efficiently within a dynamic spectrum environment, CR networks rely on spectrum-aware operations, which encompass a CR cycle [3]. After identifying the optimal channel, the network protocol needs to adapt to the available spectrum. Consequently, functionalities must be in place to facilitate this transition in the network protocols. The cognitive cycle comprises several key functions as illustrated in Fig 2.

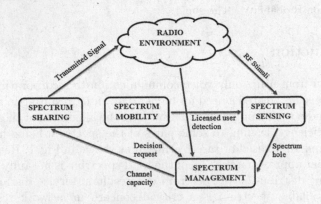

Fig. 2. CR Cycle.

Spectrum sensing (SS) serves as the fundamental module for CR by allowing SUs to detect the existence or non-existence of signals in the frequency bands. A reliable and effective SS approach is essential to prevent interference with PUs in cases where a spectrum band is already in use. Conversely, if the band is unused and the CR system fails to detect its availability, it results in under-utilization of the available radio spectrum. Therefore, Spectrum Sensing holds utmost importance in the entire CR network, ensuring optimal use of the resources.

Research indicates that the effectiveness of SS methods are compromised due to various factors such as multi-path fading, shadowing, and receiver uncertainty. In the subsequent module, SUs make decisions based on their observations. However, due to the uncertainty inherent in the detected measurements, these decisions can be incorrect or delayed, leading to sub-optimal spectrum allocation. Consequently, uncertainty propagation impacts all the processes related to radio spectrum, resulting in a degradation of CR performance. One significant source of uncertainty is NU, which relies heavily on the proper selection of threshold values. Therefore, it is crucial to address this uncertainty issue in CR by employing appropriate threshold and ensuring accurate and timely SS to enhance detection efficiency. There are situations where the PU receiver may be located beyond the radius of the PU transmitter. This scenario can result in false detection or a failure to find the availability of unused radio spectrum. It is important to acknowledge that it is generally challenging for SUs to distinguish PUs. Hence, in most cases, all received signals, including both PU and SU transmissions, are treated as a single combined signal, denoted as w(t). The SU signal, r(t), can be mathematically represented [5].

$$r(t) = \begin{cases} g\{t\} \to H_0 \\ \\ w\{t\} + g\{t\} \to H_1 \end{cases} \tag{1}$$

The noise taken as AWGN and is represented by g(t) in the given equation. The hypotheses H_0 and H_1 correspond to the non-existence and existence of PU, respectively. Therefore, the objective of SS is to make a decision between H_0 and H_1 based on the received signal r(t). The performance of the detection process is evaluated using the Probabilities of Detection (Pd), False-Alarm Probability (Pf), and Miss-Detection Probability (Pm).

The articles' sections are outlined as follows: An overview of Non-cooperative Spectrum sensing techniques, accompanied by a literature survey is found in Sect. 2. Section 3 introduces the proposal for the Modified threshold. In Sect. 4, the simulations for the Static threshold, Adaptive double threshold, and Modified threshold are presented. The paper concludes in Sect. 5.

2   Non-cooperative Spectrum Sensing Techniques and Related Works

In the last few decades, several techniques for SS have emerged and been introduced. In this study, we have categorized these approaches into cooperative and non-cooperative SS techniques, as illustrated in Fig. 3. In the Non-cooperative approach, a single SU is self-sufficient in detecting and making decisions regarding spectrum utilization. On the other hand, in the cooperative approach, multiple SUs collaborate to collectively make decisions and detect vacant spectrum bands. In the context of cooperative, multiple users work together to make collective decisions, necessitating the sharing of information. However, this approach can pose challenges for resource-limited networks due to additional tasks like channel sharing and pilot channel implementation, as well as increased overhead traffic resulting from information sharing. Despite these challenges, Cooperative approaches offer more accurate sensing performance, especially in the presence of factors like NU, fading, and shadowing. On the other hand, Non-cooperative SS techniques can be categorized into Energy Detection (ED), Matched filter-based detection (MFD), Cyclostationary feature-based detection (CSFD), and more. Table 1 presents the available and commonly used Non-cooperative spectrum sensing techniques [2–4, 7, 8].

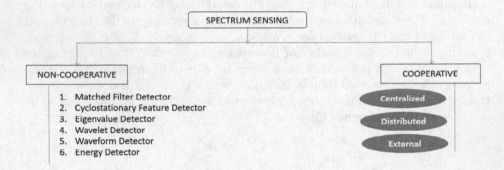

Fig. 3. SS Techniques.

It is important to highlight that ED is an appealing approach because it does not necessitate any prior knowledge about the PU. At a same time, its detection accuracy is considerably lower compared to other techniques. On the other hand, Wavelet-based and CSFD offer higher accuracy but come with the trade-off of increased complexity, longer sensing time, and higher cost. This can result in a high cost per efficiency ratio. ED stands out in terms of computational complexity, requiring minimal energy compared to other listed approaches.

The literature survey reveals that despite extensive research, CR still faces challenges in various aspects. These challenges includes:

a) Detection accuracy, which is often compromised by factors such as: (1) Hidden Primary User Problem, (2) Channel Uncertainty, (3) Noise Uncertainty (NU), and (4) Spread Spectrum Users that result in very low SNR for users. b) Lack of knowledge about primary user transmission patterns/parameters. c) Determining the optimal sensing duration and frequency. d) Ensuring self-coexistence, i.e., the ability of CR devices to coexist and operate without caus-

Table 1. Comparison Between Non-Cooperative Spectrum Sensing Techniques.

Approach	Narrowband/ Wideband	Direct /Indirect	Prior Signal Information	Accuracy	Computational Complexity	Sensing Time	Cost	Energy Efficiency
Energy Detector	Both	Direct/In direct	No	Very Poor	Very Very Low	Very Very Less	Very Very Low	Very Very Low
Matched Filter Detector	Narrowband	Direct	Yes	Very Good	Very Low	Very Less	Very Low	Medium
Waveform Detector	Narrowband	Direct	Yes	Poor	Medium	Medium	Low	Very Low
Eigen value Detector	Narrowband	Indirect	Yes	Very Poor	Low	Less	Medium	Low
Wavelet Detector	Wideband	Indirect	Yes	Medium	Very High	Very Large	Very High	Very High
Cyclostationary Feature Detector	Narrowband	Indirect	Yes	Good	High	Large	High	High

ing interference to each other. e) Addressing security concerns related to CR networks.

In conclusion, these challenges highlight the need for continued research and development to enhance the performance and efficiency of CR. Among the various spectrum sensing methods, ED stands out as an attractive option due to its simplicity and cost-effectiveness, which appeals to many researchers. However, ED is not without its limitations, including the following issues:

- Resilience against NU
- Selection of optimal design parameters such as threshold and observation window length to achieve better detection accuracy
- Performance degradation at lower SNR values Inefficiency in detecting spread spectrum signals.

Addressing these challenges is crucial for improving the reliability and effectiveness of ED in CR systems. To address the challenges associated with ED, researchers have proposed various advancements. In a study by the authors [9], they mathematically analyze the trade-off between sensing duration and throughput in CR using the ED. Additionally, the authors state the minimum number of samples required. In their study [10], the authors propose a method that utilizes ST approach. Additionally, the SS used is coherent and hence demonstrates better results compared to ED. Building upon this work, in [11], the authors further develop the method by considering eigenvalues in two ways to determine the presence or absence of the PU signal which is a coherent detector for PU signal detection. In [12], the authors discuss various non-cooperative SS approaches and their advantages and disadvantages. ED, CSFD, and MFD are specifically presented for CR ad-hoc networks in [13]. An ED algorithm based on a Double Threshold (DT) is also demonstrated in [14] to increase detection efficiency and mitigate potential miss-detections. The study [15] focuses on Adaptive Threshold for ED. The author presents simulation results for higher SNR values. A comparative analysis between single and dynamic thresholds is carried out in [16], where the dynamic threshold is determined by measuring the noise level. The outcome indicates the dynamic threshold improves detection accuracy compared to the ST. In the study [17], the detection of multiple PU signals for spectrum sensing is explored. The research focuses on investigating variations in NU levels, which commonly range from 0.5 dB to 1 dB in practical SS scenarios. In [18], authors propose an adaptive threshold method for ED-based SS. Simulation results clarify that this approach achieves good throughput for SUs with higher SNR. In [19], the efficacy of the ED approach in the presence of NU is investigated using a double threshold. Simulations are carried out within the Digital TV licensed band. The findings demonstrate that the double threshold surpasses the performance of the ST method when NU is present.

In [5], the authors explore OFDM-based SS. The study compares the performance of ED and Wavelet-based detection. The results reveal that the Wavelet-based detection approach outperforms the ED with an identical environment. In [20], the authors analyze the performance of ED-based CR systems in both AWGN and Rayleigh fading channels. They observe a performance improvement of 1.3 times in the AWGN channel and 0.5 times in the Rayleigh channel. Another study [21] introduces the concept of random sampling in ED and evaluates its performance with ROC analysis. In [22], the authors compare ED, Auto correlation-based detection, and MFD techniques with a dynamic threshold using a QPSK-modulated signal. The dynamic threshold outperforms the ST. A comprehensive analysis of different detection approaches, including ED, MFD, CSFD, and Wavelet-based detection, is presented in [7]. The results indicate that the Wavelet-based detection approach outperforms all other methods. [23] highlights the advantages and disadvantages of various sensing approaches. The efficiency of ED-based CR systems is assessed in [24] by proposing an intelligent threshold selection method based on the Constant Detection Rate (CDR) principle. The authors provide mathematical expressions for Pd with Constant False Alarm Rate (CFAR) as well as for CDR. In [6], the authors discuss both Non-cooperative and Cooperative approaches for CR, highlighting their advantages and limitations along with the associated challenges. They also introduce a hybrid spectrum sensing approach that combines MFD and ED. The implementation of the double threshold algorithm to enhance the detection performance with ED is presented in [25]. The authors demonstrate that the DT algorithm outperforms the conventional approach, resulting in improved detection efficiency. Enhancement in ED using adaptive threshold is presented in [26]. For detection, The authors have obtained the adaptive threshold (Γa) by averaging the double thresholds i.e.,

$$\Gamma a = \frac{UpperThreshold + LowerThreshold}{2} \tag{2}$$

The efficacy of the adaptive threshold is improved compared to the ST. The issue of the confused state region is addressed by the Markov model proposed in [26]. The author also considers the impact of NU. [27] introduce an enhanced

ED approach that demonstrates favorable performance even at low SNR values. A survey-based evaluation of various spectrum sensing approaches is presented in [28]. The authors assess these approaches in terms of detection accuracy, complexity, robustness, NU resilience, power consumption, requirement of PU signal, cost, sensing time, and reliability. In [29], a new adaptive threshold-based ED approach is introduced. This method aims to enhance the detection performance in scenarios where the NU is present. In a recent study [1], the Golden section search algorithm is presented to increase the efficiency of ED. The algorithm employs thresholds defined as follows:

$$\Gamma_{lower} = 0.9 * \frac{Q^{-1}(Pf) + 1}{\sqrt{N}} \tag{3}$$

and

$$\Gamma_{upper} = 1.1 * \frac{Q^{-1}(Pf) + 1}{\sqrt{N}} \tag{4}$$

Performance evaluation is conducted in [3] to assess the effectiveness of CDR in AWGN and Rayleigh channels. The study focuses on the analysis of detection performance using ED, MFD, and CSFD. Additionally, the authors investigate the performance of both ST and adaptive double threshold approaches in the context of a Rayleigh fading channel. The evaluation is performed using an OFDM signal.

From the above literature studies, it is evident that parametric approaches are not practical due to the unknown nature of the actual spectrum status. Cooperative spectrum sensing approaches suffer from drawbacks such as energy inefficiency, longer sensing time, and high cost per detection efficiency. It is acknowledged that a balance needs to be struck between energy efficiency and spectral efficiency, Also, the relationship between the sensing capability and the attainable throughput for SUs. Despite extensive research in the past decade, none of the SS approaches provide fail-safe performance in diverse environments, particularly regarding the accuracy of PU detection and the trade-off between Pd and Pf. Furthermore, the discussed SS methods fail to fully satisfy the requirements for good detection accuracy, low cost, short sensing time, and low power consumption. Some methods show promising detection performance but come with drawbacks such as high processing time, high power requirements, reliance on prior knowledge of PU at the receiver side, and the need for proper threshold setting. The detection accuracy of these methods heavily relies on the selection of the threshold.

3   Proposal for Modified Threshold (MT)

The ED approach involves matching the Average Energy (AE) of the signal received with a (Γ) to determine whether the PU signal is exist or not [3]. If the AE exceeds the (Γ), it indicates the existence of the PU signal; otherwise, it is considered non-existence. ST $((\Gamma))$ value is given as Eq. (6) [3]. This proposal is also available in our pre-print [30] and [31].

$$\Gamma = \frac{Q^{-1}(Pf) + 1}{\sqrt{N}} \tag{5}$$

where Q is represented as marcum Q function. To improve the performance in the presence of NU, an adaptive double threshold approach is introduced in [27], utilizing a Markov model. The Upper Threshold (UT) and Lower Threshold (LT) values are calculated using Eq. (8) and Eq. (9) [27], respectively.

$$UT = (\frac{2}{N}(Q^{-1}(Pf) + 1)) * NU \tag{6}$$

and

$$LT = (\frac{2}{N}(Q^{-1}(Pf) + 1)) * \frac{1}{NU} \tag{7}$$

As the NU level increases from 0.5 dB to 1 dB, the difference amongst the thresholds is also increases, aiming to reduce the likelihood of missed detections. Consequently, the ED employing the adaptive double threshold demonstrates improved performance, especially in low SNR scenarios. However, the use of a double threshold can result in increased detection time, which may be inconsistent with the requirements of efficient spectrum sensing.

Inspired by the aforementioned, this research suggests obtaining a static threshold parameter through the adaptive double threshold method. This is achieved by calculating the sum, difference, mean, and median values of the UT and LT.

$$\lambda_a = UT + LT \tag{8}$$

$$\lambda_s = UT - LT \tag{9}$$

$$\lambda_{mean} = mean(UT\&LT) \tag{10}$$

$$\lambda_{median} = median(UT\&LT) \tag{11}$$

The threshold values derived from mean, median, and subtraction techniques are consistently lower than the UT, leading to improved detection performance. Figure 4 illustrates the variation in the derived threshold for a range of Pf, considering a NU = 1 dB. The results demonstrate the mean, median, and subtraction of the UT and LT. The subtraction result in lower threshold values, which intuitively contribute to better detection performance. Additionally, during simulation, we observed that the judiciously derived value of λ_s, which is the modified threshold parameter, is the lowest among all the derived thresholds. Therefore, this study suggests utilizing λ_s as a modified threshold. To investigate the influence of NU on λ_s, another simulation is conducted as shown in Fig. 5 which illustrates the variations in the threshold for a range of Pf. It is observed that as NU increases, the value of λ_s tends to approach the ST. It is important to note that the value of λ_s is always lesser than or equal to the ST. Therefore, utilizing λ_s as a threshold parameter ensures the protection of performance when employing ED for a worst scenario. To highlight the advantages of the MT, the performance of the detector using the MT is correlated with that using the ST and the adaptive DT. The subsequent section provides a detailed explanation of the simulation for clarity.

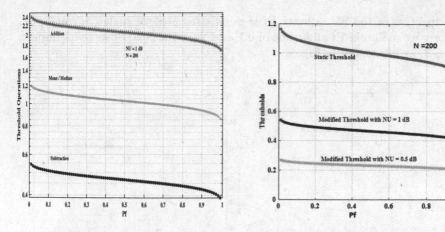

Fig. 4. Threshold against Pf.   **Fig. 5.** Efficiency of MT with respect to ST.

4 Simulations

The AE of the signal is balanced with a threshold value set in the detector. For simulation purposes, we consider the system model depicted in Fig. 6. In this model, a QPSK-modulated OFDM signal is transmitted over a Rayleigh fading channel. The FFT size is set to 2048, and as per 3gpp specification, we have taken 200 samples for analysis. The selection of the ST relies on the N and the Pf. To assess the impact of N and Pf on the ST, we present the simulation results in Fig. 7 and Fig. 8.

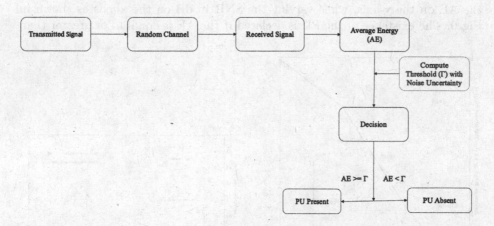

Fig. 6. General System Model.

The purpose of the simulation is to examine the influence of the Pf on the ST. It is observed that as Pf decreases, the ST also decreases. However, from the perspective of the SU, a lower Pf is desired to achieve higher throughput. Therefore, we maintain Pf at a value of 0.1 and vary the N to observe its impact on the ST, as illustrated in Fig. 8.

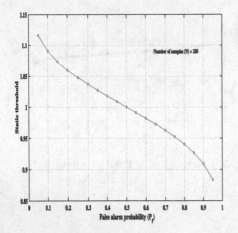

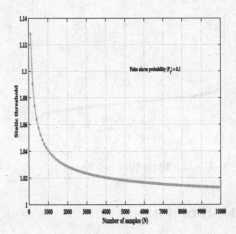

Fig. 7. Effect of Pf on ST.   **Fig. 8.** Effect of N on ST.

As the N increases, the decision threshold decreases, leading to a more complex detector. Additionally, it is crucial to carefully select the values of N and the Pf to achieve an optimal threshold for effective detection performance. Furthermore, we have investigated the influence of the ST on a QPSK-modulated OFDM system. The system is configured with N = 200 and Pf = 0.1. We plot the AE on the y-axis, while varying the SNR in dB on the x-axis as shown in Fig. 9. The existence of the PU is declared if the AE is equal to or greater than

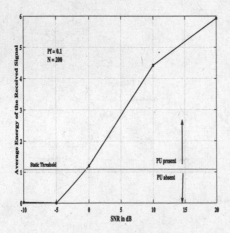

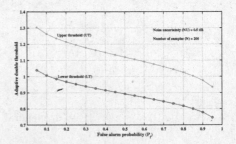

Fig. 9. Impact of SNR in dB on AE.

Fig. 10. Impact of Pf on Adaptive Double Threshold.

1.091 dB, otherwise, non-existence. The ST demonstrates reliable PU detection without considering the impact of NU. To address the issue of NU, an adaptive double threshold algorithm was proposed [27]. To evaluate the effectiveness of the adaptive DT, we conducted simulations using NU values of 0.5 dB and 1 dB, with N set to 200. The Pf values were varied on the x-axis, while the upper and lower thresholds were observed and plotted on the y-axis as per Fig. 11. By examining Fig. 10 and Fig. 11, it is observed that as NU increases from 0.5 dB to 1 dB, the gap between the LT and UT also widens. This indicates that the concept behind the adaptive double threshold is to expand or increase the difference between the thresholds in order to account for any false detections caused by NU. Furthermore, we plot to assess the influence of the parameter N on the adaptive double threshold. In these simulations, we set Pf to 0.1 and NU to 0.5 dB and 1 dB, and varied the value of N. Figure 12 and Fig. 13 demonstrate that as the NU increases, the difference between the UT and LT also increases. However, this can result in unnecessary delays and increased complexity, as the decision matrix needs to be reevaluated when the observed value falls between the UT and LT. To evaluate the detection efficiency of SS with the adaptive double threshold, we conducted simulations where we varied the SNR in dB on the x-axis and observed the AE. Figure 14 illustrates that the difference between the UT and LT increases in order to mitigate the risk of miss-detection caused by increasing NU. It is evident from the figure that if the AE exceeds the UT, the detector declares the PU as present. Conversely, if the AE falls below the LT, the detector declares the PU as absent. However, when the decision falls between the UT and LT, no decision is made, and the algorithm repeats the cycle until a decision is reached.

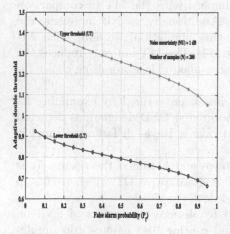

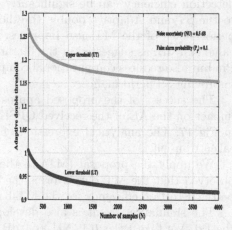

Fig. 11. Impact of Pf on Adaptive Double Threshold.

Fig. 12. Impact of N on an Adaptive Double Threshold.

This highlights the need for an MT that can account for NU. Nevertheless, it should be noted that increasing the threshold difference also leads to increased

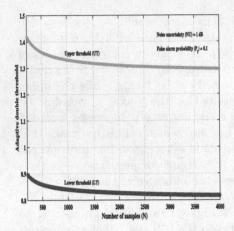
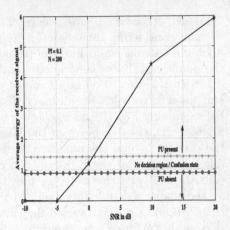

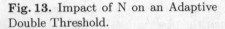

Fig. 13. Impact of N on an Adaptive Double Threshold.

Fig. 14. Impact of SNR in dB on AE.

algorithm complexity. Consequently, further results are developed to validate the usefulness of the MT. Under the same simulation parameters, it is evident that the proposed MT exhibits a lower value compared to the ST and Adaptive double threshold. Furthermore, the issue of the ST not accounting for the impact of NU is effectively addressed in the proposed MT. The decision made by the MT is accurate, leading to an improvement in detection efficiency, which was lacking in the adaptive double threshold approach. Figure 15 and Fig. 16 indicate that the detection efficiency can be significantly enhanced with the MT in comparison to the ST and Adaptive double threshold. Additionally, as NU increases, the performance of the MT also improves. In this simulation, we adopted a NU value of 1 dB, as suggested in the literature [17]. The MT not only reduces the Pm but also reduces computational complexity, making it a promising choice for improving SS performance.

The success of the proposed approach has been verified by examining its impact on the AE of the received QPSK modulated OFDM signal, as depicted in Fig. 17. The analytical expression of Pd over a Rayleigh fading channel is taken from [9].

We apply the proposal (MT) to the above and obtained the results. It is observed that the MT outperforms the ST and Adaptive DT which results in better detection efficiency for the MT-based detector.

The simulation result is also developed to observe the impact of SNR on the Pd. We take Pf as 0.1, NU as 1 dB, and run for 10e3 monte-carlo simulations. We observe that all approaches i.e. with ST, MT, and Adaptive double threshold showed a rising trend for Pd with the increase in SNR as observed from Fig. 18. Moreover, the MT outperforms the ST and the Adaptive double threshold approach. We see around 41.27 % and 26.38 % relative improvement at SNR=0 dB in the performance with MT as compared to that of the Adaptive

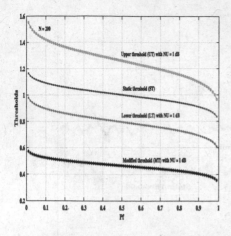

Fig. 15. MT Efficiency against Pf.

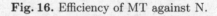

Fig. 16. Efficiency of MT against N.

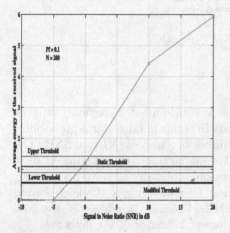

Fig. 17. Impact of SNR in dB on AE.

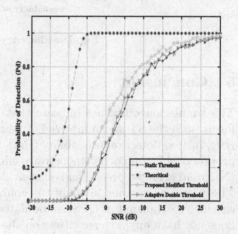

Fig. 18. Impact of SNR in dB on Pd.

double threshold and the ST respectively. The decision of PU is also judged by the ROC. The higher the area, the better the detector efficiency. Hence, to check the efficiency of the MT, we simulated ROC taking SNR=0 dB and NU as 1 dB. From Fig. 19, We observe around 23.77 % and 35.55 % relative improvement at Pf = 0.1 with an MT-based detector compared to ST and the Adaptive double threshold algorithm.

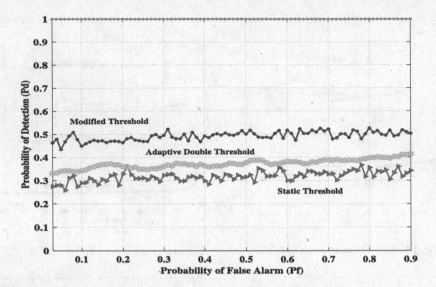

Fig. 19. Efficiency of MT on ROC.

5   Conclusion

The simulation outcomes indicate that the MT (Modified Threshold) outperforms both the ST and Adaptive DT methods in terms of false alarm probability (Pf), missed detection probability (Pm), Number of Samples (N), and SNR. The proposed MT approach demonstrates effective management of Noise uncertainty (NU) and achieves precise and efficient detection, especially at lower SNR levels. The proposed method's validity is confirmed by employing a Rayleigh fading channel to transmit a QPSK modulated OFDM signal. Importantly, the MT does not have any adverse effects on the inherent behavior of the detector.

References

1. Verma, P.: Adaptive threshold based energy detection over rayleigh fading channel. Wirel. Pers. Commun. **113**, 299–311 (2020). https://doi.org/10.1007/s11277-020-07189-2
2. Akyildiz, I.F., Lee, W.-Y., Vuran, M.C., Mohanty, S.: NeXt generation/dynamic spectrum access/cognitive radio wireless networks: a survey. Comput. Netw. **50**(13), 2127–2159 (2006). https://doi.org/10.1016/j.comnet.2006.05.001. ISSN 1389-1286
3. Chauhan, N., Shah, A., Bhatt, P., Dalal, P.: Simulation based analysis of non-cooperative spectrum sensing techniques in cognitive radio. Test Engineering and Management, pp. 5149–5162. The Mattingley Publishing Co., Inc. (2020). ISSN 0193-4120
4. Lu, L., Zhou, X., Onunkwo, U., et al.: Ten years of research in spectrum sensing and sharing in cognitive radio. Wirel. Commun. Netw. **2012**, 28 (2012). https://doi.org/10.1186/1687-1499-2012-28

5. Parekh, P.R., Shah, M.B.: Spectrum sensing in wideband OFDM based cognitive radio. In: International Conference on Communication and Signal Processing, 3–5 April 2014, India. IEEE (2014)
6. Pandit, S., Singh, G.: Spectrum sensing in cognitive radio networks: potential challenges and future perspective. In: Spectrum Sharing in Cognitive Radio Networks, pp. 35–75. Springer, Cham (2017). https://doi.org/10.1007/978-3-319-53147-2_2
7. Chauhan, N., Thavalapill, S.: Spectrum sensing in cognitive radio for multi-carrier (OFDM) signal. In: 23rd International Conference on Innovation in Electrical and Electronics Engineering (ICIEEE 2016), vol. 3, no. 9, (2016). ISSN (PRINT): 2393–8374, (ONLINE): 2394–0697
8. Arjoune, Y., Kaabouch, N.: A comprehensive survey on spectrum sensing in cognitive radio networks: recent advances, new challenges and future research directions. Sensors (2019). mdpi.com
9. Liang, Y., Zeng, Y., Peh, E.C.Y., Hoang, A.T.: Sensing-throughput tradeoff for cognitive radio networks. IEEE Trans. Wirel. Commun. 7(4), 1326–1337 (2008). https://doi.org/10.1109/TWC.2008.060869
10. Zeng, Y., Koh, C.L., Liang, Y.: Maximum eigenvalue detection: theory and application. In: 2008 IEEE International Conference on Communications, pp. 4160–4164 (2008). https://doi.org/10.1109/ICC.2008.781
11. Zeng, Y., Liang, Y.: Eigenvalue-based spectrum sensing algorithms for cognitive radio. IEEE Trans. Commun. 57(6), 1784–1793 (2009). https://doi.org/10.1109/TCOMM.2009.06.070402
12. Yucek, T., Arslan, H.: A survey of spectrum sensing algorithms for cognitive radio applications. IEEE Commun. Surv. Tutor. 11(1), 116–130 (2009). https://doi.org/10.1109/SURV.2009.090109
13. Akyildiz, F., Lee, W.-Y., Chowdhury, K.R.: CRAHNs: cognitive radio ad hoc networks. Ad Hoc Netw. 7(5), 810–836 (2009). https://doi.org/10.1016/j.adhoc.2009.01.001. ISSN 1570-8705
14. Wu, J., Luo, T., Yue, G.: An energy detection algorithm based on double-threshold in cognitive radio systems. In: 2009 First International Conference on Information Science and Engineering, pp. 493–496 (2009). https://doi.org/10.1109/ICISE.2009.257
15. Bao, Z., Wu, B., Ho, P., Ling, X.: Adaptive threshold control for energy detection based spectrum sensing in cognitive radio networks. In: 2011 IEEE Global Telecommunications Conference - GLOBECOM 2011, pp. 1–5 (2011). https://doi.org/10.1109/GLOCOM.2011.6133659
16. Plata, D.M.M., Reátiga, Á.G.A.: Evaluation of energy detection for spectrum sensing based on the dynamic selection of detection-threshold. Procedia Eng. 35, 135–143 (2012). https://doi.org/10.1016/j.proeng.2012.04.174. ISSN 1877-7058
17. Wei, L., Tirkkonen, O.: Spectrum sensing in the presence of multiple primary users. IEEE Trans. Commun. 60(5), 1268–1277 (2012). https://doi.org/10.1109/TCOMM.2012.022912.110073
18. Ling, X., Wu, B., Wen, H., Ho, P., Bao, Z., Pan, L.: Adaptive threshold control for energy detection based spectrum sensing in cognitive radios. IEEE Wirel. Commun. Lett. 1(5), 448–451 (2012). https://doi.org/10.1109/WCL.2012.062512.120299
19. Xie, S., Shen, L.: Double-threshold energy detection of spectrum sensing for cognitive radio under noise uncertainty environment. In: IEEE 2012 International Conference on Wireless Communications & Signal Processing (WCSP 2012), 25–27 October 2012, Huangshan, China (2012). https://doi.org/10.1109/WCSP.2012.6542877

20. Kalambe, S., Lohiya, P., Malathi, P.: Performance evolution of energy detection spectrum sensing technique used in cognitive radio. In: IEEE 2014 International Conference on Signal Propagation and Computer Technology (ICSPCT) (2014). https://doi.org/10.1109/ICSPCT.2014.6884975

21. Semlali, H., Boumaaz, N., Soulmani, A., et al.: Energy detection approach for spectrum sensing in cognitive radio systems with the use of random sampling. Wirel. Pers. Commun. **79**, 1053–1061 (2014). https://doi.org/10.1007/s11277-014-1917-6

22. Salahdine, F., Ghazi, H.E., Kaabouch, N., Fihri, W.F.: Matched filter detection with the dynamic threshold for cognitive radio networks. In: 2015 International Conference on Wireless Networks and Mobile Communications (WINCOM), pp. 1–6 (2015). https://doi.org/10.1109/WINCOM.2015.7381345

23. Muchandi, N., Khanai, R.: Cognitive radio spectrum sensing: a survey. In: 2016 International Conference on Electrical, Electronics, and Optimization Techniques (ICEEOT), pp. 3233–3237 (2016). https://doi.org/10.1109/ICEEOT.2016.7755301

24. Verma, G., Sahu, O.P.: Intelligent selection of threshold in cognitive radio system. Telecommun. Syst. **63**, 547–556 (2016). https://doi.org/10.1007/s11235-016-0141-y

25. TAN, R.: Research on adaptive cooperative spectrum sensing. In: Xhafa, F., Barolli, L., Amato, F. (eds.) 3PGCIC 2016. LNDECT, vol. 1, pp. 487–495. Springer, Cham (2017). https://doi.org/10.1007/978-3-319-49109-7_46

26. Alom, M.Z., Godder, T.K., Morshed, M.N., Maali, A.: Enhanced spectrum sensing based on Energy detection in cognitive radio network using adaptive threshold. In: 2017 International Conference on Networking, Systems and Security (NSysS), pp. 138–143 (2017). https://doi.org/10.1109/NSysS.2017.7885815

27. Liu, Y., Liang, J., Xiao, N., Yuan, X., Zhang, Z., Hu, M.: Adaptive double threshold energy detection based on Markov model for cognitive radio. PLoS ONE **12**(5), e0177625 (2017). https://doi.org/10.1371/journal.pone.0177625

28. Ghosh, S.K., Mehedi, J., Samal, U.C.: Sensing performance of energy detector in cognitive radio networks. Int. J. Inf. Tecnol. **11**, 773–778 (2019). https://doi.org/10.1007/s41870-018-0236-7

29. Javed, J.N., Khalil, M., Shabbir, A.: A survey on cognitive radio spectrum sensing: classifications and performance comparison. In: 2019 International Conference on Innovative Computing (ICIC), pp. 1–8 (2019). https://doi.org/10.1109/ICIC48496.2019.8966677

30. Chauhan, N.: Performance enhancement of multi-antenna correlated receiver for vehicular communication using modified threshold approach. TechRxiv (2023)

31. Chauhan, N.: Performance enhancement of multi-antenna correlated receiver for vehicular communication using modified threshold approach. TechRxiv Preprint (2023). https://doi.org/10.36227/techrxiv.22559176.v1

Improvement of Network Protocol and Analysis of Security Using Aspect of Cryptography

Nisarg Patel[1] (ID), Viral Parekh[2(✉)] (ID), and Kaushal Jani[3(✉)] (ID)

[1] Faculty of Technology and Engineering, C. U. Shah University, Wadhwan, Gujarat, India
[2] Department of Computer Engineering, Sal Engineering and Technical Institute, Ahmedabad, Gujarat, India
viral.ccet@gmail.com
[3] Department of Computer Science and Engineering, Indus University, Ahmedabad, Gujarat, India
drkmjani@gmail.com

Abstract. Wireless network protocol is the top most discussed topics and used of quantum cryptography is adding value to the network performance. In our research paper we are going to make a novel approach to create a development of quantum cryptography for wireless key distribution in 802.11 networks. Due to its mobility with fast data sharing in houses, offices, and businesses they are convenient. Users now choose a wireless network over a LAN-based network connected with Ethernet cables due to advancements in contemporary wireless technology. Unfortunately, security problems are a major worry because they frequently aren't. It is simple for someone else to obtain information sent through websites or mobile apps while someone is linked to a Wi-Fi network. Based on the theory of physics, cryptographic key can be exchanged by quantum cryptography between two remote sites without any conditional security. The origin of quantum cryptography explained in the Heisenberg uncertainty principle, which tells that the certain pairs of physical channels are related in a way that measuring one property restricts the third user from knowing the value of the other at the same time. In our current research paper, we are using quantum cryptography with AOMDV routing protocol and measure the network performance so using quantum cryptography we will have both secured and improved performance in wireless adhoc network.

Keywords: Cryptography · AOMDV · Quantum Channel · Key Distribution · Quantum Cryptography · Cryptography Techniques

1 Introduction

Everyone wants their essential information to be readily available, portable, and reachable from practically everywhere they go today, and using wireless networks makes this feasible. As their name implies, wireless networks [1] are those networks that are not physically connected by wires like Ethernet, giving the user a lot of mobility and convenience. Additionally, it saves money on the wires that would be needed to use a wired

© The Author(s), under exclusive license to Springer Nature Switzerland AG 2023
N. Chaubey et al. (Eds.): COMS2 2023, CCIS 1861, pp. 103–116, 2023.
https://doi.org/10.1007/978-3-031-40564-8_8

network and makes it simpler to move the main portion of the devices from one location to another by simply relocating a computer and wireless network station. A wired network facilitates one-to-one communication, or the transmission of data between Access points (APs), which link to a public or private (enterprise) network, wireless clients used by users, and airwave data transmission are the four fundamental parts of wireless networks. Figure 1 depicts the fundamental elements of wireless networking.

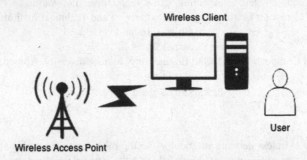

Fig. 1. Wireless Network Components [2]

Compared to wired networks, wireless networks produce a lot of sensitive data that is more susceptible to interception. Users of wireless networks may opt to use a various encryption techniques in order to reduce the danger due to this greatly increased risk. The secret to keeping data unaffected at online in a wireless network is encryption. The information gets scrambled into a code when it is encrypted, making it unreadable to outsiders. Numerous encryption methods have been developed because of heightened likelihood of information compromise linked with Wi-Fi computer networks. However, widely used data encryption techniques are also known to contain flaws and will be open to attack on confidentiality [5].

To provide more secure and reliable communications throughout a wireless ad-hoc network, the communication between nodes and base station (BS) to other nodes must be controlled carefully through the use of a suitable and secure key management protocol. Using quantum cryptography, a new secure key distribution technique called quantum key distribution (QKD) enables the broadcast of a network key with the complete confidentiality [26]. By utilizing the characteristics of quantum information. With this method, the problem of key distribution is solved and a more secure connection between two users is provided with the absolute security. This article presents the approach and supporting protocols for secure key allocation in wireless ad-hoc networks with the use of quantum cryptography. The study explores additional strategies for maintaining the security and safety of wireless networks [32].

2 Related Works

A quantum key distribution (QKD) protocol seeks to offer shared a secret key that may be utilised to discreetly communicate between two different parties through a shared secure channel. In this case, the most important thing to keep in mind is that the key generation protocol has been shown to be safe against any attack that an eavesdropper may conduct [24]. Not simply the technological limitations that come with real implementations, but also the rule of physics (or, more specifically, quantum method), guarantee of the security for the wireless network protocol. As a result, one may be sure that the protocol will be safe forever, not only until any user develops an absurdly powerful way of decryption device (or, to be more accurate, the protocol will be secure so long as quantum channel is not proven false) [9].

In general, QKD method is divided into two different parts: Alice and Bob send and measure result of the quantum states during the first section quantum transmission phase. The bits generated during the quantum phase are used to build a combination of safe keys in the second stage, which is known as the classical post-processing phase [28].

The following are some features of 802.11 WLANs that make them the ideal setting for implementing QKD:

1. **Usage:** The majority of campus and office infrastructure uses 802.11 WLANs, which makes it easier to establish a QKD network with an improved value of quantum equipment as needed.
2. **Capacity:** Compared to nodes on cellular networks, 802.11 wireless network nodes have a higher processing power and strength.
3. **Connection:** It is advantageous for QKD integration when 802.11 networks are used to give an access to internet via an access point deployed in the organisation.

Extensible Authentication Protocol (EAP) is used by 802.11 networks to efficiently maintain keys specific to access point and client and to regulate the user load [11]. The present effort will employ the authentication architecture that EAP offers. The MAC layer provides increased security for 802.11 WLAN, which is based on the WEP protocol. WEP causes security related issues in the wireless networks. The Transaction Security Network (TSN) and the reliable and strong Security Network Association (RSNA) are the two security classes that the MAC layer specifies, respectively [10].

Routing Protocol for Wireless Networks
To get the proper route between source and destination nodes, the direction conventions can be used. Planning and defining guiding norms for remote specifically appointed networks has a number of justifications. The sophisticated correspondence networks rely heavily on directing norms [26]. Every single steering convention differs in design from the others, and because of this, each one performs admirably when it comes to constraints related to the organisation. The two main categories of directing conventions are table-driven and on-request steering while looking for the courses. While based on request directing creates courses when needed by the source node have, table driven directing conventions are predictable and keep up with this steering data to all hubs at each hub. Additionally, these may be extensively divided into progressive and half and half. Each of these four characters is briefly explained here and with the help of their models [12].

A) **Reactive Routing Protocol:** The protocols use a deluge of Route Request (RREQ) packets to the nodes to find a proper path on demand. The path is only generated in reactive routing protocols when a node has to deliver data to an unidentified destination. As a result, path discovery only begins whenever it is required. Only when there is data to convey should a route be decided. These protocols feature lower routing overhead and longer delays. e.g., AODV, AOMDV [15].

The routing protocol known as AOMDV: Ad hoc on-demand multipath distance vector (AMODV) routing is one of the important wireless protocol in MANETs and other wireless ad hoc networks. In comparison to DSDV [12], which, by building routes on demand, minimizes the amount of required broadcasts, is an improvement. Nodes cannot exchange routing tables or contribute to the maintenance of routing information if they do not take the designated path. The first node initiates a route discovery procedure to identify the other nodes (and the destination) by broadcasting an RREQ packet to its neighbors [11].

AODV: It is used in MANETs and one of the other wireless ad hoc network protocol. In comparison to DSDV [12]. This is an improvement since it builds routes on demand and hence minimises the amount of broadcasts required. Nodes that don't take the designated route can't share routing tables or help maintain the routing database. In order to locate the other nodes (and the destination), a source node initiates a path discovery procedure by broadcasting an RREQ packet to its neighbors.

DSR: It is used in ad-hoc wireless networks [13]. On demand source routing is used in this case. Each host needs to maintain a route path containing all the routes it has found. The Route Discovery and Route Maintenance stages make up the protocol's main sections. When a remote node has some packets to transmit to a certain place, it first checks its path cache to identify whether it already has a path there. If the route is still viable, it will follow this path. When a path is not present, the node broadcasts a Route Request packet to begin the route discovery process.

B) **The pro-active routing protocol:** It determines the path in advance, and each node makes an effort to keep a current topological structure of the network and to constantly check the paths. When nodes wish to transmit a packet, the path is available, therefore there will not be any delay in the route discovery. It aims to maintain the consistent routing information. When the topology of network changes, the protocol responds by disseminating updates across the network to maintain a constant viewpoint. With this sort of table-driven approach, there is a significant routing overhead. as in - DSDV [16].

DSDV: Bellman-Ford-based Mobile Computers with Highly DSDV. Each mobile node maintains a routing table that indicates how many hops are required to reach each destination. Routing table updates are given out on a regular basis. Each item has a sequence number that was produced by destination node. Every node periodically broadcasts its distance vector. The broadcasting maximum is one hop.

C) **Hybrid Protocols:** It is a third kind of routing algorithm [10]. Both being proactive and being reactive are combined. It gains from both of them. It combines the benefits of proactive and reactive routing systems to overcome their disadvantages. Hierarchical network designs are commonly used by hybrid MANET routing systems. Prior to starting to process data, all routers will first configure certain proactive routes. After then, an on-demand situation can operate thanks to a flooding of numerous

RR packets. The zone routing protocol (ZRP) is one of the hybrid routing protocols [17].

D) **Hybrid Protocols:** The hierarchical level at which a node is located determines whether proactive or reactive routing should be used. The foundation of hierarchical routing is the division of nodes into groups and the assignment of distinct functionality to nodes both inside and outside of a group.

Security Issues in the Wireless Networks

In wireless networks, we cannot assure about the quality of service during data transmission since this situation uses the air rather than cables, and the possibility of infiltration into such networks is quite high. As a result, it must safeguard the transfer of users' sensitive data as well as stop unauthorised users from accessing the network. The following [2] are the general security concerns for wireless networks:

1) **Confidentiality:** Authentication of the receiver is also required since the data sent on the network is encrypted while in transmission to make sure that it only the intended the recipient can access it. The key to decrypt the information will be sent to the recipient.
2) **Integrity:** Attacks that might jeopardise the data's integrity can target wireless networks. The methods used to avoid integrity breaches are analogous to those in wired networks.
3) **Availability:** Wireless networks can be susceptible to denial of service type of attacks. Radio jamming can be used to limit network access. Unauthorised users can also conduct a battery depletion attack, which involves sending messages or data to connected devices frequently in order to drain their batteries.
4) **Eavesdropping and Authentication:** As was already said, wireless networks are broadcast, thus there are more access points that may be used to join to the network. Stopping this spying is required.
5) **Blue Snaring or Blue jacking:** These are the types of Bluetooth assaults used to change or take data.

Classical Cryptography Techniques

1. **Symmetric Key Cryptography**
   The same value of key will be used for encryption and decryption in the symmetric key distribution-based cryptosystems. That is also known as secret key cryptography. A required secure communication channel in key management can only be produced if the symmetric keys are provided before start of communication to each pair of interacting systems. The symmetric key cryptography process is shown in Fig. 2.
2. **Asymmetric Key Cryptography**
   It is a cryptosystems which uses asymmetric key distribution use a public key encryption system, which consists of two different parts: a private key that is top secret and a public key that is distributed all around the network.

   The communication between sender and receiver is encrypted by the sender using the recipient's public key. The recipient will use its private key to decrypt the transmission. This distribution is less prone to security issues since the private key is never

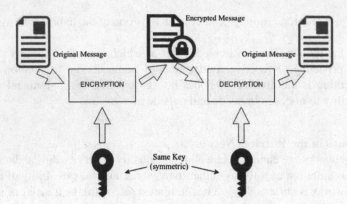

Fig. 2. Symmetric key cryptography [4]

in transit. As shown in Fig. 3, the asymmetric key cryptography process involves a device, such as a laptop, attempting to connect to an unprotected network in order to potentially collect personal data from a user of that network.

Fig. 3. Asymmetric Key Cryptography [2]

3 Quantum Key Distribution Protocols

This protocol aims to provide a distributed secret key that may be used to communicate secretly between two remote parties across a common communication medium. The most important thing to remember here is that the key generation protocol is demonstrably safe against any attack that an eavesdropper may launch. The security of the protocol is guaranteed by the law of physics, not just by technological constraints that come with actual implementations.

Six-State Protocol (SSP)

The main difference between the SSP and the BB84 protocol is that the SSP protocol allows the encoding of the bits required for inter-entity communication using three orthogonal bases. Six states are used to represent the bits as a result [7].

Quantum Node Networks

By actively conducting quantum operations on the travelling photons, a quantum node may be utilised to counteract the quantum decoherence of the signal along the quantum channel. Using quantum entanglement sources, quantum memories, and entanglement purification techniques to produce perfect entangled states that may then be stored in a section of the quantum channel is one method Cirac et al. [JC98] offer [6]. These nodes are known as quantum repeaters because they chain the recorded states together to create perfect end-to-end entanglement that can travel across virtually any distance. But until fully developed quantum computing capabilities are developed, quantum repeaters can only be used hypothetically. The Quantum Relay, a less complex quantum node proposed by Collins et al. [DC03+, is technically challenging but viable because it does not demand for a quantum memory. Quantum relays, Apart from that, do not increase the maximum possible distance over which a quantum signal may be delivered, making them unsuitable for a real-world QKD network [21].

Trusted Relay Networks

Implicit confidence is placed in a relay node to transmit the quantum signal without listening in or meddling with it. Individual keys are created across QKD connections and more securely held in the trusted nodes at both ends of links to do this in a QKD network. (The nodes are essentially a miniature Alice and Bob running a separate instance of the QKD protocol, unaffected by other messages traversing the network.) A network of trustworthy relays and their intermediary quantum connections are built to connect real Alice and real Bob when they wish to do run a QKD protocol; this is known as a QKD route. Alice and Bob's key is encrypted using a one-time pad and sent "hop by hop" between each nodes on the QKD path, where it is decrypted and then encrypted again using a separate key from the node key store (Fig. 4).

The destination now interacts with the source over the public key channel for key sifting after receiving all the photons.

Using classical channel (key sifting):

When the source asks the receiver which measurement bases he may have used, the receiver replies with a yes or no.

Bits

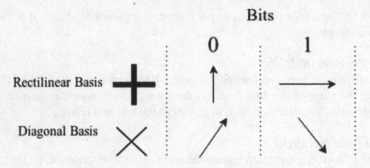

Fig. 4. Photon Polarization using Bases [9]

4 Proposed Protocol

This work uses the QKD protocol, an upgraded version of BB84, to address the security concerns associated with key distribution. Figure 5 illustrates the QKD protocol in use in the proposed handshake protocol.

The steps for the above protocol are as follows:

1. The PMK is first split between the BS and AP. After then, the quantum channel is used for transmission.
2. BS uses bases to distribute all of the polarised photons to the AP. Once the photons have done transmitting, the channel is switched to classical.
3. To eliminate all errors and acquire the ultimate encryption key, the next three phases of QKD are employed.

To enhance the quantum key and ensure secure communication, quantum transmission must carry enough photons. The PTK key is made from the quantum key's 256 bits, which are created by reducing the quantum key's (384 bit) size. After getting the PTK key, the normal handshake is carried out, during which the MIC is determined for some mutual authentication. The MIC is controlled by the XOR logical operation and the first half of equal-length bits in the PMK. This MIC (Q-MIC) is known as quantum MIC and is relayed and confirmed between the two parties. After then, the temporary key is used to begin communication and encryption. The QKD protocol is being used, thus the Nounce values that were used in the original handshake may not required. The benefits of employing this treatment are further listed in the next section [14].

Implementation Result

I have implemented the proposed Quantum cryptography with AOMDV network routing protocol and compared its result with the AOMDV without using Quantum cryptography [18].

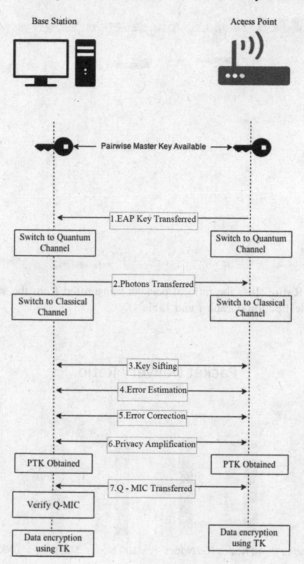

Fig. 5. Proposed Handshaking Protocol [6]

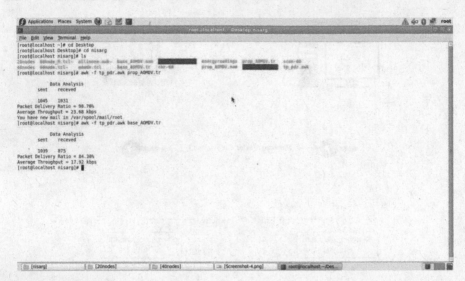

PDR Delivery Ratio: It is the ratio of packets transmitted from the source to those received at the destination (Graph 1 and Table 1).

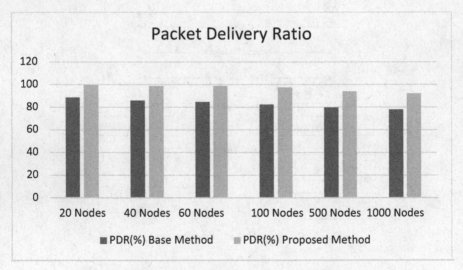

Graph 1. Packet Delivery Ratio for different number of nodes

Table 1. Packet Delivery Ratio for different number of nodes

Nodes	PDR(%) – Base	PDR(%) – Proposed
20	88.54	99.42
40	85.63	98.89
60	84.30	98.70
100	82.32	97.27
500	79.58	93.62
1000	77.83	92.10

Throughput: It is the proportion of all data sent by a sender that is received by a receiver (Graph 2 and Table 2).

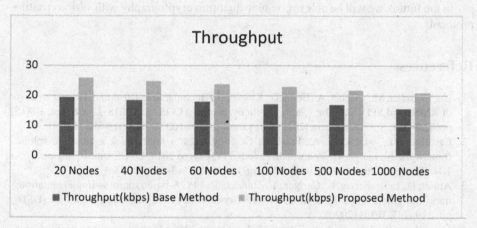

Graph 2. Packet Delivery Ratio for different number of nodes

Table 2. Throughput for different number of node

Nodes	Throughput (kbps) – Base	Throughput (kbps) – Proposed
20	19.37	25.87
40	18.48	24.73
60	17.92	23.68
100	17.10	22.93
500	16.89	21.74
1000	15.61	20.86

Advantages of Quantum Cryptography

The quantum cryptography represents a genuine advance in network security. The following are some benefits of using quantum cryptography in wireless networks [18]:

- Quantum cryptography relies on physical principles to decode encoded data rather than mathematical models, making it essentially impenetrable to hacking and requiring little upkeep [8].

QKD is beneficial for establishing connections between devices and various nearby access points in a variety of wireless network types.

5 Conclusion and Future Work

The major objective of proposed research work is to demonstrate a technique for enhancing WLAN security. It has been demonstrated that integrating quantum cryptography onto wireless networks may significantly improve network performance and security.

In the future, we will be able to combine quantum cryptography with various routing protocols.

References

1. Kannwischer, M.J., Genêt, A., Butin, D., Krämer, J., Buchmann, J.: Differential power analysis of XMSS and SPHINCS. In: Fan, J., Gierlichs, B. (eds.) COSADE 2018. LNCS, vol. 10815, pp. 168–188. Springer, Cham (2018). https://doi.org/10.1007/978-3-319-89641-0_10
2. Castelnovi, L., Martinelli, A., Prest, T.: Grafting trees: a fault attack against the sphincs framework. In: Lange, T., Steinwandt, R. (eds.) PQCrypto 2018. LNCS, vol. 10786, pp. 165–184. Springer, Cham (2018). https://doi.org/10.1007/978-3-319-79063-3_8
3. Amiet, D., Leuenberger, L., Curiger, A., Zbinden, P.: FPGA-based sphincs+ implementations: mind the glitch. In: 2020 23rd Euromicro Conference on Digital System Design (DSD), pp. 229–237. IEEE (2020)
4. Colombier, B., Dragoi, V.-F., Cayrel, P.-L., Grosso, V.: Message-recovery profiled side-channel attack on the classic McEliece cryptosystem. Cryptology ePrint Archive, Paper 2022/125 (2022). https://eprint.iacr.org/2022/125
5. Bos, J.W., Gourjon, M., Renes, J., Schneider, T., van Vredendaal, C.: Masking kyber: first-and higher-order implementations. IACR Trans. Cryptogr. Hardw. Embed. Syst. 173–214 (2021)
6. Ravi, P., Poussier, R., Bhasin, S., Chattopadhyay, A.: On configurable SCA countermeasures against single trace attacks for the NTT. In: Batina, L., Picek, S., Mondal, M. (eds.) SPACE 2020. LNCS, vol. 12586, pp. 123–146. Springer, Cham (2020). https://doi.org/10.1007/978-3-030-66626-2_7
7. Ravi, P., Roy, S.S., Chattopadhyay, A., Bhasin, S.: Generic side-channel attacks on CCA-secure lattice-based PKE and KEMs. IACR Trans. Cryptogr. Hardw. Embed. Syst. 307–335 (2020)
8. Ravi, P., Chattopadhyay, A., Baksi, A.: Sidechannel and fault-injection attacks over lattice-based post-quantum schemes (kyber, dilithium): survey and new results. Cryptology ePrint Archive (2022)
9. NIST. Post-Quantum Crypto Project - Round 3 Submissions (2021). https://csrc.nist.gov/Projects/post-quantumcryptography/round-3-submissions/

10. Moody, D., et al.: Status report on the second round of the NIST post-quantum cryptography standardization process (2020)
11. Jang, K., Baksi, A., Breier, J., Seo, H., Chattopadhyay, A.: Quantum implementation and analysis of default. Cryptology ePrint Archive, Paper 2022/647 (2022). https://eprint.iacr.org/2022/647
12. Huang, Z., Sun, S.: Synthesizing quantum circuits of AES with lower t-depth and less qubits. IACR Cryptology ePrint Archive, p. 620 (2022)
13. Jang, K., Baksi, A., Song, G., Kim, H., Seo, H., Chattopadhyay, A.: Quantum analysis of AES. IACR Cryptology ePrint Archive, p. 683 (2022)
14. Häner, T., Jaques, S., Naehrig, M., Roetteler, M., Soeken, M.: Improved quantum circuits for elliptic curve discrete logarithms. In: Ding, J., Tillich, J.-P. (eds.) PQCrypto 2020. LNCS, vol. 12100, pp. 425–444. Springer, Cham (2020). https://doi.org/10.1007/978-3-030-44223-1_23
15. Gidney, C., Ekera, M.: How to factor 2048 bit RSA integers in 8 hours using 20 million noisy qubits. Quantum **5**, 433 (2021)
16. Chailloux, A., Naya-Plasencia, M., Schrottenloher, A.: An efficient quantum collision search algorithm and implications on symmetric cryptography. Cryptology ePrint Archive, Paper 2017/847 (2017). https://eprint.iacr.org/2017/847
17. Arute, F., et al.: Quantum supremacy using a programmable superconducting processor. Nature **574**(7779), 505–510 (2019)
18. Wallden, P., Kashefi, E.: Cyber security in the quantum era. Commun. ACM **62**(4), 120 (2019)
19. Grofig, P., et al.: Experiences and observations on the industrial implementation of a system to search over outsourced encrypted data. In: Katzenbeisser, S., Lotz, V., Weippl, E.R. (eds.) Sicherheit. LNI, vol. 228, pp. 115–125. GI (2014)
20. Singh, S., Ahlawat, A.Kr., Tripathi, A.Kr.: Mechanizing wireless LAN (WLAN) using compression techniques. Free J. Int. J. Eng. Appl. Sci. Technol. (IJEAST) (2016). ISSN 2455-2143
21. Zhou, T., et al.: Quantum cryptography for the future internet and the security analysis. Secur. Commun. Netw. **2018**, 1–7 (2018)
22. Shen, J., Zhou, T., Chen, X., Li, J., Susilo, W.: Anonymous and traceable group data sharing in cloud computing. IEEE Trans. Inf. Forensics Secur. **13**(4), 912–925 (2018)
23. Li, J., Zhang, Y., Chen, X., Xiang, Y.: Secure attribute-based data sharing for resource-limited users in cloud computing. Comput. Secur. **72**, 1–12 (2017)
24. Shen, J., Shen, J., Chen, X., Huang, X., Susilo, W.: An efficient public auditing protocol with novel dynamic structure for cloud data. IEEE Trans. Inf. Forensics Secur. **12**, 2402–2415 (2017)
25. Shen, J., Miao, T., Liu, Q., Ji, S., Wang, C., Liu, D.: S-SurF: an enhanced secure bulk data dissemination in wireless sensor networks. In: Wang, G., Atiquzzaman, M., Yan, Z., Choo, K.-K. (eds.) SpaCCS 2017. LNCS, vol. 10656, pp. 395–408. Springer, Cham (2017). https://doi.org/10.1007/978-3-319-72389-1_32
26. Li, P., Li, J., Huang, Z., Gao, C.-Z., Chen, W.-B., Chen, K.: Privacy-preserving outsourced classification in cloud computing. Cluster Comput. **21**(1), 277–286 (2017). https://doi.org/10.1007/s10586-017-0849-9
27. Bennett, C.H., Brassard, G., Crépeau, C., Skubiszewska, M.-H.: Practical quantum oblivious transfer. In: Feigenbaum, J. (ed.) CRYPTO 1991. LNCS, vol. 576, pp. 351–366. Springer, Heidelberg (1992). https://doi.org/10.1007/3-540-46766-1_29
28. Winkler, S., Wullschleger, J.: On the efficiency of classical and quantum oblivious transfer reductions. In: Rabin, T. (ed.) CRYPTO 2010. LNCS, vol. 6223, pp. 707–723. Springer, Heidelberg (2010). https://doi.org/10.1007/978-3-642-14623-7_38
29. Chailloux, A., Kerenidis, I., Sikora, J.: Lower bounds for quantum oblivious transfer. Quantum Inf. Comput. **13**(1–2), 0158–0177 (2013)

30. Shen, J., Zhou, T., He, D., Zhang, Y., Sun, X., Xiang, Y.: Block design-based key agreement for group data sharing in cloud computing. IEEE Trans. Dependable Secure Comput. **16**, 996–1010 (2017)
31. Shen, J., Liu, D., Shen, J., Liu, Q., Sun, X.: A secure cloud-assisted urban data sharing framework for ubiquitous-cities. Pervasive Mob. Comput. **41**, 219–230 (2017)
32. Terhal, B.M., DiVincenzo, D.P., Leung, D.W.: Hiding bits in bell states. Phys. Rev. Lett. **86**(25), 5807–5810 (2001)

Gaussian Mixture Model-Based Clustering for Energy Saving in WSN

Mohammed Saleh Mutar[1] , Dalal Abdulmohsin Hammood[1](✉),
and Seham Ahmed Hashem[2]

[1] Electrical Engineering Technical College, Department of Computer Technical Engineering,
Middle Technical University (MTU), Al Doura, 10022 Baghdad, Iraq
`dalal.hammood@mtu.edu.iq`
[2] Technical Instructors Training Institute, Middle Technical University, Baghdad, Iraq
`dr.seham.ahmed@mtu.edu.iq`

Abstract. In wireless sensor networks, nodes have limited access to energy
sources and must make efficient use of what they have. Energy consumption may
be decreased and network life can be prolonged via the process of clustering. To
reduce the network's power consumption and increase its lifespan, we used a new
clustering technique in this work. Centralized cluster formation and decentralized
cluster heads form the basis of this stage of clustering. Clusters are determined
via a centralized Gaussian mixture model (GMM) technique, and once they are
generated, they don't change. After that, it chooses which cluster heads (CHs)
should spin. Inside those clusters to minimize energy consumption prior to the
data transmission phase to the base station (BS), taking into account the varying
quantities of energy in the nodes. Thus, the proposed approach not only effectively
addresses the energy consumption problem, but also significantly lengthens the
lifespan of the network. The results demonstrate the following ways in which the
suggested method lessens the burden on network resources. It increases network
lifetime by 301%, 131%, and 122%, decreases energy consumption by 20.53%,
6.14%, and 5%, and increases throughput by 47%, 9%, and 4% when compared
to the Flat, FUCA, and FCMDE protocols.

Keywords: Wireless sensor networks · Gaussian mixture model · clustering ·
energy consumption

1 Introduction

Wireless sensor networks, which are deployed in big numbers to collect data about their
surroundings and send it to a central location, are characterized by their low cost, small
size, and constrained resource availability [1]. Numerous applications, including habitat
these networks are used for surveillance, border surveillance, healthcare surveillance, etc.
The wireless sensor nodes are often placed in an unfriendly or unmanaged environment.
What's worse is that these nodes only have basic connection, computing, storage, and
battery capabilities [2].

© The Author(s), under exclusive license to Springer Nature Switzerland AG 2023
N. Chaubey et al. (Eds.): COMS2 2023, CCIS 1861, pp. 117–132, 2023.
https://doi.org/10.1007/978-3-031-40564-8_9

The battery that powers the remainder of the system's components (processing, sensing, receiving, and sending) is defined by its compact size and its constraints as a consequence of the sensor nodes' small size. Certain circumstances make it difficult, costly, or impossible to replace or recharge the battery [3]. In these networks, sensor nodes are placed densely to form data reading vectors that are geographically and temporally coupled. Multiple network resources are required for the processing and transmission of these vectors. The whole network's resources are impacted. Substantially while processing and sending these data vectors. These duplicate data vectors' transmission causes a number of issues for the network, including high bandwidth usage, energy consumption, and a number of overhead expenses related to data storage, processing, and communication [4].

Furthermore, a number of internal node processes, including sensing, processing, and data transfer, might negatively impact the sensor node's performance. The process that uses the most energy is data transmission [5]. As a result, it is necessary to prolong the lifespan of long-term applications like continuous monitoring systems. However, the pace of creating data for base station processing is often quite high. Energy dissipation reduction is a major issue in WSNs [6].

One practical solution for dealing with these problems and using the energy at hand is clustering. This is caused by clustering, which divides the network into clusters and requires each cluster's sensor nodes (SNs) to relay data to a cluster head (CH) [7]. Due to the sensors' close proximity to the CHs, they may reduce their transmission powers, which would save energy and lengthen the network's lifetime. CHs are chosen from the SNs to handle collecting data from sensors in their clusters, putting it all together, and sending it to the BS [8]. The popular, adaptable, and effective Gaussian-based mixture models (GMM) are used to describe both univariate and multivariate data. They've been put to use in a variety of applications, including machine learning, voice and image processing, pattern recognition, computer vision, and statistical data analysis. Using a limited mixture of Gaussian densities, it may handle issues like data analysis and grouping [9].

Similar to how k-means may be used to classify data, Gaussian mixture models can organize sensor nodes into groups. However, Gaussian mixture models provide several benefits that k-means cannot. In the first place, k-means does not include variation. The spread of a normal distribution, measured in terms of its variance, is what we mean when we talk about variance. The k-means model may be understood as if it were a set of circles, with the farthest distant point in each cluster defining the radius of the circle. When the sensor is circular, it functions as expected. Alternatively, Gaussian mixture models are capable of accommodating very elongated clusters. The second distinction is that k-means conducts hard classification whereas Gaussian mixture models do soft classification.

What follows is an explanation of the rest of the paper. The related works are included in Sect. 2. In Sect. 3, we provide a quick summary of paradigm of networks and energy use model. In Sect. 4, we cover the proposed procedure in detail. Discussions and results from the simulations are reported in Sect. 5. The last section of the article provides an overview of the main points.

2 Related Works

By introducing a model into a wireless sensor system, the energy efficiency of wireless systems will be increased. While discussing design difficulties and practical constraints, an effort is made to build an application-oriented system to enhance the functionality of wireless sensor networks while reducing their energy consumption.

Gupta et al. (2014) proposed a Gaussian mixture model (GMM), which is a collection of mixtures of multivariate Gaussian distributions and is a suitable model for clusters of various sizes that are correlated with one another. The GMM's clustering measures the associated posterior probability for each node and explains how each node connects to each cluster, i.e., the mean of the corresponding nodes. The clustering carried out by GMM is known as "soft clustering," since nodes are not limited to a single cluster [10].

Tsiligaridis et al. (2016) proposed a stochastic approximation (SA)-based distributed EM algorithm, which targets problems with sensor networks' dispersed clustering transmission cost minimization. Each node in the network in our configuration perceives an in which the world may be modeled as a collection of Gaussians, each of which corresponds to one of the basic needs. The distributed clustering issue is studied in terms of a whereby all of reality may be represented by a scattering of Gaussians, one for each of our fundamental desires. By reducing the need for network cycles and keeping calculations and communications local, The use of DEM-SA in a WSN reduces both traffic and contention [11].

Hojjatinia et al. (2021) offered a new method, namely GDECA. Which applies the premise that the distributions of nodes in the actual world are mixtures of the Gaussian distribution. Therefore, So That We Can Find out the Parameters of These Distributions by Fitting the Gaussian Mixture Model (GMM) To the Nodes, GDECA uses a distribution estimation technique that it has adopted from machine learning (ML). Additionally, the dispersion of nodes is used to calculate sinks' routing [12].

Al-Janabi et al. (2022) to enhance ES and lengthen the lifetime of sensor nodes, a k-means clustering strategy was presented. This method clusters the region of interest, which decreases the distance between the sensor nodes and the base station. Data is sent from each node to the cluster head, which in turn relays the information to the BS. Energy efficiency is improved, as well [13].

Chaubey et al. (2016) proposed a new hierarchical clustering algorithm. Some of the nodes in the proposed process must choose cluster heads that are further from the BS than they are. These nodes transmit their data to a different place, where it must travel a great distance before reaching the BS. These transmissions are referred to as "excess transmissions" and waste energy on the network. In the suggested approach, set up every sensor node in a distributed cluster environment and decide how many clusters to place there. Each sensor chooses one of the cluster's head nodes, and each cluster has its own cluster head, which communicates with the base station (BS) for communication purposes [14].

Moghadaszadeh et al. (2017) proposed a new algorithm in which expectation maximization (EM) is used. Make a suggestion for a fix to the issues the K-Means family, which is employed in many clustering algorithms, is now experiencing. The suggested approach, it uses the EM clustering technique as its foundation, increases network longevity and improves energy efficiency. Clustering is accomplished using a Gaussian mixture model using the EM technique. During the setup phase and seeks to build clusters based on the EM technique as it is specified for Gaussian mixture models (GMM). The GMM is used by the EM method to find clusters, and it gives the most likely parameters for each cluster [15].

Pancha et al. (2017) suggested a hierarchical low-energy clustering algorithm (LEACH). The first WSN clustering method is called LEACH. By using a clustering strategy with one CH in each cluster, LEACH lowers network power consumption / use. Once the sensor nodes are set up, the clustering process may begin. Here, the remaining network nodes choose the CH with the strongest received signal, which is the nearest CH. After selecting all of the CHs in the network at first using a probability-dependent threshold. Each and every CH served as a router for direct communication with the BS. Distributed clustering is carried out via LEACH [16].

Agrawal, D. and Pandey, S., (2018) proposed an approach called the "method for uneven clustering using fuzzy logic" to do just that: extend the lifespan of the network. Uneven clusters are formed using this procedure. The goal is to equalize heating and cooling needs. Fuzzy logic is used to determine which nodes in a cluster should serve as leaders. The density, the remaining energy, and Inputs consist of distance from the station's home base. The two resulting fuzzy variables are the radius of the competition and the ranking. To do fuzzy inference, the Mamdani technique is used [17].

Abdulzahra, A. and Al-Qurabat (2022) introduced a novel fuzzy c-means based clustering methodology with distance- and energy-limited termed (FCMDE) for clustering to increase the lifespan of WSN. Although FCMDE uses the fuzzy c-means approach to cluster SNs, it does not choose the node closest to the fuzzy c-means centroid as the CH but instead selects the node closest to the majority of nodes in the network. The closeness criterion ensures that all nodes in a given cluster remain in close proximity to their CH, allowing them to maintain drastically reduced transmission powers [18].

3 Preliminaries

In this part, we detail the energy usage and network model.

3.1 Network Model

In this part, we provide a common monitoring environment for applications based on WSNs. To ensure the system's low power consumption, we adopt a cluster-based layout. A square sensing field with N randomly spaced sensor nodes surround the BS. The nodes continually assess their surroundings and communicate their findings to the CH, who then periodically sends the information obtained to the BS (also known as the gateway (GW)). For our network model, we presumptively consider the following:

1. Due to the homogenous network that we have taken into consideration for the proposed study it is assumed that all of the nodes have the same initial energy and are hence static.
2. Based on the suggested packet routing scheme, each CH gets each CH sends data packets to its corresponding GW, and each GW receives data packets from its corresponding CMs. And a small number of CMs. The data aggregation procedure will thus be carried out by these CH and GHs for effective transmission and to save network energy.
3. Using the proposed method, all sensor nodes engage in single-hop communication.
4. All sensor node has a fixed initial energy and is energy-limited.
5. The GW should be unrestricted by energy, computation, and network coverage.

3.2 Energy Model

Energy is required by sensor nodes for a variety of purposes, including sensing, network maintenance, data processing, packet receipt, and packet transfer. The distance traveled and the size of the packet determines how much energy is needed to convey it [19, 20]. To broadcast a packet of $k - bits$ across a distance of d, the transmitter has to expend a certain amount of energy, as follows:

$$E_{Tx}(k, d) = \begin{cases} k \times E_{elec} + k \times \varepsilon_{fs} \times d^2 & if \ d < d_0 \\ k \times E_{elec} + k \times \varepsilon_{mp} \times d^4 & if \ d \geq d_0 \end{cases} \tag{1}$$

Receiving a $k - bits$ packet consumes the following amount of energy:

$$E_{Rx}(k) = k \times E_{elec} \tag{2}$$

E_{elec} in (1) and (2) stands for the energy spent per bit by the transmitter or reception circuits, respectively. We use ε_{fs} and ε_{mp}, transmission and receiving circuit power consumption, respectively, to characterize the energy expenditure of the amplifier for each bit in two different models: free space and multi-path fading. The letter d represents the separation between the transmitter and receiver. The d_0 threshold is formulated as having

$$d_0 = \sqrt{\epsilon_{fs} / \epsilon_{mp}} \tag{3}$$

Another component that is taken into account is the data aggregation power consumption, or E_{da}. We assume that each cluster member transmits $k - bits$ to its CH during each data collection period, and that the energy used by a CH during one data collection period may be represented as

$$E_{CH} = \frac{N}{c} \times E_{elec} \times w + \frac{N}{c} \times E_{da} \times w + \epsilon_{mp} \times w \times d_{BS}^2 \tag{4}$$

Energy is wasted by the CH when it gathers packets from nodes, aggregates them, and sends the resultant packets to the BS. Provided is the typical separation between a CH and a BS by d_{BS}, while the number of clusters is given by c.

4   The Proposed Method

The suggested procedure may be carried out in three distinct stages. Selecting an appropriate cluster number is the first Phase. During Phase 2, a centralized clustering method is suggested using the Gaussian mixture model. The last stage involves data transmission between cluster nodes and CHs. Figure 1 shows the flowchart of the proposed system.

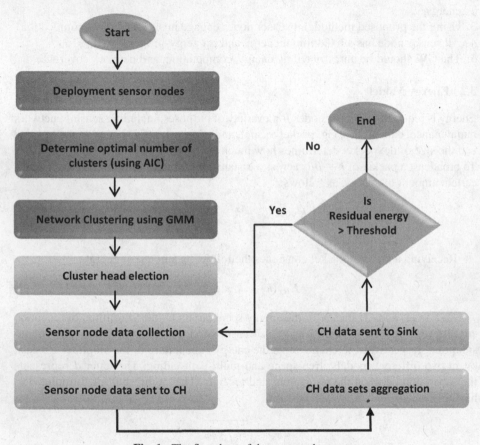

Fig. 1. The flowchart of the proposed system

4.1   Optimal Number of Clusters in a Gaussian Mixture

For clustering, a precise estimate of importance of cluster count. The quantity of clusters may be derived from the data and used as additional parameter. Akaike's information criterion (AIC) and the Bayesian inference criterion (BIC). Is used to determine the ideal number of clusters [21, 22]. The AIC is

$$AIC(G) = -2InL(\theta(G)) + 2P(G) \tag{5}$$

L $(\theta$ (G)) is the likelihood value computed at θ (G), and P is the total number of parameters to be evaluated. The vector containing the parameters' greatest likelihood estimates, in which G represents the Gaussian density function. The estimated C is the quantity of clusters (abbreviated C) with the lowest AIC value.

4.2 Gaussian Mixture Models Clustering

Several methods exist for clustering d-dimensional data sets into a predetermined size (say C). Popular clustering techniques like as model-based clustering and K-means may complete this task using a Gaussian mixture model. As previously discussed, these clustering algorithms may be divided into two categories: soft clustering algorithms and hard clustering algorithms. Mixture models make use of the probabilistic soft clustering technique. Data points provide samples from each cluster's probability distribution, which is represented as a cluster in d-dimensional space. Gaussian Mixture Models assume that each clusterable data point is selected simultaneously from a set of distributions whose parameters are unknown and is thus a mixture of Gaussian distributions. To determine the values of these unknowable factors and then create the various clusters, a learning method is used [23].

According to Eq. (6), the probability distribution p(X) of a node in a network (which is denoted by a vector X) is the weighted sum of the probability distributions of the node in each of the node's component C clusters. The distribution of each component (denoted by N (X|μC, ΣC)) is a cluster represented by a Gaussian.

$$p(x) = \sum\nolimits_{C=1}^{C} \pi C N(X|\mu C, \Sigma C) \tag{6}$$

In Eq. (6), πC is the coefficient of mixing for cluster C, which is one of C clusters; C is the mean of the normal distribution for cluster C and ΣC is the normal distribution's covariance measure for cluster C. The degree of a node's relationship with cluster Cis indicated by the mixture coefficient πC. The parameters that constitute a multivariate normal distribution that represents a cluster are mean and covariance. The value of variance or standard deviation is used in place of covariance for single-variable normal distributions.

They are probabilistic mixture models. Data samples are created using GMM clustering models. Each data point in these models, albeit to variable degrees, is a member of every cluster in the dataset. Being a part of a certain cluster has a chance of between 0 and 1, the actions listed below are done.

1. Set the starting values for μ, $\sum$ and the mixing coefficient π, and then calculate L, the logarithm of the likelihood.
2. Analyze the accountability procedure with the current settings
3. Obtain new μ, $\sum$, and π using newly acquired obligations
4. Log-likelihood L should be calculated once again. Iterate through steps 2 and 3 until convergence is reached.

Since covariance and mean are both taken into account while creating clusters, GMM will not make any errors. These factors influenced our choice to use the GMM clustering method for the suggested approach.

In order to reduce the amount of energy needed to create clusters, clustering is performed before CH selection. A node's residual energy has to be greater than a threshold in order for it to be considered for CH selection. To avoid premature death and network disconnection, this criterion is essential. Additionally, the CH is selected as the node that is closest to the largest number of other nodes. The suggested approach does not prioritize picking the cluster's epicenter node above those that are farther out since doing so would waste energy.

5   Transmission of Data

When the CHs are recognized, the sensor nodes start sending data to them. The transmission power of nodes in a cluster is decreased because the Gaussian mixture modeling technique clearly achieves the shortest geographic distance to the CHs. The CHs lower the quantity of data by aggregating it, and then they transfer the resulting data to the BS.

6   Simulation and Performance Evaluation

The recommended strategy is simulated in Python. In order to show how well the proposed method works in simulations, a scenario is developed. 100 sensor nodes are selected for a $100 \times 100 M^2$ network. When first deployed, the BS is often located centrally inside the network as shown in Fig. 2. The settings for the simulation are shown in Table 1 below. The efficiency of the suggested approach is evaluated in comparison to that of both flat and clustered networks.

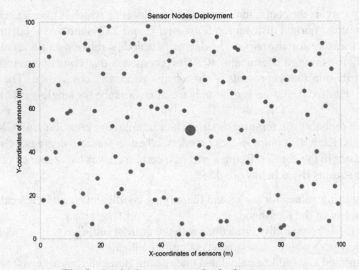

Fig. 2. Deploying sensor nodes in the target area.

Since the number of clusters must be specified in advance for the GMM technique to work, we chose 6 as shown in Fig. 3 and calculated from Eq. 5. Our proposed method

Table 1. Parameters of Simulation.

Parameters	Values
Network size(m^2)	100×100
Nodes deployment	Randomly
BS location	Center
Nodes count	100
Initial energy	$0.5\,J$
Data packet	100 readings $* 64\,bits$
E_{elec}	$50\,nJ/bit$
ε_{fs}	$10\,pJ/bit/m^2$
ε_{mp}	$0.0013\,pJ/bit/m^4$
E_{DA}	$5\,nJ/bit/signal$
d_0	$87\,m$

clusters 100 sensor nodes into six groups, each of which is illustrated by a distinct color (see Fig. 4).

The network's reliability is measured during a time interval called the stability period. Rounds till the first network node are tallied during the stability phase. (FND) completely loses power and is declared dead. When even a single node fails, the whole network is put at risk. The lifespan of a network is the number of cycles it takes for all of the nodes to run out of power.

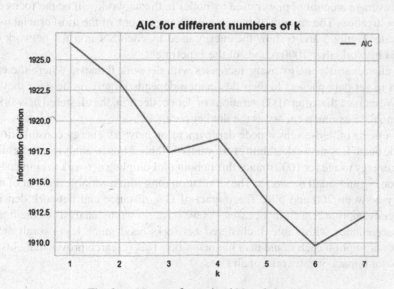

Fig. 3. AIC score for optimal No. of clusters.

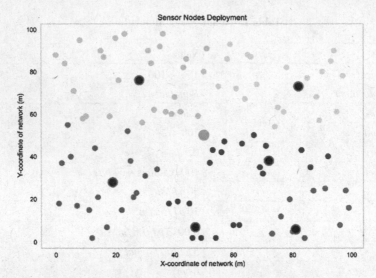

Fig. 4. Creation of Clusters using GMM.

The findings of a simulation research showing that the stability period for flat networks is 177 rounds and for clustered networks it is 534 rounds. The results suggest that the location of the BS and the overall sensor count deployed across the network are two crucial aspects that influence the lifetime of the sensor nodes (i.e., the density of the network). Clustering the nodes and placing the BS in the center of the network shortens the path data must travel, which in turn reduces the amount of energy needed to digest the data and extend the network's life.

The average amount of power used by nodes in the network will be the focus of our next investigation. The amount of energy a WSN uses is one of the most crucial metrics to evaluate. Figure 5 and 6 show the energy used by each SN in a flat network and a clustered network after 1000 rounds of the experiment.

For all scenarios, energy usage increases with network flatness. Where the energy required to get data packets to their destination depends largely on how far they must travel. We can see that after 1000 iterations of data collection, the clustered network uses less than 283% as much energy as the flat network.

The effects of dense sensor node deployment on network energy consumption and first node death (i.e. network stability) are studied. Table 2 below analyzes the results for average energy usage for 1000 rounds throughout the complete network to emphasize the impact on big and small networks. The simulation runs with a variable number of nodes, typically between 200 and 500. The impact of GW distance and network density on energy consumption is seen in all cases. As we have shown by analysis of the findings, and in accordance with Table 3, clustered networks need much less overall network energy consumption each round than flat networks. This research proves that clustering has a major impact on networks of all sizes.

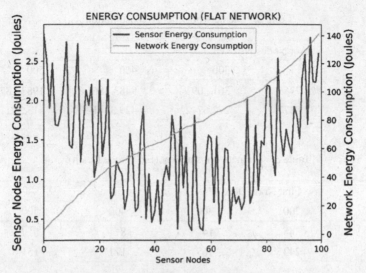

Fig. 5. The energy consumption of sensor nodes use in flat WSN.

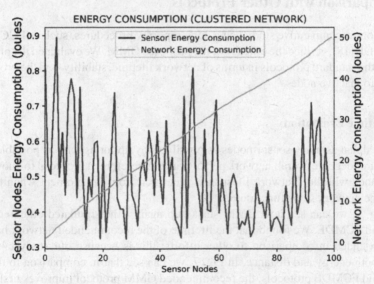

Fig. 6. The energy consumption of sensor nodes in clustered WSN.

Table 3 shows that the clustered network runs for more iterations than the flat network does. As a result of the shortened distance that data from sensors must travel, this helps to preserve the battery life of Increase the longevity of the network as a whole and the sensor nodes.

Table 2. The network energy consumption.

	Sensor Nodes No			
	200	300	400	500
Flat	924.7366	3612.09	9483.586	19834.87
Clustered	138.8371	272.6742	429.3441	613.3011

Table 3. The network stability (First Node Death).

	First Node Dead			
	200	300	400	500
Flat	34	14	8	5
Clustered	242	167	171	151

7   Comparison with Other Protocols

Furthermore, a comparative study using contemporary procedures, such as FUCA [17], and FCMDE [18], verified the efficacy of the proposed GMM. We evaluated the proposed GMM to the standard protocols in terms of network lifetime, stability, and the proportion of active to inactive nodes.

7.1   Lifetime Evaluation

It is crucial that as many sensor nodes as possible stay up for as long as possible, since node failures degrade overall network performance. Therefore, it is crucial to know when the first node will die. Network lifespan is measured from the moment when the first node in the network stops functioning.

In Fig. 7, we can see how GMM stacks up against the simulated outcomes from FUCA and FCMDE. We found that the lifetime of the recommended network has been greatly extended in comparison to other efforts; this is because our study takes into account both energy and distance. In Fig. 7, we can see that in comparison to the Flat, FUCA, and FCMDE protocols, the recommended GMM protocol improves first-SN by about 301%, 131%, and 122%.

7.2   Energy Consumption

The average Energy content that is wasted across the network is measured using the GMM protocol in this experiment. One of the most crucial criteria for evaluating a WSN's performance is its energy consumption. Energy consumption for the flat, FUCA, and FCMDE methods is also shown for comparison with the proposed GMM protocol in Fig. 8.

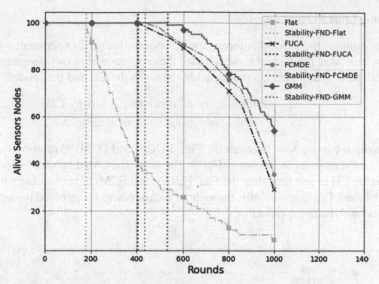

Fig. 7. FND stability time and lifespan of the network.

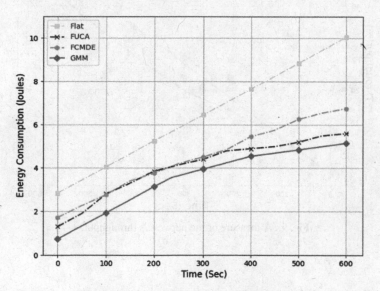

Fig. 8. The network's energy utilization level.

The experimental findings show that there was a decrease in energy use across all time periods. Compared to the flat, FUCA, and FCMDE protocols, the GMM protocol reduces energy consumption during data transmission by about 301%, 131%, and 122%, respectively, after 1000 rounds of the experiment. According to the results, the GMM procedure outperforms the other two and has the highest rate of energy savings.

7.3 Throughput Evaluation

To further evaluate the network's throughput, another simulated experiment was run. During transmission, throughput is measured as the proportion of acknowledged packets to the time spent communicating those packets between the CH and the sender.

$$Throughput = \frac{total\ number\ of\ received\ packets\ by\ CH}{delay\ in\ process\ of\ communication} \tag{7}$$

Throughput comparisons between the Flat, FUCA, and FCMDE protocols and the proposed GMM protocol are shown in Fig. 9. The proposed GMM protocol sends more packets to the CH in less time than the Flat, FUCA, and FCMDE protocols by margins of 47%, 9%, and 4%. Consequently, throughput measurement has evolved through time in comparison to earlier approaches.

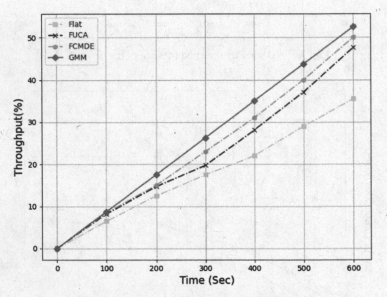

Fig. 9. A measure of the network's throughput.

8 Conclusions

In this research, a new clustering methodology based on Gaussian mixture models (GMM) for WSN was presented. The proposed approach minimizes expenses while maximizing efficiency and extending service life. During clustering, the approach selects a CH using a combination of GMM, node location, and residual power. The proposed method's efficacy has been shown via extensive simulation employing a wide range of evaluation performance metrics. One example is the average amount of energy used, while others include the stability and lifespan of the network. The suggested method was shown to be better by a comparative study of current techniques. Future projects, In order to choose the cluster head, we want to utilize an optimization approach. Also, we plan to propose a new method for scheduling the sensor node's work based on the spatial correlation.

References

1. Saeedi, I.D.I., Al-Qurabat, A.K.M.: An energy-saving data aggregation method for wireless sensor networks based on the extraction of extrema points. In: Proceeding of the 1st International Conference on Advanced Research in Pure and Applied Science (Icarpas2021): Third Annual Conference of Al-Muthanna University/College of Science, vol. 2398, no. 1, p. 050004 (2022)
2. Abdulzahra, S.A., Al-Qurabat, A.K.M.: Data aggregation mechanisms in wireless sensor networks of IoT: a survey. Int. J. Comput. Digit. Syst. **13**(1), 1–15 (2023)
3. Al-Qurabat, A.K.M., Abdulzahra, S.A.: An overview of periodic wireless sensor networks to the internet of things. In: IOP Conference Series: Materials Science and Engineering, vol. 928, no. 3, p. 32055 (2020)
4. Saeedi, I.D.I., Al-Qurabat, A.K.M.: A systematic review of data aggregation techniques in wireless sensor networks. In: Journal of Physics: Conference Series, vol. 1818, no. 1, p. 12194 (2021)
5. Al-Qurabat, A.K.M., Mohammed, Z.A., Hussein, Z.J.: Data traffic management based on compression and MDL techniques for smart agriculture in IoT. Wirel. Pers. Commun. **120**(3), 2227–2258 (2021)
6. Al-Qurabat, A.K.M.: A lightweight Huffman-based differential encoding lossless compression technique in IoT for smart agriculture. Int. J. Comput. Digit. Syst. **11**(1), 117–127 (2021)
7. Panchal, A., Singh, R.K.: EHCR-FCM: energy efficient hierarchical clustering and routing using fuzzy C-means for wireless sensor networks. Telecommun. Syst. **76**(2), 251–263 (2020). https://doi.org/10.1007/s11235-020-00712-7
8. Naeem, A., Gul, H., Arif, A., Fareed, S., Anwar, M., Javaid, N.: Short-term load forecasting using EEMD-DAE with enhanced CNN in smart grid. In: Barolli, L., Amato, F., Moscato, F., Enokido, T., Takizawa, M. (eds.) WAINA 2020. AISC, vol. 1150, pp. 1167–1180. Springer, Cham (2020). https://doi.org/10.1007/978-3-030-44038-1_107
9. Najar, F., Bourouis, S., Bouguila, N., Belghith, S.: A comparison between different Gaussian-based mixture models. In: 2017 IEEE/ACS 14th International Conference on Computer Systems and Applications (AICCSA), pp. 704–708. IEEE (2017)
10. Gupta, S., Bhatia, V.: GMMC: Gaussian mixture model based clustering hierarchy protocol in wireless sensor network. Int. J. Sci. Eng. Res. (IJSER) **3**(7), 2347–3878 (2014)
11. Tsiligaridis, J., Flores, C.: Reducing energy consumption for distributed em-based clustering in wireless sensor networks. Procedia Comput. Sci. **83**, 313–320 (2016)
12. Houriya, H., Mohsen, J., Saeedreza, S.: Correction to: improving lifetime of wireless sensor networks based on nodes' distribution using Gaussian mixture model in multi-mobile sink approach. Telecommun. Syst. **77**(1), 269 (2021)
13. Al-Janabi, D.T.A., Hammood, D.A., Hashem, S.A.: Extending WSN life-time using energy efficient based on K-means clustering method. In: Chaubey, N., Thampi, S.M., Jhanjhi, N.Z. (eds.) COMS2 2022. CCIS, vol. 1604, pp. 141–154. Springer, Cham (2022). https://doi.org/10.1007/978-3-031-10551-7_11
14. Chaubey, N.K., Patel, D.H.: Energy efficient clustering algorithm for decreasing energy consumption and delay in wireless sensor networks (WSN). Energy **4**(5), 8652–8656 (2016)

15. Moghadaszadeh, M., Shokrzadeh, H.: An efficient clustering algorithm based on expectation maximization algorithm in wireless sensor network. In: 10th International Conference on Innovations in Science, Engineering, Computers and Technology (ISECT 2017) Dubai (UAE), pp. 19–25 (2017)

16. Engineering, T., Panchal, A., Singh, A.K.: LEACH based clustering technique in wireless sensor network. Test Eng. Manag. **82**, 4185–4188 (2020)

17. Agrawal, D., Pandey, S.: FUCA: fuzzy-based unequal clustering algorithm to prolong the lifetime of wireless sensor networks. Int. J. Commun. Syst. **31**(2), e3448 (2018)

18. Abdulzahra, A.M.K., Al-Qurabat, A.K.M.: A clustering approach based on fuzzy C-means in wireless sensor networks for IoT applications. Karbala Int. J. Mod. Sci. **8**(4), 579–595 (2022)

19. Bagci, F.: Energy-efficient communication protocol for wireless sensor networks. Ad-Hoc Sens. Wirel. Netw. **30**(3–4), 301–322 (2016)

20. Wang, N., Zhu, H.: An energy efficient algorithm based on LEACH protocol. In: 2012 International Conference on Computer Science and Electronics Engineering, vol. 2, pp. 339–342. IEEE (2012)

21. Liu, Z., Song, Y.-Q., Xie, C.-H., Tang, Z.: A new clustering method of gene expression data based on multivariate Gaussian mixture models. SIViP **10**(2), 359–368 (2015). https://doi.org/10.1007/s11760-015-0749-5

22. Kim, H.-J., Cavanaugh, J.E., Dallas, T.A., Foré, S.A.: Model selection criteria for overdispersed data and their application to the characterization of a host-parasite relationship. Environ. Ecol. Stat. **21**(2), 329–350 (2013). https://doi.org/10.1007/s10651-013-0257-0

23. Vashishth, V., Chhabra, A., Sharma, D.K.: GMMR: a Gaussian mixture model based unsupervised machine learning approach for optimal routing in opportunistic IoT networks. Comput. Commun. **134**, 138–148 (2019)

Physical Layer Security Optimisation for NOMA Based UAV Communication for Optimal Resource Allocation

Monali Prajapati[1]($\boxtimes$) and Pramod Tripathi[2]($\boxtimes$)

[1] Electronics and Communication, Government Polytechnic Gandhinagar, Sector 26, Gandhinagar 382025, Gujarat, India
monalimandli79@gmail.com

[2] Information and Technology, Government Polytechnic Gandhinagar, Sector 26, Gandhinagar 382025, Gujarat, India
csharp.pramod@gmail.com

Abstract. Unmanned aerial vehicles (UAVs) have become increasingly popular for wireless communication due to their mobility, versatility in deployment, and economic advantages, particularly in catastrophic weather event scenarios and vital military operations. The utilization of Non-Orthogonal Multiple Access(NOMA) has been efficiently done to enhance channel utilization. Multiple users transmit information using similar frequency bands. This technique is helpful in enhancing the performance of UAV communication. It helps in enhancing achievable rate and robustness. Non Orthogonal as compared to the orthogonal multiple access technique provides improved spectral efficiency, reduced latency, expanded coverage, enhanced connectivity, and improved fairness. However, non-orthogonal techniques are less secure. An interceptor can intercept a transmission and can access information of multiple users that are accessing the same resources. To circumvent such issues much emphasis has been given to the physical layer. The popular matrices that are used for such a system are the probability of a link going down and the likelihood of a communication interception. This study examines the practicality of pairing trustworthy and untrustworthy users, as well as the impact of optimal power allocation coefficients using tabulation and belief MDP methods. The findings of the simulation research suggest that belief MDP is a feasible approach for enabling user pairings that are attainable while adhering to the Secrecy Outage Probability (SecOP) constraint of trusted users, thereby optimizing resource allocation efficiency.

Keywords: belief-MDP · tabulation · NOMA · Security

1 Introduction

UAV-based communication networks have garnered substantial interest and are currently the subject of extensive exploration in the existing body of literature.

N. Chaubey et al. (Eds.): COMS2 2023, CCIS 1861, pp. 133–147, 2023.
https://doi.org/10.1007/978-3-031-40564-8_10

The versatility of deploying UAVs presents possibilities for improving the coverage area, throughput, and energy efficiency of communication systems enabled by UAVs. This can be achieved through strategic placement of UAVs, controlling beam width, and optimizing power allocation. Exhibiting different approach from traditional communication where multi-antenna arrays exploit spatial diversity in a rich scattering environment, UAV-enabled downlink communication experiences limited scattering, making a single-antenna UAV the preferred choice.

In multi user scenarios a user associated with a particular UAV with a specific time slot receives a share of bandwidth. Typically performance of communication degrades as the number of users' increases. To achieve an optimal downlink communication the possible way is to increase number of transmit antennas so that served users must a one to one correspondence.

Non orthogonal techniques as mentioned serves many users in a parallel by utilizing power domain partitioning. Users out of vicinity gets benefitted by non-orthogonal techniques and thus receives desired rate. The technique followed by non-orthogonal method is to allow close users access information of distant users. There are various studies that shows the use of non-orthogonal methods can enhance performance of communication of network consist of unmanned aerial vehicles.

In [1] author has discussed the efficiency of non-orthogonal technique in the power domain. The author specifies the security challenges observed in the non-orthogonal process. The primary reason for security issues is due to the broadcast nature of the transmitter and decoding process involving successive interference cancellation (SIC) at the receiver. The combination of non-orthogonal methods and security implemented at the physical layer results in spectral efficiency as well as security however it poses various research gaps.

The design of integrated non-orthogonal methods and physical layer security techniques faces the challenge of wiretapping in the presence of untrusted users. To attain the desired level of physical layer security, it is crucial to jointly optimize multiple relevant parameters, including Pair Outage Probability and SOP, specifically for multi-UAV communications. This paper formulates a system model for two-user NOMA with two UAVs (one trusted and one untrusted user), based on their respective distances from the base station, as discussed in Sect. 3. Section 4 discussed the simulation of the proposed framework and the results obtained. We conclude the work in the last section.

2   Related Work

In [2], Extensive discussions have taken place regarding the open research challenges in the optimization and communication aspects of UAV networks. In [3] The topic of secure NOMA with multiple users in the presence of eavesdroppers has been thoroughly explored. Author has taken a network type where there is a single input to process at a time. In [4] cooperative non-orthogonal system is discussed. Such system has decode-and-forward as well as amplify-and-forward relays. The ways of dealing with eavesdropping threats have been discussed in detail. In [2], open research issues in Optimization and Communication in UAV Networks have been thoroughly discussed. In [3] the topic of safeguarding multiple users in Secure non-orthogonal networks against eavesdroppers has been a subject of discussion. In [4] the analysis of the security aspects of a cooperative NOMA (Non-Orthogonal Multiple Access) system, employing both decode-and-forward and amplify-and-forward relays, against eavesdroppers has been conducted. Apart from the primary concern of eavesdroppers author states that NOMA presents additional security challenges due to the receiver's decoding process, which relies on successive interference cancellation (SIC). In a recent work [5] the system under examination by the author involved a trusted near user and an assumed untrusted far user. The main emphasis was placed on analyzing the secrecy of the trusted user in relation to the untrusted node, while the secrecy of the untrusted user was disregarded. In [6] the researchers investigated a situation where a UAV-BS (Unmanned Aerial Vehicle Base Station) establishes communication with two ground users using NOMA. The main objective was to analyze the outage probability in this scenario. To achieve this, a UAV-BS equipped with multiple antennas was employed to create directional beams and serve multiple users. The goal was to maximize the cumulative outage rates of the users by utilizing NOMA and beam scanning techniques.

In [7], Extensive discussions have taken place regarding the optimization of capacity in next-generation UAV communication that incorporates Non-Orthogonal Multiple Access. The Authors in [8], [9] and [10] have introduced a range of diverse resource optimization algorithms specifically designed for UAV networks. However, there exists an urgent need, particularly in emergency applications, to enhance the Physical Layer Security (PLS) specifically for NOMA transmission in UAV communication. Most of the existing studies have predominantly concentrated on optimizing and enhancing PLS efficiency when addressing untrusted relay nodes and external eavesdroppers. In [11] Tthe focus of the discussion has revolved around improving Physical Layer Security (PLS) for NOMA transmission in mm-Wave drone networks. A noteworthy proposed solution involves optimizing the shape of the protected zone at various altitudes with the goal of maximizing NOMA secrecy rates. However, there is a lack of comprehensive theoretical studies that sufficiently address the feasibility of achieving enhanced efficiency when untrusted users are present. Consequently, there is a need to enhance the secrecy performance of wireless communication infrastructure when UAVs are connected to cellular networks. In [2] the researchers propose an aerial cooperative jamming scheme and conduct a study to determine its optimal design for achieving the maximum average secrecy rate.

NOMA has gained considerable recognition as a leading technology that incorporates various techniques with a shared objective of serving multiple users concurrently using the same frequency and time resources. Among the well-known NOMA types, code domain and power domain stand out for their ability to significantly improve efficiency compared to traditional methods. In this study, the transmitter side implemented the power domain approach using superposition coding, while the receiver side employed successive interference cancellation

(SIC). Consequently, users have access to the keys necessary to decode messages from other users, enabling them to effectively employ successive interference cancellation (SIC) to eliminate interference. In [12] the author's focus was on examining the impact of User Pairing on downlink transmissions utilizing 5G Non-Orthogonal Multiple Access (NOMA). The specific goal of the research was to develop a formulation for the data rate in multi-user NOMA scenarios.

In Existing literature, there are various NOMA-based methods enabling adjacent users to act as relays have been proposed. This has enhanced the efficiency of a user not in the vicinity by retransmitting data. The retransmitted data has been decoded and is being retransmitted in next time slot. Retransmission is done so that it may maximize signal-to-noise ratio and thus information from various time slots can be combined. The primary focus of the existing studies is to analyze the secrecy as well as outage parameters in the presence of an adversary. There is an immense requirement of analyzing the feasibility of required outage probability where the presence of a trusted user for a user pair is a constraint. One of the major challenges is untrusted users can become an eavesdropper by possessing decoding capabilities and spectrum sharing [1]. In [13] authors have investigated various techniques for adjusting power levels, including aided strategy, optimal power allocation, beamforming, and cooperative relaying. These techniques were explored with the aim of enhancing the secrecy of NOMA against external eavesdroppers. It has been found that untrusted user has critical issues to consider the access privileges between near and far users. This poses a significant security concern in NOMA implementation. In [5], the study made an assumption that only the far users were untrusted, and thus, the analysis of secrecy performance focused solely on the trusted (near) users. The primary objective of the investigation was to evaluate the possibility of attaining optimal outage performance for the user pair, while simultaneously meeting the secrecy outage constraint for the stronger user. In [14], The author's main focus was to examine the optimal coordination of UAVs for target tracking using tabulation. The research specifically investigated a scenario where two camera-equipped UAVs synchronized their movements to track a single target in motion on the ground. In [15], the problem of maximizing long-term cluster throughput is formulated as an optimization problem. To address this a grant-free orthogonal method is proposed that uses deep learning methods. In [16] author presents an algorithm that learns about the network contention status, allowing for subchannel and received power level selections to minimize collisions. This paper focuses specifically on optimizing the power allocation factor for Link OP and the secrecy outage probability of User1 as a research problem. The tabulation and belief Markov Decision Process (BMDP) algorithms are analyzed and compared to achieve enhanced performance.

3   System Model and Optimisation

Figure 1 illustrates a reference technique, known as NOMA-based cellular architecture, which enables multiple users to share the radio resources.

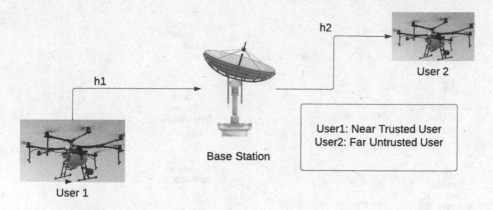

Fig. 1. Two user NOMA based UAV Communication Model.

In [5] author assumes the channel characteristic of Rayleigh fading. The main objective of the study was to optimize the key performance parameters related to physical layer security. The parameters that were used were Link Outage probability [5] between two users, namely, User1 considered as the trusted near user and User2 considered as the untrusted user, as well as a probability measure known as the Secrecy Outage Probability (SecOP) [5] associated with User 1. The goal was to achieve an optimal Pair(OP) while adhering to the specified SecOP constraint for user1. This optimization is essential for effectively allocating network resources to both users while ensuring the confidentiality of the trusted user1.

In this study we have validated the mathematical analysis presented in the reference literature [5]. We have proposed the joint optimization of Pair Outage Probability (Pair OP) and Secrecy Outage Probability (SecOP). The research extends the existing literature by introducing a more efficient approach to resource allocation through Joint Optimization, which involves optimizing the allocated power factor. In this study, tabulation and a belief MDP(BMDP) algorithm are employed, presenting a novel and enhanced method for resource allocation in a specific scenario. Initially, the impact of varying distances between the base station (BS) and the untrusted user2 is simulated. This distance plays a crucial role in influencing both Pair OP and SOP for user1, serving as a critical parameter for selection. The analysis primarily focuses on identifying feasible and infeasible pairings between trusted and untrusted users. Subsequently, the research focuses on addressing the optimal power allocation factor as a constrained problem for feasible pairings. The BMDP algorithm is utilized to optimize the power allocation factor, ensuring strict adherence to the Sum of Power (SOP) requirement for user U1. Figure 3 illustrates the proposed flow of the BMDP algorithm, demonstrating its utilization of the available channel state information, it showcases how it calculates the optimal power allocation factor for pairings between benign and malicious users.

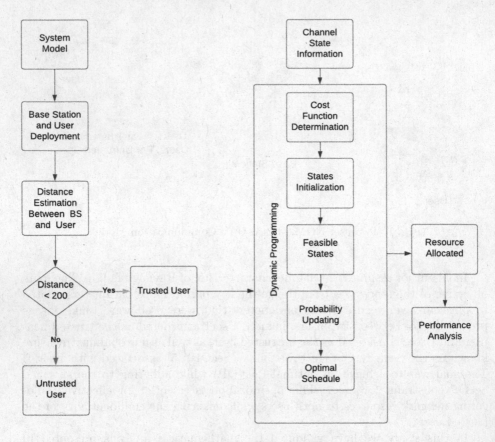

Fig. 2. Tabulation Optimisation.

The proposed optimization overall flow of work is shown in Fig. 2 and Fig. 3 as following

Upon establishing the base station, the distance between the user and the base station is assessed. If the measured distance falls below a predefined safety threshold, the user is categorized as a trusted user. On the other hand, if the distance exceeds the safe threshold, the user is considered an untrusted user. For untrusted users, The channel state information is utilized in optimization techniques such as tabulation and Contextual Decision-making Process (CDP), which are then followed by resource allocation based on the obtained results. The performance analysis is conducted based on the theoretical formulation of Pair Outage Probability (Pair OP) [5] and Secrecy Outage Probability (SecOP) derivation. The nearby user, often referred to as the adjacent or near user, possesses a higher level of security clearance necessary for physical layer security. Ensuring utmost security becomes crucial in protecting against potential threats posed by the low-security or untrusted user2, who is situated at a significant distance from the base station.

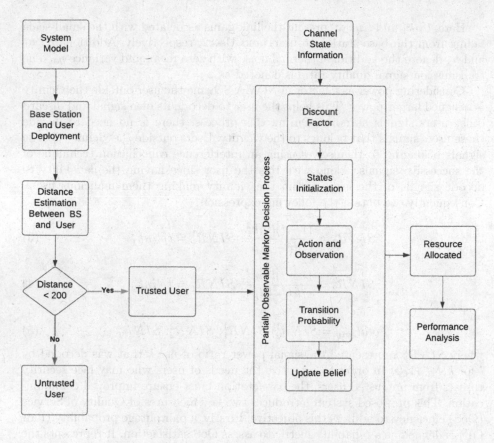

Fig. 3. belief MDP optimisation.

P_0 Denote the pinnacle power limit of the base station. In this study, it is assumed that each network node possesses a solitary antenna, and all channels are deemed uniform and autonomously quasi-static, conforming to a Rayleigh distribution. The distances between the base station and the nodes User1 and User2 are denoted as d_1 and d_2, respectively. The propagation exponent and distance-dependent attenuation parameter are represented as δ_m and ω_0, respectively. Moreover, it is presupposed that the base station possesses an awareness of the user positions, facilitating enhanced communication link condition acquisition for user pairing. The base station emits a compounded blend.

$$x_t = \sqrt{t}S_1 + \sqrt{1-t}S_2 \tag{1}$$

User1 receives a unit power signal denoted as S1, while User2 receives a unit power signal denoted as S2. The power allocation coefficient for the adjacent user is represented by "t" and satisfies the condition of $0 < t < 0.5$. The received signal at both users can be expressed as follows:

$$r_1 = link_1 x_t \sqrt{P_0} + n_1, r_2 = link_2 x_t \sqrt{P_0} + n_2 \tag{2}$$

Here, $link_1$ and $link_2$ represent the link gains associated with the small-scale fading from the base station to user1 and User2, respectively. Additionally, n_1 and n_2 denote the additional thermal noise with zero mean and variance η_0. The transmission signal quality ratio is denoted as $\rho = \frac{P_0}{\eta_0}$.

Considering power as a factor in NOMA Scheme the user outside the vicinity is assigned larger power. This helps the user to decode its own signal and discard other users signals as noise. During this process, there is no need to decode those users signals that belongs to the vicinity. Users outside the vicinity decode signals belonging to themselves using an interference cancellation technique of the successive signals. Along with this the user since having the capability to decode signals of the users within the vicinity making them malicious users. Consequently, we obtain the following expression:

$$SINR_2^1 = \frac{(1-t)link_1^2}{th_1^2 + 1/\rho}, \ SINR_1^1 = t\rho link_1^2 \tag{3}$$

$$SINR_2^2 = \frac{(1-t)link_2^2}{th_2^2 + 1/\rho}, \ SINR_1^2 = t\rho link_2^2 \tag{4}$$

and

$$Total_{sinr} = SINR_2^1; \ SINR_1^1; \ SINR_2^2; \ SINR_1^2 \tag{5}$$

where, $SINR_l^k$ represented the signal power ratio of use k that was decoded by l for $k, l \in (1, 2)$ In order to prioritize the needs of users who may face security threats from untrusted users, the base station must ensure improved communication. This proposed system introduces two key measures of Quality of Service (QoS) efficiency to address this objective. Firstly, a pair outage probability (Pair OP) is defined as a reliability metric to assess QoS satisfaction. It represents the probability that the achievable data rates for users meet or exceed a specified target threshold. Additionally, the Secrecy Outage Probability (SecOP) is introduced as another metric. SOP quantifies the likelihood that the non-negative secrecy capacity of the trusted user exceeds a predefined threshold value. This metric quantifies the level of security achieved by the trusted user. The research problem at hand focuses on optimizing the reduction of the link outage probability between two users while ensuring that the desired threshold value for the Secrecy Outage Probability of User1 (SecOP1) is achieved. This optimization objective is crucial for enhancing security. The main objective is to minimize Pair OP while taking into account the SecOP factor for user U1, as specified by the system.

$$\min_t P_0 \tag{6}$$

Subjected to $0 < t < 0.5$, and $SOP_1 \leq \beta$ in which P_0, SecOP1 and β are the link OP, SecOP(User1) and allowable threshold for the SecOP. By employing Shannon's capacity formula and taking into account the capacity thresholds of User1 and User2 as $C_1^t h$, $C_2^t h$, respectively, the SeOP of the NOMA pair could therefore be derived as shown in [5],

$$p_q = \{1 - f(t0)k_1(t0), 1 - f(t0)k_2(t0) \tag{7}$$

where $\frac{\tau_1}{\tau_1+\tau_2+\tau_1\tau_2} < t0 < 1 + \tau_2$ and, $0 < t0 < \frac{\tau_1}{\tau_1+\tau_2+\tau_1\tau_2}$ and,

$$f(t) = \exp\frac{-\tau_2}{\rho\zeta_2}\frac{1}{1-t\tau_2} \tag{8}$$

$$k_1(t) = \exp\frac{-\tau_2}{\rho\zeta_1}\frac{1}{1-t\tau_2} \tag{9}$$

$$k_2(t) = \exp\frac{-\tau_1}{\rho\zeta_1} \tag{10}$$

and Given the considering the non-negative secrecy capacity, the SOP of U1 can be given by

$$SOP_1 = 1 - \nu e^{\frac{-A}{\zeta_1}} \tag{11}$$

where $A = \frac{2^{T_s}-1}{t\rho}$ and $\nu = \frac{\zeta_1}{\zeta_1+\zeta_2 2^{T_s}}$ where Ts is defined as the target secrecy rate. Thus we can design outage optimal power allocation factor under such threshold constraints denoted as t^*. The Outage Probability of the NOMA pair is a concavity coefficient in terms of the power allocation factor t, and the optimized outage probability of the NOMA pair keeping Secrecy as constraint is shown in Eq. (6). The required condition is $0 < t_{sop} \leq t^*$. User1's SOP (Sum of Power) exhibits a continuous decrease as a function of the relevant parameters of t, Consequently, this results in the determination of the optimal power allocation factor t^* states that it must be larger than t_{sop} to ensure the compliance with the secrecy constraint. Condition to maintain secrecy and keeping outage low is $0 < t_{sop} \leq t^*$.

4 Simulaton Result and Discussion

The theoretical analysis discussed in Sect. 3 is implemented through simulations using MATLAB 2021b Version. The simulation employs the parameters listed in Table 1 to investigate the impact of increasing the distance between the untrusted user and the base station on the secrecy outage probability (SecOP) of the trusted nearby user. The simulations vary parameters such as Signal-to-Interference-plus-Noise Ratio (SINR) and target secrecy rate to observe their respective effects.

Additionally, the study explores the impact of selecting an optimal power allocation coefficient factor on the feasibility of pairings between trusted and untrusted users, while maintaining the desired SOP constraint for the trusted user. This is accomplished by employing tabulation and belief MDP optimization algorithms. A comparative analysis is conducted, considering the presence of either a passive internal eavesdropper or an external eavesdropper as the untrusted user.

Table 1. Simulation Parameters.

Notation	Parameter	Value
m	No of users	2
α	Path loss exponent	2
ω_0	Path loss constant	0.1
B	Bandwidth	100 KHz
Ts	Target Secrecy Rate	0.01
t	Power allocation coefficient	0.15
β	Sop constraint constant threshold	0.1
ρ	BS transmit signal-to-noise ratio (SNR)	0.15

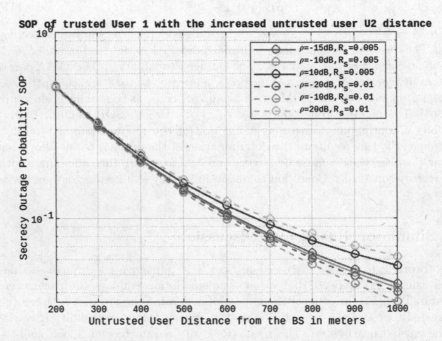

Fig. 4. Impact of increasing untrusted user distance from base station upon SOP of the trusted user for varying SNR and target secrecy rate parameters for DP Optimisation.

As shown in Fig. 4 and 5, optimization of the Secrecy and Outage Probability parameters for the users belonging in the vicinity has shown a significant performance improvement by using tabulation and belief MDP. We have increased the distance of base station and the user within vicinity during the process. The study considers various channel conditions and three different Signal-to-Noise Ratio (SNR) values: −15, −10, and 10, as well as varying target secrecy rate constraints (Ts) of 0.005 and 0.01 for the two users.

Both sets of results indicate that the SOP for User1 is a gradually decreasing function with respect to the distance of the untrusted user2 from the base station.

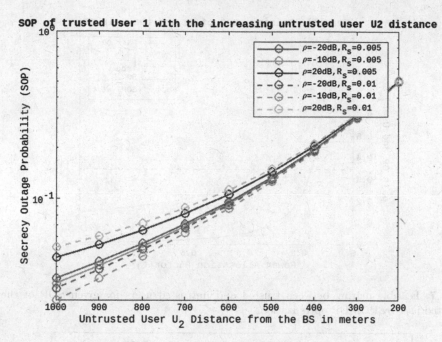

Fig. 5. Impact of increasing untrusted user distance from base station upon SOP of the trusted user for varying SNR and target secrecy rate parameters for POMDP Optimisation.

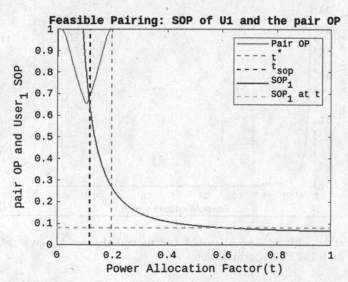

Fig. 6. Feasible pairing between trusted and untrusted users for given SOP of the trusted user by tabulation optimisation.

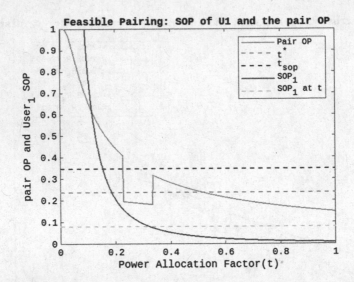

Fig. 7. Feasible pairing between trusted and untrusted users for given SOP of the trusted user by POMDP optimization.

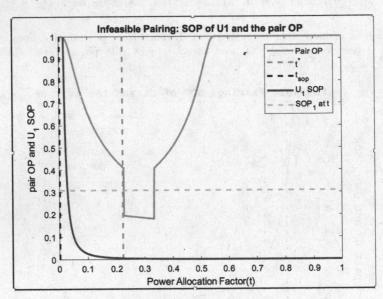

Fig. 8. Infeasible pairing between trusted and untrusted users for given SOP of the trusted user by belief MDP optimization.

This implies that increasing the distance between the untrusted user and the base station improves the SecOP of User1. As the provided SecOP threshold (β) serves as a constraint for feasible pairing of both users, the optimal value of the

SOP for the untrusted user2 must be larger than the threshold value to achieve the desired SOP for User1.

Additionally, it is expected that a higher target secrecy rate (Ts) will result in a higher SecOP for User1.

The conventional Dynamic Programming (CDP) optimization approach is designed to search for optimal policies across all possible states. However, in many cases, this exhaustive search is unnecessary. Often, when the initial and goal states are known, only a small subset of states is relevant to solving the problem. In such situations, the effort spent updating irrelevant states becomes wasteful. In contrast, belief MDP optimization approach allows agents to operate with incomplete information about the environment state. This approach has been shown to significantly enhance performance, as demonstrated in Figs. 4 and 5. Therefore, when analyzing the feasibility and infeasibility of pairing between the two users, the BMDP optimization method is more suitable. It allows for more efficient computation by focusing on the relevant states, considering the agents' incomplete knowledge of the environment.

For feasible Pairing simulation related to SecOP of link OP and User1 considering improved power allocation factor th parameters as kept as dist2 = 700 m, dist1 = 200 m, ρ = 15 decibles and β is 0.1. The results depicted that the link OP and SecOP of user1 diminishes as the power allocation factor of the untrusted user increases. The findings depicted in Figs. 6 and 7 affirm the concave curvature of both the link OP curve and the SecOP curve, as they exhibit a gradual decrease corresponding to the optimal power allocation coefficient factor th. In most instances, it has been noted that as th increases, the power allocated to the weaker user message decreases, aiming to mitigate user2's ability to discern the stronger signals. This, in turn, enhances the SecOP of User1. In Fig. 5 it is clearly evident that the value of t_{sop}, denoted by the black dotted line is above t^*, which strengthens the feasibility of the secrecy factor. The red marked line denotes the power allocation factor. The curve shows the optimal power supply keeping outage effect negligible. The green dotted line states the SecOP of User1 at $t = t^*$ is substantially low than the threshold value, β is 0.1 in this case.

Additionally, to investigate the impracticable pairing of SecOP and the pair outage probability of User 1, we have systematically varied the power allocation coefficient. For user1 we kept distance as 200 m and kept user2 at a fairly closer distance of 300 m. This distance was 700 meters in earlier case. As shown in Fig. 8 the secrecy of User1 is compromised when the SOP exceeds the desired threshold. It is noted that the performance of the proposed system model is contingent upon the relative positions of the two users with respect to the base station (BS).

5   Conclusion

This paper introduces a proposal for attaining physical layer security in power-domain Non-Orthogonal methods having two user scenarios. The study focuses specifically on utilizing non-orthogonal methods in dynamic communication models. The proposed technique focuses on addressing a menace where the base station establishes communication between trusted and untrusted users. To address this problem, tabulation and Beleif MDP optimization approaches are employed. Through simulations and analysis, it is demonstrated that joint optimization of the Pair Outage Probability (pair OP) and power allocation coefficient in the power domain non-orthogonal systems enable the feasible pairing of both users without compromising the security of trustworthy users. This ensures robust and secure communication. Moreover, the use of BMDP optimization has shown significant improvements in achieving the desired performance, therefore enhancing the system's security and efficiency.

References

1. Dai, L., Wang, B., Ding, Z., Wang, Z., Chen, S., Hanzo, L.: A survey of non-orthogonal multiple access for 5G. IEEE Commun. Surv. Tutor. **20**(3), 2294–2323 (2018)
2. Sun, H., Duo, B., Wang, Z., Lin, X., Gao, C.: Aerial cooperative jamming for cellular-enabled UAV secure communication network: joint trajectory and power control design. Sensors **19**(20) (2019). https://doi.org/10.3390/s19204440
3. Zhang, Y., Wang, H.-M., Yang, Q., Ding, Z.: Secrecy sum rate maximization in non-orthogonal multiple access. IEEE Commun. Lett. **20**(5), 930–933 (2016). https://doi.org/10.1109/LCOMM.2016.2539162
4. Chen, J., Yang, L., Alouini, M.-S.: Physical layer security for cooperative NOMA systems. IEEE Trans. Veh. Technol. **67**(5), 4645–4649 (2018). https://doi.org/10.1109/TVT.2017.2789223
5. ElHalawany, B.M., Wu, K.: Physical-layer security of NOMA systems under untrusted users, pp. 1–6. IEEE (2018). https://doi.org/10.1109/GLOCOM.2018.8647889
6. Nasir, A.A., Tuan, H.D., Duong, T.Q., Poor, H.V.: UAV-enabled communication using NOMA. IEEE Trans. Commun. **67**, 5126–5138 (2019). https://doi.org/10.1109/TCOMM.2019.2906622
7. Sarfraz, M., et al.: Capacity optimization of next-generation UAV communication involving non-orthogonal multiple access. Drones **6**, 234 (2022). https://doi.org/10.3390/drones6090234
8. Mahmood, A., Usman, M.Q., Shahzad, K., Saddique, N.: Evolution of optimal 3D placement of UAV with minimum transmit power. Int. J. Wirel. Commun. Mob. Comput. **7**, 13 (2019). https://doi.org/10.11648/j.wcmc.20190701.12
9. Sohail, M.F., Leow, C.Y., Won, S.: A cat swarm optimization based transmission power minimization for an aerial NOMA communication system. Veh. Commun. **33**, 100426 (2022). https://doi.org/10.1016/j.vehcom.2021.100426
10. Zeng, Y., Zhang, R.: Energy-efficient UAV communication with trajectory optimization. IEEE Trans. Wirel. Commun. **16**, 3747–3760 (2017). https://doi.org/10.1109/TWC.2017.2688328
11. Rupasinghe, N., Yapici, Y., Guvenc, I., Dai, H., Bhuyan, A.: Enhancing physical layer security for NOMA transmission in mmwave drone networks, pp. 729–733. IEEE (2018). https://doi.org/10.1109/ACSSC.2018.8645326
12. Ding, Z., Fan, P., Poor, H.V.: Impact of user pairing on 5G nonorthogonal multiple-access downlink transmissions. IEEE Trans. Veh. Technol. **65**, 6010–6023 (2016). https://doi.org/10.1109/TVT.2015.2480766

13. Patel, P.: Migration from 4G LTE to advanced PHY techniques for unmanned aerial vehicle (UAV) communication. Int. J. Eng. Res. Appl. **9**, 49–54 (2019)
14. Quintero, S.A.P., Papi, F., Klein, D.J., Chisci, L., Hespanha, J.P.: Optimal UAV coordination for target tracking using dynamic programming. In: 49th IEEE Conference on Decision and Control (CDC), pp. 4541–4546 (2010). https://doi.org/10.1109/CDC.2010.5717933
15. Zhang, J., Tao, X., Wu, H., Zhang, N., Zhang, X.: Deep reinforcement learning for throughput improvement of uplink grant-free NOMA system. IEEE Internet Things J. 1 (2020). https://doi.org/10.1109/JIOT.2020.2972274
16. Thapar, S., Mishra, D., Saini, R.: Secrecy fairness aware NOMA for untrusted users. In: 2019 IEEE Global Communications Conference (GLOBECOM), pp. 1–6 (2019). https://doi.org/10.1109/GLOBECOM38437.2019.9014034

DBFEH: Design of a Deep-Learning-Based Bioinspired Model to Improve Feature Extraction Capabilities of Healthcare Device Sets

Vonteru Srikanth Reddy ⓘ and Kumar Debasis$^{(\boxtimes)}$ ⓘ

School of Computer Science and Engineering, VIT-AP University, Amaravati, Andhra
Pradesh 522237, India
{Srikanth.21phd7015,Kumar.debasis}@vitap.ac.in

Abstract. Extraction of features from healthcare devices requires the efficient
deployment of high-sample rate components. A wide variety of deep learning
models are proposed for this task, and each of these models showcases non-
uniform performance & complexity levels when applied to real-time scenarios.
To overcome such issues, this text proposes the design of a deep-learning-based
bioinspired model that assists in improving the feature extraction capabilities of
healthcare device sets. The model uses Elephant Herding Optimization (EHO) for
real-time control of data rate & feature-extraction process. The collected samples
are processed via an Augmented 1D Convolutional Neural Network (AOD CNN)
model, which assists in the identification of different healthcare conditions. The
accuracy of the proposed AOD CNN is optimized via the same EHO process
via iterative learning operations. Due to adaptive data-rate control, the model is
capable of performing temporal learning for the identification of multiple disease
progressions. These progressions are also evaluated via the 1D CNN model, which
can be tuned for heterogeneous disease types. Due to the integration of these
methods, the proposed model is able to improve classification accuracy by 2.5%,
while reducing the delay needed for data collection by 8.3%, with an improvement
in temporal disease detection accuracy of 5.4% when compared with standard
feature classification techniques. This assists in deploying the model for a wide
variety of clinical scenarios.

Keywords: Healthcare · Bioinspired · Augmented · 1D CNN · EHO

1 Introduction

The Internet of Things is crucial to many different aspects of contemporary life [1].
Smart cities, intelligent healthcare, and intelligent monitoring are some examples of
IoT applications. Because of the many ways they may improve patient care, artificial
intelligence (AI) and the Internet of Things (IoT) have seen explosive growth in the
healthcare industry. It offers a broad variety of image processing, machine learning, and
deep learning approaches, as well as solutions that assist service providers and patients

in improving healthcare outcomes across a number of different industries. One of the most exciting and potentially fruitful fields of medical research is the examination of medical images [2]. Methods [3] have been investigated for use in a wide variety of medical imaging applications, ranging from the collection of images to the processing of images to the assessment of prognoses. In the process of analysing medical healthcare device scans, huge volumes of quantitative data may be acquired and retrieved for use in a variety of diagnostic applications. These approaches may also be used in the analysis of medical healthcare device scans. Scanners for medical equipment are becoming more important diagnostic instruments in many hospitals and other healthcare institutions [4]. It is inexpensive and has enormous therapeutic benefits in the diagnosis of certain infectious lung disorders [5], such as pneumonia, tuberculosis (TB), early lung cancer, and, most recently, COVID-19. Some examples of these diseases include the: This dreadful pandemic has started to spread around the globe ever since the new COVID-19 was discovered in December 2019. The respiratory infectious virus that is the root cause of this fatal illness represents a considerable risk to the health of the general population. In March of the year 2020, the World Health Organization (WHO) declared that the epidemic had reached the point where it could be considered a full-fledged pandemic because of how quickly it had spread. There are more than 50 million confirmed cases of COVID-19 in the globe, as reported by the World Health Organization (WHO). In order to monitor the spread of the virus and help put a stop to it, the medical community is investigating the most cutting-edge treatments and technologies available. When evaluating COVID-19, it is usual practice to take into account symptoms, indications, and tests related to pneumonia, in addition to scans of various medical devices [6]. The identification of the COVID-19 virus requires the use of medical equipment scanners [7]. This document contains a lot much information pertaining to the health of the patient. In spite of this, one of the most difficult aspects of a doctor's job is to come to reasonable conclusions based on the information available. The overlapping tissue structure makes it far more difficult to interpret scans that are produced by medical equipment. Examining a lesion may be challenging if there is little contrast between the lesion and the surrounding tissue, or if the site of the lesion overlaps with the ribs or pulmonary blood veins. Both of these situations make it more difficult to examine the lesion. Even for a physician with years of expertise, it might be challenging to differentiate between tumours that at first glance seem to be quite different from one another or to detect particularly intricate nodules. As a result, the examination of lung sickness using medical device scans will result in false negatives. The appearance of white spots or viruses on medical device scans is another possible obstacle for the radiologist, as it may lead to the incorrect diagnosis of illnesses such as pneumonia and pulmonary sickness such as COVID-19. Researchers are increasingly employing computer vision, machine learning, and deep learning to understand medical imagery, such as scans from medical devices for infectious illnesses [8]. This trend is expected to continue in the near future. These newly discovered approaches may be of assistance to medical professionals or doctors, as they have the potential to automatically identify the infection in scans of medical healthcare equipment. This would improve the treatment test procedure and lessen the amount of labour required. The early detection of illness via the use of these cutting-edge approaches contributes to the overall reduction in death rates. Using a smart healthcare system that is enabled by the Internet of Things (IoT), it is possible to identify infectious illnesses such as COVID-19 and pneumonia in scans of medical healthcare devices. This system was conceptualized as a direct consequence of the enhanced performance outcomes achieved by preceding systems. Transfer learning is combined with the use of two different deep learning architectures, namely VGG-19 [9] and Inception-V3 [10]. Because these designs have been trained in the past on the ImageNet data set, it is possible that they use the concept of multiple-feature fusion and selection [11]. In the course of our investigation, we made use of a method for object categorisation that is analogous to the multiple feature fusion and selection strategy that is presented in [12, 13]. In a range of applications, such as those dealing with object classification and medical imaging, this concept has been put into reality by merging numerous feature vectors into a single feature vector or space via Support Vector Machines (SVM) [14, 15]. These applications include those dealing with object classification. Using the feature selection approach, it is also possible to get rid of features in the fused vector sets that aren't necessary. As a consequence of this, a variety of deep learning models have been developed for this purpose. When applied to real-world settings, each of these models demonstrates dramatically variable degrees of performance as well as levels of complexity. In the next portion of this text, a proposal is made to construct a deep learning-based bioinspired model in order to solve the challenges that have been raised and to enhance the ability of healthcare device sets to extract features. In Sect. 4, performance assessments of the proposed model were carried out. The accuracy and latency of the proposed model were compared to those of state-of-the-art approaches for feature representation and classification. In the concluding part, the author provides some observations that are context-specific about the model that has been provided and offers some suggestions as to how it might be improved further for use in clinical settings.

2 Literature Survey

The study of medical images is a topic of medical research consider one of the most interesting and potentially lucrative areas in the profession [2, 3]. Methods have been researched for potential use in a wide range of medical imaging applications, ranging from the acquisition of images through the processing of those images to the evaluation of prognoses. The precision of diagnostics is going to be improved as a direct result of this research. Huge amounts of quantitative data may be acquired and retrieved when analyzing scans of medical and healthcare devices. This may be the case because of the nature of the data being collected. After then, this information may be put to use in a number of other diagnostic applications. The analysis of scans that were acquired by medical and healthcare equipment is another application that might make use of these approaches. Scanners that are traditionally employed as medical equipment are increasingly being put to use as diagnostic devices in a variety of hospitals and other types of healthcare facilities [4]. It is cost-effective and delivers considerable therapeutic advantages in the identification of numerous infectious lung illnesses, including pneumonia, tuberculosis (TB), early lung cancer, and, most recently, COVID-19. These diseases include: Some examples of these infectious lung disorders are pneumonia, tuberculosis (TB), and lung cancer in its early stages. The circumstances listed below are only a few examples; this is not an exhaustive list. This terrible epidemic has begun to spread over the whole world ever since the new COVID-19 strain was identified in December of 2019. The respiratory infectious virus that is the root cause of this potentially lethal disease poses a significant threat to the health of the general population. The World Health Organization (WHO) determined in March of the year 2020 that the illness had developed to the point where it could be categorized as a full-fledged pandemic [5]. This conclusion was reached as a direct result of the rapidity with which it had spread. This transpired as a consequence of the lightning-fast rate at which the illness had spread. According to the most recent statistics from the Globe Health Organization, more over 50 million confirmed cases of COVID-19 have been found in countries all over the world (WHO). In order to keep track of the virus's progression and do what they can to halt its further spread, the scientific community is doing research on the most innovative therapies and instruments that are now on the market. When doing an analysis of COVID-19, it is standard procedure to perform scans on a variety of medical equipment in addition to taking into consideration the signs, symptoms, and tests that are associated with pneumonia [6]. The use of scanners that are designed specifically for use in medical settings is required in order to achieve a positive identification of the COVID-19 virus [7]. This page contains a wealth of information that is directly applicable to the condition that the patient is in at the current time. Despite this, one of the most challenging components of a doctor's work is to be able to make sound judgments based on the data they have available to them. Because different tissue structures overlap, it is much more challenging for medical professionals to analyze scans provided by medical equipment. It may be difficult to evaluate the lesion if there is little difference between the lesion and the surrounding tissue, or if the position of the lesion overlaps with the ribs or pulmonary blood vessels. Under any of these circumstances, it can be difficult to determine whether or not there is a lesion present. Examination of the lesion will be made more challenging as a result of both of these situations. Even for a physician who has spent a lot of time working in the field, it may be difficult to differentiate between tumors that, at first glance, appear to be reasonably distinct from one another, or to recognize nodules that are extremely complex. This may be the case especially when attempting to diagnose extremely complex tumors. As a consequence of this, misleadingly negative outcomes will be obtained whenever medical equipment scans are employed to assess patients' lung health. An further potential challenge for the radiologist is the appearance of white spots or viruses on scans of medical devices. This may lead to an incorrect diagnosis of illnesses such as pneumonia and lung disorders like COVID-19. Because the appearance of these white spots or viruses might lead to an incorrect diagnosis, this could be a source of concern. Researchers are quickly turning to computer vision, machine learning, and deep learning in order to comprehend medical imaging, such as images from medical devices for infectious diseases [8]. This trend is expected to continue. It is projected that this pattern will maintain its prevalence in the not-too-distant future. It is anticipated that this pattern will go on for an extremely long period of time. It is possible that these newly found approaches, which have the capacity to automatically detect the infection in scans of medical healthcare equipment, may be valuable to medical professionals or physicians. It's possible that those in the medical field may find this extremely useful. This would result in a reduction in the amount of labor that is necessary while also enhancing the process that is used to evaluate the therapy. The use of these cutting-edge techniques for the diagnosis of diseases at an early stage results in a general reduction in the number of fatalities. Commons Utilizable Commons Utilizable Using a smart healthcare system that is made possible by the internet of things, it is feasible to discover infectious diseases such as COVID-19 and pneumonia in scans of medical healthcare equipment. This is only achievable for those who utilize the system (IoT). The improved performance outcomes that were accomplished by systems that came before it in the route of development had a direct impact on the development of this system. Transfer learning is used in conjunction with not just one but two distinct deep learning architectures, notably VGG-19 [9] and Inception-V3 [10]. Since these designs were first trained on the ImageNet data set [11], it is very probable that they integrate the idea of multiple-feature fusion and selection. This is because the ImageNet data set was used throughout the training process. This is due to the fact that these designs have already undergone training using the ImageNet data set. Throughout the course of our inquiry, we classified objects using a method that is similar to the multiple feature fusion and selection methodology that was described in [12, 13]. Specifically, this method was based on a set of rules. To be more specific, the following is the classification system that we use for things: Support Vector Machines (SVM) have been used to a variety of applications, including those that deal with object classification and medical imaging [14, 15]. SVM have also been used to combine many feature vectors into a single feature vector or space. Applications such as medical imaging and the classification of objects are two examples of the sorts of applications that suit this definition. This category also include the software that deals with organizing information into several classifications. Using the method of feature selection, it is also feasible to exclude from the fused vector sets any features that are not required for the job that is now being worked on. As a consequence of this, a wide variety of deep learning models that are particularly well-suited for the task at hand have been developed. When applied to circumstances that are more analogous to those that may be encountered in the real world, each of these models demonstrates noticeably distinct levels of performance in addition to varying degrees of complexity.

3   Design of the Proposed Deep-Learning-Based Bioinspired Model to Improve Feature Extraction Capabilities of Healthcare Device Sets

Based on the review of existing methods for feature extraction, it can be observed that a wide variety of deep learning models are proposed for this task, and each of these models showcase non-uniform performance & complexity levels when applied to real-time scenarios. To overcome such issues, this section proposes the design of a deep-learning-based bioinspired model that assists in improving the feature extraction capabilities of healthcare device sets. The design of the proposed model is depicted in Fig. 1, where it can be observed that the model uses Elephant Herding Optimization (EHO) for real-time control of data rate & feature-extraction process. The collected samples are processed via an Augmented 1D Convolutional Neural Network (AOD CNN) model, which assists in the identification of different healthcare conditions. The accuracy of the proposed AOD CNN is optimized via the same EHO process via iterative learning operations. Due to adaptive data-rate control, a model is capable of performing temporal learning for the identification of multiple disease progressions. These progressions are also evaluated via the 1D CNN model, which can be tuned for heterogeneous disease types.

From the flow of this model, it can be observed that the model initially collects large data samples from different sources, and then optimizes collection rates via an EHO process. This process assists in the estimation of deep learning hyperparameters, which enables continuous accuracy improvements under real-time use cases.

The EHO model works as per the following process,

- Initialize the following optimizer parameters,

  - Total Herds that will be configured (N_h)
  - Total iterations for which these Herds will be reconfigured (N_i)
  - Rate at which Herds will learn from each other (L_r)

- To initialize the optimization model, generate N_h Herd Configurations as per the following process,

  - From the collected sample sets, select N samples as per Eq. 1

$$N = STOCH(L_r * N_s, N_s) \tag{1}$$

  where, N_s represents the number of collected & scanned sample sets.

  - Based on the values of these samples, estimate Herd fitness via Eq. 2,

$$f_h = \frac{t_p}{t_p + t_n} \sum_{i=1}^{N} \frac{DR_i}{N} \tag{2}$$

  where, DR_i represents the data rate during the collection of the sample, while $t_p \& t_n$ represent its true positive and negative rates.

  - Estimate such configurations for all Herds, and then calculate the Herd fitness threshold via Eq. 3,

$$f_{th} = \frac{1}{N_h} \sum_{i=1}^{N_h} f_{hi} * L_r \tag{3}$$

- Once the Herds are generated, then scan them for N_i iterations as per the following process,

- Do not modify the Herd if $f_h > f_{th}$
- Otherwise, modify the Herd configuration as per Eq. 4,

$$N(New) = N(Old) \bigcup N(Matriarch) \tag{4}$$

where, $N(New)$ represents feature vectors present in the new Herd configuration, $N(Old)$ is its old features, and $N(Matriarch)$ represents feature sets present in the

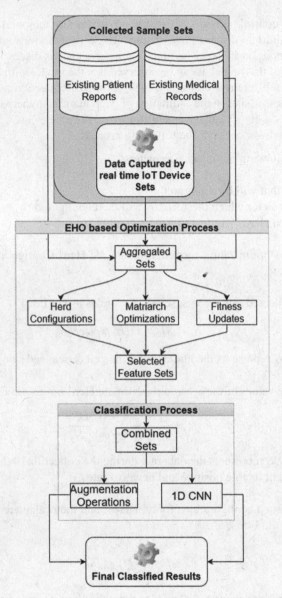

Fig. 1. The overall flow of the proposed deep learning model for healthcare analysis

Matriarch Herd, which is estimated via Eq. 5,

$$H(Matriarch) = H\left(Max\left(\bigcup\nolimits_{i=1}^{N_h} f_{h_i}\right)\right) \tag{5}$$

where, H represents the Herd Configurations.

– At the end of every iteration, estimate Herd fitness via Eq. 2, and update fitness threshold levels.

• Once all iterations are completed, then find a Herd with maximum fitness, and use its configurations for the collection of data samples Configurations of Herds with maximum fitness levels are used to estimate the Data Rate for the collection of healthcare samples. These samples are processed by a 1D CNN Model that can be observed in Fig. 2, where a combination of Convolutional layers (for feature augmentations), Max Pooling layers (for selection of high variance features), Drop Out layers (for removal of low variance features), and Fully Connected Neural Networks (FCNNs) based on SoftMax activation can be observed for different use cases.

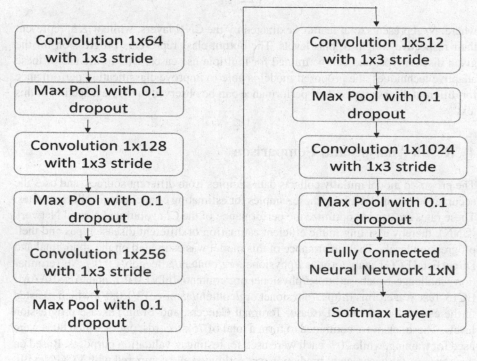

Fig. 2. Design of the CNN model for the classification of different diseases

The model initially augments collected feature sets via Eq. 6, and uses them to find feature variance via Eq. 7 which assists in the estimation of high-density features for better accuracy performance under real-time use cases

$$C_{feats} = \sum_{a=-\frac{m}{2}}^{\frac{m}{2}} FS(i-a) * ReLU\left(\frac{m+a}{2}\right) \qquad (6)$$

where, m, a represents the sizes for different convolutional Windows, and their Strides, FS represents the feature sets collected from different devices, and $ReLU$ represents a Rectilinear Unit which is used for activation of these features. These features are processed by an adaptive data-rate controlled variance estimator, which evaluates feature variance via Eq. 7,

$$v = DR * \sqrt{\frac{\left(\sum_{i=1}^{N_f}\left(x_i - \sum_{j=1}^{N_f}\frac{x_j}{N_f}\right)^2\right)}{N_f + 1}} \tag{7}$$

where, DR is the selected data rate from the EHO process. The selected features are classified as per Eq. 8, where SoftMax activation is used to identify the output class,

$$c_{out} = SoftMax\left(\sum_{i=1}^{N_f} f_i * w_i + b_i\right) \tag{8}$$

where, N_f represents total features extracted by the CNN layers, while $w_i \& b_i$ represent their respective weight & bias levels. The output class represents progression for the given disease type, and can be trained for multiple use cases. Due to the use of these adaptive techniques, the proposed model is able to improve classification performance for different disease types. This performance can be observed in the next section of this text.

4   Result Analysis and Comparison

The proposed model initially collects data samples from different sources, and uses the accuracy levels of classifying these samples for estimating efficient data collection rates. These rates are used to optimize the performance of the Convolutional Neural Network (CNN), thereby assisting in the efficient estimation of different disease types and their progression levels. The performance of this model was estimated on the abdominal and Direct Fetal ECG Database(https://physionet.org/content/adfecgdb/1.0.0/), AF Termination Challenge Database(https://physionet.org/content/aftdb/1.0.0/), and ANSI/AAMI EC13 Test Waveforms (https://physionet.org/content/aami-ec13/1.0.0/), which assisted in the estimation of Heart Disease, Terminal Cancers, and Brain Disease progression levels. These sets were combined to form a total of 75k records, out of which 80% were used for training, while 20% each were used for testing & validation purposes. Based on this strategy, the accuracy of prediction was estimated and compared with VGG Net [9], Incep Net [10], & SVM [14], which use similar scenarios. This accuracy can be observed in Table 1, where it is tabulated with respect Number of Evaluation Data Points (NED),

When compared with VGG Net [9], Incep Net [10], and SVM [14], the suggested model is able to improve classification accuracy by 6.5% when compared with VGG Net [9], 3.9% when compared with Incep Net [10], and 2.3% when compared with SVM [14] for a wide range of different scenarios. This conclusion can be drawn from the findings of this study and Fig. 3. This is because the classification was done utilizing EHO and 1D CNN, both of which lead to an improvement in accuracy for clinical use cases. As a

Table 1. Classification accuracy for different models

NED	A (%) VGG Net [9]	A (%) Incep Net [10]	A (%) SVM [14]	A (%) DB FEH
750	89.45	89.06	91.38	95.41
1500	89.64	89.45	91.80	95.67
2250	89.81	89.87	92.23	95.92
3750	89.96	90.23	92.60	96.14
7500	90.12	90.51	92.87	96.34
15000	90.29	90.83	93.19	96.57
18750	90.47	91.18	93.56	96.81
22500	90.64	91.57	93.97	97.05
30000	90.81	91.92	94.34	97.29
33750	90.98	92.27	94.70	97.52
37500	91.15	92.63	95.07	97.76
41250	91.33	92.98	95.43	97.99
45000	91.50	93.33	95.80	98.23
52500	91.67	93.69	96.16	98.46
60000	91.84	94.04	96.53	98.70
67500	92.01	94.39	96.89	98.93
75000	92.18	94.74	97.26	99.17

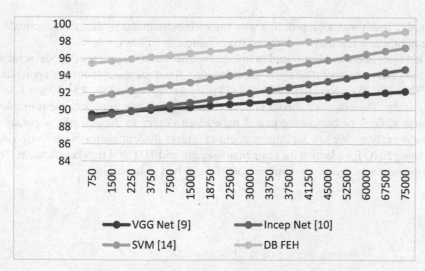

Fig. 3. Classification accuracy for different models

Table 2. Temporal analysis accuracy for different models

NED	AT(%) VGG Net [9]	AT (%) Incep-Net [10]	AT (%) SVM [14]	AT (%) DB FEH
750	84.03	83.86	86.06	89.69
1500	84.19	84.23	86.45	89.91
2250	84.34	84.56	86.78	90.12
3750	84.49	84.86	87.08	90.33
7500	84.65	85.16	87.38	90.54
15000	84.82	85.49	87.73	90.76
18750	84.98	85.83	88.08	90.99
22500	85.14	86.18	88.44	91.21
30000	85.30	86.51	88.78	91.43
33750	85.46	86.84	89.12	91.65
37500	85.62	87.17	89.47	91.87
41250	85.78	87.50	89.81	92.09
45000	85.94	87.83	90.15	92.31
52500	86.10	88.16	90.50	92.53
60000	86.26	88.49	90.84	92.75
67500	86.42	88.82	91.18	92.97
75000	86.58	89.15	91.52	93.18

result, this result was achieved. In a way somewhat dissimilar to this, the exactitude of the temporal analysis may be deduced from Table 2 as follows,

This assessment and Fig. 4 lead us to the conclusion that the proposed model achieves a higher level of temporal analysis accuracy than the three state-of-the-art approaches (VGG Net [9], Incep Net [10], and SVM [14]), by a combined 5.9%, 4.50%, and 1.88%, respectively. The proposed model is able to accomplish this goal because it employs the methodology of comparing neural networks in order to improve the accuracy of temporal analysis. We saw an improvement in temporal accuracy for clinical use cases after using EHO for adaptive data rate management and 1D CNN for classification. This improvement was due to the combination of these two technologies.

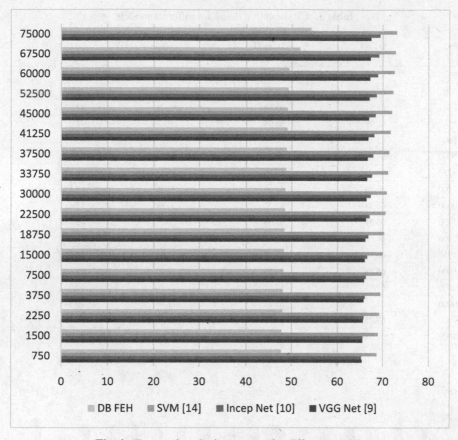

Fig. 4. Temporal analysis accuracy for different models

Similarly, the delay needed for classification can be observed from Table 3 as follows,
The results of this research are shown in Fig. 5, which demonstrates that the proposed model boosts classification speed by 10.5%, 12.4%, and 15.5% when compared to VGG Net [9], Incep Net [10], and SVM [14], respectively. It is possible that the improvement seen in classification times for clinical use cases is due to the use of EHO for the purpose of adaptive data rate control in combination with 1D CNN. After completing this study, it became very obvious that the model that was proposed might be applied in a variety of different real-time clinical scenarios. This was discovered after the research was completed & validated with different scenarios.

Table 3. Classification delay for different models

NED	D (ms) VGG Net [9]	D (ms) Incep Net [10]	D (ms) SVM [14]	D (ms) DB FEH
750	65.40	65.26	68.66	47.66
1500	65.52	65.55	68.96	47.78
2250	65.64	65.81	69.24	47.90
3750	65.76	66.05	69.48	48.01
7500	65.88	66.28	69.72	48.12
15000	66.01	66.53	69.99	48.24
18750	66.13	66.80	70.27	48.37
22500	66.26	67.06	70.56	48.49
30000	66.38	67.32	70.84	48.61
33750	66.51	67.58	71.11	48.73
37500	66.63	67.84	71.38	48.85
41250	66.76	68.09	71.66	48.98
45000	66.88	68.35	71.93	49.10
52500	67.01	68.61	72.20	49.22
60000	67.13	68.87	72.48	49.34
67500	67.25	69.13	72.75	51.78
75000	67.38	69.38	73.02	54.23

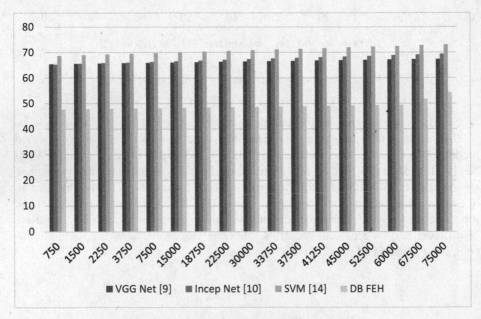

Fig. 5. Classification delay for different models

5 Conclusion

The proposed model initially collects data samples from different sources and uses the accuracy levels of classifying these samples for estimating efficient data collection rates. These rates are used to optimize the performance of the Convolutional NeuralNetwork (CNN), thereby assisting in the efficient estimation of different disease types and their progression levels. Based on accuracy analysis, it can be observed that the proposed model is able to improve classification accuracy which is due to the use of EHO & 1D CNN for classification, which assists in enhancing accuracy for clinical use cases. Based on temporal accuracy analysis, it can be observed that the proposed model is able to improve temporal classification accuracy which is due to the use of EHO for adaptive data rate control & 1D CNN for classification, which assists in enhancing temporal classification accuracy for clinical use cases. Based on delay analysis, it can be observed that the proposed model is able to improve classification speed due to the use of EHO for adaptive data rate control & 1D CNN which assists in enhancing the speed of classification for clinical use cases. Based on this analysis, it can be observed that the proposed model is useful for a wide variety of real-time clinical use cases. In future, the performance of the proposed model must be validated on larger data samples, and can be improved via integration of Transformer Models, Long-Short-Term Memory (LSTM) Models, and Adversarial Networks, which will enhance temporal analysis performance under different use cases.

References

1. Bhuiyan, M.N., Rahman, M.M., Billah, M.M., Saha, D.: Internet of things (IoT): A review of its enabling technologies in healthcare applications, standards protocols, security, and market opportunities. IEEE Internet Things J. **8**(13), 10474–10498 (2021)
2. Ray, P.P., Dash, D., Salah, K., Kumar, N.: Blockchain for IoT-based healthcare: background, consensus, platforms, and use cases. IEEE Syst. J. **15**(1), 85–94 (2020)
3. Ren, J., Li, J., Liu, H., Qin, T.: Task offloading strategy with emergency handling and blockchain security in SDN-empowered and fog-assisted healthcare IoT. Tsinghua Sci. Technol. **27**(4), 760–776 (2021)
4. Haghi, M., et al.: A flexible and pervasive IoT-based healthcare platform for physiological and environmental parameters monitoring. IEEE Internet Things J. **7**(6), 5628–5647 (2020)
5. Kumar, A., Krishnamurthi, R., Nayyar, A., Sharma, K., Grover, V., Hossain, E.: A novel smart healthcare design, simulation, and implementation using healthcare 4.0 processes. IEEE Access **8**, 118433–118471 (2020)
6. Xu, L., Zhou, X., Tao, Y., Liu, L., Yu, X., Kumar, N.: Intelligent security performance prediction for IoT-enabled healthcare networks using an improved CNN. IEEE Trans. Industr. Inf. **18**(3), 2063–2074 (2021)
7. Pathak, N., Deb, P.K., Mukherjee, A., Misra, S.: IoT-to-the-rescue: a survey of IoT solutions for COVID-19-like pandemics. IEEE Internet Things J. **8**(17), 13145–13164 (2021)
8. Vedaei, S.S., et al.: COVID-SAFE: An IoT-based system for automated health monitoring and surveillance in post-pandemic life. IEEE Access **8**, 188538–188551 (2020)
9. Ahmed, I., Jeon, G., Chehri, A.: An IoT-enabled smart health care system for screening of COVID-19 with multi layers features fusion and selection. Computing, 1–18 (2022)
10. Pal, M., et al.: Symptom-based COVID-19 prognosis through AI-based IoT: a bioinformatics approach. BioMed Res. Int. (2022)

11. Yang, Z., Liang, B., Ji, W.: An intelligent end–edge–cloud architecture for visual IoT-assisted healthcare systems. IEEE Internet Things J. **8**(23), 16779–16786 (2021)

12. Saha, R., Kumar, G., Rai, M.K., Thomas, R., Lim, S.J.: Privacy Ensured \${e}\$-healthcare for fog-enhanced IoT based applications. IEEE Access **7**, 44536–44543 (2019)

13. Bao, Y., Qiu, W., Cheng, X.: Secure and lightweight fine-grained searchable data sharing for IoT-oriented and cloud-assisted smart healthcare system. IEEE Internet Things J. **9**(4), 2513–2526 (2021)

14. Zhang, Y., Sun, Y., Jin, R., Lin, K., Liu, W.: High-performance isolation computing technology for smart IoT healthcare in cloud environments. IEEE Internet Things J. **8**(23), 16872–16879 (2021)

15. Chanak, P., Banerjee, I.: Congestion free routing mechanism for IoT-enabled wireless sensor networks for smart healthcare applications. IEEE Trans. Consum. Electron. **66**(3), 223–232 (2020)

Protecting OT Hosts with Intelligent Model-Based Defense System Against Malware Families

Manish Kumar Rai[(✉)], K. V. Srilakshmi, and Priyanka Sharma

Rashtriya Raksha University, Gandhinagar, India
manish.it.imps@gmail.com

Abstract. Over the course of the past few decades, it has been abundantly clear that modern cybercrime committed against ICS has been expanding at an exponential rate. Operational Technology, also known as OT, has been the target of different types of attacks using a variety of tactics and approaches that have been specially tailored against them. Malwares, especially like backdoors, are the most prominent types of these attacks. Major constituents of OT are the Supervisory Control and Data Acquisition systems (SCADA), Programmable Logic Controllers (PLC), and Distributed Control Systems (DCS). It is harder to patch the existing vulnerabilities due to its devastating effect on the availability of the service. Attacks against the ICS have disastrous repercussions for the nation's security. Industries have encountered many of them such as Stuxnet, BlackEnergy, CrashOverRide and many in the past years. Malwares that are polymorphic and metamorphic, both of which have efficient mutational features, are largely responsible for the exponential increase in the variability of malwares. The efficient categorization of the malware samples is a crucial and challenging task. This study mainly focuses on the efficient categorization of the huge samples of malware from nine different scandalous families, using their byte files. These byte file samples were passed into 3 different machine learning algorithms (k-neighbor, logistic regression, random forest), from which the best results were obtained from the random forest algorithm with a larger number of samples. The Identification results with the small dataset demonstrates that Random forest is not suited for the identification of malware that vary their signature. The feature extraction and the application of the machine learning algorithm aids the process and opens a wide scope for future research on this area.

Keywords: SCADA · CrashOverRide · Trisis · K-neighbor · Logistic Regression · Random Forest Algorithm

1 Introduction

One of the biggest issues in our digital age is the prevalence of security risks. Unfortunately, malicious software and agents may take advantage of flaws and vulnerabilities in any system that relies on ICT [1]. DCS (Distributed Control Systems) [2], SCADA (Supervisory Control and data Acquisition) [5], IAS (Industrial Automation System)

© The Author(s), under exclusive license to Springer Nature Switzerland AG 2023
N. Chaubey et al. (Eds.): COMS2 2023, CCIS 1861, pp. 163–178, 2023.
https://doi.org/10.1007/978-3-031-40564-8_12

[3], IACS (Industrial Automation and Control Systems) [4], and PLC (Programmable Logic Controller) are all examples of systems found within the realm of information and communication technology. SCADA [5] systems are those control systems used to oversee the industrial plants such as oil mining, traffic control systems, power grids, water treatment facilities, space stations, and nuclear systems which spread across a wide geographical area. Since modern SCADA systems employ open access networks to maximize efficiency, they have been vulnerable to a wide variety of cyber-attacks [6]. Security flaws in SCADA systems may have grave consequences. Proprietary communication protocols were implemented in these systems to ensure that they could operate to the necessary standards in terms of performance, availability, safety, and adaptability. They were often built on hardware, software, and communication protocols of proprietary nature, that are even deficient of the most basic security, safety protections and were completely cut off from the complex world of the internet. When it comes to protecting ICS [11], physical barriers between users and the network and the consoles that really did the heavy lifting were the norm. System providers have been integrating more and more innovative internet technologies and protocols to ICS under the same system constraints discussed above to meet the openness requirements brought by the evolution of IT systems [6], which increased the need for interoperability, interconnectivity, openness, transparency, and communication standardization among control systems.

Integrity attacks, in which the message or system assets are altered without permission [8, 13].

Control systems can be compromised in a variety of ways, which includes, external factors (such as hostile governments, terrorist groups, industrial spies, disgruntled employees, and malicious intruders) and internal factors (such as system complexity, human error and accidents, equipment failures, and natural disasters) [6]. A defense-in-depth [9] plan must be developed to safeguard the ICS against adversary attacks (including recognized natural threats). More than 120 incidents related to industrial cyber security have been recorded in a database kept by the Internet Engineering Lab at the British Columbia Institute of Technology (BCIT/IEL) [9]. Most facilities have been subject to cyber-attacks, according to a survey of 200 IT security executives from key energy infrastructure firms in 14 countries conducted by Baker et al. at McAfee for their 2011 sequel study. SCADA systems used to be quite secure because of their isolation, provided by their remote locations and private industrial networks [7]. Networked process historian servers are used in most modern manufacturing facilities for archiving process data and other potential business and process interfaces. Wireless technologies like IEEE 802.x [6] and Bluetooth, as well as wired technologies like Ethernet, have further broken through the isolation of SCADA networks which further increased the likelihood of SCADA attacks. It is already simpler to launch SCADA-specific attacks due to the current trend towards the standardization of software and hardware used in SCADA systems. More than fifty other incidents similar to Stuxnet are imminent [10].

2 Literature Review

Cyberattack on the Ukrainian energy system that occurred on December 17th, 2016, a year after the BE3-related strikes [14]. Consequently, one of the power substations that provides electricity to a part of Kiev was damaged, leaving residents without electricity for almost an hour. CrashOverRide (CO) was chosen as the moniker for the virus because, unlike BE3, it communicates with the underlying hardware directly and does not rely on HMIs. Both the Slovak company ESET and the American firm Dragos investigated the CO-based assault [14].

Initial step was a phishing effort to infect the host computers on the power firms' corporate network. Mimikatz and other tools might steal credentials from memory or even create Kerberos Golden Tickets, allowing unauthorized access to the whole system and all its resources [15]. Common advisory uses pre-existing features of Microsoft Windows, such as PowerShell. These instruments will aid in the download of more malware that modifies the compromised host system and allows the attacker to enter the ICS network. Once entered, within the ICS network [16], the CO malware installs itself as a service on the compromised machine. As a result, even the restart of the systems cannot mitigate the utilities of the malware.

Launchers, payloads, wipers, and even backdoors are just some of the many modules available in CO. The selected payloads are loaded into the launcher, and other activities, such as routine cleaning, may be scheduled in advance. CO determines which protocols are able to establish a connection with the target system and then downloads the appropriate payloads (in this case, the necessary capabilities) to effectively reset the circuit breakers [17]. The registry of Microsoft Windows is modified by the wipers so that the machine cannot be started. In addition to obstructing recovery efforts, wipers interrupt running programs or cause them to fail in order to force a system shutdown [18]. The attack launcher activates the wipers two hours after each assault. There are other backdoors that may have been used to get access to the compromised machine in the event that all other connections are severed. The system communicates with its command-and-control server during the CO assault, which can persist for months.

The Trisis (TS) virus targets the Triconex security system. The technology is used at a petrochemical facility in Saudi Arabia [19]. Several machines in the factory were shut down virtually with the help of TS. Because of this, there are two outcomes that may result from a successful TS attack: either the plant being shut down or being put into a dangerous physical condition. It is still unknown how TS penetrated into Saudi Arabia's ICS system. In addition, TS became successful because of a confluence of variables. In order to initiate the virtual power button, the program must first get remote access [7]. Two zero-day exploits were included into TS, making this feasible. In addition, the Saudi Arabian system was in configuration mode, either intentionally or unnoticed by the local operators [20]. The emergence of TS was traced to an unmistakable increase in the frequency of breakdowns requiring assistance. As a result of further investigation, TS was found and removed.

3 Dataset

Finding relevant malware samples for research is really challenging [12]. The data is scattered over a small number of repositories, and it's not easy to pull it out and transform it into the right format for use as input in a machine learning method. The majority of currently available datasets are too old to accurately portray the latest patterns in malware development. Most of them depend only on VirusTotal [21] to identify malicious software, despite the fact that not all antivirus programs included on VirusTotal have accurate detection rates (Table 1).

Table 1. Dataset of different malware families

Class	Family Name	Type	First Seen
1	Worm.Win32.Stuxnet	Worm(Kaspersky)	2010
2	Snake or Ekans	Ransomware(Microsoft)	2020
3	DoppelPaymer	Ransomware	2017
4	Havex	Backdoor	2013
5	TrojanDropper Win32/Stuxnet.A	Trojan(Microsoft)	2007
6	CrashOverRide	Backdoor	2016
7	Lollipop	Adware	2013
8	Tracur	Trojan Downloader	2011
9	Obfuscator.Acy	Obfuscated Malware	2012

Samples of malicious binaries from nine distinct families have been acquired from a small number of repositories for this investigation. The unique ID for each malware sample, the 20-character hash value, and the numerical code for the nine classes of malware are taken into account for the experiment. The most dangerous and damaging malwares of nine distinct sorts are categorized in the table, according to the malware family to which they belong and the year in which they were first spotted in the cyber world.

The hexadecimal representation of the binary content of the raw data for each file, without the Portable Executable (PE) header, shows that the data is unaltered, authentic and suitable for the study. The manifest, or assembly information, is provided from the malicious software samples. The goal of the research is to develop a smart model that can efficiently and accurately categorize huge numbers of harmful binary samples into distinct families using the provided training and testing data. The best method is used for training and testing the model, and further research is recommended.

4 Methodology

Constructing a model that accurately represents a subset of data is all that is required to apply machine learning to a problem. Machine learning allows for the manipulation of information in several dimensions. The machine learning algorithms may be broken down into the following categories based on their expected output: Learning-to-learn, reinforcement learning, transduction, supervised learning, unsupervised learning, and semi-supervised learning. In this research, we use supervised learning to the dataset, a technique in which the training data is labelled appropriately, in order to get the desired results. In supervised learning, a subfield of machine learning, input/output pairings or labelled data are used to train a model with the intention of creating a function that is approximate enough to predict outputs for new inputs when presented to the model. Regression problems and classification challenges are two types of supervised learning problems. In the case of continuous outputs, we have a regression issue, whereas in the case of categorical outputs, we have a classification challenge. In a basic machine learning model, training and testing make up the two halves of the learning process. During the training phase, a learning algorithm or learner uses features extracted from training data samples as input to construct a model. The learning model uses the execution engine to generate a forecast for the test or production data during the testing phase. Data that has been predicted or categorized by a learning model is called "tagged data".

Both classifier models and regression models belong to the supervised machine learning algorithm family; in the former case, the focus is on making predictions about the categories or classes to which a given input belongs, while in the latter, the prediction is about more general discrete values. Furthermore, when the inputs are used to forecast the output values in a continuous fashion using regression. Classification algorithms can be broken down into three broad categories: binary classification, multi-class classification, and multi-label classification, while regression algorithms can be broken down into three broad categories: simple linear regression, multiple linear regression, and polynomial regression.

The supervised learning method Logistic Regression uses a collection of input or independent variables to a category to identify the predictable variable. Logistic regression is a statistical method for predicting a data class by using the logistic sigmoid function with weighted input values [23]. The likelihood of a dependent variable is estimated as a function of the independent variables in a logistic regression model. The outcome (label) we are attempting to predict is the dependent variable, whereas the attributes we are using to make that prediction are the independent variables. The normality of the input data is not required for a generalized linear regression. In terms of distribution, the sample data might be anything.

Among supervised learning algorithms, K-nearest neighbor is a crucial classifier. When using this technique, fresh information is sorted according to the votes cast by its closest neighbors [22]. A distance function using Euclidean distance, Manhattan distance, and the Minkowski distance approach measures the separation between pairs of neighbors. In this context, "K" represents the total number of adjacent neighbors. The stability of the outcomes decreases as K decreases. Alternatively, one may increase the inaccuracy by raising the K value while still achieving steady results.

When it comes to machine learning, a random forest is a go-to method for addressing issues of regression and classification. Ensemble learning, in which many classifiers are combined to solve a problem, is used. Multiple decision trees make up a random forest algorithm. Training the random forest's "forest" through bagging or bootstrap aggregation. Bagging is a meta-algorithm for improving the performance of machine learning ensembles. After the decision trees have made their predictions, the (random forest) algorithm [24] determines the final result. It makes forecasts by averaging the results of many trees. The accuracy of the prediction rises as the number of trees grows.

Beginning with the acquisition of raw data from various sources, the experiment continues through its application to several machine learning algorithms and ends with a comparison of their success rates in producing the intended results. The first stage in conducting the experiment is to collect data from various sources, such as VirusTotal, Microsoft, and other repositories. The full procedure for conducting the experiment is shown in flowchart.

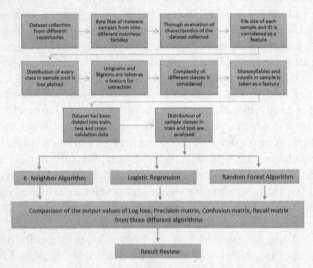

Fig. 1. Methodology Framework

The data collection, consisting of the byte files of various malwares gathered from various sources, has been rigorously evaluated to reveal the characteristics of the dangerous code contained within them. Among these characteristics are a malware's fingerprint and its classification. The file's size is also considered while trying to pinpoint the malicious executable. Another feature is the count of unique Unigrams and Bi-grams in the byte file. When the feature extraction process is complete, the data will be split into the train dataset, the test dataset, and the cross-validation dataset. We use the train data to teach the model, and the test data to check how well it learned its lessons. By contrasting the former with the latter, we may gauge the model's precision. Following this initial data preparation, three distinct machine learning algorithms (K-neighbor, Logistic Regression, and the Random Forest Algorithm) are fed into the final dataset including the chosen parameters or features. The results from the three algorithms are compared, and the one with the best overall performance is selected. The algorithms consider the measures of accuracy such as log loss, confusion matrix, recall matrix, and precision matrix while making their predictions [25]. Confusion matrix is used to depict the error in the prediction especially in a classification algorithm, which is to validate the performance of the model or the learning algorithm. Precision matrix depicts out of the positive results that we obtain, how many of them are truly positive, and the formula for the same is as follows:

$$Precision = TP/TP + FP \tag{1}$$

Recall matrix talks about how many positive examples are retrieved as positive. The formula for the recall matrix is as follows:

$$Recall = \text{TP}/\text{TP} + \text{FN} \tag{2}$$

where, TP is the number of true positives which is divided by the total number of the positive results.

5 Results and Discussion

The method that was used in the experiment was discussed in the previous part, and the results that were obtained at each stage are broken down in great detail in this part of the article. Before the acquired data could be used, it had to first be transformed into the right format, which was byte format. After that, the dataset was uploaded to Google Drive so that the individual byte files could be sorted there. The research was carried out with the assistance of the Google Colaboratory, also known as Google Colab. First, a connection is made between the Google Drive and the Google Colab. This makes it possible to read the byte files into the Google Colab and utilize them to execute the experimental code. Figure 2 illustrates this point.

```
from google.colab import drive
drive.mount('/content/mdrive')

path = "/content/mdrive/MyDrive/train1/train/"
```

Fig. 2. Command to mount the drive to Google Colab

The data in a bytes-formatted file is extracted from the various types of datasets that have been acquired and placed in a new folder with the name "train" for use in the experiment. The size of each of the 6139 samples is used to identify which class it belongs in. The identifiers of the malware samples that were provided are taken into consideration, as indicated in the (Fig. 3). The next step is to create a table that displays the serial number, size of the malware, and class that each of the 6139 samples of malware belong to. This step is repeated for all of the malware samples.

In addition to being taken into consideration throughout the process of feature extraction and classification, the byte-feature is also examined. In Fig. 4, A box plot diagram of the byte file sizes is made so that one may gain a better understanding of how the various types of malwares that are present in the sample pool that was chosen are distributed in terms of file size.

The number of monosyllables and vowels in each sample is also considered. Each sample is counted and then categorized according to its size and kind. The number of unigrams and bigrams belonging to each malware sample is counted and categorized into tables for better understanding (Fig. 5).

An increase in the effectiveness and functionality of the model can be achieved through the utilization of multivariate analysis, which is a sophisticated study of the data

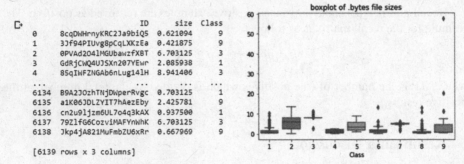

	ID	size	Class
0	8cqDWHrnyKRC2Ja9biQ5	0.621094	9
1	3Jf94PIUvg8pCqLXKzEa	0.421875	9
2	0PVAd2O4lMGUbawzfXBT	6.703125	3
3	GdRjCWQ4UJSXn207YEwr	2.085938	1
4	85qIWFZNGAb6nLug14lH	8.941406	3
...	...	...	...
6134	B9A2JOzhTNjDWperRvgc	0.703125	1
6135	a1K06JDLZYIT7hAezEby	2.425781	9
6136	cn2u9ljzm6UL7o4q3kAX	0.937500	1
6137	79Z1fG6CozviMAFYnWhK	6.703125	3
6138	Jkp4jA821MuFmbZU6xRr	0.667969	9

[6139 rows x 3 columns]

Fig. 3. Classification of the dataset   **Fig. 4.** Box plot of byte file size

	ID	0	1	2	3	4	5	6	7	8
0	8cqDWHrnyKRC2Ja9biQ5	87105	668	535	481	463	711	429	446	494
1	3Jf94PIUvg8pCqLXKzEa	19474	1135	682	571	699	586	461	407	1158
2	0PVAd2O4lMGUbawzfXBT	5709	3120	3066	3177	3152	3050	3041	3080	3065
3	GdRjCWQ4UJSXn207YEwr	93440	9304	4376	4539	7489	4299	6878	5460	10752
4	85qIWFZNGAb6nLug14lH	7572	4139	3073	3151	3055	3016	3011	3074	3079
...										
6134	B9A2JOzhTNjDWperRvgc	33951	1243	1136	1178	994	500	581	675	1090
6135	a1K06JDLZYIT7hAezEby	123315	7135	3037	3421	3408	4091	3187	2743	5908
6136	cn2u9ljzm6UL7o4q3kAX	55129	3859	3635	2398	2642	1477	810	1000	3790
6137	79ZIfG6CozviMAFYnWhK	11440	5611	3153	3292	3456	3185	3266	3139	3283
6138	Jkp4jA821MuFmbZU6xRr	87818	1132	559	1754	814	597	459	424	569

6139 rows × 258 columns

Fig. 5. Unigram and Bigram classification of malware samples

in all available factors. Figure 6 displays the complexity of the malware samples, which can be broken down into two levels of complexity: 30 and 63. These levels are used for doing multivariate analysis.

This experiment provides a clear demonstration of how the model will behave when applied to a more extensive dataset. For the purpose of this run, a total of 6139 datasets were collected; of those, 3932 were used for training, 1229 were used for testing, and 984 were used for cross-validation. There are 6139 unique malicious binaries, and their associated byte files are organized according to their size and category. The 6139 data samples that were selected were drawn at random from the overall collection of samples.

This was done to guarantee that the samples selected represent the full spectrum of malicious binaries. It is possible to safely partition the data into three separate sets by maintaining the same spread on the output variable. These sets are referred to as train, test, and cross-validation. After the selected samples had been examined to determine whether they were typical of the entire collection of samples, it was determined whether it would be appropriate to proceed with the experiment using those samples.

In this analysis, we compare the prevalence of a number of different forms of malwares in both our training dataset and our validation dataset. 14.268 percent, 22.609 percent, 4.603 percent, 0.331 percent, 7.01 percent, 3.61 percent, 11.801 percent, and 9.385 percent of the entire malware found in the train data are, correspondingly, of Malware Classes 1 through 9. To put it another way, the sample sizes for classes 3, 2, 1, 8,

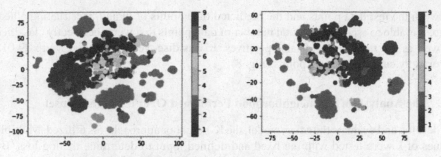

Fig. 6. Complexity when perplexity is 30 and 60

9, 6, 4, 7, and 5 are 1037, 889, 561, 464, 369, 277, 181, 142, and 13 correspondingly. For instance, while looking at the data for the trains, class 5 has the fewest observations, whereas class 3 has the most (Fig. 7).

It has been discovered, on the basis of an analysis of the distribution of the malware samples in the test data, that, just as in the training data, class 5 has the lowest distribution and class 3 has the greatest. This finding is consistent with what was found in the training data (Fig. 7).

After performing an analysis on the distribution of malware samples belonging to each class throughout the entire dataset, the dataset is then input into the appropriate algorithms. The effectiveness of the model is evaluated by comparing the values of log loss, cross validation error, the number of misclassified points, precision matrix, confusion matrix, and recall matrix respectively. After computing the confusion matrix between the test data points and the predicted data points of yi and constructing a heat map, it is able to ascertain the total number of data points that were incorrectly classified as well as the percentage of false positives. It was discovered that there were 89.015 incorrectly categorized data points (Fig. 8).

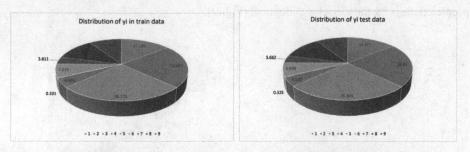

Fig. 7. Distribution of malwares families in train dataset and test dataset

After performing an analysis on the distribution of malware samples belonging to each class throughout the entire dataset, the dataset is then input into the appropriate algorithms. The effectiveness of the model is evaluated by comparing the values of log loss, cross validation error, the number of misclassified points, precision matrix, confusion matrix, and recall matrix respectively. After computing the confusion matrix between the test data points and the predicted data points of yi and constructing a heat map, it is able to ascertain the total number of data points that were incorrectly classified as well as the percentage of false positives. It was discovered that there were 89.015 incorrectly categorized data points (Fig. 8).

5.1 The Analysis of a K-neighborhood Performed Over a Large Dataset

To develop and evaluate the smart model, the K-neighbor approach was utilized. Multiple values of k were tested with the fixed and defined input to determine the log loss. By analyzing the log loss value, one may determine the effectiveness of the model using the method. With error measure on the y-axis and alpha I value on the x-axis, a graph of cross validation errors makes it clear that the optimal result is found at the third point along the x-axis. In addition to using the similarity matrix, the intelligent model may also make use of the precision matrix and the recall matrix to analyze the same. When the model was fed 6139 numbers of data, which was split evenly between train and test, the total number of misclassified points was determined to be 6.183. Results will be compared to those produced by using the other two methods on the model.

In the graph plotted below (error measure v/s cross validation error for each alpha), the log loss error for value when k = 1 is 0.27, log loss error for value when k = 3 is 0.267, log loss error for value when k = 5 is 0.2885, log loss error for value when k = 7 is 0.302, log loss error for value when k = 9 is 0.311, log loss error for value when k = 11 is 0.321, log loss error for value when k = 13 is 0.3324 respectively. Among these results, the best value of k for the given algorithm is 3, also the train log loss was found to be 0.1355.

In the matrix, the class of sample with the most interception of the original value and the predicted value is with the class of malware with maximum number of samples in the dataset, that is class 3 malware sample, and is found to be 324.

When it comes to the Precision matrix, maximum value for interception is found for the malware sample class 5 and class 7, which is 1, where the original class and the predicted class by the model are identical (Fig. 9).

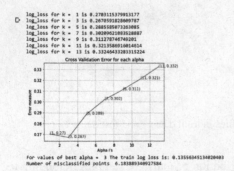

Fig. 8. Graph for cross validation error for each value of alpha

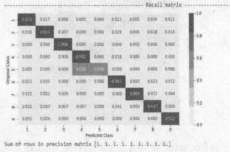

Fig. 9. Recall matrix for the Learning model

While analyzing the heat map generated for the recall matrix, the interception with maximum value is found to be for the malware sample class 3, which is 1, where the predicted class by the model and the original class of the sample is the same (Fig. 10).

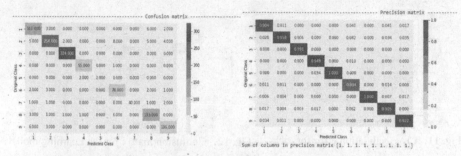

Fig. 10. Confusion matrix and Precision matrix for the Learning model

5.2 The Findings After Running the Logistic Regression Method on the Provided Data:

The Logistic Regression approach is utilized to train and test the smart model, and the log loss is determined with the assistance of the following outputs (Fig. 13) by the smart model and extensively analyzed. The cross-validation error is represented on a graph, with C in the input ranging from 0.0001 to 1000. The optimal result, located at x = 100 on the cross-validation error graph, was generated by the smart model. When compared to the previously used algorithm (K-neighbor), the number of misclassified points is determined to be 31.651, a fivefold increase. Comparing the Precision matrix, recall matrix, and confusion matrix for the identical input yields the same result.

When the cross-validation error for each alpha is plotted, as alpha I's values against error measure. The log loss values of for c at different values of alpha is calculated. It is found that the log loss for c when it is equal to 1e−05 is 1.23473, 0.0001 is 1.23470, 0.001 is 1.2315, 0.01 is 1.206,0.1 is 1.1068,1 is 1.0153, 10 is 0.9469,100 is 0.922,1000 is 0.934 respectively (Figs. 11 and 12).

Also, the log loss for train data is found as 0.927 and test data as 0.938. The minimum cross-validation error is found as 0.922, where the alpha i's value is 100. This is undoubtedly seen in the graph, where the deviation is present. When the confusion matrix is visualized over a heatmap, it is found that the maximum interceptions for the actual class and the predicted class by Logistic Regression Model is found to be for class 3, which is 324.Also the minimum number of interceptions is found to be 0 for the class 5, of which has the minimum samples in the dataset. Since the maximum number of the samples present in the dataset is for class 3 and minimum is for class 5 and the confusion matrix also gives a similar result, we can draw a conclusion on how accurate our model is (Fig. 14).

When the heatmap for the precision matrix is plotted, the maximum value for the interceptions is found as 1 for class 6 and class 7. For class 5, the model takes NaN

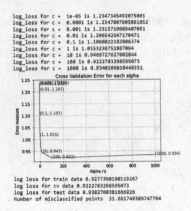

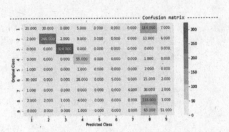

Fig. 11. Cross validation error for each alpha

Fig. 12. Confusion matrix for the Learning model

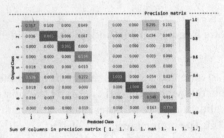

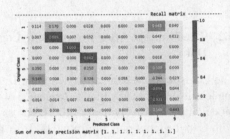

Fig. 13. Precision matrix for the Learning model

Fig. 14. Confusion matrix for the Learning model

value, since the sample distribution is very less in the dataset used for the study. The Recall matrix is analyzed thoroughly by plotting a heat map and the value for maximum interceptions is found. Class 3, with the value 1, where the true positive is high, when the predicted class by the model and the original class of the malware sample is the same.

5.3 The Findings from Running the Random Forest Classifier Algorithm on the Provided Data Set:

The smart model employs the Random Forest Classifier method, which calculates and analyzes the log loss for the target output. For the provided input, we find that the optimal value of alpha is located at the x-coordinate of 100, with a range of 10–3000. The same may be determined by meticulously analyzing the Precision matrix, the Recall matrix, and the Confusion matrix. In this case, the Random Forest Classifier method was deemed to be the best of the three algorithms used since it resulted in the last number of misclassified points (2.766) compared to the other two algorithms.

The log loss values of for c at different values of alpha is calculated. It is found that the log loss for c when it is equal to 10 is 0.1179, 50 is0.10792, 100 is 0.1071,500 is 0.10889,1000 is 0.10789,2000 is 0.10779 and 3000 is 0.10795 respectively. When the cross-validation error for each alpha is depicted using a graph which is plotted with values of alpha i which ranges from 0 to 100 in the x-axis and error measure in the y-axis, the best value for alpha is 100 where the minimum error measure, 0.107 is obtained. The train log loss is found to be 0.0361 (Figs. 15 and 16).

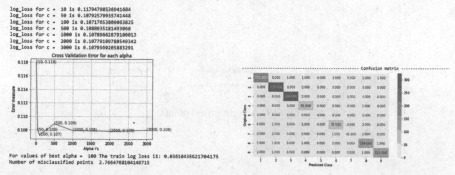

Fig. 15. Cross validation error for each alpha   **Fig. 16.** Confusion matrix for the Learning model

The heat map for studying the confusion matrix is shown in the figure, which clearly illustrates that the maximum number of intercepts is for the malware sample class 3 and is 324 as well as the sample class 5 shows minimum intercepts, which means it has a low number of true positives (Figs. 17 and 18).

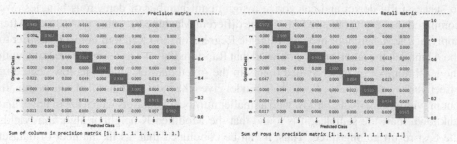

Fig. 17. Precision matrix for the Learning model   **Fig. 18.** Recall matrix for the Learning model

The precision matrix is analyzed thoroughly; the maximum intercept, otherwise called true positives, is found to be 1 which is for class 5 and class 7 of malware samples respectively. The recall matrix is illustrated using the heat map and the maximum true positives were found as 1 for the classes 2, 3 and 5 respectively. The predicted class by the random forest algorithm model and the original class of the malware intercepts are obtained. The precision matrix is analyzed thoroughly; the maximum intercept, otherwise called true positives, is found to be 1 which is for class 5 and class 7 of malware samples respectively. The recall matrix is illustrated using the heat map and the maximum true positives were found as 1 for the classes 2, 3 and 5 respectively. The predicted class by the random forest algorithm model and the original class of the malware intercepts are obtained (Fig. 19).

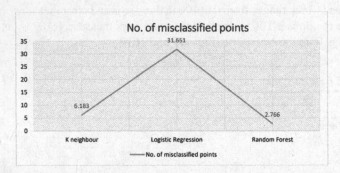

Fig. 19. Misclassified points

6 Conclusions

Due to their ever-evolving nature and sheer number, the cyber world's malwares are notoriously difficult to categorize. One of the trickiest aspects of malware is its ability to masquerade until it evades detection. The primary goal of this study was to determine "the effective approach to categorize the malware kinds, when there is an acceptable quantity of data accessible on the same." By using AI and ML, the researchers were able to successfully detect and categorize a significant number of dangerous binaries. We compared the results obtained from three different Machine Learning procedures. After applying the K-neighbor method, Logistic Regression, and Random Forest Classifier to the AI model, the latter's results showed that Random Forest was the most accurate, with the least number of misclassified points in the given dataset. Due to its low degree of effectiveness, the Logistic Regression model gives the most misclassified data points. In our previously conducted study, with a smaller number of datasets which are of novel and unknown malware samples, it is found that the Modified K-neighbor algorithm yields the best result among three. Thus, it can be concluded that, as the number of dataset increases, the accuracy of the proposed algorithm, Random Forest Algorithm, increases and the model becomes more ideal for the identification of the malware. In future, this study can be extended towards behavioral based identification of unidentified malware using different machine learning and deep learning models which are dedicated towards Industrial Control System security.

References

1. Zhu, X.: Resilient Control and Intrusion Detection for SCADA Systems. University of California, Berkeley (2011)
2. Nicholson, A., Webber, S., Dyer, S., Patel, T., Janicke, H.: SCADA security in the light of cyber-warfare. Comput. Secur. 31(4), 418–436 (2012)
3. Vieira, G.E., Herrmann, J.W., Lin, E.: Rescheduling manufacturing systems: a framework of strategies, policies, and methods. J. Sched. 6(1), 39–62 (2003)
4. Zhu, B., Joseph, A., Sastry, S.: A taxonomy of cyber-attacks on SCADA systems. In: 2011 International Conference on Internet of Things and 4th International Conference on Cyber, Physical and Social Computing, pp. 380–388. IEEE (2011)
5. Gupta, R.A., Chow, M.Y.: Networked control system: overview and research trends. IEEE Trans. Industr. Electron. 57(7), 2527–2535 (2009)
6. Geiger, M., Bauer, J., Masuch, M., Franke, J.: An analysis of black energy 3, crashoverride, and trisis, three malware approaches targeting operational technology systems. In: 2020 25th IEEE International Conference on Emerging Technologies and Factory Automation (ETFA), vol. 1, pp. 1537–1543. IEEE (2020)
7. Anson, S.: Applied Incident Response. Wiley, Hoboken (2020)
8. Al-Hawawreh, M., Den Hartog, F., Sitnikova, E.: Targeted ransomware: a new cyber threat to the edge system of brownfield industrial internet of things. IEEE Internet Things J. 6(4), 7137–7151 (2019)
9. McFail, M., Hanna, J., Rebori-Carretero, D.: Detection Engineering in Industrial Control Systems. Ukraine 2016 Attack: Sandworm Team and Industroyer Case Study. MITRE CORP MCLEAN VA (2022)
10. Reinhold, T., Reuter, C.: Towards a cyber weapons assessment model-assessment of the technical features of malicious software. IEEE Trans. Technol. Soc. 3, 226–239 (2021)
11. Alladi, T., Chamola, V., Zeadally, S.: Industrial control systems: cyberattack trends and countermeasures. Comput. Commun. 155, 1–8 (2020)
12. Chen, K., et al.: Finding unknown malice in 10 seconds: mass vetting for new threats at the {Google-Play} scale. In: 24th USENIX Security Symposium (USENIX Security 15), pp. 659–674 (2015)
13. Rathore, H., Sahay, S.K., Rajvanshi, R., Sewak, M.: Identification of significant permissions for efficient android malware detection. In: Gao, H., J. Durán Barroso, R., Shanchen, P., Li, R. (eds.) BROADNETS 2020. LNICSSITE, vol. 355, pp. 33–52. Springer, Cham (2021). https://doi.org/10.1007/978-3-030-68737-3_3
14. Akram, Z., Majid, M., Habib, S.: A systematic literature review: usage of logistic regression for malware detection. In: 2021 International Conference on Innovative Computing (ICIC), pp. 1–8. IEEE (2021)
15. Morales-Molina, C.D., Santamaria-Guerrero, D., Sanchez-Perez, G., Perez-Meana, H., Hernandez-Suarez, A.: Methodology for malware classification using a random forest classifier. In: 2018 IEEE International Autumn Meeting on Power, Electronics and Computing (ROPEC), pp. 1–6. IEEE (2018)
16. Abdualgalil, B., Abraham, S.: Applications of machine learning algorithms and performance comparison: a review. In: 2020 International Conference on Emerging Trends in Information Technology and Engineering (ic-ETITE), pp. 1–6. IEEE (2020)
17. Gao, Y., Hasegawa, H., Yamaguchi, Y., Shimada, H.: Malware detection using gradient boosting decision trees with customized log loss function. In: 2021 International Conference on Information Networking (ICOIN), pp. 273–278. IEEE, January 2021
18. Babun, L., Aksu, H., Uluagac, A.S.:. A system-level behavioral detection framework for compromised CPS devices: Smart-grid case. ACM Trans. Cyber- Phys. Syst. 4(2), 1–28 (2019)

19. Naeem, H., Guo, B., Naeem, M.R., Vasan, D.: Visual malware classification using local and global malicious patterns. J. Comput. (6), 73–83 (2019)
20. Tuptuk, N., Hazell, P., Watson, J., Hailes, S.:.A systematic review of the state of cyber-security in water systems. Water **13**(1), 81 (2021)
21. Humayed, A., Lin, J., Li, F., Luo, B.: Cyber-physical systems security—A survey. IEEE Internet Things J. **4**(6), 1802–1831 (2017)
22. Hassanzadeh, A., Rasekh, A., Galelli, S., Aghashahi, M., Taormina, R., Ostfeld, A., Banks, M.K.: A review of cybersecurity incidents in the water sector. J. Environ. Eng. **146**(5), 03120003 (2020)
23. Kirasich, K., Smith, T., Sadler, B.: Random forest vs logistic regression: binary classification for heterogeneous datasets. SMU Data Sci. Rev. **1**(3), 9 (2018)
24. Mienye, I.D., Sun, Y.: A survey of ensemble learning: Concepts, algorithms, applications, and prospects. IEEE Access **10**, 99129–99149 (2022)
25. .Priya, A., Garg, S., Tigga, N.P.: Predicting anxiety, depression and stress in modern life using machine learning algorithms. Procedia Comput. Sci. **167**, 1258–1267 (2020)

Design and Analysis of Wide-Band Planar Antenna Using Meta-material for S-Band Applications

Shefa Shah and Nimish Sunil Das(✉)

LJ Institute of Engineering and Technology University, Ahmedabad, Ahmedabad, Gujarat, India
{shefa.shah_ljiet,nimish.das}@ljinstitutes.edu.in

Abstract. A patch antenna is a low-profile antenna that may be mounted on a surface and comprise of a flat sheet metal or "patch" placed above a larger metal sheet known as a ground plane. The sheet might be rectangular, round, triangular, or any other geometric shape depending on the use. This work proposes and investigates a patch antenna with meta-surface influence for S-band applications. To reduce size and improve bandwidth performance, the recommended antenna features a single-fed architecture and is equipped with a slew of meta-surfaced unit cell. Examined and illustrated with simulated results are the precise antenna radiation characteristics. Using Ansoft HFSS software, antenna is constructed on FR4 substrate at 2.5 Ghz for S band Frequency with loss tangent of 0.02 and ε_r is 4.4. The obtained simulation results include 10.4% (2.34–2.62 GHz) for a return loss bandwidth of 10 db, which outperforms antenna without meta surface by 4%, 6.7 dBi for performance in gain and 29% decrease in the patch's size while making utilization of a meta-surface. Applications for S-band Radar using this antenna include wide range of radar systems such as weather, surface ship and space borne type radar.

Keywords: Patch · Ground plane · S-band · Meta-surface · Antenna · Dielectric · Bandwidth · Space borne radar(SAR)

1 Introduction

In 1898 J.C Bose proposed first metamaterial and it was utilized in transmitters and other microwave parts. In 2001, D.M. Smith and Pendry carried out a follow-up investigation and discovered meta-material as well as its drawbacks. The permittivity and permeability of a periodic substance known as a metamaterial are determined by its structure rather than by its component components. Today, research into microwave frequencies is expanding. Because these materials haven't been widely seen in nature, they are made artificially using their structures and electromagnetic characteristics [1].

Employed metamaterials include Swiss Roll type, SRR based wire and Chiral materials according to polarity. Metamaterial usage reduces antenna size while boosting resonance efficiency and bandwidth [2]. It also lessens mutual coupling between antenna

N. Chaubey et al. (Eds.): COMS2 2023, CCIS 1861, pp. 179–190, 2023.
https://doi.org/10.1007/978-3-031-40564-8_13

arrays. A substrate, a ground plane, array feeded network, a cloaking device, a super-strate, struts in reflector antenna and a random construction are just a few of the several ways that Meta-Material may be utilized to make antennas. Metamaterials (MTM) can be synthesized artificially. In mid of 1960's, Mr Veselago studied and researched on the behavioral properties of materials known as double negative materials as they possessed both permittivity is negative as well as permeability is also negative. Due to the Split Ring Resonators which make up such structure, the refractive index of these substance is negative. Metamaterials are used in a broad variety of fields [3].

Patch antenna provide a lot of benefits including low profile, minimal weight, simplic-ity of transportation, and compact size. Along with disadvantages including a bandwidth which is highly narrow, low efficiency as well as low gain and poor directivity, it also offers advantages. A Metamaterial unit cell placed on substrate can create a metamaterial which can be of numerous shapes and it is feed to antenna through multiple mechanism of feeding such as slot coupling or Electromagnetic coupling [4, 5].

The constraints of typical microstrip antennas include single-frequency operation, a narrow bandwidth of impedance, polarization difficulties, limited gain and large size. Improving performance of typical microstrip antenna, a number of strategies have been published. These includes various feeding methods, stacking, FSS, EBG, PBG, and metamaterials (FSS-"Frequency Selective Method", EBG-"Electro Band gap", PBG-"Photonic bandgap "). In 5th Generation sub-6 GigaHertz and mm-based wave systems, microstrip patch antennas are frequently employed [6].

For such interaction and controlling of electromagnetic waves, an artificial homoge-neous electromagnetic structure, a metamaterial can be defined as having special qualities that are not frequently observed in nature [6, 7].

Metamaterials should have a structure that is no larger than a quarter wave-length. Based on their electromagnetic properties, metamaterials can be categorized as Negative refractive Index(NRI), Right Handed (RH), Left handed(LH), Double Negative(DNG), Artificial magnetic Couplers and magneto. In addition to being known as metamaterials EBG, PBG and Defective ground Structure (DGS) [8].

Metamaterials are materials that have been developed to produce uncommon or difficult-to-obtain electromagnetic characteristics. Due to its potential to provide engi-neerable permeability, permittivity and index of refraction, metamaterials have attracted a lot of attention. This has made it is feasible for them to use in broad variety of electro-magnetic applications, especially for radiated-wave devices, from the microwave to the optical regime.

Present report comprehensively analyses the most current research initiatives per-taining to those small antennas built with metamaterials. They are discussed and divided into a number of groups, including meta resonators, metamaterial loadings, and antennas based on dispersion engineering. A few real-world obstacles or restrictions to the cre-ation of small antennas based on metamaterials are identified, and potential solutions are also shown. In order to aid general readers in comprehending, a wide range of antenna examples are included. [9, 10].

The use of metamaterials is covered in the second portion. A analysis of microstrip patch antennas employing MTM is addressed in the third section. The development of a the array of meta surface unit cells that is loaded underneath a patch antenna are covered in the fourth part. The simulation outcomes for an antenna containing and without a meta-surface are also covered in the fourth part.

2 Meta Material Applications

2.1 Antenna Miniaturisation

A keen interest is developing in ESAs have owing to their miniature size with a low profile making them feasible for application in mobile phones, airborne, IOT devices and wearables. When no ground is involved, antennas are considered tiny under condition $k\alpha < 1$ or $k\alpha < 0.5$ wave vector at the operating on corresponding frequency with radius minimal sphere around the antenna. ESAs suffices the need for compact transceivers, however their radiation efficiency and bandwidth undergoes a compromise. There is a major limitation in achieving excellent performance along with small size as a smaller antenna does not serve as an efficient radiator. The radiation properties undergo degradation by using traditional miniaturization techniques such as shortening pins, lumped elements and ceramic materials with high permittivity dielectrics. Therefore, development of tiny antennas made up of metamaterials can overcome these constrains and improve the quality of radiation.

Gain Enhancement

In a fixed point to point communication and radar systems, the critical feature of an antenna is gain. The transmission range for a given broadcast power can be extended by the use of high gain antennas which are additionally more resistant to interference. A popular method of generating higher gain is by making use of electrically massive antennas or arrays sets along with several radiating elements as directivity of the antennae is related to its aperture [6]. The use of small antennas in applications which require higher gain has become popular owing to the relationship between it's directivity and small size. Metamaterial randomness superstrates and lenses prove to be a practical, viable, low cost alternative in building otherwise complicated ultra compact and high gain antenna platforms. The use of these materials serve to increase the gain without reducing the volume of antennae considerably. The far field emission pattern is affected by the placement of these structures above the radiating elements as they interacts electromagnetic fields surrounding the radiator [9, 10].

There are two basic metamaterial-based approaches that can provide gain enhancement:

- Materials such as ZIM or NZRI are placed as superstrate.
- Materials with refractive index close to zero are known NZRI material the GRIN metamaterial lenses are placed in front of the antenna.

2.2 Isolation

For many applications, when the antenna elements are positioned closely together either by design (such as the common interelement spacing of by 2 in antenna array arrangements) or to reduce the bulk of the construction, isolation is crucial. Cross talks develop owing to interaction among antennas. Plantar antennas which are printed on the similar board,the surface waves which are considered as the primary source for development of cross talk [11, 12].

2.3 Reduction of Coupling Effects

Metasurfaces can be used in order to either mutual coupling among the antenna array elements or between the support structure and antenna. This may also boost directivity. For these goals, both grounded metasurface substrates and metasurface superstrates have been researched [12, 13].

2.4 Aperture Field Shaping– Directivity and Gain Enhancement

Metasurfaces act as lenses or transmit array for the distribution of desirable transmitted aperture field specially when high directivity is need. Metasurface which is partially reflecting can form a Fabry-Perot.In addition to this for a completely reflecting meta-surface a front feeding like a reflecting array is essential. A single radiating unit or an antenna array situated behind the metasurface forms a radiator. This leads to an increase in gain as well as rise in directivity which is brought on the metasurface and is not offset by a corresponding ohmic loss [12].

2.5 Scanning of Main Beam Direction

Varactor diodes having voltage based controlled type capacitance have been used in metamaterial to Fabry-Perot cavity antennas surface that partly reflects, composite right-left leaky wave antennas, and high-impedance reflectors in an effort to change reflection/transmission phase or propagation constant and subsequently the radiation direction [12].

3   Survey of Various Microstrip Antennae Using MTM

This section provides a variety of MTM structural variations using patch antennas to enhance the functionality of a standard patch antenna. Later, a comparison is conducted between patch antennas with and without metamaterial in terms of metrics like gain and bandwidth.

RIS acting as a metamaterial on a substrate is been used. In his paper, patch antenna with low profile circularly polarized radiation that was inspired by Metamaterials. The antenna is loaded for downsize with a composite CRLH mushroom-like framework and RIS layout structure. It features a single feed arrangement. Unit cell based on RIS being positioned at a height of 2.6 mm on the substrate based on "Megtron 6". We thoroughly study the radiation properties of a single feed patch antenna equipped with RIS & CRLH resonators. The frequency at which the suggested antenna works is 2.58 GHz [13, 14].

The tested antenna has a return loss of 10 dB as well as 3 dB axial bandwidth were determined to be 4.62% and 1.46%, respectively. The gain received is 2.98dB. The recommended antenna can be used with wire-less networks like WLAN [14, 15].

The construction of the proposed CP antenna is identical to that of in, except instead of the CRLH constructed as mushroom based structure, a pair of CSRR complementary type split ring based resonators are utilized. The CSRR functioned as a parallel LC based resonator and enabling the antenna area to be reduced. An antenna's observed 10-dB return loss that is 4.9% and 3-dB axial ratio bandwidths which corresponds 1.68%, respectively, and its gain is 3.7 dB. A frequency corresponding to 2.8 GHz is used by the proposed antenna [14, 15].

An antenna is made up of a slot-loaded with square based patch that is printed on a carefully thought-out reactive impedance's surface. The antenna, which operates at a frequency of 3 GHz, has a high gain of more than 4.15 dBi and a corresponding impedance of over 1.05%. The suggested antenna can be used with handheld and mobile communication equipment [16, 17].

In K. Agarwal study's on a small non - symmetric based slotted or slit designed microstrip based patched antenna upon RIS was shown and tested for CP radiation. Antenna has a total volume of 0.292λ0 by 0.292λ0 by 0.0308λ0 and operates at a frequency of 2.5 GHz. Compact asymmetrical crossed slot square patch antenna measurements show gain across 3-dB axial ratio bandwidth of 3.41 dBic, 5.2% for 10-decibel return loss bandwidth, and 1.6% for 3-decibels bandwidth [17].

L. Bernard et al. demonstrated a wideband antenna developed on RIS and exhibiting CP radiation. Telemetry-based applications in the region around 2300 MHz can be used to develop a wide band single-feed circular polarized patch antenna with a reduced dimension. A slot–loaded patch antenna (RIS) is used to produce and optimize the reactive impedance for the proposed structure. The fundamental role of each antenna component shown one by one comparison of statistical and experimental performance of numerous antenna designs over just one substrate as well as double layer substrate , slot loaded patch antenna , regular patch with or without RIS. The construction which has been substantially optimized has a wider bandwidth than a typically printed antenna, even though it is made up of same materials given axial-ratio of bandwidth roughly around 15% with an impedance bandwidth of 11% [18] (Table 1).

Table 1. Comparison of antenna using MTM

Antenna Configuration	Centre Frequency	10-dB Return Loss BW(%)	Gain (dBi)
Antenna structured along with CRLH mushroom and RIS	2.58 GHz	4.60	2.98
complementing split-ring resonators and RIS in an antenna	2.8 GHz	4.90	3.7
Antenna with a metasurface	3.0 GHz	2.33	5.1
Square patch with truncated corners over RIS	2.7 GHz	2.55	5.54
Square patch with ring slot on a metasurface	4.0 GHz	36.0	7.0–7.5
Metasurfaced square patch	2.3 GHz	24.0	2.5–5.7
Proposed Antenna	2.5 GHz	≥ 7.0	≥ 5.0

4   Design of Meta surface Antena

4.1   Design of Meta-Surface Cell Units

A meta surface cell unit having a dielectric constant value 4.4, 0.02 of a loss tangent, and 4.8 mm of thickness placed on FR4 substrate. The Meta- surface is 3,2 mm above the surface of the earth.

The figure below demonstrates the Meta-Surface unit cell design.

The cell unit dimensions are:

- The structure length of rectangular ring is 8.96 mm and the width of 5.6 mm
- the slot length of the rectangular ring is 7.46 mm with a slot width of 0.85 mm.

In the design and modelling of the meta- surface unit cell, master slave boundaries and unit cell's Floquet mode of excitation is utilized,mode of excitation was applied for analysis of utilizing an infinite structure. Figure 1 shows this sporadically.

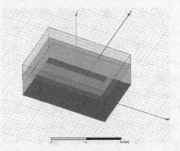

Fig. 1. Constructional Diagram of Meta-surface based Unit Cell

It's noted across a large frequency range, the unit cell's reflection phase oscillates between ±90 From 2.47 to 5.5 GHz, the range of frequency of the meta-surface unit cell is within a +90 degrees and −90 reflection phase variation. In Fig. 2, which is been displayed.

4.2   Design of Antenna in Presence and Absence of Meta-Surface

A rectangular shaped patch antenna is created at a frequency of 2.5 GHz upon a FR4 substrate with a dielectric constant of 4.4, a loss tangent of 0.02, and a thickness of 4.8 mm. The Patch Antenna has the following measurements:

- The ground plane's length and breadth are 90 mm and 180 mm, respectively.
- The patch's size is: $0.207\lambda_0 * 0.483\lambda_0$, where λ_0 is forms a free space wavelength' at 2.5 GHz.

The overall size of the antenna is 90 mm by 180 mm by 4.8 mm along with Coax-feed location: xp = −11 mm; yp = −15 mm.

Coaxial feeding is used to feed the specified antenna, and HFSS is used to mimic it.Below, in Fig. 3, is the simulation result for this antenna arrangement.

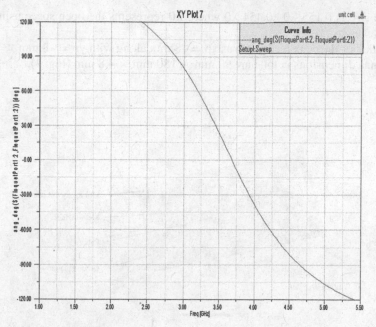

Fig. 2. Diagram illustrating the meta-surface unit cell's reflection phase

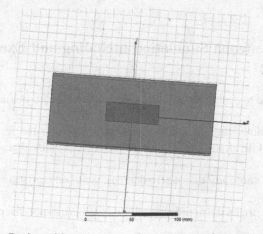

Fig. 3. Design without a meta-surface, a rectangular patch antenna

4.3 Antenna Fabricated with Meta-Surface

Following the built-up and simulation of the unit cell, the conventional antenna is designed with a 7*7 collection of meta-surface cell unit at given height of 3.2 mm, and it is positioned at 1.6 mm over the meta-surface.

The following are the overall measurements:

Ground plane dimensions are 90 mm by 180 mm.

Patch size is 0.155 λ0 *0.454 λ0 where λ0 represents the open space using a 2.5 GHz wavelength.

Location of the coax feed given as xp = –8 mm along with yp = –8 mm.

Antenna dimensions in total are 90 mm × 180 mm × 4.8 mm (Fig. 4).

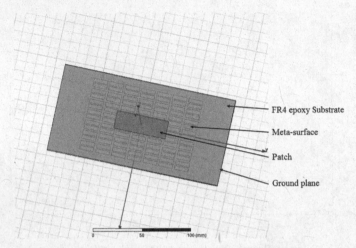

Fig. 4. Rectangular patch antenna with meta-surface

5 Results of Antenna Simulation Including and Excluding Metasurface

Ansoft HFSS is used to design the antenna and simulated outcomes are illustrated in the figure below.

Figure below shows the antenna's actual return loss, at the resonance frequency which is around –14 dB. Return loss of 10 dB has a bandwidth of around 150 MHz that is 6% (Fig. 5).

Gain (dBi), that's around 7 dBi at zero degrees, is a characteristic of far field radiation seen in Fig. 6.

Figure 7 demonstrates the approximately –13 dBi cross-pol discrimination.

5.1 Results of Meta-surface-Loaded Antenna's Simulation

Radiation pattern, gain (dBi), Figs. 8 and 9 display a meta-surface antenna's 10 dB return loss. At the resonant frequency at 2.5 GHz, return loss as much as –26 dB is seen in Fig. 9. The meta-surface antenna's 10 dB return loss having 10.4% bandwidth (2.34 GHz–2.62 GHz). Conventional antenna's return loss and a meta-surface based antenna are both contrasted in this graph.

Gain is shown against angle in degrees in Fig. 9. About 6.74 dBi of gain is attained using a meta-surface antenna. This is seen in the diagram.

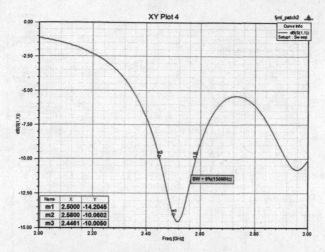

Fig. 5. A non-metasurface antenna's return loss (dB)

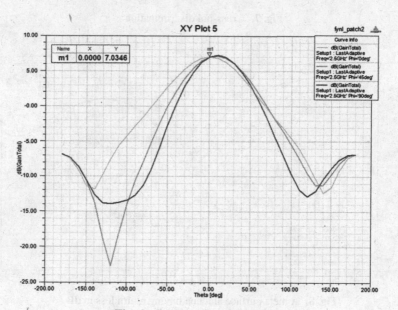

Fig. 6. Gain in dBi vs theta in deg

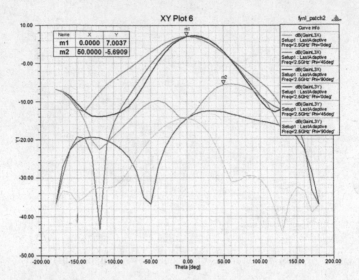

Fig. 7. Cross-pol discrimination

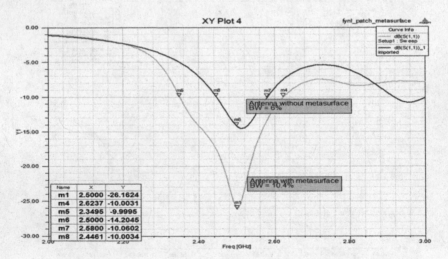

Fig. 8. A meta-surface antenna having return loss in dB

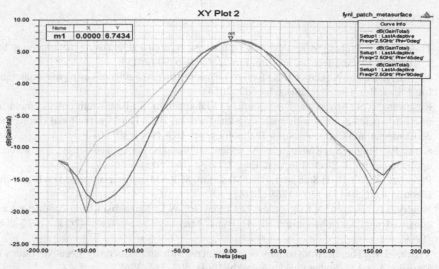

Fig. 9. Gain(dBi) versus theta(deg)

6 Conclusion

To do this, a thorough and methodical analysis of metamaterials and their properties
was conducted. Through a review of the literature, Meta-materials come in a variety
of shapes, including RIS,RIS,SRR etc. were examined and researched. This sort of
analysis has also been used to study microstrip antennas and their feeding systems.On
a FR4 epoxy substrate, a patch antenna has also been constructed and put to the test.
Its performance has been assessed both with and without a meta-surface.The gain in
dBi for a 10 dB return loss bandwidth is about 7.2 dBi without a meta-surface and 6.7
dBi with a meta-surface. Additionally, it has been discovered that the employment of
meta-surfaces causes rise in bandwidth as the strength of the link seen between patch and
indeed the meta-surface increases. Comparing the patch antenna to an antenna without
such a meta-surface can result in a size reduction of up to 29% (Table 2).

Table 2. Comparison between Conventional Antenna and Metamaterial Antenna At 2.5 GHz
frequency

No.	Parameters	Conventional Antenna	Meta-Material Antenna
1	Bandwidth	6%	10.4%
2	Gain	7.03 dBi	6.73 dBi
3	Size Reduction	(24.8*58) sq.mm	(18.6*54.5)sq.mm (29%)
4	Cross-pole Discrimination	−21 dBi	−16 dBi

References

1. Thomas, A.S., Prakash, A.K.: A survey on microstrip patch antenna using metamaterial. Int. J. Adv. Res. Electr. Electron. Instrum. Eng. **2**, 6289–6294 (2013)
2. Kumar, A., Kumar, N., Gupta, D.S.: Review on microstrip patch antennas using metamaterials. Int. J. Eng. Res. Gen. Sci. **2**(4), 678–682 (2014)
3. Kushwaha, R.S., Srivastava, D.K., Saini, J.P. Dhupkariya, S.: Bandwidth enhancement for microstrip patch antenna with microstrip line feed. In: 2012 Third International Conference on Computer and Communication Technology, pp. 183–185. IEEE 2012
4. Kaur, R., Singh, S., Kumar, N.: A review of various fractal geometries for wireless applications. Int. J. Electr. Electron. Eng. **2**(1), 34–36 (2015)
5. Pandey, G.K., Singh, H.S., Bharti, P.K., Meshram, M.K.: Metamaterial-based UWB antenna. Electron. Lett. **50**(18), 1266–1268 (2014)
6. Pendry, J.B., Holden, A.J., Robbins, D.J., Stewart, W.J.: Magnetism from conductors and enhanced nonlinear phenomena. IEEE Trans. Microw. Theory Tech. **47**(11), 2075–2084 (1999)
7. Viktor, G.V.: The electrodynamics of substances with simultaneously negative values of ϵ and M. Soviet Physics Uspekhi **10**(4), 509–514 (1968)
8. Martin, F., Sorolla, M., Marques, R.: Metamaterials with Negative Parameters: Theory, Design, and Microwave Applications (2008)
9. Lin, I.H., Caloz, C., Itoh, T.: Transmission line approach of left-handed (LH) non-uniform transmission lines (NTL). In: IEEE Asia Pacific Microw. Conference (APMC), pp. 1501–1504. IEEE (2002)
10. Belov, P.A., et al.: Strong spatial dispersion in wire media in the very large wavelength limit. Phys. Rev. B **67**(11), 113103 (2003)
11. Landau, L.D., Bell, J.S., Kearsley, M.J., Pitaevskii, L.P., Lifshitz, E.M., Sykes, J.B.: Electrodynamics of Continuous Media, vol. 8. Elsevier, Amsterdam (2013)
12. Milias, C., et al.: Metamaterial-inspired antennas: a review of the state of the art and future design challenges. IEEE Access, **9**, 89846–89865 (2021)
13. Rani, R., Kaur, P., Verma, N.: Metamaterials and their applications in patch antenna: a. Int. J. Hybrid Inf. Technol. **8**(11), 199–212 (2015)
14. Dong, Y., Toyao, H., Itoh, T.: Compact circularly-polarized patch antenna loaded with metamaterial structures. IEEE Trans. Antennas Propag. **59**(11), 4329–4333 (2011)
15. Dong, Y., Toyao, H., Itoh, T.: Design and characterization of miniaturized patch antennas loaded with complementary split-ring resonators. IEEE Trans. Antennas Propag. **60**(2), 772–785 (2011)
16. Xu, H.X., Wang, G.M., Liang, J.G., Qi, M.Q., Gao, X.: Compact circularly polarized antennas combining meta-surfaces and strong space-filling meta-resonators. IEEE Trans. Antennas Propag. **61**(7), 3442–3450 (2013)
17. Agarwal, K., Alphones, A.: RIS-based compact circularly polarized microstrip antennas. IEEE Trans. Antennas Propag. **61**(2), 547–554 (2012)
18. Bian, L., Guo, Y.X., Ong, L.C., Shi, X.Q.: Wideband circularly-polarized patch antenna. IEEE Trans. Antennas Propag. **54**(9), 2682–2686 (2006)

Performance Comparison of IEEE 802.11ax, 802.11ac and 802.11n Using Network Simulator NS3

Manav Chotalia(✉) and Sachin Gajjar(✉)

Department of Electronics and Communication Engineering, Institute of Technology,
Nirma University, Ahmedabad, Gujarat 382470, India
{21mece05,sachin.gajjar}@nirmauni.ac.in

Abstract. Wireless protocols are upgrading very rapidly. The current market scenario usually uses three wireless protocols namely 802.11ax, 802.11ac, and 802.11n. IEEE 802.11ax, a sixth-generation protocol popularly known as HE (High Efficiency) is said to have achieved 30% higher performance in terms of throughput than older protocol 802.11ac known as VHT (very high throughput). In this paper, performance evaluation of different wireless protocols namely 802.11ax, 802.11ac, and 802.11n operating on frequency bands of 2.4 and 5 GHz. The throughput of all three protocols is calculated on MCS-0 to 11 (Modulation and Coding Scheme) with a common channel width of 20, 40, and 80 MHz. Bandwidth of 160 MHz is not considered in the evaluation. Though it can achieve more throughput because, in practical urban scenarios, it is rarely used. Bandwidth sharing for all three protocols is also simulated and analyzed. For simulation, open-source Network Simulator NS3 is used which takes lesser time to set up the network, provides a precise level of simulation for wireless networks, and minutely mimics real-world wireless networks scenarios. Simulations show that for a single antenna of 5 GHz band at 80 MHz bandwidth 802.11ax achieved 18% higher throughput, whereas at 20 MHz bandwidth, it shows 50% improvement compared to 802.11ac. Further, it is seen that 802.11ax can achieve two times faster throughput than 802.11n at 20MHz bandwidth in the 5 GHz band with a single Antenna.

Keywords: Wireless protocol 802.11ax · 802.11ac · 802.11n · Network Simulator NS3 · performance comparison · throughput

1 Introduction

The Internet of Things (IoT) can have enormous potential because they enhance human's ability to interact with objects in the physical world. The field has evolved due to advancements in wireless protocol, sensors, actuators, and microprocessors. Different communication protocols are utilized for interoperability among these devices. Wi-Fi, Bluetooth, ZigBee, and LoRA are the four main networking protocols that have played a pivotal role in delivering immersive IoT applications. The protocols mentioned are commonly

N. Chaubey et al. (Eds.): COMS2 2023, CCIS 1861, pp. 191–203, 2023.
https://doi.org/10.1007/978-3-031-40564-8_14

applied in various areas such as managing homes, smart structures, sophisticated measuring, and keeping track of health and physical fitness. [1–6] The uses of IoT are limitless, and Wi-Fi provides numerous possibilities for these applications. Various versions of Wi-Fi have been created to meet the diverse needs of network applications.

Wi-Fi was developed to replace the wired Ethernet which uses fast data speed and is valued for simplicity and power efficiency. Bluetooth was developed for serial wire replacement. It has a quality-of-service overhead for voice communication but it is less power-intensive than Wi-Fi. Bluetooth can only support a network of eight devices and has a significant pairing delay. This method is the favored choice for wireless transmission of information across limited distances. It employs UHF radio waves with a wavelength that falls under the ISM band and operates within a frequency range of 2.4 to 2.485 GHz. Based on the applications, there are three different versions of Bluetooth technology: Bluetooth, iBeacon, BLE(Bluetooth Low Energy or Bluetooth 4.0). ZigBee was created to facilitate the construction of extensive sensor networks that require low-power nodes at an affordable price. Its coverage range is limited to 10–100 m, and it has a data rate of 250 Kbps, which is significantly lower than Wi-Fi or Bluetooth. The IEEE 802.15.4 radio is utilized by ZigBee, and it is commonly employed in various sense-and-control applications such as home or building automation, advanced measuring, and health or fitness monitoring.

Each of these widely used protocols is based on an industry radio standard. Several industry alliances and partnerships are in place to encourage the adoption of these protocols and ensure interoperability. The prevailing protocol employed for WLAN (Wireless Local Area Networks) is known as Wi-Fi. It adheres to the IEEE 802.11 standard and operates using the ISM frequencies of 2.4 and 5 GHz. If one of the devices within a range of 20–40 m is connected to the internet, other devices can access the internet via Wi-Fi. The highest possible data rate for the 802.11n standard can reach 600 Mbps, and this rate is influenced by factors like the frequency channel used and the number of antennas involved.

Wireless protocols have reached their capacity limitations due to recent advancements in the Internet of Things, video conferencing, low-latency online gaming, high-definition video streaming, etc. As a result, the 802.11ax wireless protocol was swiftly adopted since it can effectively handle higher client densities. This is because of its additional channel-sharing functionality that utilizes MU-MIMO.

In this paper, performance evaluation of different versions of WiFi protocols namely 802.11ax, 802.11ac, and 802.11n operating on 2.4 and 5GHz frequency bands is carried out. The throughput of all three protocols is calculated on MCS-0 to 11 (Modulation and Coding Scheme) with a common channel width of 20, 40, and 80 MHz. Bandwidth sharing for all three protocols is also simulated and analyzed. All the simulations are performed using open-source Network Simulator NS3.

The following document is structured as follows: In Sect. 2, a review of relevant literature is presented, along with an overview of all three standards. Section 3 presents the features of the Network Simulator NS3 and the simulation models. Section 4 discusses the simulation and analysis of 802.11ax, 802.11ac, and 802.11n standards. Finally, Sect. 4 concludes of the paper.

2 Literature Review

802.11ax [7], 802.11ac [8], 802.11n [9] are widely used IEEE standards for wireless local area network [10]. Additional features and amendments in 802.11ax standard are discussed in [11]. The work suggests that Unplanned wireless deployment may cause inefficiencies in the network since 802.11ax can operate up to 10 Gbps. The research concludes that incorporating Dynamic Channel Bonding (DCB) and OFDMA can increase the efficiency of spectrum usage in the standard.

Ravindranath et al. discussed the performance enhancements of the 802.11ac protocol in comparison to 802.11n in [12]. The research concluded that the 802.11ac protocol, It can be called as Very High Throughput, can attain data rates up to 2.3 Gbps when operating with 5 GHz frequency. This was accomplished by improving features from the 802.11n protocol, such as the support for wider bandwidths of 80 and 160 MHz, extended MIMO support, and better coding schemes at the Physical Layer (PHY).

The authors of [13] conducted a comprehensive review of IEEE 802.11ax. The research discusses the requirements, scope, and features of the 802.11ax amendment and why it is necessary. The coexistence of 802.11ax and LTE (Long Term Evolution) is also explored. The study highlights the suitability of 802.11ax for IoT (Internet of Things) scenarios. The research concludes that the 802.11ax amendment enables efficient spectrum utilization and provides the best user experience in high-density WLAN networks.

In [14] Machrouh et. al. Compare the performance of throughput for 802.11ax and 802.11ac. They conclude that the 802.11ax provides improved throughput by using OFDMA and a higher coding scheme. In [15] Darwish and Mohamed have also discussed the high throughput and efficiency of 802.11 wireless standards. The 802.11 versions simulated in this paper are discussed next.

2.1 802.11n

802.11n appeared at an important time in 802.11's development when smartphones were getting popular. Former PHYs were designed exclusively for the 2.4 GHz Industrial, Scientific, and Medical (ISM) band and featured direct sequence and frequency hopping PHYs. When the 5 GHz spectrum was made available for unlicensed usage, 802.11a was developed. The goal of 802.11g was to make the 802.11a technology available in the 2.4 GHz range. However, 802.11n was developed while both bands were accessible. The maximum data rate of 802.11n is 600 Mbps, as presented in Table 1. The highest modulation is 64-QAM which is based on the MCS-7 standard. It uses 0.4 and 0.8 μs guard band. The channel bandwidth supported is 20 and 40 MHz.

Backward combability is provided in 802.11n for the legacy 802.11 formats, as discussed in [16]. The latest developed Physical layer convergence protocol defines High Throughput (HT) and operates in two modes: mixed mode (802.11a/b/g and n) and Greenfield mode (802.11n). It has the capability to handle up to four spatial streams. 20 and 40 MHz channel bonding, resulting in higher throughput and low interference.

802.11n offers till 600 Mbps of data rates and increased MAC's efficiency due to its Frame aggregation approach. It divides the expense of each transmitter's access to

Table 1. 802.11n specifications

Maximum data rate	600 Mbps
RF Band	2.4 and 5 GHz
Highest modulation	64-QAM
Guard band	0.4 μs, 0.8 μs
Channel width	20, 40 MHz

the medium over several smaller frames. Aggregation increases efficiency by 50% to around 75%, depending on the type of data being transferred [16].

2.2 802.11ac

Table 2 shows the major specifications of 802.11ac. As seen in the figure maximum data rate of 802.11ac is 2.3 Gbps. This allows high-definition video streaming. The highest modulation is 256-QAM which is the MCS-9 standard. It uses 0.4 and 0.8 μs guard band. Bandwidth supported by channel are 20, 40, 80, and 160 MHz. Physical speeds greater than 500 Mbps are supported for a single connection.

Table 2. 802.11ac specifications

Maximum data rate	2.4 Gbps
RF Band	5 GHz
Highest modulation	256-QAM
Guard band	0.4 μs, 0.8 μs
Channel width	20, 40, 80, 160 MHz

802.11ac has several notable features, including multi-user MIMO [17] that can support up to 4-clients, There is backing to enable wider channels with a maximum of 160 MHz bandwidth and the adoption of more compact modulation techniques like 256-QAM. This enables a high data rate and supports up to eight spatial streams [18]. After the advent of MIMO, many of the methods were used to boost speed in 802.11ac 802.11ac builds on established strategies and elevates them to a new level. According to [19], 802.11ac's multi-user MIMO functionality empowers an Access Point (AP) to broadcast data to multiple clients concurrently, instead of merely enhancing the number of data streams intended for a single client.

2.3 802.11ax

802.11ax is the latest amendment in the WLAN protocol. It has made changes in the physical layer of legacy 802.11 for improvement. As shown in Table 3 maximum data rate of 802.11ax is 9 Gbps. The highest modulation is 1024-QAM which is the MCS-11 standard. The protocol supports guard bands of 0.8, 1.6, and 3.2 μs, as well as channel bandwidths of 20, 40, 80, and 160 MHz. The protocol maintains backward compatibility with preceding 802.11a/b/g/n/ac standards. The protocol operates in two modes: multi-user mode and single-user mode. Multi-user mode facilitates concurrent transmission whereas single-user mode, data is transferred sequentially following media access. Multi-user mode is further divided into Downlink and Uplink Multi-user. The foundation of multi-user downlink is the data that the Access Point transmits simultaneously for a number of connected wireless stations.

Table 3. 802.11ax specifications

Maximum data rate	9 Gbps
RF Band	2.4 or 5 GHz
Highest modulation	1024-QAM
Guard band	0.8, 1.6, 3.2 μs
Channel width	20, 40, 80, 160 MHz

802.11ax is also called HE (Higher efficiency) as it utilizes radio frequency more efficiently. The majority of the 802.11ax enhancement is focused on the physical layer. This includes the use of OFDM with a multi-user feature. The older 11n/ac uses OFDM with a single user. It also provides better traffic management. Another significant improvement is the Access Point (AP) can monitor both uplink and downlink transmission to multiple clients. This feature includes backward compatibility with older protocols and operates on both 2.4 GHz and 5 GHz.

Both 802.11ac and 802.11ax Access Points may receive and deliver data concurrently to multi-users (MU) using functionalities provided by multi-link MU-MIMO. This functionality gives Access Point the freedom to serve user clients in their immediate vicinity. Both protocols leverage technologies like Orthogonal Frequency Division Multiple Access (OFDMA) and multi-user MIMO. 802.11ax is also capable of transmit beam forming which is the technique of MIMO that improves SNR at receiver space [20].

3 Simulation and Analysis

3.1 Simulation Model

The Network Simulator NS3 is an open-source and freely available simulator. That is widely used by both businesses and the research community. There are several validation experiments of NS3 that makes sure that its 802.11 models are accurate [19]. Hence NS3.37 is used for the simulation and analysis of 802.11ax, 802.11ac, and 802.11n in this paper.

The source code of NS3 is written in Python and C++. It provides models for wireless and wired networks with different topologies. Figure 1 shows the network topology used in the simulation. It is an infrastructure-based wireless network with five stations connected to an Access point.

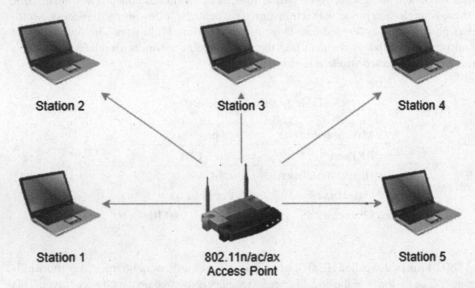

Fig. 1. Network topology used for Simulation

MCS (modulation and coding schemes) 0–11 utilised for the simulated network. Fixed-rate Infrastructure mode is used to simulate 802.11ax, 802.11ac, and 802.11n. Frame aggregation features like AMSDU and AMPDU are used to achieve higher throughput. Table 4 presents the simulation parameters. Simulation is performed on only one spatial stream as the focus of this comparison is to observe how different standards perform in the same scenario. In the simulation, the guard bands as per Table 4 are included. Simulation is carried out for 60 s for every scenario. Constant Position mobility model is used in the simulation. The transport layer protocol from Station to AP is UDP type.

3.2 Simulation Results

The network scenario used for simulation is shown in Fig. 1. It is an infrastructure-based network with one access point and five stations. Table 5 shows the basic simulation parameters. 802.11n can support MCS-7 (64-QAM) whereas 802.11ax's higher coding scheme can support up to MCS-11 (1024-QAM) which gives higher throughput as it can carry more data than 64-QAM.

Figure 2 shows that 802.11ax achieves the highest throughput irrespective of the guard interval and coding scheme. A higher coding scheme clearly transfers more packet data which results in higher throughput. Lower coding schemes transfer fewer data regardless of wireless standards.

Table 4. Simulation Parameters

MCS	MCS-0 to MCS-11	MCS-0 to MCS-9	MCS-0 to MCS-7
Guard Interval	0.8us, 1.6us, 3.2us	0.4us, 0.8us	0.4us, 0.8us
Channel Width	20, 40, 80 MHz	20, 40, 80 MHz	20, 40 MHz
Frequency	2.4, 5 Ghz	5 Ghz	2.4, 5 Ghz
Spatial Stream	1	1	1
Mobility model	Constant position mobility model		
Simulation time	60 s		

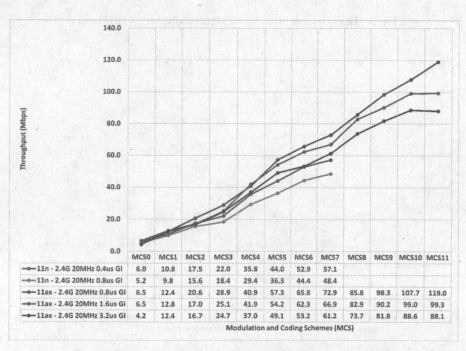

	MCS0	MCS1	MCS2	MCS3	MCS4	MCS5	MCS6	MCS7	MCS8	MCS9	MCS10	MCS11
11n - 2.4G 20MHz 0.4us GI	6.0	10.8	17.5	22.0	35.8	44.0	52.9	57.1				
11n - 2.4G 20MHz 0.8us GI	5.2	9.8	15.6	18.4	29.4	36.3	44.4	48.4				
11ax - 2.4G 20MHz 0.8us GI	6.5	12.4	20.6	28.9	40.9	57.3	65.8	72.9	85.8	98.3	107.7	119.0
11ax - 2.4G 20MHz 1.6us Gi	6.5	12.8	17.0	25.1	41.9	54.2	62.3	66.9	82.9	90.2	99.0	99.3
11ax - 2.4G 20MHz 3.2us Gi	4.2	12.4	16.7	24.7	37.0	49.1	53.2	61.2	73.7	81.8	88.6	88.1

Modulation and Coding Schemes (MCS)

Fig. 2. Throughput vs MCS for 20 MHz bandwidth 2.4 GHz band

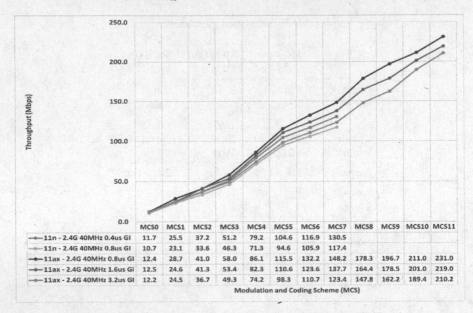

Fig. 3. Throughput vs MCS for 40 MHz bandwidth 2.4 GHz band

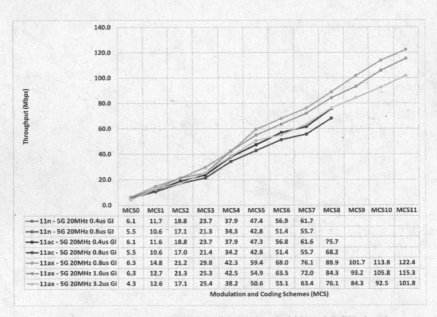

Fig. 4. Throughput vs MCS for 20 MHz bandwidth and 5 GHz band

As seen in Fig. 3, similar results are seen for 20 MHz and 40 MHz channel bandwidth for 802.11n and 802.11ax standards. 802.11ax 40 MHz can achieve 77% higher throughput than 802.11n. For 802.11n and 802.11ax, 40 MHz bandwidth achieves almost two times higher throughput.

For 802.11n protocol at 20 MHz maximum throughput achieved is 57.1 Mbps and at 40 MHz it is 130 Mbps. The results are similar for 802.1ax where 119 Mbps to 231 Mbps speed is achieved. Guard bands make difference in overall throughput as they can create overhead over actual data packets.

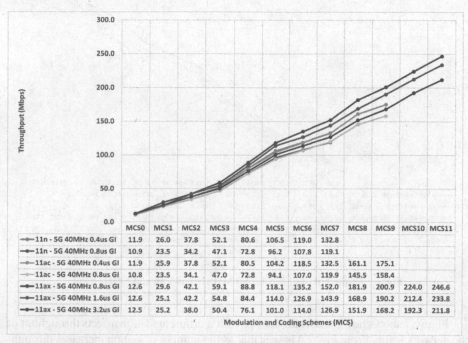

	MCS0	MCS1	MCS2	MCS3	MCS4	MCS5	MCS6	MCS7	MCS8	MCS9	MCS10	MCS11
11n - 5G 40MHz 0.4us GI	11.9	26.0	37.8	52.1	80.6	106.5	119.0	132.8				
11n - 5G 40MHz 0.8us GI	10.9	23.5	34.2	47.1	72.8	96.2	107.8	119.1				
11ac - 5G 40MHz 0.4us GI	11.9	25.9	37.8	52.1	80.5	104.2	118.5	132.5	161.1	175.1		
11ac - 5G 40MHz 0.8us GI	10.8	23.5	34.1	47.0	72.8	94.1	107.0	119.9	145.5	158.4		
11ax - 5G 40MHz 0.8us GI	12.6	29.6	42.1	59.1	88.8	118.1	135.2	152.0	181.9	200.9	224.0	246.6
11ax - 5G 40MHz 1.6us GI	12.6	25.1	42.2	54.8	84.4	114.0	126.9	143.9	168.9	190.2	212.4	233.8
11ax - 5G 40MHz 3.2us GI	12.5	25.2	38.0	50.4	76.1	101.0	114.0	126.9	151.9	168.2	192.3	211.8

Modulation and Coding Schemes (MCS)

Fig. 5. Throughput vs MCS for 40 MHz bandwidth and 5 GHz band

Figure 4, 5 and 6 show Throughput against MCS for 20, 40 and 80 MHz 5 GHz band respectively. It is observed that the 5 GHz band can transfer more data compared to 2.4 GHz for all standards in the same bandwidth. Maximum throughput of 443 Mbps is achieved in 80 MHz 0.8 us Guard Interval for 802.11ax.

Maximum throughput is 376 Mbps for 802.11ac standard. Thus, for 80 MHz band-width in the 5 GHz spectrum, 802.11ax is 18% faster. For 20 MHz bandwidth between 2.4 and 5 GHz, the 5 GHz bands can carry more data than the 2.4 GHz band because of the denser frequency band of 5 GHz and less interference in the channel.

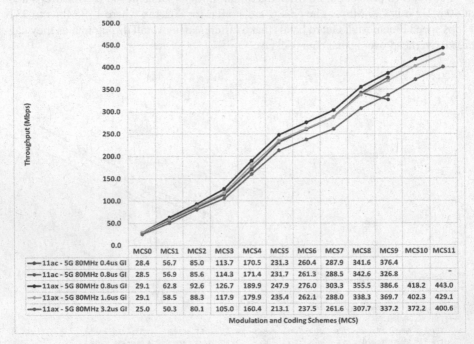

	MCS0	MCS1	MCS2	MCS3	MCS4	MCS5	MCS6	MCS7	MCS8	MCS9	MCS10	MCS11
11ac - 5G 80MHz 0.4us GI	28.4	56.7	85.0	113.7	170.5	231.3	260.4	287.9	341.6	376.4		
11ac - 5G 80MHz 0.8us GI	28.5	56.9	85.6	114.3	171.4	231.7	261.3	288.5	342.6	326.8		
11ax - 5G 80MHz 0.8us GI	29.1	62.8	92.6	126.7	189.9	247.9	276.0	303.3	355.5	386.6	418.2	443.0
11ax - 5G 80MHz 1.6us GI	29.1	58.5	88.3	117.9	179.9	235.4	262.1	288.0	338.3	369.7	402.3	429.1
11ax - 5G 80MHz 3.2us GI	25.0	50.3	80.1	105.0	160.4	213.1	237.5	261.6	307.7	337.2	372.2	400.6

Modulation and Coding Schemes (MCS)

Fig. 6. Throughput vs MCS for 80 MHz bandwidth and 5 GHz band

Figure 7 shows how bandwidth sharing with a different station affects throughput of the network setup. From Fig. 7 it is seen that as the number of station increases through-put decreases for a single antenna. Further, 802.11ax has better efficiency for multiple stations whereas legacy protocol 802.11n struggles to keep up with the throughput.

Moreover, it supports MU-MIMO technology, which allows for the transmission of up to 8 spatial streams concurrently. Due to its higher density, the 5 GHz frequency band has greater data-carrying capacity than the 2.4 GHz band for 20 MHz bandwidth between 2.4 and 5 GHz.

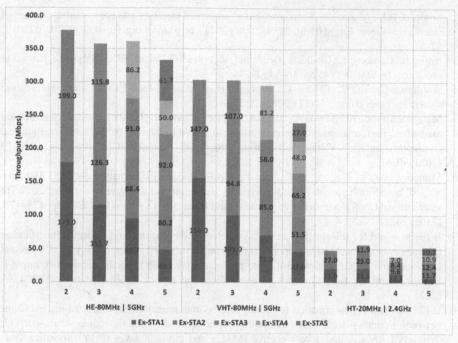

Fig. 7. Bandwidth sharing for different standard

4 Conclusion

Simulation and analysis of different Wi-Fi standards namely 802.11n, 802.11ac, and 802.11ax are carried out for 20, 40, and 80 MHz bandwidth for 2.4 and 5 GHz bands. For both bands, 20 MHz channel width does not show much improvement compared to 40 MHz and 80 MHz bandwidth. 802.11 ax standard at 2.4 GHz offers 119 Mbps and at 5 GHz it offers 122 Mbps. 2.4 GHz band offers lower throughput due to multiple reasons like lower data carrying capacity and higher interference compared to 5 GHz. The second experiment with a multi-station environment shows that as the number of station increase throughput for individual station also decrease. This is because bandwidth is shared between stations. 802.11ax performs better as it can efficiently prioritize packets, for example, it gives more priority to video calls and video streaming compared to downloading any software. In the future work range against rate, delay and jitters can be measured. The new release 802.11be popularly named Extremely High Throughput can also be simulated and its performance can be analyzed.

References

1. Cali, U., Kuzlu, M., Pipattanasomporn, M., Kempf, J., Bai, L.: Smart grid standards and protocols. In: Digitalization of Power Markets and Systems Using Energy Informatics, pp. 39–58. Springer, Cham (2021). https://doi.org/10.1007/978-3-030-83301-5_3

2. England, B.S., Alouani, A.T.: Internet-based advanced metering and control infrastructure of smart grid. Electr. Eng. **103**(6), 2989–2996 (2021). https://doi.org/10.1007/s00202-021-012 87-5
3. Breve, B., Caruccio, L., Cirillo, S., Deufemia, V., Polese, G.: Visual ECG analysis in real-world scenarios. In: DMSVIVA, pp. 46–54 (2021)
4. Stolojescu-Crisan, C., Crisan, C., Butunoi, B.-P.: An IoT-based smart home automation system. Sensors (Basel) **21**(11), 3784 (2021)
5. Mangunkusumo, K., Surya, A., Jintaka, D., Tambunan, H.: Guidance on communication media selection for advanced metering infrastructure in Indonesia. In: 2021 3rd International Conference on High Voltage Engineering and Power Systems (ICHVEPS), pp. 408–413 (2021). IEEE
6. Muneeswaran, V., Nagaraj, P., Rajasekaran, M.P., Reddy, S.U., Chaithanya, N.S., Babajan, S.: IoT based multiple vital health parameter detection and analyzer system. In: 2022 7th International Conference on Communication and Electronics Systems (ICCES), pp. 473–478. IEEE (2022)
7. IEEE standard for information technology–telecommunications and information exchange between systems local and metropolitan area networks specific requirements part 11: Wireless LAN medium access control (MAC) and physical layer (PHY) specifications amendment 1: Enhancements for high-efficiency WLAN. Technical report, IEEE, Piscataway, NJ, USA (2021)
8. IEEE standard for information technology–telecommunications and information exchange between systems—local and metropolitan area networks–specific requirements–part 11: Wireless LAN medium access control (MAC) and physical layer (PHY) Specifications–Amendment 4: Enhancements for very high throughput for operation in bands below 6 GHz. IEEE Std 802. 11ac(TM)-2013 (Amendment to IEEE Std 802.11 2012, as amended by IEEE Std 802. 11ae-2012, IEEE Std 802. 11aa-2012, and IEEE Std 802. 11ad-2012), 1–425 (2013)
9. IEEE standard for information technology– local and metropolitan area networks– specific requirements– part 11: Wireless LAN medium access control (MAC)and physical layer (PHY) specifications amendment 5: Enhancements for higher throughput. Technical report, IEEE, Piscataway, NJ, USA (2009)
10. IEEE: 8802.11–99 Wireless LAN MAC & Phy Specifications: Standard for Information Technology-telecommunications and Information Exchange Between systems-LAN/man-specific Requirements-part 11: Wireless LAN Medium Access Control (mac) and Physical Layer (phy) Specifications pt.11, 1999 edn. IEEE Press, Piscataway, NJ (2006)
11. Bellalta, B.: IEEE 802.11ax: High-efficiency WLANS. IEEE Wirel. Commun. **23**(1), 38–46 (2016)
12. Ravindranath, N.S., Singh, I., Prasad, A., Rao, V.S.: Performance evaluation of IEEE 802.11ac and 802.11n using NS3. Indian J. Sci. Technol. **9**(26) (2016)
13. Afaqui, M.S., Garcia-Villegas, E., Lopez-Aguilera, E.: IEEE 802.11ax: Challenges and requirements for future high efficiency WiFi. IEEE Wirel. Commun. **24**(3), 130–137 (2017)
14. Machrouh, Z., Najid, A.: High efficiency IEEE 802.11 ax MU-MIMO and frame aggregation analysis. In: 2018 International Conference on Advanced Communication Technologies and Networking (CommNet), pp. 1–5. IEEE (2018)
15. Darwish, M., Ali, M.B., Altaeb, M., Sati, S.O., Elmusrati, M.S.: Comparison between high throughput and efficiency of 802.11 wireless standards. In: 2022 International Conference on Innovation and Intelligence for Performance Comparison of IEEE 802.11ax, 802.11ac & 802.11n 13 Informatics, Computing, and Technologies (3ICT), pp. 470–475. IEEE (2022)
16. Kowsar, M.M.S., Biswas, S.: Performance improvement of IEEE 802.11n WLANs via frame aggregation in ns-3. In: 2017 International Conference on Electrical, Computer and Communication Engineering (ECCE), pp. 1–6. IEEE (2017)

17. Behara, A., Venkatesh, T.G.: Performance analysis and energy efficiency of MU- (OFDMA & MIMO) based hybrid MAC protocol of IEEE 802.11ax WLANs. IEEE Trans. Veh. Technol., 1–16 (2022)
18. Khalil, N., Najid, A.: Performance analysis of 802.11ac with frame aggregation using NS3. Int. J. Electr. Comput. Eng. (IJECE) **10**(5), 5368 (2020)
19. J¨onsson, A., ˚Akerman, D., Fitzgerald, E., Nyberg, C., Priyanto, B.E., Agardh, K.: Modeling, implementation and evaluation of IEEE 802.11 ac in NS-3 for enterprise networks. In: 2016 Wireless Days (WD), pp. 1–6. IEEE (2016)
20. Rochim, A.F., Harijadi, B., Purbanugraha, Y.P., Fuad, S., Nugroho, K.A.: Performance comparison of wireless protocol IEEE 802.11 ax vs 802.11 ac. In: 2020 International Conference on Smart Technology and Applications (ICoSTA), pp. 1–5. IEEE (2020)

Web Browser Forensics: A Comparative Integrated Approach on Artefacts Acquisition, Evidence Collections and Analysis of Google Chrome, Firefox and Brave Browser

Hitesh Sanghvi[1], Vismay J. Patel[2], Ramya Shah[2], Parag Shukla[2], and Digvijaysinh Rathod[2(✉)]

[1] Directorate of Forensic Science, Gandhinagar, Gujarat, India
[2] School of Cybersecurity and Digital Forensics, National Forensic Sciences University, Gandhinagar, Gujarat, India
`digvijay.rathod@nfsu.ac.in`

Abstract. Web browser is the important application and majority user users use web browsers to access the social media sites, email application, web search engines, ecommerce sites and download the video or photos. Various web browsers are available in the market for this purpose but Google chrome, Mozilla Firefox and Brave are the well-known browser application. These web browsers might be use for normal internet access also use to committee the crime. In such case it is important to use digital forensics techniques to extract evidences which will be produced to court to prove the crime. Literature survey shows that dead forensics were frequently used by researchers but very less work is carried out to use live or RAM forensics to extract the evidences. In this research paper, we created real time scenario with Google Chrome, Mozilla Firefox and Brave browser and use RAM forensics techniques to extract the evidences related to web browser activities.

Keywords: Web browser forensics · RAM forensics · digital forensics · Google chrome · Mozella Firefox · Brave · Autopsy · memory analysis · digital forensics · browser ar-tifacts · browser history

1 Introduction

One of the most common methods of retrieving the Internet is over a web browser, which gives users the ability to carry out traditional crimes or commit crimes online. Computer forensics, a more general area of study, includes web browser forensics. Computer forensics' objective is to locate, gather, protect, and analyze data that contains evidence in a way that keeps the evidence's honesty complete so that it can be used as signal in a law court. In web browser forensics, evidence pertaining to a user's Internet surfing activities is analyzed and extracted. Browser forensics is mostly used to examine a computer's browser log and universal web action in order to look for any doubtful activity or gratified access. In order to obtain precise material about the targeted system, this also relates to

N. Chaubey et al. (Eds.): COMS2 2023, CCIS 1861, pp. 204–218, 2023.
https://doi.org/10.1007/978-3-031-40564-8_15

tracking website traffic and analyzing server-generated LOG files. The goal of computer forensics, a type of forensic investigation, is to describe and analyze the digital signal that remains kept on processers and connected storage broadcasting.

Nearly everybody, including accused under examination, uses the cyberspace. A suspicious person might use a web browser to collect evidence, cover their misconduct, or look for another traditions to obligate criminalities. An important feature of digital forensic investigations is frequently penetrating for web browsing related data. Thus, nearly each action a suspicious took although by means of a web browser would be recorded on a computer. This data can therefore be helpful when a investigator inspects the accused's computer. It is likely to inspect evidence from a accused's computer, counting cookies, cache, log data, and download lists, to control the websites has been checked, when and how frequently they were retrieved, and the examination relations the suspicious used.

The digital forensics analyst either can use dead / hard disk forensics or live/RAM forensics to extract evidences related to activities carried out by the user. RAM is volatile memory but keeps important details related to recent executed programs and application by the user. In this research paper, we used RAM forensics techniques to extract important evidences related to browser activities from Google Chrome, Mozilla Firefox and Brave web browser.

The remaining part of the paper is systematized as follows - the associated research paper assessment is deliberated in Sect. 2, methodology of RAM forensics, Data modeling, Laboratory Set-up and results is discussed in Sect. 3, 4, 5 and 6 respectively. The result is discussed in Sect. 7 and paper is concluded in Sect. 8.

2   Literature Survey

To understand the current status of the research in the domain of browser forensics, we have reviews recent published research paper in this domain, Research on artefact mining of Google Chrome, Mozilla Firefox, Apple Safari, and Internet Explorer in private and moveable browsing mode has been done by Donny J. Ohan, Narasimha, and Shashidhar [1]. The forensics of Google Chrome in both normal and private mode have been discussed by Andrew and Team [2]. Evidence pertaining to internet activity has been recovered from hard disc. Browser log files were taken into consideration by Junghoon Oh and Team [3] as a source of data for potential artefact extraction. Using RAM analysis, Huwida Said and Team [4] collected evidence. D. Rathod [5, 9] has taken RAM dump to gather objects connected to cyberspace actions on windows installed Google Chrome. In their study titled "Digital Forensic Analyses of Web Browser Records," E. Akbal, Futma G., and Ayhan [6] describe how web browsers and operating systems save data. In their research paper titled "Forensics Investigation of Web Application Security Attacks," Amor. L. and Thabet S. [7] deliberated the idea of net application scientific, describing it by way of a subset of nets scientific. They also proposed a procedure that would aid in the successful completion of an examination of net application safety. The following web browser forensic tools have been chosen by J. Oh, S. Lee, and Team [8]: WEFA, Cache Back 3.17, Encase 6.13, FTK 3.2, and Net Analysis 1.52. They concluded that WEFA would be the best tool for browser forensics.

Our review of the literature reveals that the majority of researchers employed browser history, local files, or hard disk examination as their primary bases of data for material extraction linked to online practice. In this research paper we focused on extraction of evidences related to Google search, Facebook, Web WhatsApp, ecommerce sites and movie sites form Google chrome, Mozilla Firefox and Brave web browsers. We focused on RAM forensics digital forensics techniques using volatility 3, Belkasoft Evidence Center X, FTK imager, and python 3.

3 Methodology

In this section we discussed the methodology adopted to carried out web browser forensics experiment.

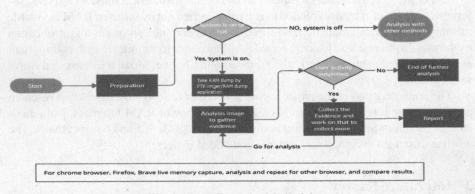

Fig. 1. RAM Forensics Methodology

As shown in the Fig. 1, whenever first responder reaches to the crime scene then he needs to check that system is switched on or off if it is switched on then take the RAM dump using FTK image or any other RAM dump application. If system is switched off then used dead forensics techniques to carried out the forensic. It is important to note down the hash worth of the picture which will be the part of chain of custodian to ensure the integrity of the evidence [10, 11]. The RAM dump is analyzed by the Autopsy and FTK analysis and examination tools. After the analysis, we used keyword search techniques to identify the evidences and this process will be continue until we found the required evidences. Once required evidences found, digital forensic analyst may prepare the report which will be produced in the court.

4 Data Modeling

Table. 1. Data modeling

No	Source	Activity
1	Google.com	The random images related to nature images searched in the Google search engine and nature images downloaded
2	Facebook	Login in to Facebook account, post photos, delete post, send friend request and also chat with friends
3	WhatsApp web	Login in the WhatsApp web, send message "Text1" and receive reply of "Text 2", made a voice call and video call, send media files and carried out chat also
4	Search for the paid product to download and also tried to find crack or key	lookingfor"adobephotoshopfree download" key word search, downloaded the same and also try to crack the same
5	Searching for free movie	free movie download site to download movies for free
6	Searching for attacks	Searching for tutorial or website which teach how to attack on any site

The goal and objective of this research paper is to represents what kind of artifacts we can get in different situation. To generate the real-world scenario, we have created data model shown in Table 1 in which various activities such as searching keywords in the Google search engine, login, post photos chatting in the Facebook and web WhatsApp etc., are carried out using Google, Facebook, web WhatsApp. Once these activates carried out, we taken RAM dump and analyzed with forensic tools to identify the evidences.

5 Laboratory Set-Up

We carried out the browser forensics with laptop and configure of the laptop is 8 GB RAM, intel i5 processor, 1 TB HDD, AMD Radeon HD 8730M - 2 GB GPU, Dell Inspiron 15R with Windows 10 home and build version 15.19042. The scenario is created with Google chrome version 90.0.4430.93, Mozilla Firefox 86.0.1(x64 en-US), Breve version 90.1.24.812. We have used following additional tools for imaging and analysis purpose,

1. FTK imager: FTK imager is used to take the memory dump
2. FTK toolkit: Its computer forensics software and we used to process the memory dump to extract the evidences.
3. Volatility 3 Framework: This is worlds widely used framework to extract digital evidences from volatile memory (RAM).
4. Belkasoft Evidence Center X: This is a digital forensics suite and it will be used to acquires, examines and analyze the evidences form computer, mobile, cloud and RAM.

6 Results

In this section we discussed the evidences extracted for Google Chrome, Mozilla Firefox and Brave web browser forensics.

6.1 Google Chrome Browser Forensics

We created various scenario list in the Table 1 and taken RAM dump with Belkasoft. The RAM dump file memChrome.mem is proceed with Volatility 3.0 shown in Fig. 2 and recovered list of process is listed in the Fig. 3. We can see list of process with their name and created time. This will be the important evidences to find the list of programs recently executed by the user.

```
Volatility 3 Framework 1.0.1

Variable       Value

Kernel Base    0xf80235a00000
DTB     0x1ad000
Symbols file:///C:/Python27/volatility3-
develop/volatility3/symbols/windows/ntkrnlmp.pdb/3FCC539FF307DD2D9C509206D352B9AA-1.json.xz
Is64Bit True
IsPAE   False
primary 0 WindowsIntel32e
memory_layer   1 FileLayer
KdVersionBlock 0xf8023660f330
Major/Minor    15.19041
MachineType    34404
KeNumberProcessors      4
SystemTime     2021-03-18 07:04:45
NtSystemRoot   C:\Windows
NtProductType  NtProductWinNt
NtMajorVersion 10
NtMinorVersion 0
PE MajorOperatingSystemVersion  10
PE MinorOperatingSystemVersion  0
PE Machine     34404
PE TimeDateStamp        Tue Sep  8 22:35:03 2082
```

Fig. 2. Image Info (Volatility 3)

```
PID    PPID   ImageFileName  Offset(V)       Threads Handles SessionId  Wow64  CreateTime                  ExitTime                    File output
13172  11468  CLIStart.exe   0x90878f4af080  0       -       4          False  2021-03-18 06:29:11.000000  2021-03-18 06:29:14.000000  Disabled
11560  13172  MOM.exe        0x90879ab77080  13      -       4          False  2021-03-18 06:29:12.000000  N/A     Disabled
15796  740    TextInputHost. 0x90879bb980c0  9       -       4          False  2021-03-18 06:29:26.000000  N/A     Disabled
13688  740    dllhost.exe    0x90879ae350c0  5       -       4          False  2021-03-18 06:29:29.000000  N/A     Disabled
7500   9352   chrome.exe     0x90879a05a0c0  0       -       4          False  2021-03-18 06:29:33.000000  2021-03-18 07:03:24.000000  Disabled
12908  1328   bdagent.exe    0x9087a63e60c0  57      -       4          False  2021-03-18 06:29:39.000000  N/A     Disabled
2168   7500   chrome.exe     0x90879a78a340  0       -       4          False  2021-03-18 06:30:13.000000  2021-03-18 07:03:23.000000  Disabled
15944  11560  CCC.exe        0x90879b0bb080  16      -       4          False  2021-03-18 06:30:34.000000  N/A     Disabled
17120  928    svchost.exe    0x9087994e60c0  1       -       4          False  2021-03-18 06:30:38.000000  N/A     Disabled
8160   740    ShellExperienc 0x908791f21080  19      -       4          False  2021-03-18 06:32:57.000000  N/A     Disabled
4256   740    RuntimeBroker. 0x90879f06d080  4       -       4          False  2021-03-18 06:32:58.000000  N/A     Disabled
12516  7500   chrome.exe     0x90879b333080  0       -       4          False  2021-03-18 06:34:16.000000  2021-03-18 06:34:22.000000  Disabled
13188  740    UserOOBEBroker 0x90879b076e0c0 2       -       4          False  2021-03-18 06:38:51.000000  N/A     Disabled
16360  7500   chrome.exe     0x90879b0570c0  0       -       4          False  2021-03-18 06:39:18.000000  2021-03-18 06:39:22.000000  Disabled
7604   7500   chrome.exe     0x90879b4790c0  0       -       4          False  2021-03-18 06:41:24.000000  2021-03-18 06:41:28.000000  Disabled
13248  7500   chrome.exe     0x90878f74a080  0       -       4          False  2021-03-18 06:49:48.000000  2021-03-18 06:49:51.000000  Disabled
10820  740    smartscreen.ex 0x90879abcc0c0  10      -       4          False  2021-03-18 07:03:24.000000  N/A     Disabled
13084  9352   FTK Imager.exe 0x908799cb0340  22      -       4          True   2021-03-18 07:03:29.000000  N/A     Disabled
```

Fig. 3. Process List (Volatility 3.0)

Fig. 4. Searched text in the Google Search Engine

Fig. 5. Visited URL by user

Extracted evidences shows in Fig. 4 depicts that user has searched nature image in the Google search engine and Fig. 5 shows the URL of the site that user has visited. Figure 6 shows image which was download by the user and this evidence is extracted by the Belkasoft.

File local offset (bytes)	359362560
File name	picture_000015687000.jpg
File size (bytes)	3211
File type	jpg
Height (px)	86
Length (bytes)	3211
Offset (bytes)	359362560
Origin	Carved
Origin path	memdumpchrome.mem
Path	picture_000015687000.jpg
PhotoDNA hash	31-45-68-19-0E-8F-25-25-1D-54-0D-64
Width (px)	86

Fig. 6. Image which was download by the user (Belkasoft).

Facebook login evidence is shown in the Fig. 7 and searched people related evidences in the Facebook is shown in Fig. 8.

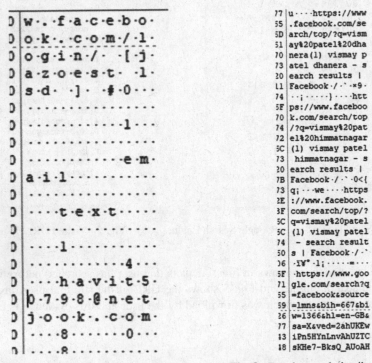

Fig. 7. Facebook login page (FTK)

Fig. 8. People search details in Facebook (FTK)

We are able to extract the evidences related to profile picture of the user from RAM shown in the Fig. 9 and original profile picture show in Fig. 10.

Vismay Patel

Fig. 9. Extracted profile of the user in the Facebook   **Fig. 10.** Original Photo

We are unable to find artifacts related to request send, message send, photo sent but able to find the video call attempt shown in the Fig. 11 using FTK. Figure 12 shows that user has search web whatsapp in the google search engine and Fig. 13 shows mobile number that user has has used to login in the web WhatsApp.

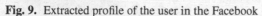

4B	LPDeBKFUhxTmxPmK
41	niraCwA-waAgrmEA
74	Lw_wcB···#··G·ht
6F	tps://www.facebo
6C	ok.com/videocall
64	/incall/?peer_id
37	=100008533205517
34	&call_id=8943154
75	39&is_caller=tru
75	e&audio_only=tru
6B	e&nonce=a60xc6tk
5F	rtto&initialize_
04	video=false·+···
66	·;·https://www.f
69	acebook.com/logi
74	n/?privacy_mutat
58	ion token=eyJ0eX

)	01	Ç···········!··
	74	··ä·½···Ç·*vhtt
;	2E	ps://www.google.
}	61	com/search?q=wha
	61	tsapp+web&oq=wha
}	68	tsapp+web&aqs=ch
?	37	rome..69i57j0i27
	63	1.4748j0j4&sourc
;	54	eid=chrome&ie=UT
?	65	F-82·whatsapp we
?	63	b - Google Searc
)	80	h:··ä·½···Ç·····
?	B5	······!····!·ɴ

31 00	_·#·!· ·2·0·2·1·
31 00	-·0·3·--1·8· ·1·
2E 00	2·:·2·0·:·5·7·,··
70 00	6·7·1·:·v·o·i·p·
6E 00	:·i·n·c·o·m·i·n·
6C 00	g·_·s·i·g·n·a·l·
72 00	i·n·g·(·p·a·i·r·
65 00	e·d· ·p·h·o·n·e·
3A 00	)·:·{·"·i·d·"·:·
44 00	"·E·1·4·0·6·E·D·
41 00	1·2·6·3·1·B·4·A·
34 00	D·C·F·F·9·F·8·4·
37 00	3·2·5·D·0·B·A·7·
65 00	0·"·,·"·t·y·p·e·
70 00	"·:·"·a·c·c·e·p·
6D 00	t·"·,·"·f·r·o·m·
30 00	"·:·"·9·1·8·2·0·
40 00	þ·9·1·0·2·8·4·@·
70 00	c·.·u·s·"·,·"·p·
22 00	l·a·t·f·o·r·m·"·
69 00	:·"·a·n·d·r·o·i·
73 00	d·"·,·"·v·e·r·s·
2C 00	i·o·n·"·:·[·2·,·
03 00	2·1·,·6·]·}·:···
00 00	····&·@···ø·{)··
12 0F	·········)······

Fig. 11. Video call through Facebook (FTK)   **Fig. 12.** Web WhatsApp Search Details (FTK)   **Fig. 13.** Web WhatsApp login number retrieved (FTK)

As far as Web WhatsApp calling and chat concern, we are able to recover a artifact of receivers mobile number shown in Fig. 14 and also able to find that with which user (mobile no) user is doing a chat shown in Fig. 15. We are not able to find the evidences related to content of the chat.

```
2·0·2·1·—·0·3·—·          _·#·!·  ·2·0·2·1·
1·8·  ·1·2·:·1·6·          —·0·3·—·1·8·  ·1·
:·3·8·.·.2·6·7·:·          2·:·2·0·:·3·6·.·.
b·i·n·—·r·e·c·v·           2·6·6·:·b·i·n·—·
:·  ·3·3·6·b·l·d·          r·e·c·v·:·  ·3·3·
8·1·9·5·f·3·f·5·           6·b·l·d·8·1·9·5·
9·b·.·—·—·6·,·a·           f·3·f·5·9·b·.·—·
c·t·i·o·n·,·c·m·           —·8·,·a·c·t·i·o·
d·,·9·1·7·3·5·9·           n·,·m·s·g·,·r·e·
5·1·8·8·0·1·@·c·           l·a·y·,·c·h·a·t·
.·u·s·,·[·o·b·j·           ,·9·1·7·3·5·9·5·
e·c·t·  ·A·r·r·a·          1·8·8·0·1·@·c·.·
y·B·u·f·f·e·r·]·           u·s·,·9·1·8·2·0·
,·1·0·6·2·8·7·0·           0·9·1·0·2·8·4·@·
9·1·7·8·0·2·4·4·           c·.·u·s·,·f·a·l·
2·9·1·9·6·2·8·3·           s·e·_·9·1·7·3·5·
5·4·0·4·5·9·2·1·           9·5·1·8·8·0·1·@·
6·8·4·5·2·5·9·7·           c·.·u·s·_·F·0·6·
5·3·9·0·9·2·3·5·           3·4·9·5·A·5·7·1·
5·6·5·8·2·4·8·3·           0·6·1·E·0·E·1·D·
8·9·1·7·7·,·i·d·           2·D·3·A·D·5·4·3·
e·n·t·i·t·y·····          8·1·2·0·C·,·····
```

Fig. 14. Web WhatsApp Receiver Mobile no. (FTK)   **Fig. 15.** Web WhatsApp Chat Receiver

6.2 Mozilla Firefox Browser Forensics

We have crated scenario listed in the Table 1 with Mozilla Firefox and taken the RAM dump using Belkasoft. The RAM dump is processed with FTK and Bulkasoft to identify the evidences related to activities performed by us. In this section, we have discussed the identified evidences for various activities.

The RAM image is processed by the Volatility 3 shown in Fig. 16 and process list is shown in the Fig. 17. We can identify the evidences related to Mozilla Firefox along with creation time.

```
Volatility 3 Framework 1.0.1

Variable      Value

Kernel Base   0xf8006f400000
DTB      0x1ad000
Symbols file:///C:/Python27/volatility3-
develop/volatility3/symbols/windows/ntkrnlmp.pdb/27FB1171F9CEB561883B586400BCEDD2-1.json.xz
Is64Bit True
IsPAE   False
primary 0 WindowsIntel32e
memory_layer  1 FileLayer
KdVersionBlock  0xf8007000f330
Major/Minor   15.19041
MachineType   34404
KeNumberProcessors   4
SystemTime    2021-03-22 11:44:41
NtSystemRoot   C:\Windows
NtProductType   NtProductWinNt
NtMajorVersion  10
NtMinorVersion  0
PE MajorOperatingSystemVersion  10
PE MinorOperatingSystemVersion  0
PE Machine    34404
PE TimeDateStamp      Fri Jul 31 16:43:11 2082
```

Fig. 16. Image info (Volatility 3)

PID	PPID	ImageFileName	Offset(V)	Threads	Handles	SessionId	Wow64	CreateTime	ExitTime	File output	
8660	820	dllhost.exe	0xbb0989e8f300	5	-	2	False	2021-03-22 11:22:16.000000	N/A	Disabled	
7412	1148	firefox.exe	0xbb0975f0b300	0	-	2	False	2021-03-22 11:22:16.000000	2021-03-22 11:22:33.000000	Disabled	
3592	7412	firefox.exe	0xbb09853a60c0	0	-	2	False	2021-03-22 11:22:22.000000	2021-03-22 11:23:05.000000	Disabled	
8572	960	svchost.exe	0xbb09881c50c0	1	-	2	False	2021-03-22 11:22:40.000000	N/A	Disabled	
8316	3592	firefox.exe	0xbb0989edd2c0	0	-	2	False	2021-03-22 11:23:01.000000	2021-03-22 11:23:05.000000	Disabled	
5248	8316	firefox.exe	0xbb09853952c0	73	-	2	False	2021-03-22 11:23:01.000000	N/A	Disabled	
7132	5248	firefox.exe	0xbb09752e3300	33	-	2	False	2021-03-22 11:23:03.000000	N/A	Disabled	
8932	5248	firefox.exe	0xbb09859650c0	24	-	2	False	2021-03-22 11:23:06.000000	N/A	Disabled	
10400	5248	firefox.exe	0xbb0983be1300	0	-	2	False	2021-03-22 11:23:07.000000	2021-03-22 11:25:07.000000	Disabled	
5208	5248	firefox.exe	0xbb097b9dd300	21	-	2	False	2021-03-22 11:23:11.000000	N/A	Disabled	
11052	5248	firefox.exe	0xbb098cf85300	0	-	2	False	2021-03-22 11:23:13.000000	2021-03-22 11:35:22.000000	Disabled	
11076	5248	firefox.exe	0xbb097b1c6300	0	-	2	False	2021-03-22 11:23:13.000000	2021-03-22 11:23:13.000000	Disabled	
5104	5248	firefox.exe	0xbb0990351300	0	-	2	False	2021-03-22 11:23:13.000000	2021-03-22 11:23:13.000000	Disabled	
10944	5248	firefox.exe	0xbb09938d82c0	0	-	2	False	2021-03-22 11:24:10.000000	2021-03-22 11:25:30.000000	Disabled	
6560	5248	firefox.exe	0xbb098f7d60c0	0	-	2	False	2021-03-22 11:24:25.000000	2021-03-22 11:26:07.000000	Disabled	
4656	5248	firefox.exe	0xbb0988bc50c0	0	-	2	False	2021-03-22 11:25:07.000000	2021-03-22 11:31:12.000000	Disabled	
2388	5248	firefox.exe	0xbb098f4e70c0	0	-	2	False	2021-03-22 11:26:07.000000	2021-03-22 11:38:39.000000	Disabled	
7752	820	CompPkgSrv.exe	0xbb0982bcf300	4	-	2	False	2021-03-22 11:28:27.000000	N/A	Disabled	
892	5248	firefox.exe	0xbb097a1e7300	6	-	2	False	2021-03-22 11:28:28.000000	N/A	Disabled	
9372	820	UserOOBEBroker	0xbb098cac50c0	3	-	2	False	2021-03-22 11:31:15.000000	N/A	Disabled	
5888	5248	firefox.exe	0xbb098a1e70c0	0	-	2	False	2021-03-22 11:31:26.000000	2021-03-22 11:34:10.000000	Disabled	
8988	5248	firefox.exe	0xbb097a6e2300	0	-	2	False	2021-03-22 11:33:09.000000	2021-03-22 11:39:20.000000	Disabled	
10688	3492	audiodg.exe	0xbb0980108080	4	-	0	False	2021-03-22 11:34:48.000000	N/A	Disabled	
8328	5248	firefox.exe	0xbb0975bf0080	0	-	2	False	2021-03-22 11:38:09.000000	2021-03-22 11:43:03.000000	Disabled	
3944	5248	firefox.exe	0xbb09884c50c0	18	-	2	False	2021-03-22 11:38:59.000000	N/A	Disabled	
9288	3500	TabTip.exe	0xbb09874d6340	8	-	2	False	2021-03-22 11:39:28.000000	N/A	Disabled	
10880	3508	SynTPEnh.exe	0xbb0985cc50c0	0	-	2	False	2021-03-22 11:43:11.000000	2021-03-22 11:43:13.000000	Disabled	
9152	10880	SynTPHelper.ex	0xbb098328a0c0	1	-	2	False	2021-03-22 11:43:12.000000	N/A	Disabled	
4888	820	smartscreen.ex	0xbb097340c8080	7	-	2	False	2021-03-22 11:43:14.000000	N/A	Disabled	
5676	1148	FTK Imager.exe	0xbb09844870c0	10	-	2	True	2021-03-22 11:43:24.000000	N/A	Disabled	

Fig. 17. Profess List (Volatility 3)

The user has searched for the in the Google search engine for the nature images and we are able to find the evidences related to search item from the RAM shown in Fig. 18. We are able to find the URL of the site from which nature image is downloaded as shown in the Fig. 19.

Fig. 18. Google Search results (FTK)

Fig. 19. URI of site to download the image (FTK)

214   H. Sanghvi et al.

6.3 Brave Browser Forensics

The Brave Browser is constructed on the open-source Chromium Web core and client code is released under the Mozilla Public License 2.0 [13]. Brave, a browser which conceits the situation in the safety and confidentiality it offers and it has more than 13 million active handlers per month [16] or 0.05% of Global Desktop Browser Market Share [17]. As Brave browser is open sources and considering the percentage share in the global desktop browser market, it is important to know that what kind of evidence a digital forensic analysis can found in case Brave browser is used to committee the crime.

We have carried out the activities list in the data model Table 1 using Brave browser and taken the RAM dump. The following evidences were obtained for the activities list in the Table 1.

The image of RAM dump created for the Brave browser is process by the volatility 3.0 framework shown in Fig. 20 and process list listed by the volatility 3.0 is shown in the Fig. 38. We observed the evidences related to Brave browser along with created date (Fig. 21).

```
Volatility 3 Framework 1.0.1

Variable        Value

Kernel Base     0xf8045d800000
DTB      0x1ad000
Symbols file:///C:/Python27/volatility3-
develop/volatility3/symbols/windows/ntkrnlmp.pdb/769C521E4833ECF72E21F0
Is64Bit True
IsPAE   False                   /
primary 0 WindowsIntel32e
memory_layer    1 FileLayer
KdVersionBlock  0xf8045e40f368
Major/Minor     15.19041
MachineType     34404
KeNumberProcessors       4
SystemTime      2021-04-14 08:58:45
NtSystemRoot    C:\Windows
NtProductType   NtProductWinNt
NtMajorVersion  10
NtMinorVersion  0
PE MajorOperatingSystemVersion  10
PE MinorOperatingSystemVersion  0
PE Machine      34404
PE TimeDateStamp        Tue Oct 11 07:04:26 1977
```

Fig. 20. Image info of Brave browser [Volatility 3]

PID	PPID	ImageFileName	Offset(V)	Threads	Handles	SessionId	Wow64	CreateTime	ExitTime	File output
10020	904	TextInputHost.	0xbb81e12a1080	9	-	1	False	2021-04-14 08:23:32.000000	N/A	Disabled
7916	904	dllhost.exe	0xbb81d1fbef080	5	-	1	False	2021-04-14 08:23:33.000000	N/A	Disabled
4812	4248	brave.exe	0xbb81e11d4080	0	-	1	False	2021-04-14 08:23:34.000000	2021-04-14 08:41:59.000000	Disabled
10228	4812	brave.exe	0xbb81e1d32080	0	-	1	False	2021-04-14 08:24:51.000000	2021-04-14 08:24:58.000000	Disabled
3628	4812	brave.exe	0xbb81e09ea080	0	-	1	False	2021-04-14 08:28:53.000000	2021-04-14 08:28:57.000000	Disabled
4832	4812	brave.exe	0xbb81e169a080	0	-	1	False	2021-04-14 08:29:48.000000	2021-04-14 08:29:51.000000	Disabled
8152	4012	brave.exe	0xbb81dfb0b080	0	-	1	False	2021-04-14 08:30:52.000000	2021-04-14 08:30:54.000000	Disabled
7760	4812	brave.exe	0xbb81e3e9a300	0	-	1	False	2021-04-14 08:31:20.000000	2021-04-14 08:31:23.000000	Disabled
10624	2288	taskhostw.exe	0xbb81e37e1340	6	-	1	False	2021-04-14 08:31:59.000000	N/A	Disabled
9728	4812	brave.exe	0xbb81e16a5080	0	-	1	False	2021-04-14 08:33:12.000000	2021-04-14 08:33:15.000000	Disabled
9060	260	svchost.exe	0xbb81e58e3340	5	-	0	False	2021-04-14 08:33:47.000000	N/A	Disabled
6416	4248	brave.exe	0xbb81de4d3080	0	-	1	False	2021-04-14 08:42:00.000000	2021-04-14 08:58:30.000000	Disabled
7512	6416	brave.exe	0xbb81e5dbf080	0	-	1	False	2021-04-14 08:42:56.000000	2021-04-14 08:42:59.000000	Disabled
7624	6416	brave.exe	0xbb81e56e5080	0	-	1	False	2021-04-14 08:43:05.000000	2021-04-14 08:43:08.000000	Disabled
2052	6416	brave.exe	0xbb81e3aea300	0	-	1	False	2021-04-14 08:47:58.000000	2021-04-14 08:48:02.000000	Disabled
4488	3660	audiodg.exe	0xbb81e607f080	4	-	0	False	2021-04-14 08:48:01.000000	N/A	Disabled
1856	904	ApplicationFra	0xbb81dc308080	2	-	1	False	2021-04-14 08:58:04.000000	N/A	Disabled
7452	904	smartscreen.ex	0xbb81de94a080	9	-	1	False	2021-04-14 08:58:37.000000	N/A	Disabled
8172	4248	RamCapture64.e	0xbb81de4d8080	4	-	1	False	2021-04-14 08:58:38.000000	N/A	Disabled
2188	8172	conhost.exe	0xbb81df317080	3	-	1	False	2021-04-14 08:58:39.000000	N/A	Disabled

Fig. 21. Process list [Volatility 3]

The user has searched for the nature images in the Google search engine and we recovered evidences for the same in the Fig. 22. We are also able to find the URL of the web site form which user downloaded the nature images (Fig. 23) .

```
 33  ··§74439f7c-3f33
 34  -4f20-bef8-c5ca4
 84  c347f36·)·······
 74  ·¦ü¥·®¹·"¿··;htt
 6F  ps://unsplash.co
 50  m/photos/vngzm4P
 6F  2BTs/download?fo
 73  rce=true···https
 61  ://images.unspla
 32  sh.com/photo-142
 37  0593248178-d8887
 62  0618ca0?ixlib=rb
 6A  -1.2.1&q=80&fm=j
 26  pg&crop=entropy&
 73  cs=tinysrgb&dl=s
 6E  tudio-dekorasyon
 73  -vngzm4P2BTs-uns
 73  plash.jpg··https
 2F  ://unsplash.com/
 70  ··"'https://unsp
 2F  lash.com/photos/
 74  vngzm4P2BTs¹·htt
```

Fig. 22. Search text in the Google search engine

```
77 77  ····%·https://ww
65 61  w.google.com/sea
6D 61  rch?q=nature+ima
73 26  ges&source=lmns&
36 36  bih=671&biw=1366
26 76  &hl=en-US&sa=X&v
44 56  ed=2ahUKEwjmzeDV
70 30  p_3vAhWihEsFHZp0
45 51  A8QQ_AUoAHoECAEQ
73 3A  AA·······https:
6F 6D  //www.google.com
72 65  /search?q=nature
63 68  +images&tbm=isch
78 3D  &source=iu&ictx=
74 64  1&fir=EdU-hizWtd
66 62  O3VM%252CHOgLtfb
```

Fig. 23. URL of the site to download image

The evidence related to keywork search "Adobe" and URL of the site from which Adobe is download is recovered from RAM and same is shown is Fig. 24 and Fig. 25 respectively.

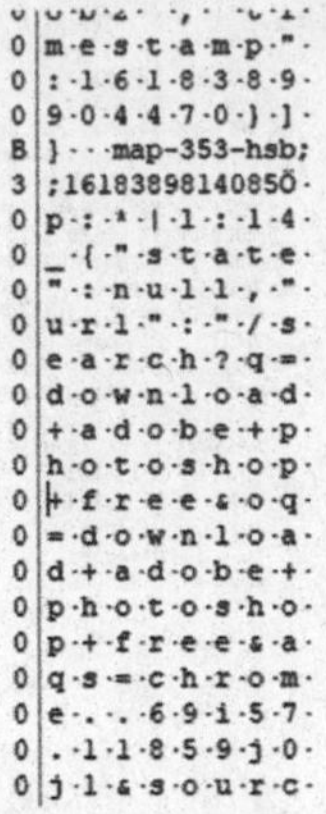

H. Sanghvi et al.

```
0 u·b·2· ·,· ·c·1·
0 m·e·s·t·a·m·p·"·
0 :·1·6·1·8·3·8·9·
0 9·0·4·4·7·0·)·]·
B }···map-353-hsb;
3 ;16183898140850·
0 p·:·*·|·1·:·1·4·
0 _·(·"·s·t·a·t·e·
0 ⁻·:·n·u·l·l·,·"·
0 u·r·l·"·:·"·/·s·
0 e·a·r·c·h·?·q·=·
0 d·o·w·n·l·o·a·d·
0 +·a·d·o·b·e·+·p·
0 h·o·t·o·s·h·o·p·
0 ┠·f·r·e·e·&·o·q·
0 =·d·o·w·n·l·o·a·
0 d·+·a·d·o·b·e·+·
0 p·h·o·t·o·s·h·o·
0 p·+·f·r·e·e·&·a·
0 q·s·=·c·h·r·o·m·
0 e·.·.·6·9·i·5·7·
0 ·.·1·1·8·5·9·j·0·
0 j·l·&·s·o·u·r·c·
```

```
0 00 ················
4 00 ····°···Y··h·t·
E 00 t·p·s·:·/·/·e·n·
9 00 ·.·s·o·f·t·o·n·i·
F 00 c·.·c·o·m·/·d·o·
1 00 w·n·l·o·a·d·/·a·
F 00 d·o·b·e·-·p·h·o·
7 00 t·o·s·h·o·p·-·7·
4 00 -·0·-·1·-·u·p·d·
4 00 a·t·e·/·w·i·n·d·
4 00 o·w·s·/·p·o·s·t·
1 00 -·d·o·w·n·l·o·a·
0 00 d·?·e·x·t·=·1···
0 00 ················
```

Fig. 24. Adobe keywork search in the Google search engine

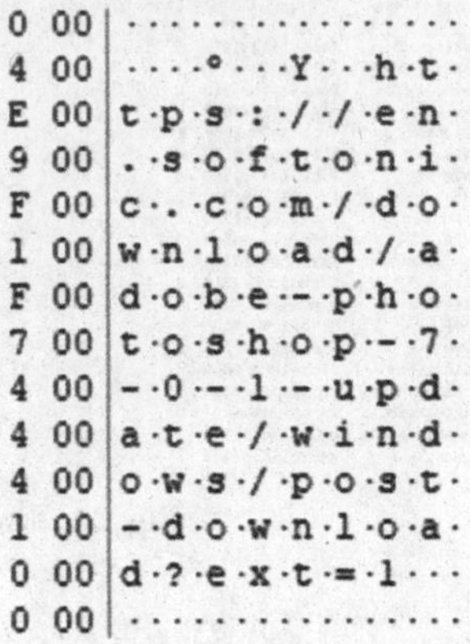

Fig. 25. URL of the site to download Adobe

The evidence related to free movie search, URL of the site from which movie is downloaded and URL of the YouTube video which user has watched is shown in Fig. 26, Fig. 27 and Fig. 28 respectively.

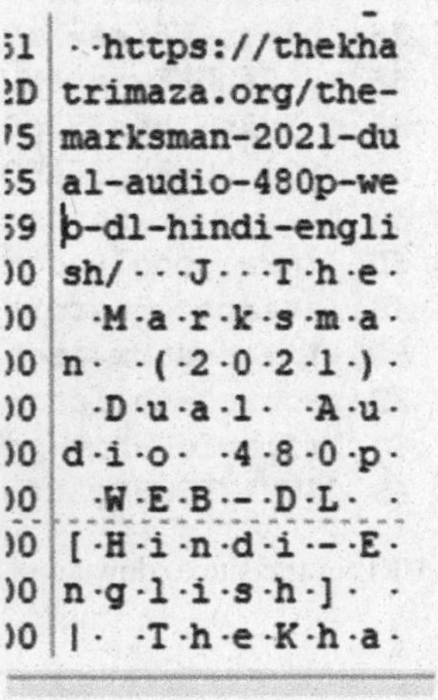

```
51   ··https://thekha
2D   trimaza.org/the-
15   marksman-2021-du
55   al-audio-480p-we
59   b-dl-hindi-engli
)0   sh/···J···T·h·e·
)0    ·M·a·r·k·s·m·a·
)0   n· ·(·2·0·2·1·)·
)0   ·D·u·a·l· ·A·u·
)0   d·i·o· ·4·8·0·p·
)0   ·W·E·B·-·D·L· ·
)0   [·H·i·n·d·i·-·E·
)0   n·g·l·i·s·h·]· ·
)0   |· ·T·h·e·K·h·a·
```

```
00 ···/·····q··1···
70 .···········http
63 s·://www.google.c
65 om/search?q=free
2B +movie+download+
76 site&oq=free+mov
65 ie+download+site
69 &aqs=chrome··69i
72 57.7043j0j1&sour
55 ceid=chrome&ie=U
00 TF-8(···f·r·e·e·
00  ·m·o·v·i·e· ·d·
00 o·w·n·l·o·a·d· ·
00 s·i·t·e· ·-· ·G·
00 o·o·g·l·e· ·S·e·
00 a·r·c·h·¬···"···
--
```

Fig. 26. Movie search in the Google Search Engine (FTK)

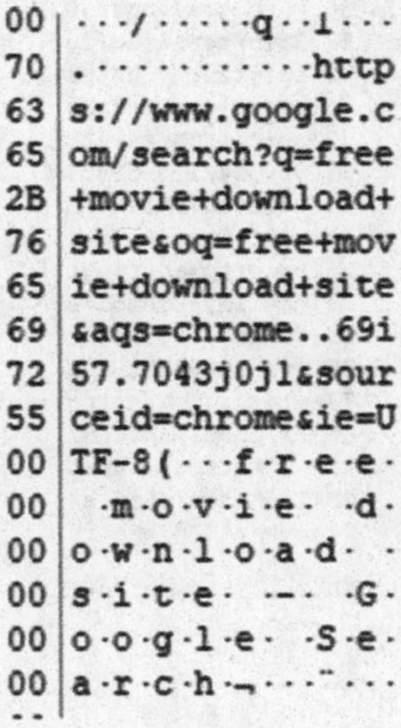

Fig. 27. URL of site to download movie (FTK)

Web Browser Forensics 217

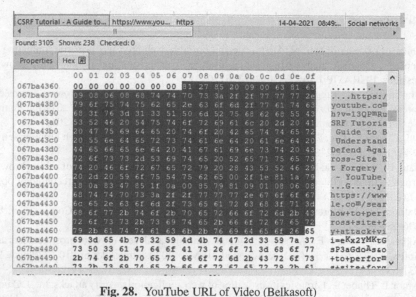

Fig. 28. YouTube URL of Video (Belkasoft)

7 Result Discussion

The results shows that in the case of Google Chrome, Mozilla Firefox and Brave web browser forensics, we are able to extract the evidences related to recent process list, Google search items along with URL of sited recently visited, images downloaded along with site and downloaded images, people search in the Facebook, Facebook profile, Facebook video call related information, web WhatsApp login details with mobile number, URL of site from which user has downloaded the movies or software. It is observed from the result that artifacts related to web WhatsApp chat found in the case of Google chrome, Facebook ID and password found in the case of Mozilla Firefox and Facebook ID in the case of Brave web browser recovered from the RAM.

8 Conclusion

A web browser remains a software program or device used to navigate the internet. Lots of persons today using web browsers to examine on Google search engine, access the social media sites and email application, view videos in the YouTube etc., Digital forensics is the branch of the forensic science which deals through acquisition, collection, analysis then reporting of the digital evidences. Today, criminals use web browser to committee the misconduct and it is significant for the digital scientific analyst know digital forensic techniques to recover the evidences form the browser. In this research paper we focused well-known browser Google chrome, Mozilla Firefox and Brave web browsers and also discussed that RAM forensics will be important techniques to recover the evidences related to recent activities carried out by the user.

References

1. Ohana, D.J., Shashidhar, N.: Do private and portable web browsers leave incriminating evidence?: a forensic analysis of residual artifacts from private and portable web browsing sessions. EURASIP J. Inf. Secur. **2013**, 6 (2013)
2. Marrington, A., Baggili, I., Al Ismail, T., Al Kaf, A.: Portable web browser forensics: a forensic examination of the privacy benefits of portable web browsers. In: 2012 International Conference on Computer Systems and Industrial Informatics, pp. 18–20 (2012)
3. Oh, J., Lee, S., Lee, S.: Advanced evidence collection and analysis of web browser activity. Digit. Invest. **8**, S62–S70 (2011)
4. Said, H., Al Mutawa, N., Al Awadhi, I., Guimaraes, M.: Forensic analysis of private browsing artifacts. In: 2011 International Conference on Innovations in Information Technology, pp.25–27 (2011)
5. Rathod, D.: Web browser forensics: google chrome. Int. J. Adv. Res. Comput. Sci. **8**(7), 896–899 (2017)
6. Akbal, E., Günes, F., Akbal, A.: Digital forensic analyses of web browser records. J. Softw. 11(7), 631–637 (2016). Accessed 10 Mar 2020. https://doi.org/10.17706/jsw.11.7. 631-637
7. Amor. L, Thabet S.: Forensics investigation of web application security attacks. Int. J. Comput. Netw. Inf. Secur. **7**, 10–17 (2015). https://doi.org/10.5815/ijcnis.2015.03.02. Accessed 10 Mar 2020
8. Oh, J., Lee, S., Lee, S.: Advanced evidence collection and analysis of web browser activity. In: The Digital Forensic Research Conference, 2001 USA (2020). Accessed 17 Mar 2020. https://doi.org/10.1016/j.diin.2011.05.008
9. "Basis Technology Corporation: Autopsy and The Sleuth", Accessed 14 Mar 2020. http://www.autopsy.com/wpcontent/uploads/sites/8/2016/02/Autopsy-4.0-EN-optimized.pdf
10. Mohammmed, S., Sridevi, R.: A survey on digital forensics phases, tools and challenges. In: Raju, K., Govardhan, A., Rani, B., Sridevi, R., Murty, M. (eds) Proceedings of the Third International Conference on Computational Intelligence and Informatics. Advances in Intelligent Systems and Computing, vol. 1090, pp. 237–248. Springer, Singapore (2020). https://doi.org/10.1007/978-981-15-1480-7_20
11. Aminnezhad, A., Dehghantanha, A., Abdullah, M.T.: A survey on privacy issues in digital forensics. Int. J. Cyber-Secur. Digit. Forensics **1**(4), 311–324 (2012)
12. https://kinsta.com/browser-market-share/. Accessed 5 Dec 2022
13. https://www.forbes.com/sites/billybambrough/2020/04/09/billions-of-google-chrome-use rsnow-have-another-surprising-option/?sh=58f2bdd45956. Accessed 5 Dec 2022

An Innovative AI Architecture for Detecting the Primary User in the Spectrum

A. Sai Suneel[1]([✉]) [iD] and S. Shiyamala[2] [iD]

[1] School of Engineering and Technology, Sri Padmavati Mahila Visvavidyalayam, Tirupati, India
saisuneel.adem@gmail.com
[2] Vel Tech Rangarajan Dr. Sagunthala R&D Institute of Science and Technology, Chennai, India
drshiyamala@veltech.edu.in

Abstract. The demand for spectrum is rising by the day as the number of consumers using the spectrum increases. However, the spectrum's coverage is constrained to a certain area dependent on the local population. Then, researchers come up with an idea of allocating secondary users in the spectrum in the absence of primary users. For this process, a new scheme has been raised known as spectrum sensing in which the primary user's presence using a variety of procedures. The device used for this process is called Cognitive radio. The spectrum sensing process involves gathering the signal features from the spectrum and then a threshold will be set depending on those values. With this threshold, the final block in Cognitive radio will decide whether the primary user is present or not. The techniques that are involved in spectrum sensing are energy detection, matched filtering, correlation, etc. These techniques cause a reduction in the probability of detection and involve a complex process to sense the spectrum. To overcome these drawbacks, the optimal signal is constructed from the original signal, and this, the spectrum is sensed. This process provides better results in terms of the probability of detection. To increase the scope of the research, the entropy features are extracted and trained with an LSTM based deep learning architecture. This trained network is tested with hybrid a feature which is a combination of both power-optimized features and entropy features. This process derives the spectrum status along with the accuracy and loss curves. The proposed method reduces complexity in sensing the spectrum along with that it produces an accuracy of 99.9% and the probability of detection of 1 at low PSNR values, outcomes when compared to cutting-edge techniques.

Keywords: Spectrum sensing · long short-term memory (LSTM) · Deep learning architecture · Cognitive radio · Optimized features, and Hybrid features · Artificial Intelligence · Entropy

1 Introduction

The electromagnetic spectrum consists of a range of frequencies that emits energy in the form of waves or photons. This spectrum consists of the different types of wave's namely visible light, radio waves, gamma rays, X-rays, etc. The waves present in the electromagnetic spectrum in the form of a periodic variance in electrical and magnetic fields [1]. They travel in the air at a speed that is equivalence to the speed of light. The frequencies may vary according to the source from which the waves are producing. The range of frequencies varies from low range to high range together forms an electromagnetic spectrum.

This spectrum is continuously monitored to determine whether the principal user is present or not. By this detection, it is possible to detect the user presence and able to reallocate with the secondary user. This spectrum sensing involves a variety of techniques includes Energy detection, Autocorrelation, a Matched filter, etc. The researchers focus on different techniques to obtain a better probability of detection. The spectrum sensing can be done using Cognitive Radio.

Cognitive radio (CR) is a wireless communication device that can intelligently detect the unused spectrum in the communication channels and made it possible for the secondary user to utilize the unused spectrum without interference with the primary user. For this technique, the energy of the spectrum is detected primarily based on measuring the noise and it is compared with the threshold.

In general, due to growth in technology, there is a rise in the consumption of the spectrum which leads to spectrum scarcity. To provide communication without any delay there is an urgent requirement of the spectrum. So, cognitive radio- an intelligent and adaptive device is developed to detect the unused spectrum in the communication channel and can transmit the information of the secondary user without interfering with the primary user. For this detection process, spectrum sensing is done to detect the existence of the primary user. The spectrum sensing approach involves various techniques. For these methods, a threshold is expected. The major consumer is present if the observed energy is substantially higher than this threshold; else, the user is not present.

2 Literature Survey

The auto-correlated spectrum sensing method [11] derives N samples from the received signal and the correlations between the samples were calculated in time-shifted translation at lag zero and lag one. To identify the user's presence, these associated samples are contrasted with the threshold value. Since the noise is uncorrelated with the signal detection is simple. But this process requires a greater number of samples and it consumes more sensing time.

Matched filter spectrum sensing [9] involves the process of convolution of N samples with the previously saved data of the user's signal characteristics and these convolved samples are compared with the threshold. Based on the result the existence of the primary consumer is recognized. However, this process necessitates previous knowledge of the key user signal properties, which is impractical.

To overcome the above problems, we put forward an Energy detection-based spectrum sensing scheme [4, 6]. Energy estimation involves the dynamic selection of threshold which can be carried on in various ways.

The dynamic threshold is generated by the Discrete Fourier Transform of the samples of the received signal. In this work, Gradient-based updates are used to set the threshold value. It also minimizes the sensing error in the spectrum caused due to the presence of noise. But this method shows poor results at low SNR [13].

Then at low SNR, for threshold estimation image binarization technique was implemented. The threshold is fixed to a certain value based on the past iteration values, number samples, false alarm, and SNR values. This process involves more sensing time.

Then to reduce the sensing time threshold is generated primarily based on the two parameters to accomplish the requirements of the chance of detection and false alarm. They are constant false alarm rate approach used to discover the probability of the fake detection in N quantity of trails and Constant Rate approach to solve the possibility of the true detection from the N number of trails. Based on these two probabilities the threshold is generated. This approach gives poor results in the fading environment [2].

Then in the Double thresholding technique [3, 12], two thresholds are evaluated to discover the presence of the primary user. If the predicted energy is below the main threshold, the user does not exist within the spectrum and if the energy is above the second threshold then the consumer is present inside the spectrum. But this process was failed to explain how the two thresholds were estimated.

Then in the Constant false alarm [8] rate approach, the false detection was restricted to a factor and the opportunity of detection may be able to increase with this reduction in false detection. The quantity of noise in the signal being received completely determines the threshold. However, this strategy falls short of explaining how the noise in the received signal was measured. These techniques reveal the various ways of sensing spectrum, but these have their drawbacks in sensing.

To reduce the drawbacks and to sense the presence of the primary user, a novel algorithm based on deep learning architecture is proposed. This architecture consists of a series of layers, it is training with entropy and optimized power features, and finally testing of the network which is explained in the next sections.

The paper is organized as follows: Sect. 3 consists of related work for the proposed method; Sect. 4 indicates the proposed deep learning architecture for spectrum sensing, Sect. 5 describes the results and discussion of the proposed process.

3 Related Works

a) Utilizing the Dynamic Threshold Technique for Noise Estimation

This technique is on sensing the spectrum by considering the energy of the signal present in it. The spectrum may consist of the signal energy values and noise energy values; these are acquired from the spectrum and compared with a threshold. The laborious situation in this technique is to fix the threshold with proper consideration. To fix this threshold, here the noise energy values were considered. The formulation of this process is as follows:

$$B_0 : y_i(n) = w_i(n) \tag{1}$$

$$B_1 : y_i(n) = x_i(n) + w_i(n) \tag{2}$$

Here B_0 and B_1 are the hypothesis functions for absence and presence of signal respectively. The term x indicates the signal coefficients and w indicates the noise coefficients. From this hypothesis, a fixed threshold is calculated through noise functions. Then the threshold is detected as λ_D [8] provided by

$$\lambda_D = \sigma_w^2 \left(Q^{-1}(P_{fa})\sqrt{2N} + N \right) \tag{3}$$

where, σ_w^2 is the noise variance, Q^{-1} is the inverse of Q-Function in which $Q(x) = \frac{1}{2\pi} \int\limits_x^\infty \exp\left(\frac{-a^2}{2}\right) da$, P_{fa} is the probability of false alarm and, N is the number of samples in the signal.

By this process, the threshold is estimated exactly and the presence of the user is estimated by comparing the threshold with the energy values which can be given as,

$$\text{Energy} > \lambda_D; B_1 \tag{4}$$

$$\text{Energy} < \lambda_D; B_0 \tag{5}$$

Where, Energy $= \sum_{n=1}^{N} (x[N])^2$.

b) **In AWGN channel**

The above process is considered using the AWGN channel [7], the additive white Gaussian noise channel is referred for a line of sight communication, it is formed by linear addition of white noise with a constant spectral density function. The bit error rate is high for this type of channel. Hence, we considered the same process in the Rayleigh fading channels.

c) **In Rayleigh fading channel**

This type of channels is considered for far distance communications. The bit error rate for this type of channel is low when compared to the AWGN channel [10]. In this channel, the coefficients are formed by passing a signal from the channel in which the magnitude of the signal varies randomly as per Rayleigh distribution. Hence, to reduce the bit error rate and for long-distance communications, the spectrum is sensed by using the Rayleigh fading channel [14].

d) **Using Optimized features**

In this process, the input signal samples are considered then the power of those symbols is calculated. Then these power values are optimized by the given formulation [15]. These optimized features are helpful to reduce the complexity in sensing the spectrum and calculating the probability of detection.

$$Inputpow = abs(X_k)^{\wedge \cdot} \tag{6}$$

The peak values are detected using the formula

$$\text{Peak}_{\text{Val}} = 10 * \log\left(\frac{\max(abs(X_k)^{\cdot 2})}{\min(abs(X_k)^{\cdot 2})}\right) \tag{7}$$

e) **Using Machine Learning Algorithms**

Spectrum is also sensed by using the machine learning algorithms namely linear SVM, Quadratic SVM, k-Nearest Neighbor, etc. These extract different kind of features from the spectrum and train the stated networks as sense the spectrum [5]. These methods are complex because it involves a complex training procedure and accuracy and probability of detections are also low.

4 Methodology

The proposed methodology is of sensing the spectrum for detecting the user presence using a deep learning process. Figure 1 displays the block diagram of the suggested technique.

a) Procedure

- The signal which is taken from the spectrum is optimized using the previous optimization algorithm.
- These optimized values are taken as features.
- These features are saved in the form of. Mat files for signal + noise which indicates primary user presence and only noise which indicates primary user absence.
- These mat files are trained using deep learning techniques like convolution neural network.
- The Convolution neural architecture and its layers are given below. This process increases the probability detection along with indicates the primary user presence.

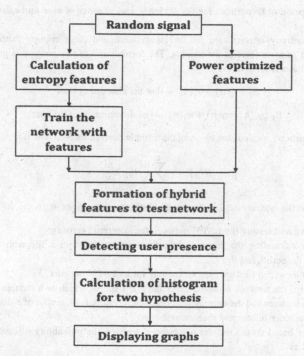

Fig. 1. Block diagram illustrating the suggested approach

b) Proposed Algorithm
The algorithm for the proposed methodology is as follows:

Algorithm: Deep learning-based spectrum sensing for user presence detection.

Input: A sequence of 1000 symbols forming a signal obtained from the spectrum.
Output: Accuracy and Loss calculation to estimate the algorithm consistency.
1: Assumption of the input signal, calculating its power and entropy values:
1.1: To sense the spectrum, the signal is acquired from the spectrum which consists of the 1000 samples which are represented by $X_1, X_2, \ldots X_{1000}$.
1.2: These symbols are modulated using the binary pulse shift keying by using the below formula,

$$S_n(t) = \sqrt{\frac{2E_b}{T_b}} \cos(2\pi ft + \pi(1-n)) \quad n=0,1$$

Where, T_b = Bit period & E_b= Symbols.
Then this modulated signal is applied to inverse Fourier transform using

$$X_{mod} = \sum_{n=0}^{N-2} S_n(t).e^{-i\frac{2\pi}{N}kn} \quad k \in [0, N-1]$$

1.3: Next, the power is calculated for the modulated signal, and then it is optimized.

$$Inputpowop = abs\ (X_{mod})\ ^.2$$

2: Assumption of Hypothesis for the presence and absence of user and calculation of Entropy:
2.1: The entropy is calculated for the input signal and these entropy features are considered as main features for training. The formulation of this entropy is given as. The hypothesis is given by:

$$B_0 : y_i(n) = w_i(n) \text{-----For the absence of User}$$

$$B_1 : y_i(n) = x_i(n) + w_i(n) \text{----For the presence of the user}$$

Then the entropy is calculated by using the formula derived by Shannon, it is

$$H(y) = -\sum_{i=1}^{L} \frac{ni}{N} log2 \frac{ni}{N}$$

Where N is the samples and L is the threshold which can be given as 16.

3. Training and testing the LSTM network for spectrum sensing:
3.1: After calculating the entropy, these features are saved in a file with ". mat" extension for both B_0 and B_1.
3. 2: Then these mat files are used for training for an LSTM network.
3.3: Finally, the network is tested using the test features which is a combination of optimized features and the entropy features, which results in an output of a dialog box with the presence of user and absence of the user.
3.4: Hence based on the number of correct detections the probability of detection is calculated as
Probability of detection

$$(P_d) = \frac{Number of detection}{Nimber of Trails}.$$

3.5: The probability of false alarm is calculated by using the

$$(P_{fa}) = \frac{Number of active deteions}{Nimber of inactive detections}$$

c) Entropy Calculation

Entropy is the randomness in the signal which will give the information about the noise coefficients and signal coefficients. This entropy explains the statistical properties of the signal obtained from the spectrum. Hence, these features are considered as the main features for training the network.

d) Deep learning architecture

The proposed deep learning architecture is given as follows

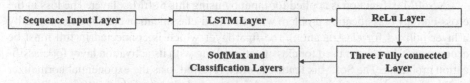

Fig. 2. Proposed deep learning architecture

In the deep learning process, various types of detections, classifications, and predictions can be achieved by forming a unique architecture for an application. In the proposed method, the features are a sequence of values. Hence, the input layer the Sequence Input Layer. This layer is the first layer in the architecture and the remaining follows a queue. Let's have a look at them in Fig. 2.

e) LSTM Layer

The expansion of LSTM is a Long short-term memory Layer which is a recurrent layer used for training an ordered data taken from the sequence layer. This layer consists of small cells called LSTM cells which learn the data in the forward process. First, the data entered into the cells and they decide whether the data is sufficient for training or not. Based on this information it accepts the data or rejects it. If the data got rejected then the output will be inexact. Hence, the data should be processed and in an ordered form.

This layer is complex in the entire deep learning architecture because it learns according to the given input.

f) Fully Connected Layer

The data derived from the previous layers are multiplied by a weight matrix formed by a fully connected layer and then a vector of bias is applied. This layer consists of one layer or more than one layer which follows the convolutionary (and down-sampling) operation. All neurons in this layer, as the name indicates, interact with all features obtained from the previous layer. This layer incorporates all the features of the previous layers across the picture (local information) to detect the broad patterns. For classifying the data, the last layer among these layers combines all the features obtained from the previous layers. Hence, the size which is given as input to the fully connected layer resembles the total number of groups.

By determining the related name-value pair, we can change the learning rate and controlling parameters for this layer. If the training network does not change the training options, then the training framework uses the parameters specified by the global training options. The weight matrix W multiplies the data given as input through a layer that is connected through links and adds a bias vector b. The completely connected layer operates separately on each stage when the input is the sequence (e.g. in an LSTM Network).

g) Output Layers: Softmax and Classification Layers

A SoftMax function is applied for input by using this SoftMax layer. The loss in the cross-entropy classification problem with the multi-classification class is determined by a layer utilized for classification. The final layer which is connected in full must be accompanied by a layer used for classification along with its activation layer for classification problems. The SoftMax feature is often referred to as the exponential normalizer and the logistic sigmoid function can also be regarded as a multiclass generalization. Traditional classification networks require that the classification layer come after the activation layer. Train Network uses the values from the SoftMax function in the classification layer. Hence, by designing the above architecture the training and testing of the spectrum will be done.

5 Results and Discussion

The probability of detection is explained as a graph for accuracy and loss when comes to deep learning-based spectrum sensing which is given below.

Case I

If the user selects the input value as a $= 1$, then

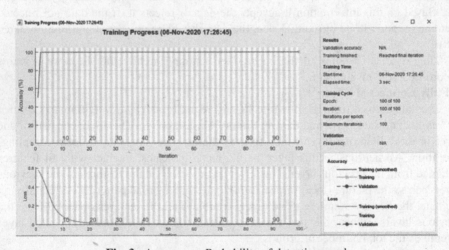

Fig. 3. Accuracy or Probability of detection graph

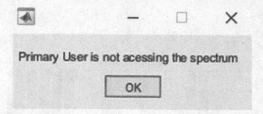

Fig. 4. Dialog box showing the absence of primary user

The above Fig. 3 and Fig. 4 reveals that the presence of the user is detected by using the deep learning process. As we are simulating the results, we are giving the results from the input, in real-time, the values are derived from the spectrum.

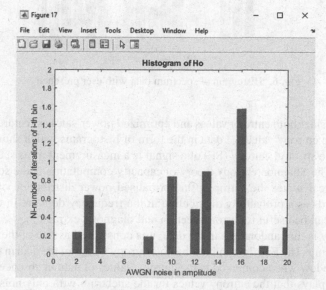

Fig. 5. Histogram of spectrum data without user presence

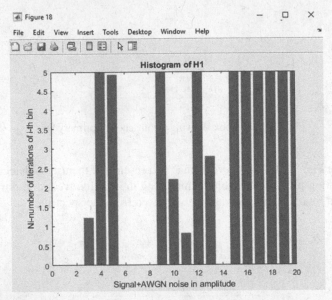

Fig. 6. Histogram of spectrum data with user presence

As we consider both entropy values and optimized power vales as features, here I am visualizing the entropy values of data in the form of histograms which shown in Fig. 5 and Fig. 6. The spectral entropy (SE) of a signal is a measurement of its spectral power distribution. The Shannon entropy theory of capacity computation is the source of this idea. The SE calculates the entropy of a normalised power distribution of the signal, which it regards as a probability distribution in the frequency domain. In this context, this function can be useful for error detection and diagnosis extraction.

As entropy is the randomness in the data, it is considered as one of the features for spectrum sensing. The Fig. 7 resembles that the entropy values of the data in the presence of the user are low when compared to the entropy values of data in absence of the user. The graph displays that the entropy values for the spectrum with only noise are nearer to 1 J/K and the spectrum with both data and noise is -8 J/K.

Case II

If we select the input as 2, then the spectrum is equipped with the user, then the results appear as follows.

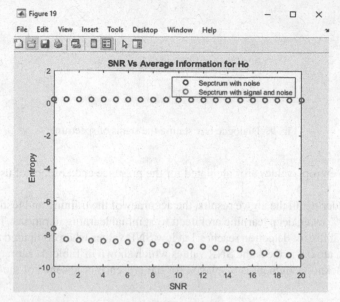

Fig. 7. Comparison graph between SNR vs Average information

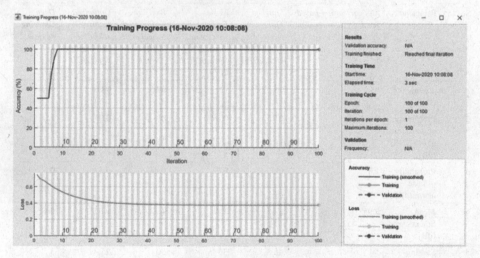

Fig. 8. Training process

The above Fig. 8 indicates the training accuracy and loss values for each epoch/iteration in the presence of the user. The Fig. 9 indicating the presence of the user is as follows:

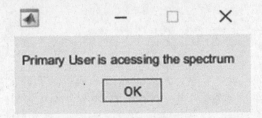

Fig. 9. Dialogue box stating the status of spectrum

Then the entropy values are calculated for the presence and absence of user as in the above case.

By considering all the above results, the accuracy of the training and testing process reaches 99.9% using deep learning architecture at initial learning iterations. This reveals that the probability of detection reaches 1 at low SNR values when compared to previous values which are 0.9 at the same SNR values which shown in Table. 1. Moreover, in this process, an acknowledgment is displayed for the presence or absence of the user.

Table 1. Comparison between existing and Proposed Methods at SNR = −5 dB

S. No	Parameter	Autocorrelation-based sensing (Subramaniam et al. 2012)	Matched Filter Detection (Shobhana et al. 2013)	Noise Estimation spectrum sensing (Pawan et al. 2014)	Rayleigh Fading (Sai Suneel et al. 2019)	Optimized feature selection (Sai Suneel et al. 2020)	Deep Learning method
1	Accuracy (%)	85	90	97	97.5	98.6	99.9
2	Probability of detection at low SNR (dB)	0.6	0.75	0.89	0.9	0.95	1.0
3	Probability of false alarm (dB)	1.0	0.95	0.9	0.85	0.77	0.65
4	Mean Square error (dB)	2.95	2.45	1.48	1.32	1.22	0.4
5	Sensing Time (ms)	50	48.5	35	30	25	3

6   Conclusions

Hence in the proposed method, the entropy features were extracted and trained with an LSTM based deep learning architecture. This architecture was created using different layers as explained. This trained network was tested with hybrid features which were a combination of both power-optimized features and entropy features. This process helped to derive the spectrum status along with the accuracy and loss curves. The experimental results of the proposed method reduced the complexity in sensing the spectrum with an accuracy of 99.9% and the probability of detection of 1 at low PSNR values, results when compared to state of art methods.

In the future, we can extend this process to real-time implementation by constructing a fully equipped cognitive radio.

References

1. Centre for Remote Imaging, Sensing and Processing (CRISP). https://crisp.nus.edu.sg/~research/tutorial/em.htm. Accessed 13 Feb 2023
2. Electronic notes, 'Rayleigh Fading'. https://www.electronics-notes.com. Accessed 13 Feb 2023
3. Wu, J., Luo, T., Yue, G.: An energy detection algorithm based on double-threshold in cognitive radio systems. In: International Conference on Information Science and Enginneering, pp. 493–496. Zhanjiajie (2009)
4. Maleki, S., Pandharipande, A., Leus, G.: Two-degree spectrum sensing for cognitive radios. In: IEEE International Conference on Acoustics, Spe. and Sig. Proc., IEEE, pp. 2946–2949, Texas, USA (2010)
5. Plata, D.M.M., Reatiga, A.G.A.: Evaluation of strength detection for spectrum sensing based at the dynamic desire of detection threshold. J. Procedia Eng. 35, 135–143 (2012)
6. Zhang, X., Chai, R., Gao, F.: Matched cleanout based spectrum sensing and energy degree detection for the cognitive radio network. In: IEEE Global Conference on Signal and Information Processing, IEEE, pp. 1267–1270, Atlanta (2014)
7. Sutanu, G.: Performance analysis based on a comparative study between multipath Rayleigh fading and AWGN channel in the presence of various interference. Int. J. of Mob. Netw. Commun. Telematics, 4, 15–22 (2014)
8. Subramaniam, S., Reyes, H., Kaabouch, N.: Spectrum occupancy measurement: an autocorrelation based scanning approach using USRP. In: IEEE Wireless and Microwave Technology Conference on IEEE, pp. 1–5, Barcelona (2015)
9. Al-Badrawi, M.H., Kirsch, N.J.: An EMD-based double threshold detector for spectrum sensing in cognitive radio networks. In: Vehicular Technology Conference. IEEE, pp. 1–5. Glasgow, UK (2015)
10. Sai Suneel, A., Prasanthi, K.: Multiple input multiple output cooperative communication technique using for spectrum sensing in cognitive radio network. In: IEEE Int. Conference on Signal Processing Communication Power and Embedded System, IEEE, pp. 2052–2063, Chennai (2016)
11. Arjoune Y., Mrabet Z. E., Ghazi H. E. and Tamtaoui A. : Spectrum sensing: Enhanced energy detection technique based on noise measurement. In: IEEE 8th Annual Computing and Communication Workshop and Conference, IEEE, pp. 828–834, Las Vegas (2018)
12. Arjoune, Y., Kaabouch, N.: On spectrum sensing, a machine learning method for cognitive radio systems. In: IEEE International Conference on Electro Information Technology IEEE, pp. 333–338. Ecuador (2019)
13. Sai Suneel, A., Shiyamala, D.S.: A novel energy detection of spectrum based on noise measurement a review. J. Adv. Res. Dyn. Control Syst. 11, 870–873 (2019)

14. Sai Suneel, A., Shiyamala, D.S.: Dynamic threshold selection through noise variance for spectrum sensing. Int. J. Eng. Adv. Tech. **8**, 23–234 (2019)
15. Sai Suneel, A., Shiyamala, S.: Peak detection based energy detection of a spectrum under Rayleigh fading noise environment. J. Ambient Intell. Humanized Comput. **12**, 4237–4245 (2021)

Power Optimization for Millimeter Wave MIMO System

Aisha Chauhan$^{(\boxtimes)}$, Sarvjit Singh, and Preeti Gupta

UIET Punjab University, Chandigarh, India
aishachauhan014@gmail.com

Abstract. Water filling algorithm can be used for mmWave (millimetre wave), MIMO (Multiple Input Multiple Output) systems. It offers channel optimality for AWGN and ISI (Additive White Gaussian Noise and Inter Symbol Interference) respectively. In this article we proposed the water filling algorithm for equal power allocation. In this we study the decomposition of MIMO wireless channel with the help of Singular Vector Decomposition (SVD). SVD is used for generating parallel channels and is a factorization of real and complex number. For optimality of MIMO power allocation constrained maximization problem occurs to solve this problem we use Lagrange multiplier. The performance of water filling algorithm may be approach the channel capacity. In this the result when SNR is high the suggested method with equal power allocation of water filling is studied.

Keywords: Water filing algorithm · mmWave · MIMO · SVD

1 Introduction

Millimeter wave MIMO is considered to be the key enablers for 5G wireless network. In 5G mobile network the a projected millimeter-wave (mmWave) with a bandwidth of 30–300 GHz [1]. MmWave technologies have great potential to satisfy the requirement of wireless communication systems such as high data rates, low cost and good user experience. In mmWave MIMO systems, there is precoding and combining for one user. An algorithmic solution was proposed utilising orthogonal matching pursuit for the MmWave precoder design problem of sparsity limited signal recovery. As a result, by using the SVD (Singular Value Decomposition) technique, it can effectively capture the governing Eigen modes, expand the number of channels, and remove interference. This allows mmWave systems to estimate channel capacitance [4]. For uplink broadcasts with the same power allotment, the AIA digital transmitter design method is advised. A low hardware complexity precoding approach was devised using a realistic spatial channel model [8]. Without real-time channel state information, spectral efficiency performance can get close to the best general transceiver design performance.

In this article we consider the millimeter wave MIMO systems. The space between different information transmitter and receiver antenna for multiplexing different information stream and hence it is called spatial multiplexing. It is based on MIMO technology, which carries several data streams concurrently within the same frequency range

N. Chaubey et al. (Eds.): COMS2 2023, CCIS 1861, pp. 233–244, 2023.
https://doi.org/10.1007/978-3-031-40564-8_17

234   A. Chauhan et al.

by using multiple antennas at both the transmitter and receiver. We consider the SVD receiver for decomposition of MIMO systems. The SVD exist for any matrix even for non square matrix whereas other types of decomposition occur for square matrix e.g. Eigen values. In order to distribute the best amount of power among the various channels in multicarrier schemes, we thus take into account the water filling method, where the power distribution changes nonlinearly with the highest average transmit power to each channel.

1.1   The Main Contribution of this Article is:

- We suggested the water filling strategy for mmWave MIMO systems optimal power distribution.
- We model the singular vector decomposition because it exist any matrix even for square matrix.

2   Literature Review

Omar El Ayach et al. [3] in this paper is focusing on large millimeter wave MIMO systems using low complexity precoding. This is based on the water filling capacity. In this paper also include the large antenna array with one user beamforming and precoding in millimeter wave structure. In single user channel a layered transceiver design for millimeter wave systems are generated. The low hardware complexity precoding method is generated for the realistic spatial channel model.

Shiyu Zhou et al. [6] in this paper mmWave MIMO systems works on the Attitude information aided digital beamforming. For unequal power allocation case water filling power allocation is proposed. The UE (User Equipment) may assess its transmitter and choose to ignore the sequence impact rather than compensating for it, according to this paper. This research suggests an equal power distribution attitude information-aided transmitter design algorithm.

Renwang Li et al. [8] in this paper focusing in mmWave MIMO using Reconfigurable intelligent surfaces (RIS). To control the blockage case RIS algorithm is generated. Ergodic capacity is used for RIS aided model for mmWave MIMO systems under the Saleh Valenzuela channel model.

Wenbin Zhang et al. [2] This work uses combined beam and mmWave small cell system resource allocation for 5G. To solve the issue of resource allocation, the tiny cell base station's hybrid beamforming shape was presented. In this study, analogue, digital, and analogue precoding are accomplished using identity switched and matrix beam. To solve the problem of Lagrange duality it proposes the water filling algorithm for optimal power allocation.

Woo-Hee Lim et al. [9] in this paper is focusing ZF (Zero Forcing) Hybrid downlink-based precoding and aggregation is provided by the mmWave multi-user MIMO system. Optimising the minimal use rate while allocating electricity to each user using the gradient descent method. This paper ZF precoding is used for transmission into download under the perfect CSI (Channel State Information). The MMSE (Minimum Mean Square Error) based precoding and combining are used to balance the hybrid precoder and combiner.

Jianwei Zhao et al. [7] focused on millimetre wave MIMO communication for tracking channels with unmanned aerial vehicle flight control system. This research also suggests the use of the Kalman filter to track the movement of unmanned aerial vehicles. The spatial channel was proposed to be represented by a 3D geometry-based total channel model, where the channel is chosen based on information about UAV movement status and remaining channel advantage.

3   Methodology

- We use the decomposition of MIMO wireless channel with help of SVD to generate parallel channel.
- SVD (Singular Vector Decomposition) receiver is used, now let us some manipulation at the transmitter .With SVD we can show that a MIMO channel with m antenna at each side can be treated as m separate single antenna channel.
- We proposed the optimally MIMO power allocation to maximize the capacity or information rate of different transmission streams. The subject to restrictions problem arises while attempting to maximise overall MIMO capacity.
- The constraints maximization problem occurs to solve this problem we use the Lagrange multiplier. Now all the power depends upon the $1/\lambda$.
- We developed the water filling method to allocate the greatest amount of electricity among the several channels in multicarrier systems.

4   Proposed Work

Figure 1 depicts our system model. We consider a transmitter and receiver. In MIMO can increase the data rates by transmitting several information streams in parallel at same transmit power. This is as if i am utilizing this space between different transmitter and receiver antenna for multiplexing different information streams hence in context with MIMO is called spatial multiplexing.

In Fig. 1 shows that

$$\begin{bmatrix} x_1 \\ x_2 \\ - \\ - \\ x_3 \end{bmatrix}$$ Passed through MIMO channel

MIMO channel →

$$\begin{bmatrix} y_1 \\ y_2 \\ - \\ - \\ y_t \end{bmatrix}$$

$\bar{x}$ = called transmit symbol vector (t dimension)

$\bar{y}$ = called received symbol vector (r dimension)

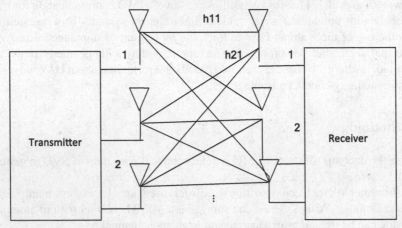

Fig. 1. System model for mmWave MIMO system

$$\begin{bmatrix} y_1 \\ y_2 \\ - \\ - \\ y_t \end{bmatrix} = \begin{bmatrix} h_{11} & h_{12} & - & h_{1t} \\ h_{21} & h_{22} & - & h_{2t} \\ - & - & - & - \\ h_{r1} & h_{r2} & - & h \end{bmatrix}_{rt} \begin{bmatrix} x_1 \\ x_2 \\ - \\ - \\ x_3 \end{bmatrix} + \begin{bmatrix} n_1 \\ n_2 \\ - \\ - \\ n_r \end{bmatrix}$$

$$y_1 = h_{11}x_1 + h_{12}x_2 + \cdots\cdots + h_{1t}x_t \tag{1}$$

$$y_2 = h_{21}x_1 + h_{22}x_2 + \cdots\cdots + h_{2t}x_t \tag{2}$$

Therefore

$$\bar{y} = H\bar{x} + \bar{n} \tag{3}$$

$\bar{y}$ = received signal power
$\bar{x}$ = transmit signal power
$\bar{n}$ = noise vector

• Assume variance (power) of each noise component at each receiver antenna.

$$E = \left\{ |n_i|^2 \right\} = \sigma_n^2$$

- Further assume that power of each antenna is uncorrelated i.e. independent (Gaussian).

$$E\{n_i n_j\} = 0$$

n_i = noise at i^{th} receiver antenna
n_j = noise at j^{th} receiver antenna

4.1 Decomposition of MIMO Wireless Channel

SVD (Singular Vector Decomposition) used to generate parallel channel.
  SVD of any matrix H is given by

$$H = u \mathcal{E} V^H \tag{4}$$

$$H = u \mathcal{E} V^H$$

$$H = \begin{bmatrix} u_1 \ u_2 \ \cdots \ u_t \\ \vdots \ \vdots \ \vdots \ \vdots \\ \vdots \ \vdots \ \vdots \ \vdots \\ \vdots \ \vdots \ \vdots \ \vdots \end{bmatrix}_{rxt} \begin{bmatrix} \sigma_1 \ 0 \ \cdots \ 0 \\ \sigma_2 \ \ddots \ \cdots \ 0 \\ \vdots \ \cdots \ \ddots \ \vdots \\ 0 \ \cdots\cdots \ \sigma_t \end{bmatrix} \begin{bmatrix} V_1^H \\ V_2^H \\ \vdots \\ V_T^H \end{bmatrix}$$

Properties of Matrix
These columns of 4 matrixes are orthogonal i.e.

$$\|u_i\|^2 = u_i^H u_j = 0; \quad \text{if i} \neq \text{j} \tag{5}$$

$$\|V_i\|^2 = v_i^H v_j = 0; \quad \text{if i} \neq \text{j} \tag{6}$$

$$V^H V = V_V^H = \text{I (unitary matrix)}$$

$$u^H u = u_u^H = \text{I (unitary matrix)}$$

$$u^H u = I \ for \ \ r = t$$

$$u^H u \neq I \ for \ \ r = t$$

Now the structure of singular matrix is $\sigma_1 \sigma_2 \cdots\cdots \sigma_t$ are known as the singular vectors such that $\sigma_1 \sigma_2 \cdots\cdots \sigma_t \geq 0$ they are non negative. $\sigma_1 \geq \sigma_2 \geq \sigma_t \geq 0$ [singular values are ordered (decreasing order). This SVD exist for any matrix even for non square matrix. Whereas other types of decomposition occurs for square matrices (e.g. Eigen value decomposition).

4.2 SVD Receiver

Recall

$$H = u \mathcal{E} V^H \tag{7}$$

$$\bar{y} = H\bar{x} + \bar{n} \tag{8}$$

Using equation (7) in (8)

$$\bar{y} = u \mathcal{E} V^H \bar{x} + \bar{n} \tag{9}$$

At receiver multiple $\bar{y}$ with u^H

$$u^H \bar{y} = \tilde{y} = u^H (u \mathcal{E} V^H \bar{x} + \bar{n}) \tag{10}$$

$$\tilde{y} = u^H u \, \mathcal{E} V^H \bar{x} + u^H \tilde{n} \tag{11}$$

$$[u^H u = I] \quad [u^H \tilde{n} = \tilde{n}]$$

$$\tilde{y} = \mathcal{E} V^H \bar{x} + \tilde{n} \tag{12}$$

Now let us do some manipulation at transmitter also i.e. before transmission $\bar{x}$ i.e called precoding.

Let

$$\bar{x} = v\tilde{x} \tag{13}$$

(Transmit vector $\bar{x}$)

$$\tilde{y} = \mathcal{E} V^H v\tilde{x} + \tilde{n} \quad [V^H v = I]$$

$$\tilde{y} = \mathcal{E} \tilde{x} + \tilde{n} \tag{14}$$

where,

$$\begin{bmatrix} \tilde{y}_1 \\ y_2 \\ - \\ - \\ \tilde{y}_t \end{bmatrix} = \begin{bmatrix} \sigma_1 & 0 & \cdots & 0 \\ \sigma_2 & \cdots & \cdots & 0 \\ \vdots & \ddots & \cdots & \vdots \\ 0 & \cdots & \ddots & \sigma_t \end{bmatrix} \begin{bmatrix} \tilde{x}_1 \\ x_2 \\ - \\ - \\ \tilde{x}_t \end{bmatrix} + \begin{bmatrix} \tilde{n}_1 \\ \tilde{n}_2 \\ - \\ - \\ \tilde{n}_t \end{bmatrix}$$

Decoupling of MIMO channel (or parallelization of MIMO systems).

Now observed

$$\tilde{y}_1 = \sigma_1 \tilde{x}_1 + \tilde{n}_1$$
$$\tilde{y}_2 = \sigma_2 \tilde{x}_2 + \tilde{n}_2$$
$$\vdots$$
$$\tilde{y}_t = \sigma_t \tilde{x}_t + \tilde{n}_t$$

(15)

Now SNR of ith parallel channel $= \frac{\sigma_i^2 P_i}{\sigma_n^2}$

Maximum rate is given by Shannon's capacity. Therefore

Maximum rate (capacity of channel) $= log_2 (1 + \text{SNR})$

Therefore maximum rate of ith parallel channel (or capacity of ith parallel channel)

$$\dot{c}_i = log_2(1 + \frac{P_i \sigma_i^2}{\sigma_n^2})$$

Total MIMO capacity,

$$c_i = c_1 + c_2 + \cdots \cdots + c_t$$

$$\sum\nolimits_{i=1}^{t} c_i = \sum\nolimits_{i=1}^{t} log_2 \left(1 + \frac{P_i \sigma_i^2}{\sigma_n^2}\right)$$

(16)

4.3 Optimally MIMO Power Allocation

This is to maximize the capacity i.e.

Maximize (capacity or rate) $= \max \sum_{i=1}^{t} log_2(1 + \frac{P_i \sigma_i^2}{\sigma_n^2})$

Subject to constraints,

$$\sum\nolimits_{i=1}^{t} P_i = P$$

(17)

This is called constraints maximization problem to solve this, I have to consider Lagrange multiplier.

Let,

$$f = \sum\nolimits_{i=1}^{t} log_2 \left(1 + \frac{P_i \sigma_i^2}{\sigma_n^2}\right) + \lambda(P - \sum P_i)$$

(18)

($\lambda =$ Lagrange multiplier)

Differentiate w.r.t P_i

$$\frac{df}{dP_i} = 0$$

$$\frac{\sigma_i^2/\sigma_n^2}{\left(1 + \frac{P_i\sigma_i^2}{\sigma_n^2}\right)} + \lambda(-1) = 0$$

$$\frac{\sigma_i^2/\sigma_n^2}{\left(1 + \frac{P_i\sigma_i^2}{\sigma_n^2}\right)} = \lambda$$

$$\frac{\sigma_i^2}{\sigma_n^2}\left(\frac{1}{\lambda}\right) = \left(1 + \frac{P_i\sigma_i^2}{\sigma_n^2}\right)$$

$$\frac{1}{\lambda} = \frac{\sigma_n^2}{\sigma_i^2}\left(1 + \frac{P_i\sigma_i^2}{\sigma_n^2}\right)$$

$$\frac{1}{\lambda} = \frac{\sigma_n^2}{\sigma_i^2} + P_i$$

$$P_i = \left(\frac{1}{\lambda} - \frac{\sigma_n^2}{\sigma_i^2}\right) \tag{19}$$

Considering $i = 1, 2, 3, 4 \cdots\cdots\cdots t$

$$P_1 = \left(\frac{1}{\lambda} - \frac{\sigma_n^2}{\sigma_1^2}\right)^+$$

$$P_2 = \left(\frac{1}{\lambda} - \frac{\sigma_n^2}{\sigma_2^2}\right)^+$$

$$\vdots$$

$$P_t = \left(\frac{1}{\lambda} - \frac{\sigma_n^2}{\sigma_t^2}\right)^+$$

Now here all the power depends upon $\frac{1}{\lambda}$ so how to find $\frac{1}{\lambda}$ or λ
Using the condition of total power allocation to find more about the λ

$$P = \sum_{i=1}^{t}\left(\frac{1}{\lambda} - \frac{\sigma_n^2}{\sigma_i^2}\right)^+ \tag{20}$$

Now optimally power allocation P_i is given by

$$P_i = \left(\frac{1}{\lambda} - \frac{\sigma_n^2}{\sigma_i^2}\right) \tag{21}$$

To solve the problem of capacity a water filling algorithm of ideal power allocation. We use the water filling algorithm to fill the area with water below $1/\lambda$.

4.4   Water Filling Algorithm

In multicarrier systems, the water filling algorithm is a method for dividing up the best amount of power among the many channels.

It offers the channel's best performance when combined with AWGN and ISI (Inter Symbol Interference).

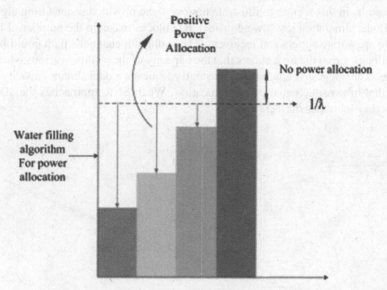

Fig. 2.   Water filling algorithm (source: ScienceDirec.com)

Considering there are 4 channels here

$\frac{1}{\lambda} > \frac{\sigma_n^2}{\sigma_1^2}$ i.e this power allocation is positive

$\frac{1}{\lambda} > \frac{\sigma_n^2}{\sigma_2^2}$ i.e this power allocation is positive

Likewise similarly for 3rd but

$\frac{1}{\lambda} > \frac{\sigma_n^2}{\sigma_4^2}$ i.e this power allocation is negative

Now if i want to fill the area with water below $\frac{1}{\lambda}$ then first three will be filled with water is known as water filling algorithm. The water filling algorithm distributes the energy according to the channel circumstances. When the channel condition is good, more power is allocated, and when it is bad, less power is allocated.

In Fig 2 since the channel is too short, more power is given to this sub channel, but since channel 4 is too big, no power is sent to it. The water filling algorithm's output demonstrates the sub channel's features, which include a big power allocation to a significant channel gain in order to increase the sub channel's capacity or information rate. It guarantees that the effective channel can transport more data. If the circumstances are bad enough, the transmit power cannot be given for that channel. The water filling algorithm uses useful channels and ignores useless ones.

5 Result and Discussion

The simulation results are obtained through MATLAB 2015a. We demonstrate the simulation results in this section to illustrate how well the provided water filling algorithm works. In the simulation result we consider 100 blocks make up the number of blocks, and there are 4 transmitters and receivers. The multipath channel's path count is set to 1: numBlocks. From the fig it shows that the capacity of the channel various when SNR increases. The suggested approach consistently achieves a data stream capacity that is near to that of possible equal power allocation. When SNR approaches the 10dB the capacity may increases the 12.

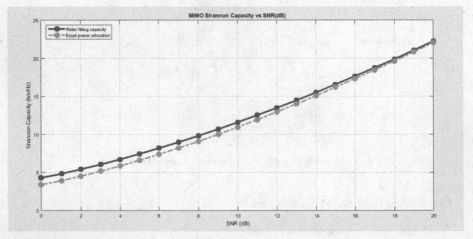

Fig. 3. Transceiver designs for a 4 × 4 mmWave system are shown to have varied Shannon capacities.

We can utilising a water filling model, determine the production of equitable power allocation. We take into account the 10db SNR for the 4 × 4 and 8 × 8 mmWave systems. The outcome in Fig. 3 demonstrates that the suggested water filling procedure outperforms earlier simulation. Additionally, when the SNR is large, the suggested equal power allocation technique resembles the water filling algorithm. When the SNR in Fig. 4 is 10 dB, the capacity gets close to 24. Similar to how the SNR increases, so does the channel's ability to hold water.

Therefore, the performance of the algorithm is well defined by the various numbers of data symbols. Additionally, the suggested method for allocating water filling power performs quite well.

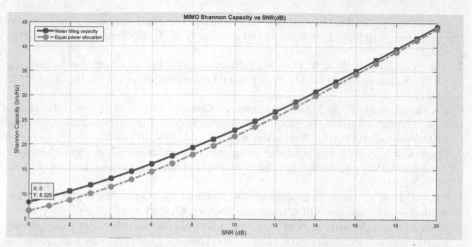

Fig. 4. Shannon capacity for an 8×8 mmWave system displaying several transceiver configurations

6 Conclusion

In this article we consider the water filling algorithm for mmWave MIMO systems. We establish the relationship between Shannon capacity and SNR. We develop water filling algorithm with proposed algorithm the decomposition of MIMO wireless channel we use the singular vector decomposition. This SVD exist for any matrix even for non square matrix where as other types of decomposition occurs for square matrices (e.g. Eigen value decomposition). For estimation of optimal power allocation in MIMO the constraint maximization problem occurs to solve this problem we use Lagrange multiplier.

References

1. Niu, Y., Li, Y., Jin, D., Su, L., Vasilakos, A.V.: A survey of millimeter wave communications (MmWave) for 5G: opportunities and challenges. Wireless Netw. **21**(8), 2657–2676 (2015)
2. Zhang, W., Wei, Y., Wu, S., Meng, W., Xiang, W.: Joint beam and resource allocation in 5G MmWave small cell systems. IEEE Trans. Veh. Technol. (2015). https://doi.org/10.1109/TVT.2019.2932190
3. El Ayach, O., Heath Jr., R.W., Abu-Surra, S., Rajagopal, S., Pi, Z.: Low complexity precoding for large millimeter wave MIMO systems. In: Signal Processing for Communications IEEE ICC (2012)
4. Dutta, S., Barati, C.N., Ramirez, D., Dhananjay, A., Buckwalter, J.F., Rangan, S.: A case for digital beamforming at mmWave. IEEE Trans. Wireless Commun. **19**(2), 756–770 (2020)
5. Zhou, S., Chen, L., Wang, W.: Attitude information aided digital beamforming in millimeter-wave MIMO systems. IEEE Syst. J. **16**, 1820–1831 (2021). https://doi.org/10.1109/JSYST.2021.3092430
6. Zhao, J., Gao, F., Kuang, L., Wu, Q., Jia, W.: Channel tracking with flight control system for UAV mmWave MIMO communications. IEEE Commun. Lett. **22**, 1224–1227 (2018). https://doi.org/10.1109/LCOMM.2018.2824800

7. Li, R., Guo, B., Tao, M., Liu, Y.-F., Yu, W.: Joint design of hybrid beamforming and reflection coefficients in RIS-aided mmWave MIMO systems. IEEE Trans. Commun. **70**, 2404–2416 (2022)
8. Lim, W.-H., Jang, S., Park, W., Choi, J.: ZF-Based downlink hybrid precoding and combining for rate balancing in mmWave multiuser MIMO systems. IEEE Access **9**, 162731–162742 (2021)
9. González-Coma, J.P., Rodríguez-Fernández, J., González-Prelcic, N., Castedo, L., Heath, R.W.: Channel estimation and hybrid precoding for frequency selective multiuser mmWave MIMO systems. IEEE J. Sel. Topics Signal Process. **12**, 353–367 (2018)
10. Duan, K., Du, H., Wu, Z.: Hybrid alternating precoding and combining design for mmwave multi-user MIMO systems. In: IEEE International Conference on Communications in China (ICCC) (2018)
11. Choi, J., Han, S., Joung, J.: Low-complexity multiuser MIMO precoder design under per-antenna power constraints. IEEE Trans. Veh. Technol. **67**, 9011–9015 (2018)
12. Uwaechia, A.N., Mahyuddin, N.M., Ain, M.F., Latiff, N.M.A., Za'bah, N.F.: On the spectral-efficiency of low-complexity and resolution hybrid precoding and combining transceivers for mmWave MIMO systems. IEEE Access **7**, 109259–109277 (2019)
13. Y. Lin, C. Shen, and Z. Zhong: Sensor-aided predictive beam tracking for mmWave phased array antennas in Proceedings of IEEE Globecom Workshop*s*, pp. 1–5 (2019)
14. Bao, J., Li, H.: Motion aware beam tracking in mobile millimeter wave communications: a data-driven approach. In: Proceedings of IEEE International Conference on Communication (2019)
15. Ali, A., González-Prelcic, N., Heath, R.W.: Spatial covariance estimation for millimeter wave hybrid systems using out-of-band information. IEEE Trans. Wireless Commun. **18**(12), 5471–5485 (2019)

Performance Evaluation of VBF, DBR and Modified CARP for Underwater Acoustic Sensor Network

Nisha A. Somani[1]([✉]) and Nirbhay Kumar Chaubey[2]([✉]) [iD]

[1] Guarat Technologcal University, Ahmedabad, Gujarat, India
nishasomani@yahoo.com
[2] Ganpat University, Kherva, Gujarat, India
nirbhay@ieee.org

Abstract. Underwater sensor network (UWSN) faces heavy transmission losses due to the presence of different types of noises, which consumes a vast amount of transmission energy compared to the terrestrial data transmission. Routing algorithms play a vital role in route selection and forwarding data packets from source to destination. In multiple hop networks, if packet forwarder node selection is identified efficiently, the amount of energy consumption can be regularized. Vector-Based Forwarding (VBF), Depth Based Routing (DBR), and Channel Aware Routing Protocol (CARP) are designed especially for UWSN based on the stringent environmental requirements. VBF and DBR follow a conventional protocol stack for routing decisions whereas CARP is based on a cross-layer approach. This paper discusses the packet forwarder selection methodology of VBF, DBR, and CARP protocols, implemented in network simulator ns-3, aquasim-ng2, and obtained results among the three algorithms, reflect that the cross-layer approach in CARP enables less energy usage as compared to VBF and DBR. Based on this finding, we proposes a new model of CARP protocol in which data packet transmission is initiated only when environment parameters exceeds the predetermined threshold range thereby reducing the transmission of redundant data and decreasing the network traffic.

Keywords: UWSN · CARP · VBF · DBR · ns-3

1 Introduction

Acoustic communication is one of the best alternatives for sending and receiving data packets from the source point to the sink node in the Under-water Sensor Network. In UWSN, node positions are not static due to the water currents and activities of aquatic animals as well as vehicles moving under the water. Localization of node is one of the important parameters as sensed data carry meaning only when it is received from the required point of interest. Another major issue that is affecting underwater sensor networks is energy saving. Most of the energy competent protocols designed for terrestrial communication networks become inefficient because of node mobility and rapid change

N. Chaubey et al. (Eds.): COMS2 2023, CCIS 1861, pp. 245–255, 2023.
https://doi.org/10.1007/978-3-031-40564-8_18

in network topology in underwater sensor networks. Perhaps there are a few protocols specially designed keeping in mind the adverse conditions of the water environment that result in saving the energy of the entire network.

Three of the others are Vector-Based Forwarding (VBF), Depth Based Routing (DBR), and Channel Aware Routing Protocol. Discussion of each of the protocols is explained in further sections with its experimental setup and results are compared for further analysis. Parameters like bit error rate is compared of the three protocols.

2 Background

2.1 Vector Based Forwarding (VBF) [1]

It is inspired by Trajectory Based Forwarding (TBF) protocol designed for terrestrial Network Communication. VBF is one of the geographical routing algorithms. Each packet carries the position of the sender, target, and forwarder. A virtual routing vector from the sender to the target is generated which specifies the forwarding path.

Every node which receives a packet from the source sender node, by knowing its distance from the forwarder and signal's angle of arrival (AOA), it calculates its relative position. Figure 1 shows S1 as a sender node and S0 as the target node. The node which is close to the routing vector it puts its own computed positions and forwards the packet toward the target. The other node simply discards it. Although VBF is a robust protocol it suffers from energy usage as each node essentially performs a broadcast. In the case of multiple nodes in the network, the amount of energy used is considerable.

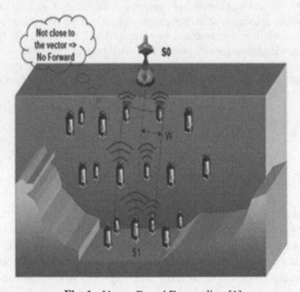

Fig. 1. Vector Based Forwarding [1]

2.2 Depth-Based Routing Protocol (DBR) [2]

It is the greedy routing protocol designed for UWSN applications. As Vector-Based Forwarding protocol is a geographical routing algorithm it requires full-dimensional location information of all sensor nodes, Depth Based Routing protocol requires only information on the Depth level of sensor nodes. Thus based on the depth information of each sensor, DBR forwards data packets greedily toward the water surface (i.e., the plane of data sinks). Figure 2 shows multiple sink nodes and the sensor nodes that transfer the data packet over the acoustic link. In DBR, a data packet has a field that records the depth information of its recent forwarder and is updated at every hop.

Forwarder node when receives a packet, it checks the field, depth d, and forwards packet if and only if, its position field, depth d' is smaller that is $(d' < d)$. Otherwise, it discards the packet. DBR is suitable in scenarios where multiple sinks are on the water surface so the packet can be transferred to any one of the nearest sinks. With limited sinks, DBR results are not well suited. [3] Presents the analysis of VBF and DBR where results presented show that DBR output is good for a higher number of sink nodes than VBF.

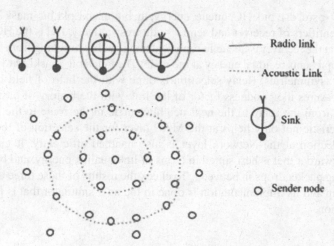

Fig. 2. Depth Based Routing Protocol [2]

2.3 Channel Aware Routing Protocol (CARP) [4]

Underwater communication is affected the most by challenges like long propagation delays, slow power signal attenuation, and physical parameters like noise, and temperature which cause multipath fading of the signals. As a result, channel selection algorithms at the MAC layer suffer. High mobility in the environment affects the channel quality and bit rate. Routing algorithms that select the forwarder gets affected as well. This ultimately causes the depletion of energy in the network. Hence UWSN applications require special attention while designing the routing algorithm that not only selects the forwarder based on the location information but also the parameters like link quality, and the history of a number of successful transmissions among the neighbouring nodes in past from the MAC layer. These parameters help in the selection of the best forwarder in the path. This is called the cross-layer approach. Channel Aware Routing Protocol (CARP) [4] emphasizes the concept of a Cross-Layer Approach rather than the conventional layered approach as used in terrestrial communication. It also considers information about the simple topology in the form of hop count for routing and connectivity. Other parameters like residual energy and buffer space help in the selection process of the best forwarder. CARP algorithm works in two phases. i) Network Initialization phase ii) Data Forwarding phase. Every node in the network has location information in the form of hop count (HC) from the sink node for the network initialization and setup phase. When a node has a data packet to send it first broadcast a control packet PING to search for a suitable neighbor node. Fields of PING [4] are PING = < src; HC; pid; Lpkt >. The field src is the node's unique identifier; HC is the hop count value of the sender node; pid is the unique identifier of the current PING packet, Lpkt is a list of pairs that the node has a data packet to transfer. Only node that receives PING packet from sender node such that HC (sender) < = HC(receiver) replies to a PONG [4] control packet with the following information.

PONG = < src, dst, pid, HC, queue, energy, lq, bit_maskLpkt,bit_mask JR > where src,dst are identifiers of receiver and sender nodes respectively, HC is the HC(receiver). Buffer space at the receiver is queue,lq represents link quality outgoing from the receiver, and energy represents residual energy at the node. The fields bit_maskLpkt,bit_mask JR handles link asymmetries. Relay selection is done with the help of field link quality, lq, which measures the goodness factor of the link with the history of past successful transmission from the relay to the next neighbor node in the route to the destination. This characteristic not only helps at the MAC layer for the selection of the best relay but route selection at the Network layer is also handled efficiently. It guarantees to select the forwarder that is best suited in terms of link quality, energy, and buffer space. Thus avoiding packet drops in between. To check the results of these three algorithms a network setup and its implementation is done in the ns-3 simulator that is presented in the next section.

3   Simulation Setup

Simulation is developed using **ns-3 simulator.** It is a discrete-event network simulator for Internet systems, targeted primarily for research and educational use. ns-3 is free, open-source software, licensed under the GNU GPLv2 license, and maintained by a worldwide community.

Implementation from physical layer up to application layer is facilitated. Network parameters and their values are shown in Table 1 below.

Table 1. Simulation Parameters

Sr No	Parameters	Value
1	Network size	250 m × 250 m × 250m
2	Deployment	Random uniform
3	Node Initial energy	50 J
4	Packet size	40 bytes VBF 50 bytes DBR 100 bytes CARP
5	Data Rate	16kbps
6	Transmission range	100 m
7	Transmission power consumption	1.6W
8	Receiving power consumption	1.2W
9	Idle power consumption	0.008W
10	Frequency	4 kHz
11	No. of sink	1
12	No of Nodes	3, 4, 5, 6, 7

4 Experimental Result

Experimental results are achieved for variation in a number of nodes. Table 2 presents the number of packets transmitted and received with varying sender nodes for VBF DBR and CARP respectively. The packet delivery ratio of the three algorithms is shown in Table 3. A graphical representation of Table 3 is shown in Fig. 3. The graph reveals that as the number of nodes is increasing, packet loss increases gradually for VBF. Packet loss is observed highest in the DBR as location information is available in the form of depth of node from the sink.

Due to the mobility of nodes under the water, the location information changes, and hence the packet loss is higher. In comparison to VBF and DBR, CARP proves to be the best as packet loss is less. The link quality (lq) parameter of the MAC layer decides the next relay over the route.

The experimental results reveal that up to sender nodes equal to 5 packet loss is almost the same in each case but as the node size increases the performance of DBR decreases and in DBR it suddenly reaches zero whereas CARP outperforms. This leads to the idea of using the cross layer approach for UWSN applications.

Table 2. Packets transmitted and received in VBF, DBR, CARP by varying node size

Nodes	VBF		CARP		DBR	
	Packet Transmitted	Packet Received	Packet Transmitted	Packet Received	Packet Transmitted	Packet Received
3	513	511	4	4	5	5
4	684	681	11	11	13	13
5	855	851	11	11	18	18
6	1197	1191	19	17	2	0
7	1364	1242	23	18	1	0

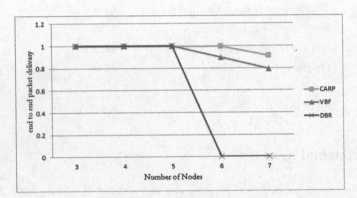

Fig. 3. End to End packet delivery

Table 3. Packet delivery ratio

Nodes	VBF	DBR	CARP
3	1	1	0.996101
4	1	1	0.995614
5	1	1	0.995322
6	0.894737	0	0.994987
7	0.794333	0	0.91055

5 Proposed Model

Experimental results obtained from above simulation reveals that cross layer approach yields better performance. In CARP, Link quality L_q parameter plays important role in forwarding node selection. Along the same line, we propose a model in which environment parameter temperature (T) is also considered for initiating data transmission from

Table 4. Tx and Rx energy in VBF,DBR and Modified CARP

Number of nodes	VBF		DBR		Modified CARP	
	Tx	Rx	Tx	Rx	Tx	Rx
3	1.929554	2.960168	1.939666	2.124589	3.994587	4.253554
4	1.920219	2.241751	1.785989	1.996587	2.047857	2.414777
5	3.02939	3.245805	4.888859	5.125633	4.541237	4.685922

the source node. We consider a scenario for monitoring temperature of the area where fishes are observed more in water bodies (Fig. 4).

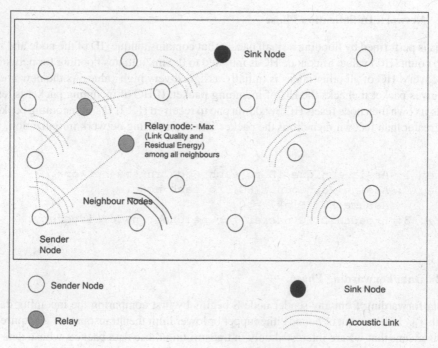

Fig. 4. Proposed Model

We consider underwater wireless sensor network architecture that consists of nineteen common nodes and one sink node. We assume that all common nodes are homogeneous in terms of the computational ability, initial energy and communication range. Common nodes collect data from environment at a fix source rate. The sink acts as the network terminal to accumulate collected data. Unlike in CARP where data transmission from source node is initiated after <PING> and <PONG> control packet generation. We incorporate a new Temperature threshold (T_{th}) parameter for initiating data transmission from the source node. Temperature threshold (T_{th}) is an ambient water temperature range considered as safe atmosphere for fishes.

In order to avoid unnecessary periodic data transmission, collected data is compared with T_{th} before forwarding to sink node. Data transmission is initiated only if collected data is beyond the threshold with both lower and upper bound.

Temperature threshold (T_{th}) range we select is between 16 degree centigrade to 29 degree centigrade. The range selection is done after reviewing with few fisheries near the Gujarat coastal area. The threshold range helps in avoiding periodic data transmission and will initiate the data transmission only when data is out of the range either upper bound or the lower bound thus enabling less transmission and eventually saving the energy of the source nodes. That ultimately results in longer network life. To explain proposed model following algorithm is designed.

Network is set up in two phase viz. Network Initialization phase and Data Transmission phase.

5.1   Network Initialization Phase

This is performed by flooding a small packet that contains unique_ID of the node and its hop count (HC) value. Sink node HC is initialed to 0. Sink initiates flooding for network discovery. HC of all other nodes is initially assigned very high value. As the new node receives packet it checks the HC of incoming packet. If HC of incoming packet is less than its own then node resets HC by adding one to received HC. If HC of incoming packet is greater than its own then drops the packet.Thus completing network initialization.

```
Step 1: Assign unique ID to each node in the network.
Step 2: Assign Hop Count (HC) to each node.
        Assume HC( Sink) = 0.
Step 3: Broadcast HC packet for neighbor node discovery.
```

5.2   Data Forwarding Phase

Data forwarding from any sender node S begins by first comparing the incoming data with T_{th}. If data is out of bound either upper or lower limit then transmission is required. This means that we are interested only in transmitting those data packets whose data is out of the range and not sending any data that lies within the predetermined range.

Data within the range signifies that there is no or minimum change in the surrounding environment. Thus data transmission can be ignored. And network energy can be saved. For reverse scenario where data is out of range then forwarding is essential. Hence a control packet <PING> and reply from the neighbor node as a candidate forwarder <PONG> are generated [4]. Information carried in <PING> is <src,HC,pid,L_{pkt}> where src is sender node address, HC of sender node, pid is unique id of the packet and L_{pk} is length of data packet. Any neighboring node, upon receiving < PING > checks HC if HC(Sender) <HC(neighbor),if yes then that node drops the packet. Otherwise creates a reply control packet <PONG> that carries information about its buffer space, residual energy, link quality.

PONG = < src; dst; pid; HC; queue; energy; lq; bit maskLpkt;bit maskJRi> where src is node's own address, dst is address of sender node which initiated PING. Algorithm for two phase is mentioned below.

```
    // Temp: environment parameter.
    // Tth : Threshold Temperature range
Step 1: Begin
Step 2:  If (Temp < Tth ) OR (Temp > Tth ) then goto step
3; step 9 otherwise.
Step 3: Create Control packet <PING>
Step 4: Broadcast <PING>
Step 5: Delay(Network turnaround time)
Step 6: Get Max( Lq and residual energy) from all the
received PONG packets.
Step 7:Assign
        Relay_node:= node with Max(Lq<PONG> AND
energy<PONG>)
Step 8: Create and Send Data Packet to Relay_node
Step 9: End
```

The above algorithm is implemented using ns-3, aqua-sim-ng module. The experiment is run by varying size of sender nodes and the obtained results are compared with VBF and DBR. The results reveal that performance of modified CARP is better than the other algorithms in terms of energy consumption. Table 4 presents the energy utilized in transmission (Tx) and received (Rx) of packets. Figure 5 the obtained results in graphical form. The improvement in result is due to data transmission is initiated only when data is beyond the range. This suffices our proposed model condition that data transmission is avoided if there is slight change in environment to be monitored (Fig. 5).

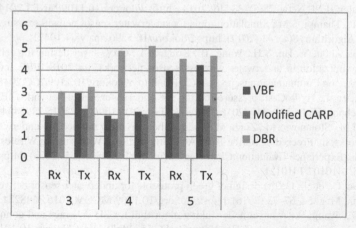

Fig. 5. Tx and Rx energy

6 Conclusion

Experimental results depict that among the existing three protocols, VBF, DBR and CARP, CARP performance is better than the other two. CARP is based on cross layer approach for UWSN communication. Due to large propagation delays and noisy channels in underwater surfaces, it is anticipated to transmit only essential data over the channel to save the network energy. Keeping these criteria at importance, we propose a model based on CARP and incorporate environment parameter together with residual energy and Link quality. In our model data transmission is initiated only if environment parameter changes beyond predetermined threshold range. Thus periodic data transmissions are avoided, data transmission energy is saved and thereby entire network life is increased.

References

1. Xie, P., Cui, J.-H., Lao, L.: VBF: vector-based forwarding protocol for underwater sensor networks. In: Boavida, F., Plagemann, T., Stiller, B., Westphal, C., Monteiro, E. (eds.) NETWORKING 2006. LNCS, vol. 3976, pp. 1216–1221. Springer, Heidelberg (2006). https://doi.org/10.1007/11753810_111
2. Yan, H., Shi, Z.J., Cui, J.-H.: DBR: depth-based routing for underwater sensor networks. In: Das, A., Pung, H.K., Lee, F.B.S., Wong, L.W.C. (eds.) NETWORKING 2008. LNCS, vol. 4982, pp. 72–86. Springer, Heidelberg (2008). https://doi.org/10.1007/978-3-540-79549-0_7
3. Somani, N.A., Chaubey, N.: Experimental analysis of vector based forwarding and depth based routing protocols in underwater acoustic sensor network (Uw-Asns) by varying network size. Tianjin Daxue Xuebao (Ziran Kexue yu Gongcheng Jishu Ban)/Journal of Tianjin University Science and Technology, vol. 55 no. 01, pp. 137–148 (2022). ISSN (Online): 0493–2137, E-Publication: Online Open Access. https://doi.org/10.17605/OSF.IO/QDXFM
4. Basagni, S., Petrioli, C., Petroccia, R., Spaccini, D.: CARP: a channel-aware routing protocol for underwater acoustic wireless networks. Ad Hoc Netw. 34, 92–104 (2015). https://doi.org/10.1016/j.adhoc.2014.07.014
5. Casari, P., et al.: Open source suites for underwater networking: WOSS and DESERT underwater. IEEE Netw. 28(5), 38–46 (2014). https://doi.org/10.1109/MNET.2014.6915438
6. Das, A.P., Thampi, S.M.: Simulation tools for underwater sensor networks: a survey. Netw. Protoc. Algorithms 8(4), 41 (2017). https://doi.org/10.5296/npa.v8i4.10471
7. Yang, H., Zhou, Y., Hu, Y.H., Wang, B., Kung, S.Y.: Cross-layer design for network lifetime maximization in underwater wireless sensor networks. In: 2018 IEEE International Conference on Communications, pp. 1–6 (2018). https://doi.org/10.1109/ICC.2018.8422176
8. Noh, Y., et al.: HydroCast: pressure routing for underwater sensor networks. IEEE Trans. Veh. Technol. 65(1), 333–347 (2016). https://doi.org/10.1109/TVT.2015.2395434
9. Jornet, J.M., Stojanovic, M., Zorzi, M.: Focused beam routing protocol for underwater acoustic networks. In: Proceedings of the Third ACM International Workshop on Wireless Network Testbeds, Experience Evaluation Character - WuWNeT 2008, p. 75 (2008). https://doi.org/10.1145/1410107.1410121
10. Coutinho, C., et al.: On the design of green protocols for underwater sensor networks. IEEE Commun. Mag. 54, 67–73 (2016). https://doi.org/10.1109/MCOM.2016.7588231
11. Wang, Z., Wang, B.: A novel node sinking algorithm for 3D coverage and connectivity in underwater sensor networks. Ad Hoc Netw. 56, 43–55 (2017). https://doi.org/10.1016/j.adhoc.2016.11.009. ISSN: 1570–8705

12. Chaubey, N.K., Patel, D.H.: Energy efficient clustering algorithm for decreasing energy consumption and delay in wireless sensor networks (WSN). Int. J. Innov. Res. Comput. Commun. Eng. **4**(5), 8652–8656 (2016). https://doi.org/10.15680/IJIRCCE.2016. No: 0405084

13. Chao, H.-C., Chen, C.-Y., Shih, T.K., Cho, H.-H.: Survey on underwater delay/disruption tolerant wireless sensor network routing. IET Wirel. Sens. Syst. **4**(3), 112–121 (2014). https://doi.org/10.1049/iet-wss.2013.0118

14. Raj, C., Sukumaran, R.: Modeling UWSN simulators–a taxonomy. Int. J. Comput. Inf. Eng. **9**(2), 585–592 (2015)

15. Ismail, N.: Simulation and visualization of acoustic underwater sensor networks using aquasim and aqua-3D : an evaluation. Int. J. Adv. Trends Comput. Sci. Eng. **8**, 943–948 (2019). https://doi.org/10.30534/ijatcse/2019/93832019

16. Coutinho, R.W.L., Boukerche, A., Vieira, L.F.M., Loureiro, A.A.F.: Geographic and opportunistic routing for underwater sensor networks. IEEE Trans. Comput. **65**(2), 548–561 (2016). https://doi.org/10.1109/TC.2015.2423677

17. Domingo, M.C., Prior, R.: Energy analysis of routing protocols for underwater wireless sensor networks. Comput. Commun. **31**(6), 1227–1238 (2008). https://doi.org/10.1016/j.comcom. 2007.11.005. ISSN: 0140–3664

18. Liao, W.-H., Huang, C.-C.: SF-MAC: a spatially fair MAC protocol for underwater acoustic sensor networks. IEEE Sens. J. **12**(6), 1686–1694 (2012). https://doi.org/10.1109/JSEN.2011. 2177083

19. Guo, X., Frater, M.R., Ryan, M.J.: A propagation-delay-tolerant collision avoidance protocol for underwater acoustic sensor. In: OCEANS 2006 - Asia Pacific, Singapore, pp. 1–6 (2006). https://doi.org/10.1109/OCEANSAP.2006.4393849

20. Kuo, L.C., Melodia, T.: Cross-layer routing on MIMO-OFDM underwater acoustic links. In: 2012 9th Annual IEEE Communications Society Conference on Sensor, Mesh and Ad Hoc Communications and Networks (SECON), Seoul, Korea (South), pp. 227–235 (2012).https://doi.org/10.1109/SECON.2012.6275782

21. Melodia, T., Vuran, M.C., Pompili, D.: The state of the art in cross-layer design for wireless sensor networks. In: Cesana, M., Fratta, L. (eds.) EuroNGI 2005. LNCS, vol. 3883, pp. 78–92. Springer, Heidelberg (2006). https://doi.org/10.1007/11750673_7

22. NS-3, www.nsnam.org

Performance Analysis of Smart Antenna in Wireless Communication System

Pradyumna Kumar Mohapatra[1] , Saroja Kumar Rout[2(✉)] , Ravi Narayan Panda[3],
N. Sujata Gupta[2] , and Nirmal Keshari Swain[2]

[1] Department of Electronics and Communication Engineering, Vedang Institute of Technology,
Bhubaneswar, Odisha, India
[2] Department of Information Technology, Vardhaman College of Engineering (Autonomous),
Hyderabad, India
rout_sarojkumar@yahoo.co.in
[3] Department of Electronics and Communication Engineering, Gandhi Institute for Technology
(GIFT), Bhubaneswar, Odisha, India

Abstract. Wireless communication services have been in high demand, increasing the capacity of the system. Increasing bandwidth would be the most straightforward solution. However, the electromagnetic spectrum is becoming increasingly congested, making this a more and more challenging task. In this paper, we present a standard LMS algorithm that can detect taps based on NLMS and active detection. The proposed scheme takes advantage of refining the convergence rate and special filtering to reduce data transmission bandwidth requirements. The NLMS algorithm which is based on the frequency domain was simulated with a MATLAB simulator under multipath effects and multiple users. Comparing the results of the simulations with those of previous work suggests an improvement in the convergence rate, which leads to better efficiency of the system.

Keywords: FDLMS · SAS · DOA · Active tap detection

1 Introduction

The idea behind smart antennas is to increase the gain in a chosen direction to systematically improve wireless communication performance. The primary lobes of the antenna-beam patterns can be directed in the direction of the intended users to accomplish this. The radiation and/or reception pattern of a smart antenna system are automatically optimized in retort to the indication environment by combining several antenna rudiments with a signal processing capacity. The smart antenna system can automatically guide one or more nulls of the directivity pattern towards one or more sources of interference in addition to pointing the main lobe's direction in the direction of a selected user. Consuming a smart antenna system for a wireless system has several advantages, including greater coverage, better SNR and capacity, using less energy for equivalent performance, giving spatial diversity, etc. Long projected to perform significantly better than smart antenna systems [1, 2] Smart antennas need the Direction-of-arrival (DOA)

N. Chaubey et al. (Eds.): COMS2 2023, CCIS 1861, pp. 256–265, 2023.
https://doi.org/10.1007/978-3-031-40564-8_19

algorithm to be able to determine upon arrival, the direction of the signal is determined and, consequently, aim the array beam in that direction with the help of adaptive beam shaping. Earlier work on DOA estimation typically fails to consider the mutual coupling between isotropic parts [3–7]. Systems of multiple inputs and outputs (MIMO) and smart antennas provide performance improvements over omnidirectional antennas as well as communication on 5G systems thanks to their advantages over omnidirectional antennas[8]. Various experimental works using directional antenna arrays and DOA algorithms, including Bartlett [9], MUSIC [10–12], and Matrix Pencil [11], are also available. The management of nonlinear adaptive smart antenna resources for 5G communications through surveillance systems was well described by Subha et al. [13]. A new technology called 5G evolution in mobile telecommunications can transmit data at a rate of about 10 Gbps. High-frequency waveforms with increased bandwidth are needed to achieve such high-speed data. 5G uses a technique called massive MIMO beam forming (BF) for providing higher frequency and it uses Millimeter Wave (mm). Printing antennas are integrated into a multifunctional composite structure called a skin antenna structure. An antenna structure embedded with fiber Bragg grating strain sensors is described in [14].

Using the same channel, smart antennas can broadcast (or take delivery of) several packets simultaneously in diverse beams. Nevertheless, transmission scheduling greatly affects network performance. There are two transmission scheduling schemes proposed to improve the throughput of networks and reduce transmission delays [15]. It takes into account communication restrictions and packet sizes as well as exploits parallel transmission opportunities to ensure network throughput is maximized and latency is minimized. Mobile ad hoc networks (MANETs) require DMAC tactics to overcome the restrictions caused by omnidirectional antennas. The overall MAC performance can be enhanced by a sectorized antenna approach and a frame scheduling mechanism [16]. Channel equalization is the major criterion in a communication channel. There is some research work proposed by Mohapatra et al. [17–22] on channel equalization problems.In this work, the purpose of this study is to examine how the frequency domain normalized LMS method is used for the identification of active taps and beam patterns for two white signals with three DOAs each.

The following is the organization of this paper. The smart antenna system describes in Sect. 2. Section 3 describes the NLMS and FDNLMS algorithms followed by active tap detection in Sect. 4. Simulation and conclusion describe in Sects. 5 and 6.

2 Smart Antenna Systems (SAS)

Among the various types of SAS are phased array, adaptive antenna systems, and digital beam shaping systems. However, switching beam or adaptive array systems are the typical classifications for smart antennas. Regarding the manner of operation, smart antennas may be categorized into two groups.

2.1 Switched Beam

Patterns with a fixed number of predefined and fixed parameterswithout channel feedback. Multi-beam systems with high sensitivity in desired directions are used in this system. As the mobile moves through the sector, the antenna switches from one beam to another depending on the signal strength. Rather than combining the output of multiple antennas into finely directional beams with more spatial selectivity than conventional, single-element approaches can, switched beam systems combine the output of multiple antennas to form finely directional beams with the metallic properties and physical design of a single element, as shown in Fig. 1.

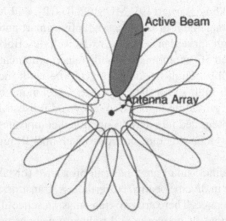

Fig. 1. Switch beam

2.2 Adaptive Array

Variable parameters, such as channel noise conditions, can modify this pattern in real time. The most advanced smart antenna approach is based on adaptive array antenna technology. The adaptive system uses an array of new signal-processing algorithms to dynamically minimize interference while maximizing intended signal reception by effectively locating and tracking various types of signals. The adaptive system provides optimal gain while simultaneously detecting, tracking, and minimizing interference while simultaneously identifying, tracking, and optimizing gain based on the location of the user. Figure 2 shows a main lobe that extends toward a co-channel interferer and a null pointing toward it.

Multiple fixed beams can be formed in some directions by switching beam antennas. A mobile device moving about a specific area can switch between a fixed, predefined beam and one of these antenna systems, which monitor signal strength. As a result, they create a static beam that becomes automatically controllable. A more efficient approach to locating and tracking signals is to use adaptive antenna technology, which relies on adaptive algorithms to dynamically reduce interference and improve signal reception. In this instance, the shaped beam is changeable and adjusts to the state of the broadcast channel with a dynamically changing weight array over time. In this situation, nodes estimate the DOA or AOA using the spatial structure. However, both systems make an effort to boost gain based on the user's location. The following graphic provides a summary of the fundamental SAS operation principle.

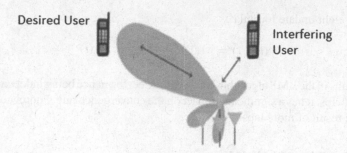

Fig. 2. Adaptive Array

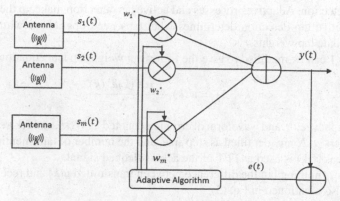

Fig. 3. Principles of SAS operation

Figure 3 inputs $s_1(t), s_2(t), \ldots \ldots s_m(t)$ are multiplied by elements of the weight vector $\overline{w} = w_1, w_2, \ldots \ldots w_m$ The output is y(t) and the error is e(t), and both are functions of discrete time t, a version of the algorithm using adaptive arrays is the only one that uses the adaptive algorithm. Switching beams can, however, be compared to not running an adaptive algorithm at all, since there is no weight array involved. SAS can be divided into several categories according to the type of created geometry pattern. The circular, hexagonal, and rectangular arrays are the most prevalent types. In contrast, antenna arrays in 5G technology must be adaptive and must be able to guide the key beam in the required path while directing the nulls in the unwanted interfering directions. When this adaptive mechanism is adjusted, the system's output will always attain the best signal-to-interference noise ratio [23]. An efficient and dynamic genetic algorithm was developed based on the received signal strength indicator (RSSI) of the node to find its optimal location value with the smallest localization error [24].

3 Normalized Least Mean Square Algorithm

The stability, convergence time and volatility of the LMS and step size is always determining factor in the adaptation process. The update step size can be effectively overcome by the normalizing variance of the input signal, $\sigma_u(t)^2$. Therefore, the following equation shows the weight update formula:

$$w(t+1) = w(t) + \frac{\mu}{N\sigma_u(t)^2}x(t)e^*(t) \tag{1}$$

This results in the LMS algorithm's asymptotic performance being independent of the N number of taps, it has a significant impact on the convergence rate. Poorer convergence rates are the result of more taps.

3.1 Modified Form of LMS [25]

Figure 4 shows the suggested algorithm which is a modified form of LMS(FDLMS) with active taps detection. Adaptive processes and active tap detection make up the suggested approach. Active tap detection determines what taps need upgrading, while adaptive processes update tap weights.

Equation 1 can be modified to give the following weight update equation:

$$w(k+1) = w(k) + \frac{\mu X(k)e^*(k)}{N} \tag{2}$$

Here, the weight vector, and waveform of error are denoted as W(k), and e(k)respectively. The parameters μ, N are identified as step size, and the number of taps mentioned in the figure, whereas X(k) is used as FFT of the acknowledged signal.

The error is nothing but the difference between transmitted $u(k)$ and received signal $x(k)$ which also mentioned in Eq. (3).

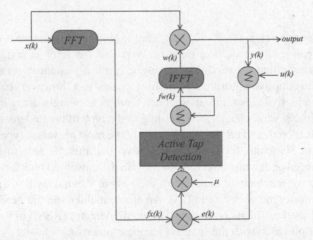

Fig. 4. LMS algorithm with frequency domain normalization

However, when there are a lot of adaptive taps, it is noted that the NLMS method has a poor convergence rate and high processing requirements. For mobile communication situations with extensive multipath components, this poses a serious issue because the numerous active taps needed could result in a lower convergence rate. To solve this issue, researchers suggested a detection-guided NLMS estimator. To distinguish between dynamic and sedentary sections or taps inside the channel is the function of the detection technique. We only need widely spaced elements since the taps or elements of a smart antenna correspond to various DOAs in the spatial domain to develop an NLMS algorithm in the spatial frequency domain, we propose to:

$$w(k+1) = w(k) + \frac{\mu X(k)e^*(k)}{\sum_{j=1}^{N} A_j(k)} \tag{3}$$

Here, the tap number is $A_j(k)$, while tap j is the active tap. If the tap is active then $A_j = 1$, or else for an inactive tap $A_j = 0$.

4 Detection of Active Tap

The key to using the "active" tap detection method is figuring out if a certain unknown channel tap is active or not. Similar to research, this strategy is based in part on intuition. As was already noted, different DOAs correlate to various Smart Antenna elements or taps in the spatial domain. Using the active taps that match the required signal, we can then create an activity measure and to understand the unknown channel, we begin by assuming that it's linear, time-invariant, and stationery.

$$x(k) = r(k) + n(k) \tag{4}$$

Here, the acknowledged signal is r(k), noise n(k) at sampling prompt k from the activity measure M. Now, we have

$$\Upsilon = [\Upsilon_1, \Upsilon_2, \ldots . \Upsilon_N] \tag{5}$$

$$\Upsilon = \sum_{k=1}^{k} u(k)x_j^*(k) \tag{6}$$

At sampling instant k, a measure of activity M is derived from a signal r(k) and noise n(k). $\acute{\Gamma}$,

$$\Gamma = [\Gamma_1, \Gamma_2, \ldots . \Gamma_N] \tag{7}$$

Finally, the spatial angle activity metric M is given by,

$$M = \Gamma(k)\Gamma *(k) \tag{8}$$

Here, the $\acute{\Gamma}$ is the discrete Fourier transform of γ.

Based on the following threshold, active and inactive taps can be distinguished.

$$T(k) = \frac{2\log(KN)\left(\sum_{i=1}^{k} X(i)X^*(i)\right)\left(\sum_{i=1}^{k} u(i)u^*(i)\right)}{KN} \tag{9}$$

Therefore, the jth tap at the instant k is active if, the threshold spread is controlled by this parameter.

$$M > \alpha T(k) \tag{10}$$

The active tap detection which is based on FDNLMS is described in Fig. 5. A sample interval of k is measured separately in the array utilizing Eq. 10.

5 Simulation and Results

Based on the suggested algorithm (FDNLMS), we estimate its convergence rate, active tap number, and beam pattern. For those simulations with many multi-paths, each multipath experiences a variable gain, which incorporates both amplitude and phase components to recreate genuine mobile settings.

Receiving 2 signals with 3 DOA will allow us to evaluate the performance of the suggested algorithm critically. Figures 5 & 6 shows received signal error and beam pattern for white Signals with DOAsThe Smart Antenna system used for analysis is displayed in this choice. To maintain a level of accuracy, the following will be kept constant throughout all smart antenna simulations:

- To imitate a transmitter delivering binary values, each of the 640 input signals has a signed value of 1 or -1.
- Convergence parameter μ *was taken as* 0.006
- 400MHz is the carrier frequency, fc
- Here, 0.84m is considered as the wavelength (λ.)
- A value of 0.375 is set for element spacing

Transmission to the first antenna element is delayed by 100 μs for simulations with a single transmitted signal, and 150 μs for simulations with a second transmitted signal.

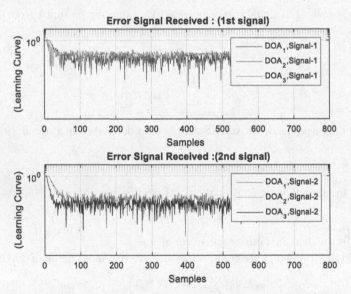

Fig. 5. Received Signal error for FDNLMS algorithm, with $\alpha = 0.1$

Figure 6 illustrates four beam patterns from both signals, with the third multipath pattern having two lobe-like projections pointing in the right direction for the second and third multipath. Figure 6 describes different Beam patterns for FDNLMS, $\alpha = 0.1$ with respect to DOA's of signal 1 and signal 2. Figure 7 shows FDNLMS-based active tap detection with respect to DOA's of signal 1 and signal 2.

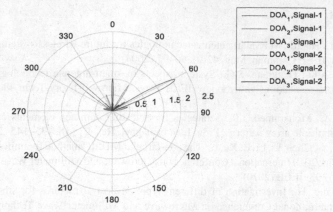

Fig. 6. Beam patterns for FDNLMS, $\alpha = 0.1$,

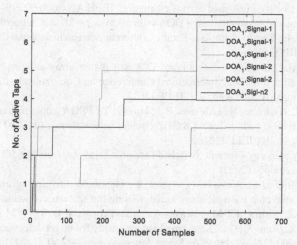

Fig. 7. Number of active taps for proposed algorithm, $\alpha = 0.1$

6   Conclusions

The idea of smart antenna systems and how they affect mobile communication networks has been effectively discussed in this research. This paper analyses active tap detection, beam pattern, and signal error of two signals. Our goal was to develop an algorithm for Smart Antenna systems that integrates frequency domain normalized LMS algorithms. The proposed activity threshold for the detection-guided FDNLMS algorithm, however, yields a variety of results. The system's performance is considerably hampered by the narrower threshold levels, although it exhibits noticeably quick convergence rates and reduced computational cost.

References

1. Alexiou, A., Haardt, M.: Smart antenna technologies for future wireless systems: trends and challenges. IEEE Commun. Mag. **42**(9), 90–97 (2004)
2. Boukalov, A.O., Haggman, S.G.: System aspects of smart-antenna technology in cellular wireless communications-an overview. IEEE Trans. Microw. Theory Tech. **48**(6), 919–929 (2000)
3. Karim, D.A., Mohammed, J.R.: Strategies for selecting common elements excitations to configure multiple array patterns. Prog. Electromagnet. Res. C, **118**, 135–145 (2022)
4. Li, R., Shi, X., Chen, L., Li, P., Xu, L.: The non-circular MUSIC method for uniform rectangular arrays. In: 2010 International Conference on Microwave and Millimeter Wave Technology, pp. 1390–1393. IEEE (2010)
5. Jin, L., Wang, H.: Investigation of different types of array structures for smart antennas. In: 2008 International Conference on Microwave and Millimeter Wave Technology, vol. 3, pp. 1160–1163. IEEE (2008)
6. Aboumahmoud, I., Muqaibel, A., Alhassoun, M., Alawsh, S.: A review of sparse sensor arrays for two-dimensional direction-of-arrival estimation. IEEE Access **9**, 92999–93017 (2021)
7. Bo, W.: Realization and simulation of DOA estimation using MUSIC algorithm with uniform circular arrays. In: The 2006 4th Asia-Pacific Conference on Environmental Electromagnetics, pp. 908–912. IEEE (2006)
8. Kayithi, A., et al.: Design and simulation of smart planar array antenna for sub (6 GHz) and 5G applications. In: 2022 International Conference on Communication, Computing and Internet of Things (IC3IoT), pp. 1–4. IEEE (2022)
9. Abusultan, M., Harkness, S., LaMeres, B.J., Huang, Y.: FPGA implementation of a Bartlett direction of arrival algorithm for a 5.8 GHZ circular antenna array. In: 2010 IEEE Aerospace Conference, pp. 1–10. IEEE (2010)
10. Mustafa, I.A.Y.: Energy Efficient Switched Parasitic Array Antenna For 5G Network and Iot (Doctoral dissertation) (2022)
11. Hirata, A., Taillefer, E., Yamada, H., Ohira, T.: Handheld direction of arrival finder with electronically steerable parasitic array radiator using the reactance-domain MUltiple signal classification algorithm. IET Microwaves Antennas Propag. **1**(4), 815–821 (2007)
12. Kong, D., Li, X., Ren, X., Gao, S.: A smart antenna array for target detection. In: WSA 2021, 25th International ITG Workshop on Smart Antennas, pp. 1–5. VDE (2021)
13. Subha, T.D., Perumal, C.A., Subash, T.D.: Nonlinear adaptive smart antenna resource management for 5G through to surveillance systems. Mater. Today: Proc. **43**, 3562–3571 (2021)
14. Zhou, J., Cai, Z., Kang, L., Tang, B., Xu, W.: Deformation sensing and electrical compensation of smart skin antenna structure with optimal fiber Bragg grating strain sensor placements. Compos. Struct. **211**, 418–432 (2019)
15. Chang, C.T., Chang, C.Y., Wang, T.L., Lu, Y.J.: Throughput enhancement by exploiting spatial reuse opportunities with smart antenna systems in wireless ad hoc networks. Comput. Netw. **57**(13), 2483–2498 (2013)
16. De Rango, F., Inzillo, V., Quintana, A.A.: Exploiting frame aggregation and weighted round robin with beamforming smart antennas for directional MAC in MANET environments. Ad Hoc Netw. **89**, 186–203 (2019)
17. Kumar Mohapatra, P., et al.: Application of Bat algorithm and its modified form trained with ANN in channel equalization. Symmetry **14**(10), 2078 (2022)
18. Acharya, B., Parida, P., Panda, R.N., Mohapatra, P.K.: A novel approach for BOA trained ANN for channel equalization problems. J. Inf. Optim. Sci. **43**(8), 2121–2130 (2022)

19. Mohapatra, P.K., Rout, S.K., Bisoy, S.K., Sain, M.: Training strategy of Fuzzy-Firefly based ANN in non-linear channel equalization. IEEE Access **10**, 51229–51241 (2022)

20. Mohapatra, P.K., Rout, S.K., Panda, R.N., Meda, A., Panda, B.K.: Performance analysis of fading channels in a wireless communication. In: Innovations in Intelligent Computing and Communication: First International Conference, ICIICC 2022, Bhubaneswar, Odisha, India, 16–17 December 2022, Proceedings, pp. 175–183. Springer, Cham (2023). https://doi.org/10.1007/978-3-031-23233-6_13

21. Mohapatra, P.K., Panda, R.N., Rout, S.K., Samantaroy, R., Jena, P.K.: A novel application of HPSOGWO trained ANN in nonlinear channel equalization. In: Proceedings of the 6th International Conference on Advance Computing and Intelligent Engineering: ICACIE 2021, pp. 159–174. Springer, Singapore (2022). https://doi.org/10.1007/978-981-19-2225-1_15

22. Mohapatra, P.K., Panda, R.N., Rout, S.K., Samantaroy, R., Jena, P.K.: A novel cuckoo search optimized RBF trained ANN in a nonlinear channel equalization. In: Proceedings of the 6th International Conference on Advance Computing and Intelligent Engineering: ICACIE 2021, pp. 189–203. Springer, Singapore (2022). https://doi.org/10.1007/978-981-19-2225-1_18

23. Mohapatra, P., Sahu, P.C., Parvathi, K., Panigrahi, S.P.: Shuffled frog-leaping algorithm trained RBFNN equalizer. Int. J. Comput. Inf. Syst. Ind. Manag. Appl. **9**, 249–256 (2017)

24. Rout, S.K., Mohapatra, P.K., Rath, A.K., Sahu, B.: Node localization in wireless sensor networks using dynamic genetic algorithm. J. Appl. Res. Technol. **20**(5), 520–528 (2022)

25. Haykin, S.S.: Adaptive Filter Theory. Pearson Education India, Noida (2002)

Low-Light Video Enhancement on a Mobile Device Using Illumination-Reflection Model Based Retinex Envelope

G. R. Vishalakshi[1]([⊠]) [iD], M. T. Gopalakrishna[2] [iD],
and M. C. Hanumantharaju[3] [iD]

[1] Dayananda Sagar College of Engineering, Affiliated to VTU,
Belagavi, Karnataka, India
vishala.gr2005@gmail.com
[2] SJB Institute of Technology, Affiliated to VTU, Belagavi, Karnataka, India
[3] BMS Institute of Technology and Management, Affiliated to VTU,
Belagavi, Karnataka, India
mchanumantharaju@bmsit.in

Abstract. A low-light video usually exhibits features like low brightness, poor contrast, a narrow color spectrum and distortion. Low-light videos are also subjected to considerable noise, which significantly affects the viewing experience for humans and limits the effectiveness of computer vision algorithms. The main feature of the paper is to enhance low light videos using an illumination-reflection envelope model corrupted by poor lighting conditions. A luminance function and cost parameter are used to estimate illumination in the proposed method. Piecewise spatial smoothing is applied to the estimated illumination in the low-light videos to remove halo artifacts. Low-pass filters improve details and correct illumination dynamics. In addition to improving low-light videos' contrast, our method preserves the natural appearance of the original videos. Color shifting is prevented by performing all operations on the hue-saturation-value (HSV) value component. A red-green-blue (RGB) format is then used to display videos. Metrics such as discrete entropy, a measure of enhancement, absolute mean brightness error, and pixel distance are used to estimate the method's performance. The experimental results presented clearly demonstrate that the proposed method enhances ill-posed videos more effectively and clearly than other existing methods.

Keywords: Low-light · Video Enhancement · HSV color space · Illumination-Reflection · Retinex Algorithm

1 Introduction

Advancement in the science and technology enabled many handheld devices such as smartphones, tablets, laptops etc. In addition, accessibility of network made

N. Chaubey et al. (Eds.): COMS2 2023, CCIS 1861, pp. 266–277, 2023.
https://doi.org/10.1007/978-3-031-40564-8_20

human to use them widely in all fields such as education, traffic management, crime investigation, military etc. Although there is an advancement in advancement in electronic gadgets, specifically camera and corresponding software features but, still there exists a gap. Smartphones plays vital role in image or video processing by assisting to click pictures and record videos of desired carry out basic vide or image processing operations instantly. On the other hand due to camera shakes, environmental conditions, and lack of expertise in taking photos or recording videos results in a ill posed images or poor quality videos.

In image acquisition and video capturing, the main challenge is to get clear, vivid, and high-quality videos regardless of the problems stated earlier. Digital cameras on mobile devices have been improved by technological advancements. The human visual system (HVS) still prevails over a machine-made imaging system. A huge gap exists between recorded video and human observation. Moreover, it has outstanding abilities to adapt to light or color under extreme environmental conditions. In addition, it discriminates between different types of visual content under extreme conditions. It is difficult to process such ill-posed images or videos captured on a mobile device due to limitations such as restricted dynamic range, inadequate ambient lighting, and poor weather conditions. There have been a few efficient, adaptive algorithms developed by various scholars to improve the performance of such images or videos. When videos are not uniformly illuminated, improving video details without affecting naturalness is a challenge. In the resulting image, halo artifacts and the loss of naturalness are two drawbacks associated with such low-light enhancement techniques. The tradeoff between naturalness and detail enhancement is very difficult. Low-pass filters employed in the proposed work improve details and correct illumination dynamics.

There are typically low-light areas in outdoor scenes in real life [12]. This is because images captured at night have poor lighting conditions, as well as camera problems. These low-light images cannot produce accurate results with conventional algorithms such as image identification, tracking, surveillance, etc. The low lighting in the recorded videos has caused a significant reduction in video quality due to the loss of local details.

Numerous researchers [5,13,14] have worked to avoid ill-posed images under various ill-posed conditions of the environment. Shin et al. [19] presented effective approach to enhance poor quality videos. Chen et al. [1] Presents an improved method for dynamic range adjustment and compression. Enhances bright and dark regions in an image by enhancing color. Due to unavoidable and unnatural effects on the video, the development of efficient and effective algorithms for enhancements is very difficult.

Our paper is categorized as follows: Sect. 2 contains the literature survey that other researchers have contributed to low light video enhancement. In Sect. 3, presents our illumination-reflection model based retinex envelope. A Sect. 4 represents experimental results with database, results, performance evaluation and comparative analysis. In the Sect. 5, conclusions on the overall approach is presented.

2   Related Work

An image's contrast can be enhanced both on an overall and local level through different enhancement techniques. Improving the detailed features, and transforming low-light images into images that can be more easily observed by humans is the need of the hour. Processing poor quality images using computers with noise reduction and high real-time performance is challenging. Many researchers have proposed various algorithms for low-light video enhancement [14].

The conventional method of Histogram equalization (HE) is very effective in adjusting the brightness globally and is widely used in enhancing low-light videos. HE proposed by Le et al. [9] provides good results for global contrast enhancement but, fails for local contrast enhancement. An Adaptive HE (AHE) method proposed by Karel [22] to achieve local contrast enhancement. Therefore, AHE is an effective method for enhancing local details in an image compared to HE.

Histogram related methods [9] are widely extended to implement effective and adaptive algorithms for enhancement of low-light images. Some of the extended version of HE based methods are Brightness preserving Bi-Histogram equalization method (BBHE), Dualistic sub-image Histogram Equalization (DSIHE), Minimum mean brightness error bi-Histogram equalization (MMBEBHE), Many researchers proposed local histogram equalization methods such as Partially overlapped sub-block Histogram Equalization (POSHE), Cascaded multistep binomial filtering Histogram Equalization (CMBFHE), etc.

Land et al. proposed retinex theory in 1968. Retinex is a theory modelling visual perception [8]. Retinex-type algorithms are used for dynamic range compression, coloured illumination correction, or general image enhancement. Kimmel et al. [15] contribution is based on Horn's physical prior work that is using retinex algorithm and the results are comparitively better. However, halo artifacts still exists. Fu et al. [3] presented an algorithm based on illumination and reflectance model using estimated weighted variational model.

According to this model, the estimated reflectance can be preserved in greater detail than conventional variational models, and noise to some extent can be suppressed. Guo et al. [4] proposed a simple and effective low-light image enhancement method (LIME). A pixel's illumination is calculated separately for the R, G, and B channels. Xu et al. [11] implemented a STAR to decompose illumination and reflectance into a single image based on texture and structure. This method is very hard to extend for low-light videos because it is based on vectorized least squares regression with closed-form solutions.

Deep learning has become increasingly popular in recent years because of its development, many researchers have developed algorithms using machine learning algorithm for low light enhancement of images or videos. Fu et al. [21] presented a method using color estimation model (CEM), which eliminates the over saturation. Numerous researchers uses Convolution neural network (CNN) as basic to propose their work. Tao et al. [20] presented a low light CNN (LLCNN), a few researchers proposed CNN as basis algorithm such as a global illumination-aware and detail-preserving Network (GLADNet), a low light image enhancement network (LLIE-net), kindling the darkness (KinD) network, a GAN (generative adversarial network).

Chih et al. [18] Presented a robust envelope algorithm for enhancing color retinex images. The V component of an RGB image is enhanced when it is converted into an HSV color image. This robust envelope was developed to overcome holographic artifacts along the edges and corners caused by gray-world violation or color-shifting. Setty et al. [17] a retinex enhancement algorithm that enhances contrast in spinal cord images, described an envelope-based algorithm that enhances retinex. However, this method works very well for medical images.

Li et al. [11] developed a Structure-Revealing Low-Light Enhancement (SRL-LIE) using retinex model. Fu et al. [2] developed an algorithm to enhance poorly illuminated images using fusion.

Experimental results show enhancement for various ill-posed images, and this method is effective in computation and better than other methods. Haidi et al. [6] have extended the idea of conventional HE to brightness preserving dynamic histogram equalization (BPDHE) extension of HE. In spite of its benefits, BPDHE over-enhances the dark regions of a video.

3   Proposed Illumination-Reflection Based Retinex Envelope Model

The following section describes an illumination reflection model based retinex envelope that can preserves the naturalness of the input. The proposed method suppresses noise and improves details as well as overall quality of the images or videos with reduced halo artifacts.

3.1   Motivation

It is evident from the literature review that the existing work on low light video enhancement on mobile device focus on the quality of videos, databases, performance metrics. Although, there is substantial improvement in data driven methods as compared to model-based techniques, deep learning methods have increased database complexity and also the noise remains intact with the videos. Therefore, development of efficient pre-processing system such as ours is highly essential. The proposed method addresses common problems such as halo artifacts, color shifting and noise encountered while capturing low light videos. Machine learning systems are negatively affected by these issues and their performance is diminished. The proposed method transforms composite video into frames in RGB domain followed by HSV conversion. Hue component is preserved to avoid color distortion. The value and saturation components are processed in accordance with the process flow described in the following sections.

3.2   Illumination Estimation on a Mobile Video for Low Light Enhancement

The conventional retinex algorithm assumes that reflectance and illumination are both important factors in forming color images. As shown in Eq. (1).

$$f_i(x,y) = l_i(x,y) \times r_i(x,y) i \in \{R, G, B\} \tag{1}$$

where (x,y) denotes the spatial coordinates, $f_i(x,y)$ indicates the color image formed, $l_i(x,y)$ denote the illumination component of an image, $r_i(x,y)$ represents the reflectance component of an image with values in the range $0 < l_i(x,y) < \infty$ and $0(total absorption) < r_i(x,y) < 1(total reflectance)$.

The Eq. 1 can be re-written as follows:

$$l_i(x,y) = \frac{l_i(x,y)}{r_i(x,y)} \ge f_i(x,y) \tag{2}$$

This work generally ensures that the estimated illumination is close to the intensity. In addition, this model considers that the illumination component changes steadily, with its frequency spectrum remaining in the narrow band of the frequency spectrum. On the other hand, reflectance quickly fluctuates such that its frequency remains in the image's high-frequency detail. In Eq. (1), the color image formation model is depicted by the value component of the HSV image. A robust envelope approach is used in this work to determine illumination estimation which is based on Shen et al. [18] Retinex algorithm. In order to achieve spatial smoothness and closeness to intensity, the following equation is used:

$$F(L(x,y)) = \int \left(\|\nabla L(x,y)\|^2 + \alpha \|L(x,y) - I(x,y)\|^2 \right) dx dy \tag{3}$$

where ∇ represents differential operator of first order and $\|.\|$ is modulus value. The cost minimum operation and is given as

$$L_j(x,y) = L_{j-1}(x,y) - \beta.G \tag{4}$$

where $L_j(x,y)$ and $L_{j-1}(x,y)$ shows the luminance images at step j and j-1; indicates the linear step, G shows the gradient of $F(L(x,y))$. Next, the grad. operation given by Kim at al. [7] as shown below

$$G = -L(x,y) * K_{lap}(x,y) + \alpha.(L(x,y) - I(x,y)) \tag{5}$$

where Δ is the Laplacian operator of 2nd order that is averaged as a convolution using filter K_{lap}

$$K_{lap} = \begin{bmatrix} 0 & 1 & 0 \\ 1 & -4 & 1 \\ 0 & 1 & 0 \end{bmatrix} \tag{6}$$

Finally, we write eqn. to find the brightness

$$L_j(x,y) = max\{w(\nabla I).I(x,y) + (1-w(\nabla I)).L_j(x,y).I(x,y)\} \tag{7}$$

$$\nabla I = \|I(x,y) * H(x,y)\| + \|I(x,y) * H^T(x,y)\| \tag{8}$$

where H reveal the strong edge details and is given by

$$H = \frac{1}{34} \begin{bmatrix} 1 & 1 & 1 & 0 & -1 & -1 \\ 1 & 2 & 2 & 0 & -2 & -1 \\ 1 & 2 & 3 & 0 & -3 & -1 \\ 1 & 2 & 3 & 0 & -3 & -1 \\ 1 & 2 & 3 & 0 & -3 & -1 \\ 1 & 2 & 2 & 0 & -2 & -1 \\ 1 & 1 & 1 & 0 & -1 & -1 \end{bmatrix} \tag{9}$$

3.3 Reflectance Estimation and Video Enhancement

In order to improve the system, Saponara et al. [16] proposed a Retinex-based enhancement scheme which achieves reflection estimation. In order to calculate reflectance, we use the ratio of V channel to estimated illumination. Low-pass edge-preserving RRFs result in output as shown in equation (12).

The following equations are utilized to correct the illumination dynamically and improves the details.

$$\Gamma(y) = N \left(\frac{L}{N}\right)^{k\left(1 + \frac{y}{N}\right)} \tag{10}$$

$$\beta(r) = e^{\left(g\left(\frac{1}{1 + e^{-b.log(r)}} - \frac{1}{2}\right)\right)} \tag{11}$$

where k range from 0 to 1, b ranges from 1 to 10, and N = 255. An easy way to process video sequences is to process each frame individually. It is, however, annoying to observe temporal effects on consecutive frames when they have been processed independently. This occurs, for example, when luminance correction is performed differently on adjacent frames. A temporal filter may be used to resolve this issue.

4 Experimental Results

4.1 Database

We have selected test images of resolution 1024 × 768 an extended graphics array (XGA) standard from the digital single lens reflex cameras (DSLR) photo enhancement dataset (DPED). The images were captured by a numerous photographers in a variety of places, under different lighting and weather conditions during the day. Data collection for this study was conducted using four device models: iPhone 3GS, BlackBerry Passport, Sony Xperia Z, and Canon 70D DSLR. Wireless control of mobile phones enabled the simultaneous capture of photos while mounted on a tripod. Throughout the entire collection process, all cameras were operated in automatic mode with default settings. We have chosen one group of four images that has text in the name plates in out-door environment. The second group consisted of natural images captured under varying conditions such as cloudy, ill-posed conditions.

The images are available freely for the public and can be downloaded using the url: http://people.ee.ethz.ch/~ihnatova/#dataset

4.2   Results

We experimented with several images using the combination of low light and cloudy conditions. As an example, Fig. 1 and Fig. 2 shows results in two groups based on the type of images chosen for experimentation. An analysis of competitive enhancement techniques is conducted to compare the proposed method with others. We have started with classical HE followed by BPDHE, FEM method, SRLLIE techniques. As it is found from the results presented in Figure that images enhanced by our method has enhanced details and overall quality appears vivid, brilliant and natural.

4.3   Performance Evaluation

The performance of the image or video enhancement methods are objectively assessed using the four quality metrics presented in Ref. [10]: discrete entropy (DE), the measure of enhancement (EME), absolute mean brightness error (AMBE), and PixDist. Image variations and information conveyed by a high DE are usually more apparent when there is a high DE. Secondly, in EME, a score is calculated according to the minimum and maximum gray levels in each block of an image and added together to approximate the average contrast. Thirdly, AMBE measures the arbitrary distinction among the gray-level means of input and output. Lower the value, the better the algorithm at maintaining the brightening of the input image. Pixel brightness is measured by PixDist.

4.4   Comparative Analysis

Information processing inequality prevents transformation functions from producing higher DE outputs than their inputs. There are more details provided by this algorithm than any conventional algorithm, but the average DE is lower than the input. The proposed algorithm, however, provides comparitively higher details than any conventional algorithm. HE [9] provides the most accurate EME score, but it is prone to overstretching and overenhancement artifacts. BPDHE [6] technique has better EME score and its moderately correlate with the enhanced image. Due to the incorporation of 2D contextual information and the enhancement of local details featured in SRLLIE and the proposed algorithm, these algorithms gives substantial EME scores than FEM. The linear transformation function is averaged with the FEM transformation function to obtain the lowest brightness change. In terms of ranking, the proposed algorithm is third. Despite this, FEM [2], SRLLIE [11], and our algorithm produces significantly higher AMBE scores than the HE algorithm. Whenever the gray-level

Fig. 1. Comparison of mobile Phone Images Captured Synchronously using Four Cameras. First Row: Input Images, Second Row: Histogram Equalization [9], Third Row: BPDHE [6], Fourth Row: FEM [2], Fifth Row: SRLLIE [11], Sixth Row: Proposed Method.

components of histograms are uniformly distributed, pixel distance can yield a high score. As far as PixDist is concerned, our algorithm shows better results, except for the contrast overshooting HE algorithm (Fig. 3).

Fig. 2. Results of Natural Images Captured under Cloudy, Low-light, and Non-uniform light conditions.

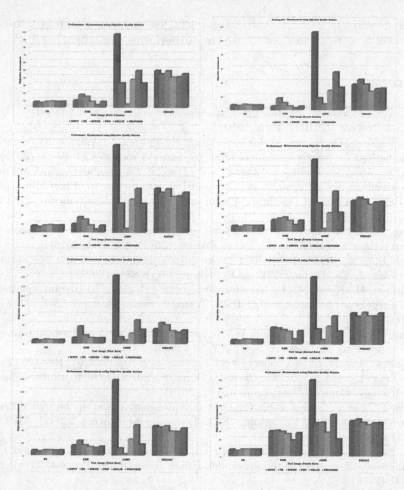

Fig. 3. Performance Comparison of Results Presented in Fig. 1: First and Second Row, Performance Comparison of Results Presented in Fig. 2: Third and Fourth Row.

5   Conclusion

Low-light images or videos captured using a mobile phone are subjected to poor brightness, color shifting, and halo artifacts. In addition to these problems, noise significantly affects the quality of videos, diminishing the effectiveness of computer vision algorithms. To overcome these problems, an illumination-reflection model based on the retinex envelope is presented. The proposed method efficiently estimates illumination using luminance and cost functions. Further, piecewise spatial smoothing functions have been applied to the estimated illumination to remove halo artifacts. The low pass filter significantly suppresses noise, improves details, and accomplishes overall video enhancement. Our method is measured using DE, EME, AMBE, and PixDist metrics. Compared to other researchers' contributions, our algorithm outperforms the others.

References

1. Chen, S., Beghdadi, A.: Natural enhancement of color image. EURASIP J. Image Video Process. **2010**(1), 1–19 (2010)
2. Fu, X., Zeng, D., Huang, Y., Liao, Y., Ding, X., Paisley, J.: A fusion-based enhancing method for weakly illuminated images. Signal Process. **129**, 82–96 (2016)
3. Fu, X., Zeng, D., Huang, Y., Zhang, X.P., Ding, X.: A weighted variational model for simultaneous reflectance and illumination estimation. In: Proceedings of the IEEE Conference on Computer Vision and Pattern Recognition, pp. 2782–2790 (2016)
4. Guo, X., Li, Y., Ling, H.: LIME: low-light image enhancement via illumination map estimation. IEEE Trans. Image Process. **26**(2), 982–993 (2016)
5. Hai, J., et al.: R2RNet: low-light image enhancement via real-low to real-normal network. J. Vis. Commun. Image Represent. **90**, 103712 (2023)
6. Ibrahim, H., Kong, N.S.P.: Brightness preserving dynamic histogram equalization for image contrast enhancement. IEEE Trans. Consum. Electron. **53**(4), 1752–1758 (2007)
7. Kimmel, R., Elad, M., Shaked, D., Keshet, R., Sobel, I.: A variational framework for retinex. Int. J. Comput. Vis. **52**, 7–23 (2003)
8. Land, E.H.: The retinex theory of color vision. Sci. Am. **237**(6), 108–129 (1977)
9. Le-Peng, L., Sun, S., Xia, C., Chen, P., Dong, F.: Survey of histogram equalization technology. Comput. Syst. Appl. **3**, 1–8 (2014)
10. Lee, C., Lee, C., Kim, C.S.: Contrast enhancement based on layered difference representation of 2D histograms. IEEE Trans. Image Process. **22**(12), 5372–5384 (2013)
11. Li, M., Liu, J., Yang, W., Sun, X., Guo, Z.: Structure-revealing low-light image enhancement via robust retinex model. IEEE Trans. Image Process. **27**(6), 2828–2841 (2018)
12. Li, Y., Liu, T., Fan, J., Ding, Y.: LDNet: low-light image enhancement with joint lighting and denoising. Mach. Vis. Appl. **34**(1), 1–15 (2023)
13. Li, Z., Wang, Y., Zhang, J.: Low-light image enhancement with knowledge distillation. Neurocomputing **518**, 332–343 (2023)
14. Liu, X., Ma, W., Ma, X., Wang, J.: LAE-Net: a locally-adaptive embedding network for low-light image enhancement. Pattern Recogn. **133**, 109039 (2023)
15. Ma, W.: Variational models in image and signal enhancement. University of California, Los Angeles (2011)
16. Saponara, S., Fanucci, L., Marsi, S., Ramponi, G., Kammler, D., Witte, E.M.: Application-specific instruction-set processor for retinex-like image and video processing. IEEE Trans. Circuits Syst. II Express Briefs **54**(7), 596–600 (2007)
17. Setty, S., Srinath, N., Hanumantharaju, M.: Details enhancement of MRI image using illumination and reflectance estimation. In: 2017 International Conference on Signal Processing and Communication (ICSPC), pp. 421–424. IEEE (2017)
18. Shen, C.T., Hwang, W.L.: Color image enhancement using retinex with robust envelope. In: 2009 16th IEEE International Conference on Image Processing (ICIP), pp. 3141–3144. IEEE (2009)

19. Shin, H., Yu, T., Ismail, Y., Saeed, B.: Rendering high dynamic range images by using integrated global and local processing. Opt. Eng. **50**(11), 117002 (2011)
20. Tao, L., Zhu, C., Xiang, G., Li, Y., Jia, H., Xie, X.: LLCNN: a convolutional neural network for low-light image enhancement. In: 2017 IEEE Visual Communications and Image Processing (VCIP), pp. 1–4. IEEE (2017)
21. Xu, J., et al.: Star: a structure and texture aware retinex model. IEEE Trans. Image Process. **29**, 5022–5037 (2020)
22. Zuiderveld, K.: Contrast limited adaptive histogram equalization. Graph. Gems 474–485 (1994)

Author Index

Printed in the United States
by Baker & Taylor Publisher Services